Overturning the Culture of Violence

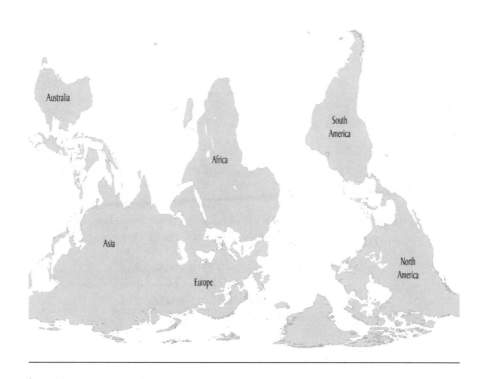

Australia

South America

Africa

Asia

North America

Europe

Penny Hess

Burning Spear Uhuru Publications
P.O. Box 3757
St. Petersburg, FL 33731
727-894-6997
BSUP@uhurumovement.org

ISBN 1-891624-02-4

Many thanks to Tim Seibles for the use of his poem "You" from *Hammerlock*,
published by Cleveland State University Poetry Center.

Cover design by Burning Spear Uhuru Publications.
Cover photo: Culver Pictures, Inc.
All other photos credited with image.

African People's Socialist Party
1245 - 18th Avenue South
St. Petersburg, Florida 33705

DEDICATION

To Omali Yeshitela without whose leadership not one word of this book could have been written. Through his lifelong dedication to the liberation of African people, he has provided the world with the key to overturning the culture of violence.

And to African, indigenous and oppressed peoples who carry in their hearts the memory of freedom, the spirit of resistance, the commitment to liberation and the vision of a new and just world;

To those who once lived free in the lush beauty of Africa and the Americas;

To those who were ripped from their homelands, severed from their loved ones, subjected to genocide, coerced into human bondage, forced to bear unspeakable violence and made to endure poverty, injustice and degradation;

To those who are today the targets of the undeclared war on African, indigenous and oppressed peoples in the inner cities, the barrios, the reservations and the concentration camps known as prisons...

Your suffering is the price of our prosperity and freedom.

This book represents a step from white society towards shouldering our responsibility and righting this historic wrong.

Reparations Now!

TABLE OF CONTENTS

Foreword

A year or so ago, prior to publication of this book, an acquaintance peripherally associated with the African Liberation Movement, enough to retain some semblance of revolutionary legitimacy, mischievously let me in on a bit of gossip from a contending organization. The story went that a mysterious white woman is the real author of the various books, pamphlets and articles ascribed to me.

Within a movement that is generally permeated with race nationalism, this was a serious charge, designed to cause me maximum discomfort, no doubt. Just as with most gossip, no names were mentioned, either of the group from whence the rumor originated, or of the white woman whose genius I was said to have appropriated for my own use. However, I suspect the mystery white woman must be Penny Hess, author of this most important book presently before us.

Penny Hess was won to participation in the Uhuru Movement under my leadership in 1976. She was one of many North Americans who came to a meeting in St. Petersburg, Florida to form the African People's Solidarity Committee. Penny Hess came to the meeting from Louisville, Kentucky. Others came from California, Florida, Alabama, Maine, New York and various other places.

Most of those who participated in that Florida meeting have long since discovered better things to do; many did so within days of the meeting's ending. For many of the North Americans who initially stepped forward, it seemed that the idea of whites working under the leadership of the African Liberation Movement was a good concept as long as it was not put into practice.

Not only did Penny Hess remain in the group, she has grown tremendously in the process. She has set examples for everyone with her principled political stance. She has shown her willingness to abandon the assumptions of imperialism that keep most white people in the world wedded to the imperialist ruling class and the parasitic relationship that whites enjoy at the expense of the peoples of the world.

It will not do to argue with any race nationalists, either African or European, that Hess is not the author of my works. Indeed, in such quarters there is an underlying assumption that if there is a relationship between Africans and Europeans, it is the European who leads. It is not an unreasonable assumption. It is generally supported by history. What *is* unusual is that the African People's Socialist Party, which I lead, has come to certain philosophical conclusions that make it necessary for Penny Hess and the African People's Solidarity Committee to work directly under the Party's leadership.

These philosophical conclusions are the bases for this work by Penny Hess. It is a work that strips bare many of the most popular radical assumptions within the U.S. and Europe regarding the fundamental underlying cause of oppression in the world. *Overturning the Culture of Violence* gives flesh to our premise that world capitalism has its basis in and owes its continued existence to slavery, the slave trade, the rape and pillage of the world by Europe and North America. It exposes the political and economic structures put in place by white power to facilitate this parasitic relationship.

Hence, this book is not a simple recitation of bad things done by Europeans to others designed to make white people "feel bad," as some have claimed upon knowing of our views. Rather, it is a thumb-nail sketch of history as experienced by most peoples of the world who have had the misfortune to come into contact with Europe and/or white people.

It is history as we, the raped and pillaged, the bludgeoned and garroted, the starved and colonized victims of white power have experienced it. Anyone with a smidgen of objective intellectual capacity would understand that this is not an understanding that Hess could have come to on her own. Clearly, it is not she who is the author of my works. Rather it has been the African People's Socialist Party's influence on Hess that has equipped her to write such an incredibly significant work.

This book presents objective truth, something white people have great difficulty accepting when it comes to their relationship to other—oppressed—peoples. This is because, generally speaking, white people live in a world created by and maintained off of the suffering and brutalization of the vast majority of the world's peoples. In the short term white people benefit from this relationship immensely.

This objective truth challenges the notion that white people are wealthier, healthier and generally better off than the rest of the world because of some inherent genius of whites. For if it is the genius of whites that is responsible for the vast difference in conditions of existence of whites and others, then Europeans have no greater obligation or responsibility than that informed by their own sense of generosity.

However, if it is true that white wealth has its origin in genocide, pillage and brutality reinforced by the incredible institutional devices of today—including the prisons, the police, enforced poverty—then the implications are obviously very different. One shudders to think about the deep implications of this reality, so one doesn't. Hence, it is a rarity that we find whites capable of dealing with objective truth. There is a stake in falsifying history, in covering up objective truth.

On the other hand, the slave, the colonized, the oppressed and despised African must know the truth. Unlike the case of the oppressor nation, which experiences some interest in disguising or falsifying truth, the oppressed nation must know objective truth as a condition for liberation.

Hess has been able to write this book because she has learned to see the world through the eyes of the oppressed, of the enslaved colonized African. She has done this not through "unlearning her racism" or some other idealist fantasy, which has no real bearing on the real world. Rather she has leapt into the fray under the leadership of the African Revolution, by understanding as Che Guevara did, that it is not about well wishing but about sharing the same fate whether in victory or in death.

Obviously, Penny Hess is not colonized and hence cannot share the same fate as we in absolute terms. But she can and has relinquished all claims to a world built on the labor and resources of the enslaved masses of the world. And, unlike most white people of the United States and Europe, she has come to terms with the fact that the foundation of European wealth and civilization is the resources and genius of Africa and the colonized world. Moreover, Penny Hess has made it her profession to turn the world right side up by uniting, in absolute terms, with the objectives of the African Liberation Movement.

The leadership of the African People's Socialist Party and the Uhuru Movement is what has made this possible for Hess, just as it makes it possible for many others of us.

I am profoundly proud of this book and my relationship to it. I will be flattered if my detractors get the authorship of this work confused with me.

— *Omali Yeshitela*
Chairman
African People's Socialist Party

Introduction

Uhuru Means Freedom

Overturning the Culture of Violence is not an "objective" book. It represents the biased point of view that there must be justice for those so long enslaved, colonized, victimized by genocide and oppression.

The ideological foundations of this book are the political, yet very human, theories and perceptions of Omali Yeshitela, Chairman of the African People's Socialist Party and leader of the Uhuru Movement.

In the process of spending most of his life actively engaged in struggle for the liberation of African people, Chairman Yeshitela has formulated an analysis of the world. Because his work represents such a dramatic advance over earlier Euro-centric political theories, the Uhuru Movement called his analysis "Yeshitelism." This theory systematizes the worldview of oppressed peoples, forging it into a cogent tool in the struggle for freedom.

With this theoretical basis, *Overturning the Culture of Violence* looks at history through the eyes of those whose lives, land, culture and resources were—and are—plundered for the benefit of white society.

Overturning the Culture of Violence

Yeshitela often speaks of turning the world right side up. Indeed, even maps have historically been positioned from the standpoint of Europeans. Hence, the use of the map turned "right side up" shown on the title page.

In this book, we are attempting in particular to reach white people who, like myself, are interested in understanding this standpoint, so different from our own, which represents the experiences of the majority of humankind.

Overturning the Culture of Violence unearths the bitter truth about the part played by white people from all strata of our society in the enslavement and genocide of colonized peoples. The book delineates our historic role as passive or active enforcers of the culture of violence, a role that has had very lucrative consequences for the American social system, as well as for us, the beneficiaries of white power.

The information on these pages may at times be painful, wrenching, even overwhelming—as it certainly was to research and write. As much as possible we soften no blows and cover over none of the reality. As white people we feel that it is our responsibility to go deeply into the crimes and complicity of white society, as part of the process of making reparations and a self-criticism to African people and the majority of humanity.

Overturning the Culture of Violence tries to chip away our long-held assumptions. It challenges the fact that we are able to abide on tree-lined streets with our cats, dogs and appropriate numbers of children, with our vacations, benefits and experience of democracy, while most of the world is suffering in poverty, misery and political terror. On these pages we demonstrate Yeshitela's point that there is a dynamic relationship between the two experiences—a dialectic between the wealth of a few and the poverty of many, the well-being of white people and suffering of most other peoples. This is the overriding theme of this book.

We hope that by looking honestly at the truth, we can begin to take responsibility for our brutal history and move towards an equitable future for all who share this planet. Though challenging, this book is at the same time hopeful and optimistic, offering a vision presented by African people of a world in which justice and peace prevail. There is a place for us in this new world, a place that opens up as we take on the task of righting the historical wrong.

OMALI YESHITELA AND THE UHURU MOVEMENT

Every understanding, insight, overview and perception that might be found in this book comes from Omali Yeshitela. There is really nothing on these pages that generates originally from the author. Nor could it. As white people sitting on the pedestal of the oppression of others, these are conclusions to which we could never come on our own. It is possible, however, for us to open our minds and spirits and embrace this worldview shared by the vast majority of humanity. By so doing we begin to experience for the first time a commonality with the rest of the world, a unity that releases us from the fears, xenophobia, violence and alienation which characterize white society.

Yeshitela's theory poses the very simple question: why *shouldn't* African and oppressed peoples be free? Why shouldn't they control their homelands, resources, cultures and destinies without economic, political and armed intervention from white power and white people? Why shouldn't they experience the economic and political benefits that we take for granted? These questions must be resolved if there is ever to be an end to war, anger and violence in the world.

Yeshitela begins from the premise that African people inside the United States are not the victims of "racism." Rather they constitute a nation of people colonized inside the borders of the United States. As such, black people are *African* people wherever they are located in the world. The hyphenated attachment of "American" belies reality.

Overturning the Culture of Violence

Chairman Omali is a fully committed leader of African people everywhere. His theory is ascendant; his influence extends from the streets of Brooklyn to the continent of Africa, and increasingly penetrates to every corner of the globe where oppressed peoples are struggling for freedom.

A brilliant political strategist and a charismatic orator, Omali Yeshitela has the ability to bring his profound theoretical analysis down to Earth with wit, persuasion and raw emotion. His consistently unique observations of white power are painted in a hilariously funny light one moment, while he brings the listener to tears with poignant descriptions of oppression the next. He has the rare ability to make white people laugh at our own arrogance and white nationalism. He radiates the optimistic African spirit and paints a vision for the possibilities of all humanity in the process of liberating Africa and her people.

Years ago Yeshitela adopted "Uhuru" for his slogan. The entire movement which he leads is now known by this Swahili word for freedom popularized by the struggle of the Mau Mau in Kenya in the 1950s. The aim of the Uhuru Movement is the liberation of African people in this country, in the African homeland, and wherever African people have ended up as a result of being kidnapped into slavery.

In 1976, the African People's Socialist Party formed the African People's Solidarity Committee (APSC), made up of white people whose mission is to organize solidarity with the struggle of African people from our own communities. Years of research for presentations at forums, teach-ins and panel discussions geared at organizing other white people laid the basis for *Overturning the Culture of Violence*. Moreover, nearly a quarter of a century of studying the books, articles and speeches of Omali Yeshitela, as well as participation in numerous community campaigns directly under his leadership, prepared us for the task of writing this book.

Located in Oakland, California; Philadelphia, Pennsylvania; Chicago, Illinois and St. Petersburg, Florida, the work of the African People's Solidarity Committee has long involved building a mass movement for raising funds and resources for the Uhuru Movement, as a means of white reparations to African people. The question of white reparations to African people has become the central focus of the work of the African People's Solidarity Committee over the years. Our dedication to reparations stems from the simple fact that the stolen resources of African and oppressed peoples are found in the white community and create the economic pedestal upon which our society sits.

In Oakland and Philadelphia, APSC manages Party institutions that function as a base of the Uhuru Movement in white communities. These popular institutions include Uhuru Concessions and Uhuru Furniture stores.

REVISED EDITION

An earlier version of this book was published in 1991 as *Culture of Violence*. Much has taken place in the world since the publication of that original book, which was less than 200 pages long. During the past decade, the voice of the oppressed has grown stronger; the movements of African and indigenous peoples have continued to expose "the lies my teacher told us."

No longer can the rape and crimes of slave masters like Thomas Jefferson and George Washington be hidden. No longer can Christopher Columbus be held up as anything other than an agent of genocide. Many new and excellent books have appeared during the 1990s, detailing much more of the true history as experienced by those who make up capitalism's pedestal.

When we decided to reissue *Culture of Violence* in 1999, we felt that it needed some revision. In the process of revision, the book ended up being more than 600 pages long—and even then we had to cut out enormous amounts of material. The result was a completely different entity which we named *Overturning the Culture of Violence.*

The scope of this book encompasses ancient history up through the current situation today. With this enormous time frame, we can only present an overview and do not pretend to make a thorough and exacting study of history. There are many, many more past and present-day events which could have been included had we the time and the space.

We consciously used easily accessible books for source materials for *Overturning the Culture of Violence,* rather than scholarly and esoteric material. Thus, the information put forward here is available to most people in books found at libraries and book stores. We have used many direct quotes because we felt that it was important that certain points be made in the authors' own words. We recommend that all of the books listed in the bibliography be studied for their contributions to a more thorough understanding of the culture of violence.

Chapter 1 takes a look at the greatness of African and indigenous civilizations prior to the European invasion. It gives a history of the European onslaught and the genocide, enslavement and colonization of Africa and the Americas as the basis for the system of parasitic capitalism. It introduces the theory of Omali Yeshitela and points out the shortcomings of traditional left analysis based on Marxism-Leninism. The enthusiasm of Europeans for profound savagery toward other peoples is exposed.

Chapter 2 continues on in the same vein with a focus on slavery and genocide in the United States. Chapter 3 deals with twentieth century America beginning with the Spanish American War and on through the 1960s. It covers the Garvey Movement and the Civil Rights and Black Power Movements. Again, it looks at the opportunism of the white left and the violence and brutality of white people towards oppressed peoples.

Chapters 4, 5 and 6 examine the U.S. government's counterinsurgency against the Black Power Movement of the 1960s and against the African community as a whole. It attempts to provide data and a human face to back up Yeshitela's point that the conditions facing African people today are the consequence of a public policy stemming from this undeclared government war. This "war without terms" inside the U.S. is put in the context of the U.S. foreign military policy of counterinsurgency against the liberation movements of oppressed peoples around the world. Producing a war economy, this counterinsurgency, both internationally and domestically, has proven to be economically beneficial for white society.

Chapter 7 details the political situation in St. Petersburg, Florida, the national headquarters of the African People's Socialist Party. The Uhuru Movement there has won a measure of political power for the African community since 1996 when the police murder of a young African motorist sparked rebellions.

Chapter 8 raises the issue of reparations from white people to the African community and addresses our role and interest in contributing to the building of a new and just world.

The Uhuru Movement often uses the term "North American" for white people. The reader will find that although we mainly use the term "white" since it is in common usage, there are times when "North American" and "European" are used interchangeably. The African People's Socialist Party initiated the term "North American" to take the issue of white people out of the realm of racism, the ideas in our heads. The use of this term does not imply that we have any claims to this land stolen from the indigenous people. Rather the term "North American" makes the issue our political, economic and social relationship to the capitalist system and the U.S. government, on the one hand, and to African people on the other.

We have used materials from many sources, including from the books of Ward Churchill. The African People's Socialist Party and the African People's Solidarity Committee recognize that struggles revolving around Ward Churchill are currently taking place inside the American Indian Movement. The Uhuru Movement affirms that our use of his research in no way indicates a position in those struggles.

The APSP asserts its complete unity with the right of the indigenous people to regain their stolen land and resources and to define their struggle for self-determination and sovereignty as they see fit. The Party has demonstrated its solidarity with the liberation of native peoples throughout the years and in no way wants to intervene in the internal struggles of that movement. However, we made the decision to use certain books by Churchill, just as we would any other source, simply because some of them contain pertinent information which contribute to the overall understandings of the book.

We hope that this book will provide the reader with a new approach to the world. We see *Overturning the Culture of Violence* as a journey embarked upon by a traveler with an open mind and honest spirit. It takes us from genocide to liberation, from oppression to reparations. For North Americans it gives us a picture of what we must do to rectify our relationship with African people. It provides us with a way to understand that true solidarity with the struggles of oppressed peoples is the only path to a viable future for all humankind.

We want to thank all the comrades and friends who contributed resources, time and real commitment to the production of this book. We hope that with the next edition of this book we can provide a more thorough index.

For more information about the African People's Socialist Party, visit the web site at www.uhurumovement.org, call 727-821-6620; write to APSP, 1245 18th Avenue South, St. Petersburg, FL 33705 or email APSPuhuru@aol.com. For the African People's Solidarity Committee write to P.O. Box 883, St. Petersburg, Florida 33731. Call 727-898-1042 or email APSC@uhurumovement.org.

Uhuru!

Introduction Uhuru Means Freedom

King Tutenkhamen: ancient Egypt was African.
Credit: Photodisc.com.

Olmec head: Africans visited Central America in
ancient times.

Credit: Anthroarcheart.org

Mayan Temple of the Inscriptions: showing the influence of the Egyptian pyramids.
Credit: Anthroarcheart.org

1

The Inescapable Dialectic

There is an inescapable dialectic, a unity of opposites to be found in the emergence of Euro-Americans as the subjects of history and Africans and others becoming its objects. Clearly there is an inescapable relationship between the great wealth of the "white" world and the impoverishment of the rest of us upon whose backs the entire, intricate capitalist edifice, and capitalist activity, rest with ever growing anxiety.[1]

— *Omali Yeshitela*

A frican life along the Nile is depicted in the beautiful paintings of Thebes (modern-day Luxor, Egypt), created by skillful artists some 3,500 years ago. Portrayed is the daily reality of a society that unraveled the mysteries of astronomy, probed the realm of higher mathematics and left us an enduring legacy of splendid architecture. It is a harmonious life that is shown, warmly social, close to nature, collectivist and free from want. Enriched with music, the arts and science, we see a society capable of fulfilling the material, spiritual and creative needs of its people.

These paintings reveal lush gardens with trees and multi-colored flowers, fishponds, birds and lotus blossoms. In this setting the homework of schoolchildren is being corrected; artists are at work. Magistrates sit on their benches, a girl pauses while gleaning grain and someone's hair is being braided outdoors in an open meadow. A goldsmith is putting the finishing touches on beautiful jewelry, a gardener is planting, and craftsmen are making furniture. Men and women are celebrating around a banquet table, entertained by musicians and dancers.[2]

Representative of human culture prior to the European onslaught, these paintings, at once magnificent and simple, provide a glimpse into a past—and perhaps future—world. There is much to be gained by studying a society in which oppression, prisons, hunger and homelessness were nonexistent.

We North Americans, however, are often complacently indifferent to history; its lessons are lost on us. We tend to see ourselves as the center of the universe, and our ignorance of convenience serves us well. The less we know, the easier it is to never question our place in the world. We carefully cherish our denial about the fact that our lives are built on the suffering of so many others.

Now, at the start of a new millennium, things are changing. The voice of the enslaved is rising to new authority as the people of the colonies strive to regain power over their stolen land, resources and destinies. The strength of this voice has begun to force us from the white community to question the "lies my teacher told me," and to unmask the fabrications that make up the myths of white power.

This book is an attempt to help us open the door that many have preferred for so long to keep shut. It lets us see the world from the point of view of African people and all those whom we have treated as nameless objects of history. It is an attempt to understand the past in order to begin to play a part in the inevitable transformations of a future shaped by the hands of those who are now enslaved.

Overturning the Culture of Violence *came about as the result of years of participation in the African People's Solidarity Committee (APSC). Formed by the African People's Socialist Party, APSC is composed of white people who organize in our own communities under the leadership of the black-led Uhuru Movement.*

This book is based on research and lectures directed at other North Americans as part of the process of building solidarity with the movement for African liberation. All the understandings on these pages derive directly from the theoretical, political and human vision of the Party's chairman, Omali Yeshitela, who has in effect codified the worldview of the oppressed in this era. His theory is known as Yeshitelism.

There are no conclusions, no insights in this book that we, as a white people, could have come to on our own, no matter how astute our perceptions, thorough our research or Marxist our spectacles, as one African scholar put it. Our perspective, on the backs of other peoples, would never permit us to comprehend the experience of the oppressed majority of humankind, past and present, whose lives, resources and civilizations have provided the fuel for the Western imperialist engines. It took the clarity and wisdom of Chairman Omali Yeshitela and the African working class to inform us.

The Uhuru Movement has opened itself up to white people who are interested in taking responsibility to rectify the past in the process of building a just world for tomorrow. To the extent that we, as the beneficiaries of white power, can unite with this vision and rise to its tasks, we are able to enter into the embrace of humanity, instead of being its policeman, executioner, exploiter and slave driver.

This book is an attempt to help turn the world right side up, as Omali Yeshitela says. It is an invitation for the reader to walk through that door to examine the world as it really is, rather than as we would like it to be.

As we break our bonds with white power we can truly join the world community. It is not always an easy process—for we carry on our shoulders the accumulated assumptions of generations that have lived on imperialism's pedestal—but it is profoundly fulfilling. Perhaps we could say this is the price of our redemption.

CIVILIZATION SINCE TIME IMMEMORIAL

For thousands of years before an Italian ex-slave trader[3] and mercenary named Christopher Columbus sailed to the Caribbean, financed by the Spanish crown, world trade, culture and civilization flourished.

By 1492, Portugal had already been attacking Africa for a century or more, stealing human beings and extracting vast amounts of gold. It was the Portuguese king who told Columbus that "boats had been found which started out from Guinea and navigated to the west [to the Americas] with merchandise."[4]

Since ancient times, well-traveled trade routes over land and sea provided the means for the interchange of commodities and ideas among African, Arabic and Asian peoples. Evidence long suppressed by Europeans also proves that African people regularly sailed to the Americas hundreds, indeed, thousands of years ago.[5]

From time immemorial, these long-standing spice and silk routes enabled Africans in Timbuktu, Mali, for example, to be linked with other cosmopolitan world centers in northern Africa, the Persian Gulf, Constantinople, India[6] and China.[7] Trade winds and ocean currents to Asia and the Americas created water routes used since antiquity by African mariners.[8] Widely diverse civilizations were thus connected in this way. Gold, salt, silk, spices, oils and precious stones were disseminated, in addition to philosophical and scientific advancements.

It was along these routes that the Swahili people in southeastern Africa shipped an elephant to the court of the Emperor of China nearly a thousand years ago, and African secrets of building pyramids and mummifying the dead were taken to the peoples of Central America as long ago as 850 B.C.[9] One book notes, "The fact that the banana, which seems to derive from Asia, had reached West Africa before the Europeans suggests an international interconnection of great range."[10] For millennia humanity participated in world commerce, enjoyed by all, controlled by none.

Isolated from the global interchange between sophisticated cultures in Africa and other parts of the world, Europe, for all practical purposes, did not exist. What is today known as Europe was made up of warring tribes alienated from the rest of the human race, and desperately competing for scarce resources on cold, barren lands. While Africa enjoyed advanced civilization, Europeans still lived in caves. Notoriously impoverished and ignorant, nomadic European clans from the forests of the north wreaked destruction and violence at every turn. Far from being civilized, the reputation of these early Europeans gave us negative and anti-social concepts still in use today, such as *vandalism* and *barbarity*.

The emergence of southern European cultures along the Mediterranean came about because of their proximity to Africa. Ancient Greece and Rome were directly attributable to the much more ancient African civilization of Egypt, which had been the dominant political and intellectual force in the world for more than 4,000 years. A conscious European identity only manifested itself far later with the advent of slavery and colonialism, which created a world economy benefiting Europe at the expense of everyone else.

The African historian Hosea Jaffe explains in his book, *A History of Africa*:

> Before capitalist colonialism there was no Europe, only a collection of feudal, mercantile and tribal towns, farms, villages, discrete states and kingdoms vying and warring with each other....When [Europe] became connected with and dependent on, first Africa, then the Americas and finally Asia, it began to become a reality and idea. Only when Portuguese, Spanish, French, Italian, Dutch, English, German, Danish and Swedish confronted and clashed with Africa, America and Asia did the need arise for them to consider themselves as a set, a whole, different from, hostile to and, eventually, superior to Africans, Americans and Asians. Colonialism gave them a common interest.[11]

ABUNDANCE, BRILLIANCE AND BEAUTY

Africa is unquestionably the birthplace of civilization and humanity itself. Its glorious history dates back tens of thousands of years and includes, but did not begin with, the great civilization of ancient Egypt. Africa is splendid and it is huge (nearly 11.7 million square miles);[12] all of Europe, India, China and the United States could fit within its borders.[13] The late African scholar W.E.B. DuBois describes it very poetically:

> Africa is a beautiful land; not merely comely and pleasant, but haunted with swamp and jungle; sternly beautiful in its loveliness of terror, its depth of gloom, and fullness of color; its heaven-tearing peaks, its silver of endless sand, the might, width and breadth of its rivers, depth of its lakes and height of its hot, blue heaven. There are myriads of living things, the voice of storm, the kiss of pestilence and pain, old and ever new, new and incredibly ancient.[14]

Warm in climate and abundant in food and natural resources, the life-giving environment of Africa was conducive to the early rise of civilizations. "Somewhere between 50,000 and 100,000 years ago, it seems that man in Africa became a regular user of fire," Howard University professor Joseph E. Harris tells us, in *Africans and Their History*.[15]

African civilization arose in the valley of the Nile River, which flows north for 4,160 miles[16]—more than half the length of Africa—into the Mediterranean. It was in the fertile Nile valley that agriculture was developed and iron tools were first wrought. The late brilliant African scholar Cheikh Anta Diop places the earliest beginnings of Egyptian civilization at 17,000 B.C., when African society developed in the cradle of the Upper Nile and slowly descended to spread out along the Mediterranean basin.[17]

By 7,000 B.C., Africans had domesticated animals and developed agriculture, growing rice, corn, sorghum and yams in several parts of the continent.[18] Africans in Egypt first set a calendar in 4241 B.C. In the most ancient of times, Africans had musical instruments, chairs, beds, jewelry and art as well as advanced concepts of science and technology—including architecture, astronomy and mathematics.[19]

Attesting to the great age and breadth of African civilizations, Diop wrote:

> From the appearance of Homo sapiens—from earliest prehistory until our time—we are able to trace our origins as a people without significant breaks in continuity. In early prehistory, a great South-North movement brought the African peoples of the Great Lakes region into the Nile Basin. They lived there in clusters for millennia.[20]

Characteristically democratic, these first African civilizations were governed by constitutions and a "People's Council on which the various social strata were represented." These states were each headed by a leader whose "mission was to serve the people wisely, and his authority depended on his respect for the established constitution."[21] Throughout his writings, Cheikh Anta Diop demonstrated the cohesive cultural and linguistic legacy of African civilizations, a legacy that continued through centuries.

Egypt was one of the most brilliant and influential of African civilizations, but there were many other remarkable African states which were unique, yet notably similar. Nubia, with its ports on the Red Sea, was one such example. Like Egypt, Nubia (now the Sudan) was a bustling hub that attracted people from Southern Africa as well as the Middle East and Asia. Both Egypt and Nubia "emerged as viable economic, political, and cultural centers in Northeastern Africa with links to other regions of the continent," writes Professor Harris in *Africans and Their History*.[22]

The kingdom of Kush on the Blue Nile was "urban, materially advanced, literate, and existed in the interior of the continent for about a thousand years, with dynamic relations not only with its immediate neighbors but, through trade, with an international community."[23]

Axum, or Ethiopia, was a "wealthy cosmopolis" which "included residents from Egypt, the eastern Roman Empire, Persia, and India." The Ethiopians developed their own written language and became skilled architects and builders in stone, as well as producers of bronze, silver and gold coins.[24]

Egypt and Ethiopia were the first countries in the world to have been ruled by women; Hatshepsut, who reigned for 20 years during Egypt's New Kingdom, and Ethiopia's legendary Queen of Sheba are remembered by history as powerful leaders.[25]

African societies in other parts of the continent also became as powerful creators and traders. Carthage (modern-day Tunisia) in the north, and Ghana, Mali and Songhai in West Africa were long-standing African civilizations, which, though they emerged later, continued to carry Egypt's cultural heritage.

On the eastern coast, south of the Horn, Africans have engaged in commerce and trade with India, China and other parts of Asia since ancient times. Ivory, gums, shells, copper, leopard skins, gold and many other commodities have been exported from this area for millennia. It was here that the civilization of Zimbabwe grew up, and its medieval ruins of enormous stone walls, built skillfully without mortar, draw tourists from around the world today.[26]

DISTORTION OF HISTORY

European historians have long falsified African history in order to justify slavery, colonialism and the plunder of Africa. A speaker from Zimbabwe's liberation movement of the 1970s once told an American audience that the British colonial school system taught him the magnificent stone walls found in his country were "built by Vikings."

White archeologists and "Egyptologists" not only attack Africa ideologically; in typical colonial fashion, they routinely loot Africa of its great artistic treasures. Consequently, any serious African art historian must go to London or Paris or New York to see the masterpieces of his or her own people.

When the British colonial grave robber, Lord Carnarvon, opened and desecrated the tomb of Egyptian King Tutankhamen in 1922, he crudely remarked in a letter, "There is enough stuff to fill the whole upstairs Egyptian section of the B[ritish] M[useum]. I imagine it is the greatest find ever made."[27]

In an effort to wipe out the truth about the magnificence and integrity of African history, Europeans separate Egypt from Africa and propagate the ridiculous myth that the ancient Egyptians were white. Despite the fact that even the briefest look at Egyptian statues and paintings in museums reveals them to be unmistakably African, Europeans have gone to great lengths to maintain this lie.

One cannot help noting, while walking through the stolen Egyptian exhibit in the British Museum, that the noses of so many of the busts and statues are missing. Legend has it that Napoleon shot off the noses of many figures, including the Sphinx, when he invaded Egypt in 1798. No one was to know that the legacy of ancient Egypt with all of its wonders was irrefutably African, not European.

While Europe tries to claim that Egypt was somehow part of the white world, in reality European scientific, artistic, philosophical, theological and even technological understandings derive from African civilization.

Ancient Greece and Rome, upheld by Europeans as the apex of civilization, invaded, sacked, burned and looted Egypt for its science, agriculture and wealth. Europeans didn't just "adopt" or "annex" African ideas. Without the stolen intellectual, artistic and economic foundation of African Egypt there could have been no Roman or Hellenistic cultures in Europe. Egypt was undeniably black. Cheikh Anta Diop has set the record straight:

> The Egyptians were Negroes. The moral fruit of their civilization is to be counted among the assets of the Black world. Instead of presenting itself to history as an insolvent debtor, that Black world is the very initiator of the "western" civilization flaunted before our eyes today. Pythagorean mathematics, the theory of the four elements of Thales of Miletus, Epicurean materialism, Platonic idealism, Judaism, Islam, and modern science are rooted in Egyptian cosmogony and science....To his great surprise and satisfaction, [the African] will discover that most of the ideas used today to domesticate, atrophy, dissolve, or steal his "soul," were conceived by his own ancestors.[28]

ANCIENT TOURISTS FLOCKED TO AFRICA

With the centrality of its location, the beauty of its environment and the attraction of its scientific and artistic achievements, Africa has always been cosmopolitan. Thirty-five hundred years ago tourists from all over the world were flocking to the Nile delta to see the already ancient wonders of Egypt. During the lifetime of King Tutankhamen, about 1300 B.C., the great Sphinx and the pyramids at Giza were well over 1,000 years old.

King Tutankhamen's era was known as the New Kingdom, in the Egyptian Bronze Age. Rich poetic, philosophical and scientific writings from this period survive today. It can be noted that the Bronze Age in Europe has no recorded history whatsoever. One scholar remarks, "Except for a few hundred clay tablets from Greece—most of which appear to be accounting and inventory lists, and none of which seem to be older than about 1400 B.C.—no writings at all have come down to us from Europe's Bronze Age."[29]

For thousands of years B.C., travelers came to Egypt "simply to enlarge their intellectual horizons or out of curiosity....Alexandria had an international reputation for scholarship and medicine....The sick could be cured. Then there were notorious pleasure resorts at Alexandria," explains Brian M. Fagan in *Rape of the Nile.* Fagan continues:

> ...[T]he tourist [of the Bronze Age] could then venture southward up the Nile to another world, where the monuments of antiquity overlooked fertile fields and centuries-old irrigation systems. Although the more serious traveler might examine hundreds of temples, most tourists followed an itinerary which took them from Alexandria to Memphis, the pyramids, the Valley of the Kings, and the lovely island of Philae. These places were easily visited by boat or road. Numerous small inns catered to the needs of the weary traveler. Private contractors hired out their boats or pack animals to organized parties of visitors.[30]

When the Greek historian and traveler Herodotus visited Egypt about 450 B.C., he wrote, "Concerning Egypt itself I shall extend my remarks to a great length, because there is no country that possesses so many wonders, nor any that has such a number of works which defy description."[31] In *Black Spark, White Fire,* Richard Poe notes that:

> [Herodotus] exemplified the respect that the Greeks felt for Egypt. He attributes to the Egyptians the invention of geometry, the solar calendar, stone carving, medicine, and astronomy....Surviving papyri have shown that the

Egyptian mathematicians knew how to calculate the area of circles, triangles and trapezoids, as well as the volume of cylinders, pyramids and other solids, centuries before these skills were known in Greece. Medical texts from Egypt show that its surgeons were skilled at setting bones, removing tumors and stitching wounds.[32]

The harmonious African societies provided Europe with its first introduction to the concept of democracy. The bases of both Plato's *Republic* and Aristotle's *Politics* are taken from Egyptian ideas. Richard Poe quotes the Greek philosopher Krantor summing up Plato around 300 B.C. Krantor observed that "Plato's contemporaries mocked him, saying that he was not the inventor of his republic, but that he had copied Egyptian institutions."[33]

ENGINEERS AND NAVIGATORS

The awe-inspiring Egyptian pyramids attest to a profound and unequaled knowledge of architecture, mathematics, astronomy and engineering. It is still not known how the pyramids could possibly have been built, and attempts by modern-day European and North American engineers to replicate this monumental task have been unsuccessful. Made of stones weighing from 2.5 tons to as much as 70 tons apiece, and rising to heights of as much as 481 feet, "even trying to calculate the logistics of such work, in modern terms, is too overwhelming," states one observer.[34]

Europeans have historically dismissed the African ability to engineer the pyramids, claiming that the monuments were constructed by anyone other than African people. Some popular books by Europeans attribute the great Egyptian monuments to aliens from other planets. One such white nationalist book is *Chariots of the Gods?* by Erich von Däniken, who "invents a divine species from outer space to account for the building of both the Egyptian pyramids and the gigantic stone figures of Easter Island."[35]

Another falsification commonly put forward by Europeans is that African people knew nothing of navigation. Recent discoveries reported by *The London Times* show that 12,000 year old skulls found in Brazil and Colombia are African, pre-dating *by about 3,000 years* the Asian immigration. According to *The Times* article, Africans sailed to Australia and from there to South America as long as 40,000 years ago, a fact evidenced by "charcoal, a chipped stone stool and scraps of food."[36]

By the time of Egypt's New Kingdom in 1500 B.C., sailing was a time-tested art. Reigning during the height of Egypt's power and prosperity, the New Kingdom pharaohs most certainly launched great sea-faring excursions to the many corners of the globe. According to Poe, it was "a time when every port bustled with merchants and travelers from a dozen different countries."[37]

Phoenician ships found on the bottom of the Mediterranean in the late 1990s help to illuminate our knowledge of this period of African navigation. Many scholars believe that the Phoenicians were mercenary seamen for the Egyptians.[38]

The *San Francisco Chronicle* reported on June 24, 1999 that the perfectly preserved 2750 year old ships were laden with large "ceramic containers of wine" which were "probably headed to the pharaoh's table in Egypt."[39]

Although European historians still suppress it, there is considerable evidence that African mariners crossed the Atlantic during many periods of history. Distance was never an obstacle for African sailors, as *The London Times* article substantiates. In 1969 and 1970 the Norwegian explorer Thor Heyerdahl made an Atlantic crossing in models of Egyptian boats constructed from papyrus reeds. In 1970, Heyerdahl set sail from the Moroccan port of Safi in an exact replica of an Egyptian vessel which he named the *Ra II*.[40] Richard Poe tells us:

After 57 days, Heyerdahl sailed triumphantly into Bridge-town Harbor in Barbados, ending an epic journey of 3,270 nautical miles. He had not proved that the ancient Egyptians ever crossed the Atlantic. But he had shown, beyond question, that they were fully capable of such a voyage. Contrary to expert opinion, neither the alleged flimsiness of the boat nor its flat bottom had proved to be a problem.[41]

Poe believes that the Egyptians were accomplished navigators who "knew no frontiers, needed no passport or identity papers or tickets. The Earth was free, the world lay open, and they wandered across it as though a thousand miles was nothing but a joyous adventure."[42]

Further evidence reveals that Africans lived for centuries on the East Coast of South America, which is only about 1,500 miles from the West Coast of Africa. The magnificent sculptures of African heads from the Olmec civilization found in Mexico and Central America date back more than 2,700 years.[43]

These massive six- to eight-foot high, unmistakably African heads are carved from single blocks of basalt. Among the clusters of these enormous statues are found engravings "closely resembling an Egyptian sphinx and the Egyptian god Ra."[44] In all, 11 African colossi have been found in the Olmec world of Central America.[45]

According to Ivan Van Sertima, who published well-researched evidence in *They Came Before Columbus: The African Presence in Ancient America*, the Aztec and Mayan pyramids date back no earlier than the Olmec sculptures. This fact, along with many other cultural similarities, asserts Van Sertima, further indicates direct African contact with the indigenous peoples of the region.[46]

Chinese scholars have uncovered relics attesting to on-going visitation by Africans dating from 206 B.C. Professor Joseph Harris tells us, for example, in "1954 a figurine with 'typical African features' was unearthed in a Tang tomb near Xi-an where it had been buried in 854 A.D. as a funerary object."[47]

Despite this and other impressive data, European historians and "Egyptologists" continue to obscure the truth about Africa.

DEMOCRATIC, MATRIARCHAL SOCIETIES

Resilient and cohesive in the face of the onslaught against it, African civilization survived, according to Diop's earlier quote, "without significant breaks in continuity" well beyond the 4,000 year reign of the pharaohs. Nubia and Ethiopia kept alive much of the Egyptian tradition for centuries after it was conquered by the Persians in 525 B.C., the Greeks in 332 B.C. and the Romans in 30 B.C.

African people fought back against these early invasions, waging what is known as the Punic Wars from 264 to 201 B.C. Hamilcar Barca and his son Hannibal of Carthage led these wars of resistance. Hannibal was a military genius who in 218 B.C. "astounded the Romans by crossing the Alps with an army of troops and elephants and descending into Italy" in a mere two weeks time, an achievement regarded as one the greatest feats of ancient warfare.[48]

Even though North Africa was unable to repel wave after wave of invasions, looting, rape and destruction by Europeans and Arabs, Professor Harris points out that Egypt's "political, economic, and cultural tentacles" long exerted a profound influence in Africa as well as the world. "In that way," Harris concludes, "Africa became a touchstone of ancient world civilization which continued to be fed for centuries by a continuous and abounding input from Africans and Africa."[49]

Africa was known for its sense of justice. It had collective, prosperous and healthy societies in which there was no need for prisons, police, welfare or unemployment. Orphans, widows and others with difficulties were taken care of by the collective. The Arab traveler

Ibn Battuta who visited Timbuktu in the 1300s, and whose journal survives today, wrote that African people "detest injustice."[50]

In addition, Battuta noted the "complete and general safety one enjoys throughout the land. The traveler has no more reason to fear brigands, thieves, or ravishers than the man who stays at home."[51]

For many foreigners throughout the ages, the free and unself-conscious position of women in Africa was always remarkable and sometimes shocking.

The stunning golden walls of a shrine found in King Tutankhamen's tomb contain pictures in bas-relief of the king and his wife, Queen Ankhesenamum, which beautifully portray an equitable, loving, and companionable relationship between the two. They depict scenes of life in Africa 3,500 years ago: Ankhesenamum is fastening a necklace around Tutankhamen's neck; the king is pouring a perfumed liquid into the queen's hand and the queen is hunting with the king.[52]

A thousand years after the death of Tutankhamen, the position of African women was still noteworthy. Herodotus observed in 450 B.C.:

> Not only is the climate different from that of the rest of the world and the rivers unlike any other rivers, but the people also, in most of their manners and customs, exactly reverse the common practice of mankind. The women attend the markets and trade, while the men sit at home at the loom.[53]

An editor's footnote to Herodotus' statement in the Everyman edition of *Herodotus' Histories* comments:

> If...Herodotus had told us that the Egyptian women enjoy greater liberty, confidence and consideration than under the hareem system of the Greeks and Persians, he would

have been fully justified, for the treatment of women in Egypt was far better than in Greece.[54]

Another millennium passed by the time the rather ill-humored traveler, Ibn Battuta, rode his camel across the Sahara Desert into Mali in the 1340s. Battuta wrote quite a bit about the freedom that African women enjoyed—apparently much to his dismay. In one episode of his journal, Battuta was so outraged at the casual friendships between African women and men that he rushed out of the house of his wealthy African host in a huff, never to return. Battuta chronicled:

> One day I entered upon Abu Muhammad Yandakan....I found him sitting on a mat and in the middle of his house was a bed with a canopy. On it was a woman and with her a man was sitting, and the two were conversing. I said to him, "Who is this woman?" He said, "She is my wife." I said, "What is [the relationship of] the man with her to her?" He said, "He is her companion." I said, "Do you accept this when you have lived in our country and have known the matters of the *shar* [divine law]?" He said to me, "Women's companionship with men in our country is honorable and takes place in a good way: there is no suspicion about it. They are not like the women in your country." I was astonished at his thoughtless answer and I went away from him and did not go to him after this. Though he invited me many times, I did not respond.[55]

Yandakan and his wife probably had a good laugh at poor Battuta.

Cheikh Anta Diop has brilliantly summed up that it was the different material conditions in Africa and Europe which shaped their very different and opposing worldviews, cultures and societies. Diop shows that while the "northern cradle" of Europe was nomadic, patriarchal, oppressive, individualist and violent, Africa and the "southern cradle" were sedentary, matriarchal, collective, democratic and peaceful in nature.

Diop believed that matriarchy, a society in which the family line is passed to the children through the mother instead of the father, was a significant characteristic affecting all of African life, including its state organization. His thesis is that a matriarchal society lends itself to collectivity. Diop describes African society as characterized by

> ...[an] unconcern for tomorrow, a material solidarity of right for each individual, which makes moral or material misery unknown to the present day; there are people living in poverty but no one feels alone and no one is in distress. In the moral domain, it shows an ideal of peace, of justice, of goodness and an optimism which eliminates all notion of guilt or original sin in religious and metaphysical institutions.[56]

"HOW CAN YOU BUY OR SELL THE SKY?"

The profound and ground-breaking Diop analyzed the European character as well, pointing out that Europe's topography contributed to the singular social and psychological traits of its people. Cold climate, barren land, nomadic lifestyle and geographic isolation from world culture produced poverty, ignorance, violence, disrespect for other peoples, oppression of women, patriarchy. Diop summed up the European succinctly: "He was cruel."[57]

It was out of these conditions in Europe that the rather uncommon concept of private property evolved. This notion was very different from the tradition of collective use of land which, deriving from of a sense of unity with the environment, was the norm throughout most of the world. This uniquely European idea of private land ownership has been the basis of countless campaigns of genocide against African and indigenous peoples, many of whom had no linguistic concepts for owning a piece of the Earth. Thus the seizure of land became one of the tools for European domination and exploitation of others. Diop observes:

> Giving a divine character to property is an Aryan custom: in Rome, Greece, and India* it led to the isolation from society of an entire category of individuals who had no family, had neither hearth nor home, and no right of ownership.[58]

Indeed, the European worship of the "divine character of property" continues to result in millions of colonized peoples who have no rights to their homelands, nor even food, clothing and shelter which they once abundantly enjoyed.

"[N]either king nor lord in Black Africa," Diop continues, "ever felt he possessed the land. Land possession there never polarized the consciousness of political power."[59]

The incomprehensibility of land ownership to the majority of human societies was expressed eloquently centuries later by Chief Stealth (also known as Seattle). He stated in 1854:

> How can you buy or sell the sky, the warmth of the land? The idea is strange to us. If we do not own the freshness of the air and the sparkle of the water, how can you buy them? Every part of this earth is sacred to my people. Every shining pine needle, every sandy shore, every mist in the dark woods, every clearing and humming insect is holy in the memory and experience of my people. The

---

* Many historians believe India was conquered by Aryans who set up the caste system there about 1500 B.C.

sap which courses through the trees carries the memories of the red man.[60]

VANDALS, BARBARIANS AND PREDATORS

The European has historically measured his worth by conquest. His main strategy for obtaining the material resources for life has always been pillage and looting of other peoples and cultures. Indeed, pillage and looting were to become the basis of capitalism.

One European historian acknowledges without a second thought the fact that European looting is the basis for its economic system when he stated that "Vikings...were pirates, and piracy is the first stage of commerce."[61] This statement betrays the Eurocentrism of the author. Piracy is the basis of commerce for white people. The rest of the world had been trading quite amicably and equitably for thousands of years as we have seen.

The assault that Europe unleashed upon Africa and the world in the process of building capitalism was a logical outgrowth of the concept that "piracy is the first stage of commerce." With violence, brutality and ruthlessness, Europeans, when they set out from the forests and caves of the north, destroyed world civilization and altered the course of history. While various peoples resisted European attacks fiercely, many were not prepared militarily or emotionally to repel the incessant invasions. As with the question of private property, most cultures had neither words nor historic precedent for the kind of terror the Europeans brought.

In short, Europe's barbarous assault on world civilization was to culminate in the complete expropriation of the life-giving resources and labor of the peoples of the world for the benefit of white people. This is a relationship that could only be maintained by constant violence and economic dependency imposed by the oppressors.

Africans and many other peoples of the world were long wary of Europeans. Aryans, Goths, Celts, Vandals, Barbarians, Vikings and other Europeans reportedly provoked more concern than an encounter with savage beasts. Africans and their eastern neighbors were for the most part content to let the Europeans stay in the northern regions. Richard Poe comments:

> Europe's most dangerous predators were not animals, but men....perhaps the fiercest barbarians were the Celts. In battle, they made a hideous spectacle, stripping themselves naked and howling like beasts....Celts would carry back the heads of their victims dangling from their saddles, embalm them in cedar oil and hang them outside their houses or display them to guests. Sometimes the Celts used captured heads as footballs.[62]

The Scythians drank the blood of men they slew in battle and took the scalps from their victims, using them to wipe their dirty hands on. Herodotus noted, "The Scyth is proud of these scalps and hangs them from his bridle-rein."[63]

Poe also notes that cannibalism "appears to have been widespread in Darkest Europe."[64]

Europeans used these traditional practices of scalping and eating human beings as part of their attacks on African and indigenous peoples. In white power's usual manner it then attributed scalping and cannibalism to the victims of such terroristic practices.

IGNORANCE AND POVERTY IN EUROPE

As the centuries passed, Greece and subsequently Rome were overrun by barbaric northern tribes, while Egypt and northern Africa were conquered by Turks and Arabs. In the process, Europe lost all contact with Africa, which had long provided its intellectual and economic lifeblood. Possessing neither inherent cultural nor material resources, all of Europe—including the Mediterranean regions which once basked in Africa's reflected light—were plunged into social backwardness.

Like a parasite without a host, Europe spent half a millennium withering in poverty, ignorance and disease. This was the European Dark Ages, defined, according to one source, as the "period of European history between the fall of the Roman Empire in A.D. 476 and about A.D. 1000, for which there are few historical records and during which life was comparatively uncivilized."[65] It is interesting to note that the word Europe reportedly comes from a Semitic word meaning "darkness."[66]

By contrast, North Africa and the Middle East in this period were rich in natural wealth and characterized by a sophisticated cultural and intellectual life. The region continued to be dominated by the profound heritage of Egyptian civilization, and everyone wanted a piece of it.

On the heels of the earlier Persian and Greek conquests of Egypt, the Romans overtook and colonized Egypt and Carthage in 30 B.C. when Julius Caesar sacked Alexandria. The Romans were dependent on Africa to supply gold and resources including grain, linen, papyrus and beautiful glass to Europe, extracted "by imperial authorities without payment of any sort."[67]

When the Germanic tribes then conquered Rome early in the fifth century A.D., the Vandals seized control of Carthage and its resources, until they were then routed by the army of Justinian, the Byzantine emperor, in the year 527.

While Europe was mired in the poverty and ignorance during these centuries, the regions around Palestine were resplendent with "lush gardens and towns full of wine, bread, cheese and oil."[68] Eyeing the treasures of Palestine and Africa, Europe responded characteristically by looking for solutions to its problems at the expense of others. Late in the eleventh century, Europeans launched the Crusades, "holy wars" of aggression and plunder. The Crusades were early attempts to seize the regions around Palestine from the Saracens (Turks) and to colonize them.

CRUSADES OF PLUNDER

The Roman Catholic Pope Urban II made the call for the first Crusade, admonishing Europeans in a telling statement:

> Your land is shut in on all sides by the sea and the mountains, and it is too thickly populated. There is not much wealth here, and the soil scarcely yields enough to support you....Set out on the road to the Holy Sepulcher, take that land from the wicked people and make it your own![69]

A millennium or so earlier, the same words could have been uttered by Alexander of Greece or Julius Caesar of Rome; 800 years later the British imperialist Cecil Rhodes or the American Theodore Roosevelt might have pronounced them. Africa was always used to solve Europe's problems.

So in April of the year 1096, 15,000 Europeans set out for Constantinople (today's Istanbul, Turkey) and ultimately Palestine in what is called the "People's Crusade." One imagines a Monte Python movie,* except that it wasn't very funny for the victims of the holy warriors. Jay Williams testifies about this crusade in his book, *Knights of the Crusades*:

> Consequently, wherever they traveled they ate up the land like a mass of hungry locusts....Many were no better than thieves or cutthroats. Their passage through Hungary and Bulgaria....was marked by the slaughter of inno-

---

* Monte Python was a British comedy troupe of the 1970s. Their movie, *The Holy Grail* depicted King Arthur and the exploits of hapless, wayward medieval knights.

cent farmers, the wholesale plundering of villages and towns and even the burning of entire cities.

They arrived on August 1 in Constantinople, where they were received patiently and kindly by the Emperor Alexius....Here they began pillaging and looting the countryside, even butchering the Christian Greeks who lived in surrounding villages. They fought constantly among themselves, and a large section split off from the leadership...and went raiding as far as the city of Nicaea.... [Meanwhile] the Turks had gathered troops and attacked the invaders. In a swift campaign against the crusading commoners they killed or captured all but a small number....The People's Crusade, begun with such high hopes ended in blood, having accomplished nothing.[70]

Europeans waged these crusades of plunder, pillage and attempted colonization for 200 years until Palestine was definitively conquered by the Turks in 1291. The Europeans were driven back to their northern countries, soon chased by another family of Turks, the Ottomans, who occupied much of eastern Europe for centuries.

Despite its military defeat by the Turks, Europe and ultimately the face of the Earth had been altered by these years of aggression. As a result of two centuries of plunder, enormous wealth was appropriated by Europeans. The Crusades introduced Europe to the splendor of the African world and the riches tied to the ancient trade routes, which Europe now attempted to dominate.

An international Italian textile industry was built after the Crusades with wool from England, cotton from Egypt and silk from Persia. "Italy ran a consistent trade surplus [in] North Africa. The bill was settled in gold, which enabled the north Italian cities to issue a gold coinage, the first to be seen in the west for 500 years."[71] As a result of the loot from the Crusades, Europe faced an unprecedented prosperity.[72]

Many of the knights of the Crusades became so incredibly wealthy from the pillage that they gained more power than kings and the Catholic pope. One organization of knights, known as the Templars, built castles and centers all over Europe that were repositories of stolen wealth taken from Africa and the Middle East.

The Templars represented one of Europe's first attempts at international banking and corporate power. Their stolen wealth was so great that a Templar could "deposit" his loot in their Palestine castle and write a check for it back at another castle in Europe. The Templars were money-lenders to the kings of Europe, who often became deeply indebted to them.[73]

"HOLY WARS" AMASS STOLEN LOOT

The 200 years of ravishing Africans and Arabs began the process of accumulating the start-up resources for early European capitalism. This process would later be consolidated by the trade in African people and the plunder of Africa, Asia and the Americas. Indeed, the Crusades continued the Greek and Roman precedent for developing Europe by "underdeveloping" others.

More than material wealth was plundered. As in ancient times, scientific and artistic knowledge, as well as elements of a more sophisticated lifestyle, were taken. It was through this period of plunder that Europe came out of its "Dark Ages," at least for those of the upper classes. The majority of Europeans were no more than serfs, near-slaves tied to the land of the feudal lords.

The Italian Renaissance, which sprang up in the fourteenth century and spread throughout Europe, was both financially and intellectually indebted to the cultured African and Arabic world. Arguably the sudden burst of building cathedrals and castles throughout Europe during this period became possible through secrets of architecture that Arabs may have learned from Africans when they conquered Egypt in 639 A.D. The Freemasons, a European secret society dating from the period of the Crusades, still use the Egyptian pyramid for its symbol today, as does the American dollar bill.

European knowledge of navigation was most likely learned in Africa where the ancient sea-faring arts were retained. As we showed earlier, Portugal, one of the earliest European sea-going countries, had learned much about sailing from its invasions of Africa, as well as, no doubt, from the African Moors who had inhabited the country for centuries.

Through contact with Africans, Turks and Arabs during the Crusades, Europeans encountered world civilization for the first time in half a millennium. From the North Africans, Europeans were exposed to and began to adopt qualities that were quite foreign to the European character: romantic love, an appreciation for poetry, music and art, and a code of conduct known as chivalry. Even sports, cuisine and the enjoyment of leisure time were learned during the attacks on North Africa.

Knights of the Crusades "developed a taste for spices in their food."[74] In place of their customary bland, tasteless meals, Europeans now learned to season their food in the manner of peoples around the world. In the usual European style, however, they overdid it. A medieval European cookbook calls for rabbit to be prepared with "ground almonds, saffron, ginger, cypress root, cinnamon, sugar, cloves, and nutmeg."[75] Notably, none of these ingredients except the rabbit were indigenous to Europe. The book, *Tastes of Paradise*, concludes that plunder from the Crusades had a

> ...direct and obvious effect upon medieval Europe... [with] luxuries that ushered in an entirely new way of life. And many of these new items even brought along their original Arabic names to the West. The carpet, the sofa—with which previously bare and uncomfortable living quarters were now furnished, were Arabic, as were silk, velvet, damask, and taffeta, in which the upper classes now

dressed—in contradistinction to the coarse linen of their subjects.[76]

To African people the art of living well emanated from a culture that reflected an easy-going interaction with humanity, the Earth and the universe. Europe was characteristically at war—with other people and with the forces of nature itself, which it sought to dominate. For Europeans, social skills and the fine arts were but a veneer, more stolen booty from other peoples.

The affectation of culture, chivalry and romantic love did nothing to change the violent and oppressive character of Europeans. It did not bring about equality for women or just societies such as those in Africa. The newly found chivalric regard for women was but a European distortion of the genuine political power of and societal respect for women in Africa, qualities which flowed naturally out of the matriarchal societies there. In Europe, romantic love and chivalry were adopted as weapons *against* women, enforcing the constriction of female social mobility and creating the basis of the patriarchal family.

Dating from the era of the Crusades, upper-class European women became idealized as part of the property rights of men, and the general oppression of women became formalized. Typically, Europeans turned a stolen African concept into its opposite. It is notable that during this period of European "chivalry," the torture and burning of European women as "witches" became a common practice. Thus, while romantic love arose out of matriarchy in Africa, it became a tool of patriarchy in Europe.

EUROPEAN SQUALOR

Newly acquired European "culture" was enjoyed only by the privileged elite. Europeans were unable to also annex the collective and humanitarian African spirit. For the majority of Europeans, life was miserable. Though the "chivalrous" rich feasted gluttonously on well-seasoned fare, the rest of the population literally starved to death. England and France were fighting incessantly over the spoils of the Crusades. Plagues swept through the European cities every few years. Fleas from rats in the filthy European urban centers spread what was known as the "Black Death," killing up to 75 percent of the population, mostly from the masses of the poor.

However, the enormous casualties from the plagues seem "to have had astonishingly little impact on the political and economic life of Europe. England and France were kicking each other to bits again within a few years; the armies were a little smaller but the national strategies were unchanged," one account notes.[77]

In his excellent book, *American Holocaust: The Conquest of the New World*, David Stannard gives a graphic picture of life for the European masses in the good old days:

"Roadside ditches, filled with stagnant water, served as public latrines in the cities of the fifteenth century, and they would continue to do so for centuries to follow."

When poor people died, their bodies were thrown "side by side, row by row" into large, deep open pits. "Only when the pit was filled with bodies was it finally covered over with earth."[78]

Professor Stannard goes on:

Along with the stench and repulsive appearance of the openly displayed dead, human and animal alike, a modern visitor to a European city in this era would be repelled by the appearance and the vile aromas given off by the living as well. Most people never bathed, not once in an entire lifetime. Almost everyone had his or her brush with smallpox and other deforming diseases that left survivors partially blinded, pock-marked, or crippled, while it was the norm for men and women to have "bad breath from the rotting teeth and constant stomach disorders which can be documented from many sources, while suppurating ulcers, eczema, scabs, running sores and other nauseating skin diseases were extremely common, and often lasting for years."[79]

In medieval Europe, moreover, alcoholism was rampant. Before the potato was stolen from the native people of the Americas, "beer was second only to bread as the main source of nourishment for most central and north Europeans." The English family "consumed about three liters of beer per person daily, children included."[80]

"Street crime in most cities lurked around every corner," Stannard notes. He quotes another scholar as saying, "This was a time when it was one of the festive pleasures of Midsummer Day to burn alive one or two dozen cats...." Stannard adds:

> But what Lawrence Stone has said about the typical English village also was likely true throughout Europe at this time—that is, that because of the dismal social conditions and prevailing social values, it "was a place filled with malice and hatred, its only unifying bond being the occasional episode of mass hysteria, which temporarily bound together the majority in order to harry and persecute the local witch."[81]

During many years, Stannard tells us, as many as a third of the population of many towns was accused of witchcraft with one-tenth being executed for it in a single year.

> Violence, of course, was everywhere...but occasionally it took on an especially perverse character. In addition to the hunting down and burning of witches, which was an everyday affair in most locales, in Milan in 1476 a man was torn to pieces by an enraged mob and his dismembered limbs were then eaten by his tormentors. In Paris

and Lyon, Huguenots were killed and butchered, and their various body parts were sold openly in the streets. Other eruptions of bizarre torture, murder, and ritual cannibalism were not uncommon.[82]

During the Middle Ages, torture was routinely practiced throughout Europe. The most infamous device for torment was the "rack," an insidious device used by the English and the Spanish to stretch the body "until the ligaments, and then the fibers of the muscles themselves, are torn." Further stretching ruptured the muscles of the abdomen, and, if the torture is continued, the limbs will be dislocated, and finally torn from their sockets."[83] These and other methods were used by Europeans against Africans and the indigenous people in the Americas.

TRADE ROUTES CONQUERED

The social system during the time of the Crusades was known as feudalism, characterized by masses of serfs tied to lands ruled by aristocratic lords. At the same time, plunder and the growing European domination of world trade routes created a new class, the rising bourgeoisie.* This new business class included bankers, merchants and moneylenders.

By the fifteenth century, Europeans controlled the traffic on the Mediterranean, having conquered the trade routes from Constantinople to Syria, and around the northern coast of Africa to Gibraltar. With this wealth Europe developed an "economic and strictly capitalistic activity which was gradually to communicate itself to all the lands north of the Alps."[84] One historian observes the process that is taken for granted as the method of European development:

---

* The term "bourgeoisie" is literally French for "city dwellers."

While Europe forged ahead, the Near East stood still or even slipped back. Egypt, for example, which had been exporting paper to Europe in the eleventh century, was importing it from Italy in the fifteenth.[85]

With a taste of the riches outside its borders, Europe aspired to command the wealth of the world; it was hungry for land to colonize and gold to steal. It looked to Africa, the richest of all the continents, known for its abundance of precious ores and diamonds, which lay scattered on the ground.

Hosea Jaffe records some of the early European plunder of Africa, which provided the stolen wealth necessary for the birth of capitalism:

The first recorded commercial explorations by Genoese merchants in Africa were as early as 1291, in Dante's life-time. In 1341 Portuguese merchants were going to the Canaries with the Italians, and three years later the Vatican ordered the French admiral de la Cerda to seize the Canaries. By 1364 Normans from France were trading and raiding along the Cape Verde coast; by 1375 the Spanish in Majorca knew enough to enable Cresques to show Timbuktu and Gao on a map, with other Mali and Niger towns. In 1402 merchants from Toulouse were settling in Timbuktu and Gao, and in the same year de Bethencourt seized the Canaries. Thus the fourteenth century saw considerable penetration of west and north Africa by Italian, Portuguese, French and Spanish colonialists. This period of primitive or primary accumulation prepared the "take-off" of capitalism, which Marx put at the year 1500.[86]

The primary accumulation was no small sum. Jaffe calculates that already by the year 1500, Portugal alone had expropriated at least 700 tons of gold from Africa, a sum worth billions of dollars today. The value of the gold, diamonds and other precious metals, gems and resources along with the human beings forcibly extracted from Africa is probably incalculable. Certainly it accounts for the ability of white people everywhere to enjoy the highest standard of living in the world. The human price extracted by Europeans from African people in terms of terror, slaughter, rape and genocide is hardly mentioned in European history books.

Onslaught Begins

In the fourteenth and fifteenth centuries, Mali in western Africa experienced a golden age, and its capital city, Timbuktu, had a lively population of more than 100,000. Timbuktu's Sankore University was renowned for law and medicine, and delicate cataract operations were routinely performed by accomplished surgeons. The intellectual life of Timbuktu "was brisk and stimulating" and its citizens "sophisticated and knowledgeable."[87]

It is a testament to the on-going slander of African people and their history that in the United States today "Timbuktu" is commonly used to designate a spot as remote as possible from civilization.

W.E.B. DuBois asserts that there can be "no doubt that the level of culture among the masses of...West Africa in the fifteenth century was higher than that of northern Europe, by any standard of measurement—homes, clothes, artistic creation and appreciation, political organization and religious consistency."[88] But Europeans were hungry for land, gold and human labor, and thus the devastating onslaught on Africa began.

Portugal's Prince Henry the Navigator was instrumental in institutionalizing the enslavement of African people a half century before

Columbus sailed to the Americas. One account describes the onslaught of his men:

> Excited by stories of the great wealth of Africa and Asia, [Henry] ordered his ships to explore the coast of Africa. There on a fateful day in 1444, Henry's men came upon the first large group of Africans. They tiptoed through the high grass and crept to the edge of the village and then, said a contemporary, "they looked towards the settlement and saw that the Moors, with their women and children, were already coming as quickly as they could out of their dwellings, because they had caught sight of their enemies." But [the Portuguese], shouting out...attacked them, killing and taking all they could...[89]

Soon the rest of Europe was following in the footsteps of Portugal to share in the rape of Africa, feast on its resources and enslave its people. As Diop pointed out, Europeans used Africa's own philosophical and scientific concepts to conquer and exploit it.

BLOODY HANDS REACH ACROSS OCEAN

Even as Europe was tightening its grip on Africa, it was extending its bloody fingers across the Atlantic, setting out to conquer new territories. Within a year of Columbus' first deadly excursion to the Americas, the Catholic Pope Alexander VI "divided the world into Spanish and Portuguese spheres of interest, in effect pronouncing for the first time that Europe was to rule the world."[90]

Brazil was handed over to Portugal, which is why Portuguese, not Spanish, is spoken there today. Thus the Catholic Church, the so-called moral leader of Europe, sealed the fate of genocide and enslavement for countless millions of people from Africa and the Americas.

The Inescapable Dialectic

Like Africans and Asians, the peoples of the so-called Americas lived for thousands of years in magnificent civilizations before their invasion by bloodthirsty, gun-wielding white men. They were open and hospitable to foreigners. Columbus' own journals reveal his brutality and cynicism in the face of the welcoming stance of the indigenous peoples:

> As soon as I arrived in the Indies, on the first island which I found, I took some of the natives by force, in order that they might learn and might give me information of whatever there is in these parts. And so it was that they soon understood us, and we them, either by speech or signs, and they have been very serviceable. At present, those I bring with me are still of the opinion that I come from Heaven, for all the intercourse which they have had with me. They were the first to announce this wherever I went....So all came, men and women alike, when their minds were set at rest concerning us, no one, small or great, remaining behind, and they all brought something to eat and drink, which they gave with extraordinary affection.[91]

David Stannard reveals in *American Holocaust* that everywhere Columbus landed on his voyages his troops raped and murdered:

> Wherever the marauding, diseased, and heavily armed Spanish forces went out on patrol, accompanied by ferocious armored dogs that had been trained to kill and disembowel, they preyed on the local communities— already plague-enfeebled—forcing them to supply food and women and slaves, and whatever else the soldiers might desire. At virtually every landing...Columbus' troops had gone ashore and killed indiscriminately, as

though for sport, whatever animals and birds and natives they encountered, "looting and destroying all they found," as [Columbus'] son Fernando blithely put it.[92]

The Americas were by no means empty lands as the colonizers so deceitfully portray. The indigenous civilizations were ancient, varied and magnificent. Professor Stannard emphasizes this point. Tenochtitlán, the Aztec city located on the site of present-day Mexico City, had about 350,000 residents at the end of the fifteenth century, with a total of about 25 million in the surrounding region. In the sixteenth century, the city's population was at least five times greater than that of either London or Seville. When Europeans arrived at Tenochtitlán they found this magnificent city overwhelmingly beautiful.

Led by Montezuma, Tenochtitlán reflected a quality of life far superior to anything in the ugly, disease-ridden and violent towns of Europe. The mountainous city contained about 60,000 stucco houses with "very pleasant gardens of various sorts of flowers both on the upper and lower floors," according to the journal of conquistador Hernando Cortés, which is quoted by Stannard.

The Spanish conquerors were filled with awe at the city's floating gardens and fresh drinking water piped in by a huge aqueduct system. Located at 7,200 feet above sea-level and situated on a series of interconnected lakes, Tenochtitlán viewed from a distance was breathtaking.

Being typical Europeans who bathed rarely if ever, Cortés and his men were astonished by the hygiene and colorful dress of the people who used soaps, deodorants and breath sweeteners.

There was an enormous Great Market on the city's north side where "more than sixty thousand people come each day to buy and sell, and where every kind of merchandise produced in these lands is found; provisions, as well as ornaments of gold and silver, lead, brass, copper, tin, stones, shells, bones, and feathers." So wrote

Cortés who went on for pages about the splendors of the market which was unparalleled in all of Europe.

"And," states Stannard, "this was only the market. The rest of Tenochtitlán overflowed with gorgeous gardens, arboretums, and aviaries. Artwork was everywhere, artwork...dazzling in conception and execution."[93]

Bernal Díaz traveled with Cortés and wrote about the "multi-colored birds—parrots, hummingbirds, falcons, jays, herons, owls, condors, and dozens and dozens of other exotic species—who lived in public aviaries that the government maintained."[94] The splendors of Tenochtitlán were beyond description for the Europeans, and the quality of life for the entire population was unheard of in Europe.

HOLOCAUST IN THE AMERICAS

Montezuma welcomed Cortés and his band of soldiers who claimed that they were visiting Tenochtitlán in peace. The great Aztec leader invited the Spanish to participate in a festive ceremony that was taking place at that moment. As Professor Stannard describes, "Once the Spanish were inside the city's gates, however, it soon became apparent that this was a far from conciliatory mission."[95]

Wasting no time, the vicious Spanish got right down to business. According to a report of the scene quoted by Stannard:

> The first Spaniards to start fighting suddenly attacked those who were playing the music for the singers and dancers. They chopped off their hands and their heads so that they fell down dead. Then all the other Spaniards began to cut off heads, arms, and legs and to disembowel the Indians. Some had their heads cut off, others were cut in half, and others had their bellies slit open, immediately to fall dead.[96]

But the Aztecs fiercely and brilliantly resisted the Spanish. Stannard tells us:

> As the European interlopers' own accounts make clear, individual Indian warriors repeatedly showed themselves the equal, and more, of any among the Spanish militia. The story of one Aztec soldier who, in hand-to-hand combat, fought off a handful of Spanish horsemen...was but one among innumerable such reports from the conquistadors themselves.[97]

The Spanish were routed in this battle, but they left behind a deadly weapon: the smallpox germ that swept through the Aztec population for two months, seriously decimating the population. Once the disease wiped out most of the Aztec leadership, Cortés attacked again.

Eduardo Galeano in *Open Veins of Latin America*, quotes Cortés' journals of 1521 as the Spaniards leveled the magnificent city and wiped out its incredible people, sparing no cruelty. "Devastated, burned and littered with corpses, the city fell," writes Galeano of the ravishing of Tenochtitlán.

Their admiration of Tenochtitlán not withstanding, it took only a few years for the Spanish destroyers to completely devastate the city and the Aztec civilization. Cortés and his band of murderers razed the vast agricultural lands surrounding the city and plundered the incredibly rich gold mines. Galeano quotes indigenous writings which reflect the disdain that the original peoples had for the bloodthirsty, barbaric, gold-hungry Europeans:

> The Spaniards "were in seventh heaven," says the Nahuatl text preserved in the Florentine Codex. "They lifted up the gold as if they were monkeys, with expressions of joy, as if it put new life into them and lit up their

hearts. As if it were certainly something for which they yearn with a great thirst. Their bodies fatten on it and they hunger violently for it. They crave gold like hungry swine."[98]

When Columbus arrived in the Americas, as many as 300 million people lived between what is now Alaska and Chile and in the Caribbean islands. The Europeans helped themselves to the native people's land, which was already quite "settled."

James W. Loewen explains in *Lies My Teacher Told Me: Everything Your American History Textbook Got Wrong*:

> The invaders followed a pattern: throughout the hemisphere Europeans pitched camp right in the middle of Native populations—Cuzco, Mexico City, Natchez, Chicago. Throughout New England, colonists appropriated Indian cornfields for their initial settlements, avoiding the backbreaking labor of clearing the land of forest and rock....The new settlers encountered no wilderness....[99]

TORTURE AND TERROR

The genocide against the native peoples of this hemisphere was swift and vast. To read the history of this ghastly slaughter in *American Holocaust* or *Open Veins of Latin America* is extremely disturbing. As in Africa, great and ancient civilizations, some dating back tens of thousands of years, were annihilated. Suddenly, after only a few years of European invasion, nothing was left but concentration camps called "reservations," and in some places spectacular ruins to feed the colonizers' tourist industry.

In addition to the Aztecs, millions of other indigenous peoples in this hemisphere were killed at the first contact with Europeans by diseases for which the peoples of the Americas had no defenses. Because of the lack of hygiene, diseases and plagues raced through

Europe for thousands of years. Ultimately many Europeans developed immunities to these microbes which were unknown among the indigenous peoples.

Just to be breathed upon by a European was deadly. Smallpox, tetanus, intestinal and venereal diseases, yellow fever, leprosy, typhus and dental cavities wiped out more than half of the indigenous population of America, Australia and Oceania following the European invasion.[100]

Exposure to these plagues greatly weakened the ability of the indigenous people to resist the European invasions. Ninety percent of the population in Mexico was wiped out by epidemics within 50 years of the first invasion by Cortés. The Tainos of Española were decimated by a strain of influenza transmitted by hogs being transported from the Canary Islands by Columbus.[101]

The Europeans soon learned that the germs they carried were effective tools for genocide. Ward Churchill comments in *A Little Matter of Genocide*:

> There can be no question that Christopher Columbus and his crew—and undoubtedly others of the early Spanish invaders as well—were unaware at the outset that they were carrying pathogens to which America's native peoples had never been exposed and therefore possessed no immunity, and of the extent of the lethal effect these microbes would unleash. Onsets do not, however, last forever. By 1550 at the latest, and probably earlier, it was common knowledge in Europe that there was a firm correlation between the arrival of "explorers, settlers and military expeditions" on the one hand and massive die-offs of native peoples—and diseases on the other. This is frequently remarked upon—piously attributed to the "hand of God" and often celebrated—in the literature of the day.[102]

Besides their germs, the Europeans used gunpowder and lethal weapons against the native peoples, a practice they had begun to perfect in Africa. It was the advantage of deadly and unequaled firepower that eventually overwhelmed the fierce and often brilliant indigenous and African resistance. An explosive made up of potassium nitrate, charcoal and sulfur, the substance known as gunpowder had been used by the Chinese peacefully in pyrotechnics for centuries.[103]

Diop points out that although the African was the "first to discover iron, he had built no cannon; the secret of gunpowder was known only to the Egyptian priests, who used it solely for religious purposes at rites such as the Mysteries of Osiris."[104] Learning of the powder from the Arabs during the Crusades, Europeans immediately put it to use in their well-known deadly manner.

Once in command, the Europeans relished their ability to torture and terrorize the indigenous people. The Spanish were infamous for their creative new methods of terror. Vicious dogs were used against the indigenous population—wolfhounds raised on human flesh, trained to disembowel on command. "Rape, forced concubinage, and compulsory prostitution..."[105] were part of the spoils of the victor that European colonizers enjoyed with impunity.

Professor Stannard quotes the journals of the sixteenth-century Spanish priest Bartolomé de Las Casas in which he notes the atrocities which he witnessed:

> The Spaniards found pleasure in inventing all kinds of odd cruelties, the more cruel, the better, with which to spill human blood. They built a long gibbet, low enough for the toes to touch the ground and prevent strangling and hanged thirteen [native people] at a time in honor of Christ our Savior and the twelve Apostles. When the Indians were thus still alive and hanging, the Spaniards tested their strength and their blades against them, ripping chests

open with one blow and exposing entrails, and there were those who did worse. Then straw was wrapped around their torn bodies and they were burned alive. One man caught two children about two years old, pierced their throats with a dagger, then hurled them down a precipice.[106]

In Central and South America, millions of native people were worked to death in freezing-cold silver mines or just openly slaughtered by the conquistadors. Galeano writes:

> In 1581, Philip II told the *audiencia** of Guadalajara that a third of Latin America's Indians had already been wiped out, and that those who survived were compelled to pay the tributes for the dead. The monarch added that Indians were bought and sold; that they slept in the open air; and that mothers killed their children to save them from the torture of the mines.[107]

A CONTINENT KIDNAPPED

When it was clear that the indigenous peoples of the Americas were "unsuitable" for slavery because of resistance and rapid genocide, Europeans looked to Africa for the backbreaking labor of making the lands of the Americas profitable. The Spanish priest Bartolomé de Las Casas, quoted above, was famous for demanding the end of the genocide and enslavement of the indigenous people. His plan for saving the native people, however, was to use African people as slaves in the Americas.

Only 26 years after Columbus' first voyage, Europeans began the process of kidnapping African people to the Americas in bondage. Sugar, cotton, tobacco and rum—highly profitable commodities for

---

* An *audiencia* is a judicial district.

the growing capitalist economy—needed bodies for their production regardless of the price.

Like the peoples of the Americas, Africans fought brilliantly and tirelessly to retain their independence in the face of the deadly European firearms. Queen Nzinga of Angola was famous for leading armies in the fifteenth century in a courageous attempt to expel the Portuguese.

Nzinga led her army in battle until she was in her 80s. "A visionary political leader, competent, self-sacrificing, and devoted to the resistance movement," Queen Nzinga was a brilliant speaker and military strategist who worked to gain "new recruits for the defense of her country against the occupation of the Portuguese."[108]

"Resistance saved whole villages, untold millions of lives, engineered many escapes, frightened off many slaving expeditions," reports Hosea Jaffe. Jaffe goes on:

> Resistance arose everywhere—against the collaborator King Alphonso I in Mbanza, Congo, against Çao and da Gama, against the Portuguese Viceroy of the East Indies, D'Almeida, who was killed in 1509 by Khoi-Khoin herders, against the sacking of Kilwe and other Zanj towns. Portuguese forts were destroyed at Kilwe and Mombasa in 1529, a mass rebellion in Mbanza after 1534, a mass armed Islamic rising under Granye against the Portuguese in Ethiopia in 1540—drove the Portuguese out of Ethiopia forever....[109]

But by the opening of the seventeenth century, white people were on a wild rampage for gold and spices, salt, gems, sugar and human bodies. Armed to the teeth with guns and cannons, the Europeans overran Africa. The trade in African people was the most lucrative commodity that the world has ever known and an explosion of wealth hit Europe. All of Africa and South America were ripped apart and dug up for gold, natural resources and labor to feed the burgeoning capitalist system in Europe.

"Plunder," reiterates Galeano, "internal and external, was the most important means of primitive accumulation of capital" for Europe. The wealth stolen from Mexico alone between 1760 and 1809—barely half a century—through silver and gold exports has been estimated at many billions of present day dollars.[110] Galeano continues:

> [T]he most potent force for the accumulation of mercan-
> tile capital was slavery in the Americas; and this capital in
> turn became "the foundation stone on which the giant
> industrial capital of modern times was built."...[S]lavery
> had miraculous qualities: it multiplied the ships, factories,
> railroads, and banks of countries that were not originally
> involved in Africa—or with the exception of the United
> States—in the fate of the slaves crossing the Atlantic.
> From the dawn of the sixteenth to the dusk of the nine-
> teenth centuries, many millions of Africans—no one
> knows how many—crossed the ocean; what is known is
> that they greatly exceeded the number of white emigrants
> from Europe, although many fewer survived. From the
> Potomac to the Rio de la Plata, slaves built the houses of
> their masters, felled the forests, cut and milled the sugar-
> cane, planted the cotton, cultivated the cacao, harvested
> the coffee and tobacco and were entombed in the mines.
> How many Hiroshimas did these successive extermina-
> tions add up to?[111]

Hosea Jaffe reports that at least 200 million Africans were mur-
dered by European slavers. "The death toll was about one in every three of the 600 million Africans who lived during those centuries of Dark Europe in Africa."[112]

Millions of people were hunted down like animals, thrown into chains, separated from family and children and those who spoke the same language, stuffed into the cargo holds of ships, brutalized and worked to death.

This long and violent process destroyed the civilizations of Africa and pushed African people backward into poverty and degradation, while Europe was catapulted forward into "progress." African people who loved and were loved, who had dreams and aspirations in life, who were talented, skilled and had a great joy for living were tortured, captured and enslaved by the millions. Today they are but nameless statistics in history books. Anxiety, fear and great sorrow were introduced into the traditionally optimistic and joyful societies of Africa. Mothers feared for their babies and their husbands, and thousands fled further and further into the interior of the continent.

SCENE OF HORROR

In 1562, Captain John Hawkins sailed to the Caribbean under the English flag with a ship full of enchained African people. Africans were imprisoned in outdoor camps on the west coast of Africa until Europeans were ready to load them into the holds of ships. They were chained two by two, right leg and left leg, right hand and left hand. Each African had less room to move than a body in a coffin. Everyone, including children and pregnant women, was packed into a dark, airless space for the months of the voyage. If for some reason there were not enough Africans to fill the space, cattle were loaded into the holds next to the human cargo.[113]

An enslaved African named Olaudah Equiana chronicled his own brutal journey across the Atlantic in the 1750s:

> The stench of the hold while we were on the coast was
> so intolerably loathsome that it was dangerous to
> remain there for any time, and some of us had been

permitted to stay on the deck for the fresh air; but now that the whole ship's cargo were confined together, it became absolutely pestilential. The closeness of the place, and the heat of the climate, added to the number in the ship, which was so crowded that each had scarcely room to turn himself, almost suffocated us. This produced constant perspirations, so that the air soon became unfit for respiration...and brought on a sickness among the slaves, of which many died, thus falling victims to the improvident avarice, as I may call it, of their purchasers. This wretched situation was again aggravated by the galling of the chains, now become insupportable; and the filth of the tubs, into which the children often fell, and were almost suffocated. The shrieks of the women, and the groans of the dying, rendered a scene of horror almost inconceivable.[114]

Women and children were forced into the airless cargo compartments of ships "as if they were herrings in a barrel. If any one wanted to sleep they lay on top of each other," reports Hugh Thomas in *The Slave Trade*.[115] A Dr. Thomas Trotter testified before the British House of Commons in the seventeenth century:

The slaves that are out of irons are locked "spoonways," according to the technical phrase, and closely locked to one another. It is the duty of the first mate to see them stowed in this manner every morning; those which do not get quickly into their places are compelled by the cat [o' nine tails] and, such was the situation when stowed in this manner, and when the ship had much motion at sea, that they were often miserably bruised against the deck or against each other...I have seen [the Africans'] breasts heaving and observed them draw their breath, with all those laborious and anxious efforts for life which we observe in expiring animals subjected by experiment to bad air of various kinds.[116]

HUMAN BONDAGE

The terrible impact that slavery has had on the continent of Africa cannot be calculated: the destruction of magnificent civilizations, the break-up of family and kinship circles, the massive depopulation, forced impoverishment, famine and starvation, the ravishing of an environment which had been so conducive to human civilization for millennia. From open, educated, prosperous and democratic societies, African people now lived in sheer terror, never knowing when their village or town would be raided for human loot by these white invaders.

Some North American people cynically place the blame for the enslavement of African people on the shoulders of African collaborators who participated in the kidnapping of their own people. Impacted by the social destruction wreaked by invading Europeans, a tiny minority of the conquered people did find their own survival by participating in this treachery.

The setting up of collaborators among the colonized population has been a successful tool of domination in every instance of European colonialism around the world. Africa is no exception. Europeans attack societies in Africa, Asia or the Americas, destroying their traditional economies and long-standing social relationships. A unilateral colonial economy, which starves the people and creates dependency on the colonial power, is militarily enforced.

The European invader gets richer and richer through this blood-sucking relationship, and offers resources, guns and special status to a minority sector of the oppressed population. The selected "elite" of the colony can themselves become enslaved or carry out the will of white power. If they take any kind of stand independent of the colonizer as have, say, Panama's Manuel Noriega or Iraq's Saddam Hussein in today's world, white power spares them none of its wrath.

This plan has worked well over the centuries. A few people in every colony have participated in the devious imperialist schemes of slavery, genocide, torture and exploitation against their own people, a collaboration which benefits no one more than the European or North American "mother" country.

The statement that "Africans enslaved their own people" separates out African people from other colonial subjects, all of whom have had their share of betrayal among their ranks. It is a statement of imperialism's historic need to mobilize public opinion against African people.

Like the general white attitude toward the government-imposed drugs and dependent drug economy in today's African communities, this statement lets the parasitic colonial economic system off the hook. It is an anti-black expression of unity with the oppression of African people, saying, "they did it to themselves." Meanwhile all white people everywhere still benefit from the parasitic economic system which has as its foundation the enslavement and continued exploitation of African people.

Most Africans resisted enslavement with all of their energy. Rebellions on slave ships were common. According to one source, "Many deaths on slave journeys across the Atlantic derived from violence, brawls, and, above all, rebellions. There was probably at least one insurrection every eight to ten journeys." For example, Africans successfully rebelled in 1532 aboard the Portuguese slave ship the *Misericordia*. The 109 Africans on board "rose and murdered all the crew except for the pilot and two seamen. Those survivors escaped in a longboat...but the *Misericordia* was never heard of again."[117]

Slave ship owners often threw Africans off the ships just to collect the insurance money. One famous case was that of a ship owned by William Gregson and George Case (both former mayors of Liverpool, England). The captain threw 133 Africans into the sea because if Africans were to die naturally the owners would lose money, but if the African people were "thrown alive into the sea," supposedly for the safety of the crew, "it would be the loss of the underwriters."[118]

So many African people died en route that it has been said that sharks followed slave ships all the way from Africa to the Americas.

Africans who survived the notoriously brutal middle passage, as the Atlantic crossing was known, reached the Americas barely alive. If they were too ill, they were left to die on the shore. They were sold like animals on public auction blocks, naked or in rags, weakened and emaciated, having survived the months below deck with disease and malnutrition, not to mention the emotional ravages of such an experience. Many Africans committed suicide to avoid enslavement, a practice otherwise unknown in African culture.

White buyers came to the market for slaves, "feeling the Africans' limbs and bodies much as butchers handled calves. The slaves were often asked, as they had been told to do before leaving Africa, to show their tongues and teeth, or to stretch their arms."[119]

In the Americas, Africans were "broken in" by submitting them to inhuman terror in an attempt to crush out any resistance. The "breaking" process was psychological as well as physical, and included being forced to learn a version of a European language and to take a European name, something many Africans militantly resisted.

Under the domination of their white slave masters, African people of all ages were branded, women on the breasts. Africans were whipped until they were deeply scarred, and their ears or ear lobes were cut off. People were slashed in the face, and their hands and feet were cut off to prevent them from running away. Men were castrated; women were raped. Women's babies were cut out of their bellies for "punishment," and any man, woman or child could be forced to wear iron collars on their necks for life.[120]

Under such brutal conditions, normal human relationships between men and women or parents and children were interrupted and nearly impossible. Mothers were forced to work the full nine months of pregnancy, often giving birth in the field. They were then forced to abandon their children, as they had to keep on working or nurse the children of the slave master.

OPIUM TRADE

It was this incredible brutality of the slave trade and hundreds of years of plunder of the world by Europeans which gave birth to the capitalist world economy. This economic system today binds most of humanity in the shackles of oppression and exploitation while bene-fiting the minority white population.

This is the "inescapable dialectic" described by Omali Yeshitela: advancement and prosperity for white people which needs for its existence starvation and economic dependency for everyone else. Brought under the whip of the European-dominated imperialistic system, the world was profoundly altered. The once-feared northern barbarians so hostile to the world's civilization now dominated the world.

No corner of the Earth escaped the bloody hand of the European and his burgeoning capitalist system. While raping Africa and the Americas in the 1500s, Europeans were also attempting to foist opium onto the people of China and other countries of Asia in order to make them economically dependent. Portugal sent slave ships to Africa and drug ships to China. Pushing drugs has been a major European enterprise since the dawn of capitalism, as Karl Marx noted. By the nineteenth century, the majority of the wealth of France resulted from the sale of opium that it forced upon the sub-ject people of Viet Nam. Historically the Asians were completely disinterested both in opium and in trading or dealing with Europe-ans on any level. Hatred of the imposed European traffic by the

Chinese was strong, and later in the 1840s and '50s, this aversion erupted in a sustained, organized resistance known as the Opium Wars. Alfred McCoy states in *Politics of Heroin*:

> Before the first Portuguese ships arrived in the 1500s opium smoking and drug smuggling were almost unknown in Asia. Most of the traditional Asian states were inward-looking empires with only a marginal interest in sea trade. Their economies were self-contained, and they only ventured abroad to trade for luxury goods, rare spices, or art treasures.[121]

BIRTH OF CAPITALISM

We have been looking at the process which brought about the birth of capitalism. We have seen the emergence of a world economy that is incredibly beneficial for a small percentage of the world's population and enormously destructive for the majority. The ability to view the world in such a way comes from the political and philosophical theory of Omali Yeshitela. It is a theory which is based simply on examination of reality through the lens of the African slave, the indigenous person, the Asian peasant.

We are used to looking at the world sitting on top of everyone else. We take it for granted that our worldview is correct. But "our" worldview is simply history written by the victor, the oppressor. Millions and millions of people see and experience life quite differently.

Omali Yeshitela is Chairman of the African People's Socialist Party and leader of the Uhuru Movement. For more than 30 years since the 1960s he has tirelessly led struggles and movements for the interests of the African working class and poor community, continuing to keep alive the aspirations of the Black Power Movement of the 1960s. At the same time that he has been immersed in heated campaigns for the liberation of African people, Chairman Yeshitela has always brilliantly summed up and analyzed the theoretical basis for this struggle, unearthing how the roots of the oppression of African people emerged.

The body of his dynamic political theory, called Yeshitelism, shows unequivocally that slavery, plunder, genocide and colonialism form the pedestal upon which capitalism was born and which it continues to rest. He has shown that capitalism had no benign beginnings, but was born and continues to be parasitic.

Capitalism would not have emerged as a social system and cannot continue to exist without expropriating the lifeblood of the majority of the peoples on the planet. Cold, barren, barbarous Europe had nothing within itself to develop the capitalist system. It needed the resources from the external plunder of Africa, the Americas and Asia to come to life.

Years ago, Chairman Yeshitela observed that buried in the back of Volume I of Karl Marx's *Capital* was a little noticed section in which Marx discussed the "primitive accumulation of capital." This section of Marx's work was seldom if ever discussed by the white leftists. Marx stated:

> The discovery of gold and silver in America, the extirpation, enslavement and entombment in mines of the aboriginal population, the beginning of the conquest and looting of the East Indies, the turning of Africa into a warren for the commercial hunting of black skins, signalized the rosy dawn of the era of capitalist production. These idyllic proceedings are the chief momenta of primitive accumulation. On their heels treads the commercial war of the European nations, with the globe for a theater. It begins with the revolt of the Netherlands from Spain, assumes giant dimensions in England's Anti-Jacobin War, and is still going on with the opium wars against China."[122]

Concretizing Marx's abstract European style, Chairman Omali observed, "We [African people] are primitive accumulation!" Primitive accumulation of capital simply means the start-up resources for the capitalist system. Europe was impoverished, backward and uncivilized. Where did the money come from to transform its society?

As Marx said, and as we have seen, it came from plunder, rape, slavery, imposed drugs and massive theft. It came from science, technology, the arts and literacy, along with the notions of civilization and democracy themselves—stolen from others, expropriated at their expense. Hosea Jaffe notes in relation to the parasitic nature of capitalism, "Colonial conquests and trafficking in slaves provided the precious metals and general wealth that permeated the ages of Leonardo, Galileo, Newton and Beethoven."[123]

Yeshitela asserts that the "slave trade was the prime force which gave birth to the world economy and to the development of capitalism which in its present form we call imperialism."[124]

Yeshitela quotes a statement by Marx that "the veiled slavery of the wage workers in Europe needed for its pedestal slavery pure and simple in the new world." To which Yeshitela adds: "This statement by Marx is simply another way of saying that capitalism, the entire basis and superstructure of white power as it exists, has its origin in and rests upon a pedestal of African oppression."[125]

Chairman Yeshitela shows how Marx, Engels and Lenin, though communist theorists, were nevertheless bound by the white nationalist limitations of their era. Their theories reflect the Eurocentric views of white men living in nineteenth or early twentieth century Europe, sitting on the pedestal of capitalism. To them, African and colonized peoples were little more than unfortunate "uncivilized" victims of "progressive" European development.

Marx and Engels based their understandings on such thinkers as Hegel, the German philosopher who wrote, "At this moment we leave Africa, not to mention it again. For it is no historical part of the world; it has no movement or development to exhibit."[126]

In looking for the means to create revolution, Marx and Engels could only conceive of solving problems for white workers through the process of the development of capitalism. They were not able to hear the voice of the slave, which would emerge powerfully as the twentieth century progressed. It has been the struggles for national liberation by colonial peoples which have thrust this voice upon us today. To the extent that we are willing to embrace that voice we can begin to see beyond our narcissistic Eurocentrism. Marx, Engels and Lenin had no such ability.

For them, the question of the parasitic origins of capitalism was nothing more than a footnote to Marx's *Capital*. Marx never made any condemnation of the unspeakable rapine of colonialism. Nor did he ever call for demonstrations of international solidarity by white workers with the African, indigenous and other peoples whose genocide and slaughter were providing the resources and raw materials for white workers' jobs in Europe.

Certainly Marx and Engels never imagined that, in fact, the parasitic capitalist system will ultimately be brought down by the leadership of African workers, along with the millions and millions of colonized laborers throughout the world.

In his pamphlet "Dialectics of Black Revolution," Yeshitela writes, "Primitive accumulation is not a contradiction inside the society. It is a pre-condition for the development from feudalism to capitalism...." In other words, Europe could have languished indefinitely under feudalism without the external impetus of its pillage of other peoples. Yeshitela adds:

> The slave trade, according to Karl Marx, was the pre-condition for the emergence of capitalism itself. It was the thing that gave birth to the world economy, that was the pre-condition for the existence of capitalism.
>
> This so-called primitive accumulation has also served to undermine the consciousness of the victims, of those

people who are now being defined as "primitive accumulation." We have become objects of history as opposed to subjects of history. Our value is now defined by how we impact on the development of Europe and white people in general.[127]

EUROPE TRANSFORMED

The benefits of slavery were hardly restricted to feeding the wealth of the U.S. Southern planter class as we are told in many history books. In fact, the plantation owners benefited most ephemerally from the bondage of African people. The long-term wealth and power of New York, Boston, Liverpool, Amsterdam and eventually all of Europe and North America came from the trade in human beings.

It seems highly symbolic that an African cemetery from the era of enslavement was unearthed at a construction site on New York's Wall Street in 1992—the capitalist world economy rests literally on the foundation of the bodies of African people.

With its cataclysmic origins, "capitalism emerged as white power," as Chairman Omali says. It bred racism as its ideological underpinning. In regard to the rest of the world, "...the general European view, expressed in a rich vocabulary of abuse and manifested in gratuitous insult and brutality, was one of disapproval and contempt."[128]

Europeans came out of the northern caves to destroy the world in order to build a self-serving social system. The days of pure joy of living for the majority of humankind were over. The ancient system of equitable and reciprocal world trade was destroyed. Brilliant life-giving civilizations dating from the dawn of humanity lay in ruins. The entire Earth and the majority of the human beings on it were reduced to commodities to be wasted and spent with impunity. Unless one had white skin, the value of one's human life was nothing.

The business of buying and selling African people, and the rape and genocide in Africa, the Americas and Asia, did indeed transform European society.

Suddenly the unhealthy "European diet was enlarged and enriched."[129] Europeans killed the people but stole their food so white people could live. They took the potato from the indigenous peoples of the Americas and called it "Irish." They took noodles from Asia and covered them with sauce made by the native American's tomato; now it became "Italian spaghetti."

But despite the foods stolen from peoples around the world, European eating habits continued to expose the culture of violence. While most of the world eats their food with chopsticks or wrapped in flatbreads, Europeans bring weapons—knives and forks—to the table. This is surely more than just a matter of style. Europeans had to protect their stolen loot from other plundering white people even at dinner.

Historian G.V. Scammell sums up the overall results of the slave trade in Europe:

> [T]here was a massive influx of precious metals and precious stones and a substantial flow of oriental [sic] books, manuscripts, textiles, porcelain, artifacts, seeds, plants and archeological fragments, together with treasures of every sort from the Americas. Natural history specimens, wonders and works of art were assiduously collected, like the magnificent Chinese library assembled for Louis XIV of France.[130]

Collected? Stolen would be more accurate. As Omali Yeshitela has often stated, the rape of Africa and the stolen African labor set Europeans up to wield absolute power of life and death over the rest of the world.

The explosion of wealth from the slave trade enabled the crude and unwashed Europeans to discover poetry, art and music. William Shakespeare's career as a playwright arose in the sixteenth century as the slave trade was opening up in England under Queen Elizabeth I. Elizabeth, the "Virgin Queen" knighted Captain John Hawkins after he initiated the English slave trade and granted him the ship *Jesus*. Holland, France, Portugal and Spain all built fortunes on the human cargo, but it was England that ultimately controlled the trade after defeating the Spanish Armada in 1588.

Thus the trade in African bodies motivated Europe's countless wars, affording a profusion of wealth even to the losers of the battles. It was the slave trade that gave us our self-identity and shaped even the very concept of Europe. Hosea Jaffe sums it up astutely:

> With capitalism arose Europe, and with Europe the myth of "European civilization"—a civilization based on African slavery, American plantations, Asian spices, precious metals from all three "non-European" continents—based, too, on Indian numerals, Arabic algebra, astronomy and navigation...and Chinese gunpowder, paper and compasses. This non-European European civilization was the narcissus-like admiration of its own conquests. The sword, gunfire, murder, rape, robbery and slavery formed the real material basis for the idea of European superiority.[131]

Despite its newfound trappings from the spoils of subjecting virtually the entire world to its will, however, European society remained alienated and without a human core. W.E.B. DuBois noted the empty basis of European "civilization":

> Mechanical power, not deep human emotion nor creative genius nor ethical concepts of justice, has made Europe ruler of the world. Man for man, the modern world marks

no advance over the ancient; but man for gun, hand for electricity, muscle for atomic fission, these show what our culture means and how the machine has conquered and holds modern man in thrall. What in our civilization is distinctly British or American? Nothing. Science was built on Africa and Religion on Asia.[132]

TRADE IN SUGAR, RUM AND AFRICAN BODIES

All classes of European society emerged on the pedestal of slavery and plunder, from the ruling classes to working people. Former illiterate serfs were freed to become workers who could ultimately scramble up the proverbial "ladder of success" on the backs of African people. It was through slavery that European peasants became workers to begin with, and it was the same parasitic rise of capitalism that transformed a growing merchant middle class and bourgeoisie into the ruling class.

In *Capitalism and Slavery*, the late Eric Williams, formerly the Prime Minister of Trinidad and Tobago, showed how the slave trade financed all levels of European society, giving the example of England:

> The development of the triangular trade and of shipping and shipbuilding led to the growth of the great seaport towns. Bristol, Liverpool and Glasgow occupied, as seaports and trading centers, the position in the age of trade that Manchester, Birmingham and Sheffield occupied later in the age of industry.
>
> It was said in 1685 that there was scarcely a shopkeeper in Bristol who had not a venture on board some ship bound for Virginia or the Antilles. Even the parsons talked of nothing but trade, and it was satirically alleged

that Bristol freights were owned not by merchants but by mechanics....

It was the slave and sugar trades which made Bristol the second city of England for the first three-quarters of the eighteenth century. "There is not," wrote a local annalist, "a brick in the city but what is cemented with the blood of a slave. Sumptuous mansions, luxurious living, liveried menials, were the produce of the wealth made from the sufferings and groans of the slaves bought and sold by the Bristol merchants."[133]

Coffee, spices, sugar, tobacco, opium and rum flowed into Europe on the slave ships returning from ports in Africa and the Americas. These fashionable luxuries became the basis of the triangular trade, and by 1700 there were 3,000 coffee houses in London alone, one cafe for every 200 people.[134]

Eric Williams delineates other industries that sprang up as a result of the trade in African people. They included woolen goods, cotton, cotton manufacture, sugar refining, rum distillation, metallurgy. A single voyage of a slave ship brought in profits of 100 to 300 percent for the English operating out of Liverpool. The banking and insurance industries mushroomed; Barclay's Bank was founded by two immensely wealthy Quaker slave traders who held plantations in Jamaica.[135] Lloyds of London, which began as a coffee house, became incredibly rich and powerful by insuring slaves, slave ships and plantations.

"From the beginning, *London Gazette* announcements advised that fugitive slaves should be returned to Lloyds," reports Eduardo Galeano in *Open Veins of Latin America*.[136] In addition, profits from the African trade built railroads and financed the steam engine.

In the Americas there was a burst of wealth from the slave trade in the colonies that would become the United States. Slavery not only shaped the banking and insurance industries but, as in England, created new and lucrative enterprises such as the New England distilleries. The United States exported machinery, timber and food to the sugar plantations of the Caribbean. Galeano's words reflect Yeshitela's view of parasitic capitalism:

> Ships built in the colonists' yards carried to the Caribbean massive cargoes of fresh and smoked fish, grain, beans, flour, fats, cheese, onions, horses and oxen, candles and soap, textiles', pine, oak and cedar...barrel staves, hoops, rings and nails.

> The whole process was a pumping of blood from one set of veins to another: the development of some, the under-development of others.[137]

DuBois wrote:

> "That the slave-trade was the very life of the colonies had, by 1700, become an almost unquestioned axiom in British practical economics. The colonists themselves declared slaves "the strength and sinews of this western world"...as the settlements "cannot subsist without supplies of them."[138]

FROM SLAVERY TO COLONIALISM

Institutional slavery was ended only when it became untenable due to the constant resistance and escape of African people and as it began to be more profitable to enslave Africans on their own land. By the turn of the nineteenth century, African resistance was fierce, better organized and more broadly executed. Winthrop Jordan details some of the resistance in *White over Black*:

> The newspapers which carried the ubiquitous runaway advertisements not infrequently carried reports of more

alarming manifestations of slave discontent. *The Maryland Gazette* in 1795, for example, took note of a "Horrid Murder," perpetrated by a slave upon his master. Two years later the same paper reported that Negroes had killed two white men on a Georgia plantation and that a Negro woman in Maryland, upon hearing that her master's will provided for her freedom should he leave no heirs, had enterprisingly poisoned his three children. In 1806 two Negroes killed an overseer in Georgia; one was hanged and the other burned, tied to a tree. Next year the *Richmond Enquirer* announced the trial of a Negro girl for poisoning her master and mistress. Slaves sometimes turned to arson: the great fire of 1793 in Albany was set by Negroes....[139]

The abolition of slavery in 1863 coincided conveniently with a more lucrative form of parasitic extraction—direct colonialism. The slave system did not end because of moral sentiments on the part of certain sectors of the liberal white upper classes. Many who had already made millions of dollars from the slave trade were now champing at the bit to dig their claws into Africa directly. Certainly the vast majority of North Americans (white people), including those in the northern states, was firmly against abolition.

Catholics, Protestants and Jews had all been among the slave ship and plantation owners who operated for generations without twinges of conscience. The Quakers who proclaim that they were abolitionists, were, in fact,

> ...important in the slave trade in the eighteenth century in New England...and also prominent in the slave trade in Pennsylvania, often carrying slaves from the West Indies to their own city....

One or two doubts occurred, all the same, to some North
American slave traders. A few Quakers in Philadelphia in
the early eighteenth century questioned the ethics of
what they were doing—but many of them...continued
trading slaves nonetheless.[140]

Suddenly in the mid-nineteenth century, however, the slave system became unconscionable.

An abolitionist movement was afoot among the genteel Europeans and North Americans of the upper classes. King Leopold of Belgium was one of the staunchest opponents of the slave trade, but his
motivation, like that of many others, was far from altruistic. The aims
of the Belgian king were to rid the Congo of the external slave trade
in order to enchain the people on African ground, claim the land,
and exploit it for rubber and ivory.

At the Berlin Conference of 1884-85, the European powers
launched a parasitic scramble for Africa by agreeing that all countries
should have free access to the African interior, and that the slave
trade should be abolished so that direct colonial exploit could com-
mence. It was decided that "no new European colonies would be
recognized unless they were effectively occupied, which meant that
European officials had to establish visible and effective power in the
areas claimed."[141]

Leopold's occupation in the Congo set the example of sheer
genocide in colonial Africa. In the course of making $1.1 billion in
today's dollars for himself and ultimately the people of Belgium by
expropriating rubber to sell on the European and American market,
the Belgians killed at least 10 million African people in the Congo.
Millions more were terrorized, raped, tortured and mutilated.[142]

Under this more profitable colonial system, African people were
forced to extract the rich natural resources of their continent for the
benefit of Europeans. For those who refused the backbreaking work
of going into the forest to extract the rubber, their villages were

burned, their women were raped and the hands of millions of people were cut off. Or they were simply slaughtered and decapitated, at which point the Belgians stuck the heads on the village fence as a means of demoralizing other townspeople.

Accounts tell of the huge mounds of hands, including those of children, which were gleefully sliced off by European soldiers. The African historian Chinweizu, in his excellent book, *The West and the Rest of Us*, quotes the letter of one white missionary:

> It is blood-curdling to see them [the soldiers] returning with hands of the slain, and to find the hands of young children amongst the bigger ones evidencing their bravery....The rubber from this district has cost hundreds of lives, and the scenes I have witnessed, while unable to help the oppressed, have been almost enough to make me wish I were dead....This rubber traffic is steeped in blood, and if the natives were to rise and sweep every white person on the Upper Congo into eternity, there would still be left a fearful balance to their credit.

Chinweizu goes on to comment that one European mercenary soldier employed in the Congo "wrote home boasting that he had killed 150 men, cut off sixty hands, crucified women and children, and hung the remains of mutilated men on the village fence."[143]

GENOCIDE IN THE CONGO

In the Congo, as throughout Africa, the people resisted powerfully. In the end, as always, they were no match for the firepower of Europeans. In *King Leopold's Ghost*, Adam Hochschild describes the African fight and the European counterinsurgency:

> The Force Publique [the terroristic Belgian colonial shock troops] had its hands full. Many of the king's new subjects

belonged to warrior peoples who fought back. More than a dozen different ethnic groups staged major rebellions against Leopold's rule. The Yaka people fought the whites for more than ten years before they were subdued, in 1906. The Chokwe fought for twenty years, inflicting heavy casualties on Leopold's soldiers. The Boa and the Budja mobilized more than five thousand men to fight a guerrilla war from deep within the rain forest. Just as Americans used the word pacification in Viet Nam seventy years later, so the Force Publique's military expeditions were officially called *reconnaissances pacifiques*.[144]

An African woman in the Congo described her experiences under the terroristic Belgian rule:

We were dragged into the road, and were tied together with cords about our necks, so that we could not escape. We were all crying, for now we knew that we were to be taken away to be slaves. The soldiers beat us with the iron sticks from their guns, and compelled us to march to the camp of Kibalanga....[They] ordered the women to be tied up separately, ten to each cord, and the men in the same way. When we were all collected...the soldiers brought baskets of food for us to carry, in some of which was smoked human flesh.

We then set off marching very quickly....So it continued each day until the fifth day, when the soldiers took my sister's baby and threw it in the grass, leaving it to die, and made her carry some cooking pots which they found in the deserted village.

One of the soldiers caught [a] goat, while two or three others stuck the long knives they put on the ends of their guns into my husband. I saw the blood spurt out, and then saw him no more, for we passed over the brow of a hill and he was out of sight. Many of the young men were killed the same way, and many babies thrown into the grass to die....[145]

Inside the Congo, the Belgians set up three "children's colonies, the aim of which," wrote King Leopold, "is above all to furnish us with soldiers." These children's prisons were "ruled by the chicotte [a whip made of hippopotamus hide] and the chain. There were many mutinies. If they survived their kidnapping, transport, and schooling, most of the male graduates of the state colonies became soldiers, just as Leopold had ordered. These state colonies were the only state-funded schools for Africans in Leopold's Congo."[146]

The genocide of millions of Africans in the Congo was no secret. By 1890, a steady stream of at least a thousand European and North American journalists had visited the African country to see Leopold's wonders of rubber production. Not one of them mentioned the outrage of mounds of severed hands and the incessant carnage of the people.

It wasn't until an African from the United States traveled to the Congo that the atrocities were exposed. George Washington Williams went to the African country in 1890 in the belief that it could be a place of employment for Africans from the U.S.

He was horrified by what he found, writing a lengthy open letter to King Leopold exposing the monarch's atrocities and "crimes against humanity." Williams' letter was printed as a pamphlet which was widely circulated throughout Europe and the United States. Calling for an end to the "oppressive and cruel Government," Williams demanded a new regime that would be "local, not European; international, not national; just, not cruel."[147]

Despite the exposures, the genocide continued. Leopold blamed the vastly diminished population in the Congo on "sleeping sickness."[148] It wasn't until 1909, nearly 20 years after Williams' pamphlet, that a movement among liberals began to grow up in Europe protesting the atrocities against the African people. This movement forced Leopold to turn over the Congo, which he held personally, to the Belgian State. This move seemed to assuage the European conscience but changed no conditions for African people.

As always the outrage was after the fact, and the sudden moral consciousness of white people had an economic basis: the wild rubber vines were becoming scarce and a shift to cultivated rubber was in the making. In addition, the Belgian State found it far more persuasive to impose a colonial head tax that forced the African people to go to work on the plantations or starve to death.[149]

By the time the "reforms" were made, the holocaust in the Congo had destroyed the lives of countless millions of people. And untold billions of dollars were made for the benefit of Europeans.

This genocidal exploitation of the Congo is the reason that Belgium is now one of the richest countries in Europe. Today any tourist can visit a monument in a park in downtown Antwerp. The stone structure with Leopold's face etched on it, has an inscription from the populace of Belgium which reads simply: "Thank you, King Leopold, for giving us the Congo."

"I THOROUGHLY ENJOYED THE OUTING"

The history of Belgian atrocities in the Congo is only one example of the terror that Europeans inflicted on Africa in their colonial orgy of genocide and exploitation. Britain, France, Germany and the United States have similar legacies throughout the continent. During the 1890s all of Europe was scrambling madly for a piece of Africa.

Direct colonialism meant open genocide of African people by Europeans. Britain alone ruled a fourth of the planet Earth, becoming the most powerful empire in history. The British imperialist, Cecil Rhodes (who later bequeathed the well-known British scholarship in his name) was carrying out a program of genocide in Zimbabwe, which he named Rhodesia. He amassed an enormous fortune working African people to death in the diamond and gold mines there.

Sir Henry Morton Stanley (the one who says, "Dr. Livingston, I presume," in the old movies) was leading the British massacre in the Sudan. A young Winston Churchill participated as English soldiers killed 16,000 unarmed Sudanese resistors in one day. Armed with Enfield rifles, the British hardly dirtied their white uniforms. Churchill delighted at the sport of slaughtering African people. Prior to the annihilation, Churchill and the British officers dined on beef and champagne.

"This kind of war was full of fascinating thrills. It was not like the Great War," Churchill later wrote in his memoirs. "Nobody expected to be killed....To the great mass of those who took part in the little wars of Britain in those vanished light-hearted days, this was only a sporting element in a splendid game."[150]

An English-born American citizen, Henry Morton Stanley, went about Africa, colonizing the continent in the employment of any source from whom he could get money. For five years during the 1890s, he worked for King Leopold in the Congo where he earned his reputation as a viciously brutal invader. Hochschild writes:

> His crews of workmen carved a rough track, more a trail than a road, around the big rapids, using existing paths in some areas, in others cutting through brush and forest, filling in gullies, and throwing log bridges over ravines. Then they moved more than fifty tons of supplies and equipment up the trail. Draft animals like horses and oxen could not survive the Congo's climate and diseases, so supplies traveled mostly on porters' heads.[151]

Meanwhile, Sir Robert Baden-Powell (the founder of the Boy Scouts) was leading an attack on the Ashanti people in 1896.

Unarmed and aware of the European slaughter all around them, the Ashanti surrendered. One account relates:

> To his disappointment, Baden-Powell did not fire a single shot at the natives. To get hostilities going, the British planned extreme provocations. The king of the Ashanti was arrested together with his whole family. The king and his mother were forced to crawl on all fours up to the British officers sitting on crates of biscuit tins, receiving their subjugation.

> Baden-Powell later wrote to his mother, "I thoroughly enjoyed the outing except for the want of a fight, which I fear will preclude our getting any medals or decoration."[152]

The Europeans' favorite torture tool, the infamous hippopotamus hide chicotte whip, was used everywhere on African people. This whip "at every blow slashes bloody runes." The Europeans trained their forces to administer a beating with a stone cold face: "If you have to order physical punishment to a savage, have this punishment carried out with not a muscle in your face betraying your feelings."[153] By all accounts, Europeans *enjoyed* inflicting the torture on African people immensely.

HEROIC AFRICAN RESISTANCE

Uprising, rebellion and sabotage were commonplace throughout Africa, and the colonizers, like the plantation owners in the Americas, could never rest easy. As late as 1879, the Zulu people of southern Africa dealt British colonialists a resounding defeat. Richard Poe describes the battle:

> ...(W)hen Lord Frederick Chelmsford led an army into Zululand in the winter of 1879, his worst fear was that the

Zulus would be so frightened that they would never come out to fight. But Chelmsford need not have worried. On January 22, an army of Zulu warriors obligingly descended on one of Chelmsford's isolated columns....

A Lieutenant Curling, who survived the ensuing battle, later recalled that the British were not concerned at first, even when the Zulus charged them en masse.... "The British never dreamed," said Curling, that "the Zulus could charge home." But they did. Braving rockets, artillery, and concentrated rifle fire, the Zulus hurled themselves at the British lines, climbing over the bodies of their own dead.

In the end, the British were slaughtered, almost to a man. Over 800 British soldiers, 52 officers, and some 500 of their African allies were massacred and ritually disemboweled—1,300 in all. More British officers were killed that day than in the entire battle of Waterloo.[154]

During the same period, in Namibia, the poorly armed Herero and Nama people brilliantly and fiercely fought 10,000 German colonizing shock troops for more than three years. The Germans had invaded the lands, raping women, burning villages and looting.

The Herero uprising marked the beginning of "Germany's bloodiest and most protracted colonial war."[155] One book notes the strikingly humane actions of the Herero in defense of their land as compared to the vicious genocidal German attackers led by the savage General von Trotha:

The Herero were very humane in their conduct of the war. They were fighting exclusively against German men, the missionaries being spared as were women and children. Contrary to newspaper reports pretending otherwise, only three white women were killed (apparently inadvertently) and not a single child. It is a well-known fact that the Herero took the wives and children of German settlers killed in battle to sites near the German lines in a great number of cases, often at the risk of their own lives.

The German conduct of the war was diametrically opposed to that of the Herero. The Germans did not spare the wives and children....

By 1904 the Germans had surrounded the courageous Herero and driven them into the Omaheke desert. There "the bulk of the Herero met a slow, agonizing death. The study of the General Staff noted that the Omaheke had inflicted a worse fate on the Herero than 'German arms could ever have done, however bloody and costly the battle.'"

The German "victory" in Namibia is summed up: "German imperialism crushed the Herero uprising by committing genocide" some 40 years before the slaughter of Jews in Europe.[156]

"YOU MUST BECOME IMPERIALISTS!"

The colonial rape of Africa brought almost unimaginable wealth into to the white world. Countless men in Europe and the United States were joining the ranks of the bourgeoisie, which flaunted its wealth ostentatiously. At the same time, the wealthy middle class (petty bourgeoisie) grew exponentially as imperialist colonialism expanded.

In response, European workers organized themselves into trade unions and staged massive demonstrations. Their aspirations were not to destroy the colonial system, but instead to share its wealth. The European working class was no longer the mass of homogenous poor; it now experienced for the first time the real possibilities of improving its lot. Charles Dickens and others, through such stories as "A Christmas Carol," called for capitalism to put on a more human face in regards to English workers.

Cecil Rhodes, the British colonizer who was raping Zimbabwe, was very clear that colonialism was the solution to the unrest of white workers in Europe. The Russian revolutionary leader V.I. Lenin reported on speeches by Rhodes. Lenin—and Omali Yeshitela—use Rhodes' statement to expose that the plunder of Africa and the Americas created a fat and self-interested European and North American working class:

> I was in the East End of London [working class quarters] yesterday and attended a meeting of the unemployed. I listened to the wild speeches, which were just a cry for "bread, bread!" and on my way home I pondered over the scene and I became more than ever convinced of the importance of imperialism....My cherished idea is a solution for the social problem, i.e., in order to save the 40,000,000 inhabitants of the United Kingdom from a bloody civil war, we colonial statesmen must acquire new lands to settle the surplus population, to provide new markets for the goods produced in the factories and mines. The empire, as I have always said, is a bread and butter question. If you want to avoid civil war, you must become imperialists.[157]

The *American Heritage Dictionary* defines "imperialism" as "The policy of extending a nation's authority by territorial acquisition or by the establishment of economic and political hegemony over other nations."[158]

PARASITES ON THE BODY OF MANKIND

In his pamphlet, "Imperialism and the Split in Socialism," Lenin defined imperialism this way:

> Its specific character is threefold: imperialism is:
> (1) monopoly capitalism;
> (2) parasitic, or decaying capitalism;
> (3) moribund capitalism....
>
> There is the tendency of the bourgeoisie and the opportunists to convert a handful of very rich and privileged nations into "eternal" parasites on the body of the rest of mankind, "to rest on the laurels" of the exploitation of Negroes, Indians, etc., keeping them in subjection with the aid of excellent weapons of extermination provided by modern militarism.[159]

Lenin's definition of imperialism came about as the entire continent of Africa was soaking in the blood of African people at the end of the nineteenth century. Lenin was struggling to lead an anti-capitalist revolution of the Russian people against the czarist rulers during the same period that King Leopold's troops were torturing, mutilating and committing genocide against African people in the Congo.

Yet even Lenin, the leading revolutionary of his time, put no human face on his definition of imperialism, nor did he—like Marx before him—urge white workers to stand in solidarity with the struggling African people. By the turn of the century, the European atrocities were being debated widely in public forums, yet Lenin made no definitive condemnation or even mention of the genocide in Africa outside of his statements quoted above.

The widespread lynchings in the United States were also well-known, and the annihilation of the indigenous people was nearly complete. America in this period was also stealing and colonizing the Philippines, Cuba and Puerto Rico.

Lenin was relatively silent on the question of African and colonized peoples, and denunciation of the imperialist genocide in down-to-earth human terms was forthcoming from missionaries and novelists far more than from him. Despite the significant discussion on imperialism that he initiated in socialist circles, Lenin was not able to come to the conclusion that African and colonized peoples would themselves be the leading force against imperialism.

At the height of the colonial attack on Africa in 1896, Lenin was making only Eurocentric statements regarding proletarian internationalism, the "worldwide" unity of workers:

"The fight against the domination of the capitalist class is now being waged by the workers of all European countries and also by the workers of America and Australia."

Presumably, Lenin is not including African people in America or indigenous peoples in both countries. Lenin continues:

> Working class organization and solidarity is not confined to one country or one nationality: the workers' parties of different countries proclaim aloud the complete identity (solidarity) of interests and aims of the workers of the whole world....Capitalist domination is international. That is why the workers' struggle in all countries for their emancipation is only successful if the workers fight jointly against international capital. That is why the Russian worker's comrade in the fight against the capitalist class is the German worker, the Polish worker and the French worker, just as his enemy is the Russian, the Polish, and the French capitalists.[160]

Meanwhile, throughout Africa and the Americas the slaughter continued, and resources benefiting white workers flowed into Europe.

IGNORANCE OF CONVENIENCE

Out of the material conditions of African people, experienced inside the United States and around the world, Omali Yeshitela has been able to formulate a cogent analysis of imperialism as it is found in the real world. Yeshitela shows that when Lenin looked at imperialism, he was talking about the same set of circumstances that Marx was dealing with when he described primitive accumulation of capital. Capitalism has always been parasitic, Yeshitela tells us. It was born from plunder, slavery and genocide and it survives and thrives on plunder, slavery and genocide today.

Yeshitela has shown that, because the slave trade forcibly dispersed African people around the world, African people inside U.S. borders are colonial subjects. It is colonialism—economic and political oppression—which is the major problem facing African people today. The problem does not lie in racism, the ideas in the heads of white people. Political power is needed to change the conditions of African people—not sensitivity on the part of whites.

The empty slogan of the white left, "black and white unite and fight," liquidates the reality of colonialism and the responsibility that white people as a whole must take for our ongoing unity with and benefits from the oppression of African people. Genocide, plunder, slaughter, slavery—these were not things that imperialist governments carried out in secret, without the knowledge of their citizens.

As white people, we have always voluntarily and enthusiastically upheld colonialism; we have participated in it, been exhilarated by it, gotten rich by it, used it as the solution to our problems. As we will show throughout this book, white workers in particular have welcomed colonialism as a means to attain affluence and "success."

The Inescapable Dialectic

The white left in Europe and the United States has traditionally done nothing more than fight for a greater share of the spoils of the colonial system to go to white workers. We have all of us—workers, middle class and rulers alike—been thoroughly united in our willingness to pick up the whip, the gun, the hanging rope, the bomb or the vote to protect our place on the backs of the world's oppressed peoples. All of us sit on the pedestal of the oppression of African human beings; our only fight has been who would sit where.

Yeshitela shows that the white left and progressive movements have historically manifested the same stance as the colonial government and the white population as a whole when it comes to African people.

The left and "communists" have always defended the anti-African brutality and genocidal practices of the white population by saying that white people are "duped" and divided by the ruling class.

If this is true, why were the majority of native people never duped by the same government? They welcomed African people as they escaped from slavery and gave them asylum on their lands, fighting side by side against the oppressors. Native people didn't hang Africans from trees.

As Chairman Omali says, the white population lives under a self-imposed ignorance of convenience, a self-appointed alienation from the majority of the world in unity with capitalist white power. We "dupe" ourselves in order to cover atrocities perpetrated against others—atrocities that provide us our enjoyable lifestyle gained at the expense of humanity.

Marx and Lenin lived in an era in which the voice of colonized people had been temporarily silenced by imperialism. We have no such excuse. As Chairman Omali observes:

> Marx's and Lenin's world was white. For them the enslaved Asian, African and "Indians" of North and South America were essentially objects of history which had

more or less significance for European development. [Marx's and Lenin's] perceptions, however, were constantly developing, and...with the era of imperialism, of decaying, parasitic, and moribund capitalism which might also be called the ascendancy of the slave, Lenin's understanding of the significance of the underdeveloped world in the struggle against world capitalism developed.

Lenin didn't understand that his imperialism rested precisely on the "development" of the relationship of the contradiction inferred in Marx's primitive accumulation. But Lenin died [a long time ago], marking the end of the process of his development. Unfortunately, most of those who swear by his and Marx's name were not interred with Lenin. For not only have they not progressed, they have moved backwards beyond Lenin and Marx and exist in a state of political zombieism preserved for what can only be called the walking political dead of the left....[161]

TAKING RESPONSIBILITY

European and North American history is nearly overwhelming in its legacy of brutality and plunder. Yet, what appears on these pages is only a tiny sample of our true past. Many of the books cited contain enormous amounts of similar information and should be studied. The more that we look at this reality, the more we begin to understand that genocide and plunder are the essence of the American and European "way of life."

Ultimately Yeshitelism, the theoretical basis for this book, challenges all the assumptions that we have grown up with and taken for granted. Yeshitela gives voice to the enslaved and the colonized, and also gives us an opportunity to finally take responsibility for the historic crimes, not of just white power, but of white people who have upheld white power.

In so doing it offers to us a whole new possibility of taking a principled stand in relation to African and colonized peoples. We can change ourselves and our relationship to the other inhabitants of the world whom we have so long exploited. The choice is up to us.

Omali Yeshitela takes the reality of the parasitic beginnings of capitalism out of the lofty theoretical sphere and brings it down to Earth. He makes it simple, then invites us to join humanity in the struggle for liberation.

African and other colonized peoples are fighting to destroy white power. They are attempting to rebuild a world in which human beings can live once again. If we unite with the leadership of struggling humanity instead of the leadership of white power, we can work for this future as well. Yeshitela sums up:

> Capitalism emerged in the world as white power. It was built at the expense of African freedom, liberty and resources as well as that of other peoples on the planet Earth. We want to remove ourselves from the fallacies and superstitions which have posed as history to us for the longest period of time, pretending to be what political economy is all about....
>
> These white nationalist theories cannot explain in any kind of meaningful terms why a minority of people seem to have everything including that which is produced by the majority of the people on the planet Earth who have nothing. It seems to us to be a totally irrational assumption that this handful of people somehow would have developed naturally and be more civilized and better off than the rest of the people.
>
> If we examine history we see that the people who seem to be so well off have a history of brigandage, rape and enslavement of all the other people who seem not to be

doing so well. We say that capitalism was always para-sitic—It was born parasitic.[162]

A quote from the Maya book of *Chilam Balam*, written centu-ries ago, cited in *American Holocaust*, states quite simply and elo-quently the essence of parasitic capitalism—white power—from the point of view of the enslaved. In this haunting stanza, the Mayan writer describes "what the white lords did when they came to our land":

> They taught fear and they withered the flowers. So that
> their flower should live, they maimed and destroyed the
> flower of others...Marauders by day, offenders by night,
> murderers of the world.[163]

1. Omali Yeshitela, 1987, *The Road to Socialism Is Painted Black: Selected Theoretical Works* (Oakland: Burning Spear Publications), p. 148.
2. Christiane Desroches-Noblecourt, 1963, *Tutankhamen: Life and Death of a Pharaoh* (London: Penguin Books Ltd.), pp. 44-47.
3. David E. Stannard, 1992, *American Holocaust: The Conquest of the New World* (New York: Oxford University Press), p. 62.
4. Ivan Van Sertima, 1976, *They Came Before Columbus: The African Presence in America* (New York: Random House), p. 6.
5. Same as above.
6. Colin McEvedy, 1992, *The New Penguin Atlas of Medieval History* (London: Penguin Books), p. 24.
7. Joseph Harris, 1987, *Africans and Their History*, Revised Edition (New York: Mentor Books), p.92.
8. Richard Poe, 1997, *Black Spark White Fire: Did African Explorers Civilize Ancient Europe?* (California: Prima Publishing), pp. 244-255.
9. Van Sertima, pp. 61-155.
10. Hugh Thomas, 1997, *The Slave Trade: The Story of the Atlantic Slave Trade: 1440-1870* (New York: Touchstone), p. 62.
11. Hosea Jaffe, 1985, *A History of Africa* (London: Zed Books), p. 45.
12. Anne H. Soukhanov, ed., 1999, *Encarta World English Dictionary* (New York: St. Martin's Press), p. 27.
13. W.E. Burghardt DuBois, 1972, *The World and Africa* (New York: International Publishers), p. 82.
14. Same as above, p. 85.
15. Harris, p. 31.
16. William Morris, ed., 1982, *The American Heritage Dictionary, Second College Edition* (Boston: Houghton Mifflin Company), p. 1509.
17. Cheikh Anta Diop, 1974, *The African Origin of Civilization: Myth or Reality* (Westport: Lawrence Hill & Company), p. 22.
18. Harris, pp. 32-35.
19. DuBois, *The World and Africa*, pp. 101-105.
20. Cheikh Anta Diop, 1978, *Black Africa: The Economic and Cultural Basis for a Federated State* (Westport: Lawrence Hill & Co.), p. 3.
21. Diop, *African Origin*, p. 23.
22. Harris, p. 40.
23. Same as above, p. 45.
24. Same as above, p. 46.
25. Cheikh Anta Diop, 1978, *Cultural Unity of Black Africa: The Domains of Patriarchy and of Matriarchy in Classical Antiquity* (Chicago: Third World Press), pp. 55-56.
26. Harris, p. 70.
27. Nicholas Reeves, 1990, *The Complete Tutankhamun: The King, The Tomb, The Royal Treasure* (London: Thames and Hudson Ltd.), p. 10.
28. Diop, *African Origin*, pp. xiv-xv.
29. Poe, pp. 16-17.
30. Brian M. Fagan, 1975, *Rape of the Nile: Tomb Robbers, Tourists and Archaeologists in Egypt* (Rhode Island: Moyer Bell), pp. 21-23.
31. Herodotus, 1997, *The Histories* (Vermont: Charles E. Tuttle Co., Inc.), p. 134.
32. Poe, p. 97.
33. Same as above, p. 109.
34. "The Egyptian Pyramids" from "Rediscover Ancient Egypt with Tehuti Research Foundation," November 11, 1998, p. 3. (www.egypt_tehuti.com/pyramids).
35. Van Sertima, p. 78.

36. Sarah Toyne, August 22, 1999, "Aborigines Were First Americans," *The Sunday Times (London)*.

37. Poe, p. 250.

38. Van Sertima, p. 135.

39. Dina Kraft, June 24, 1999, "Phoenician Ships Found Intact in Mediterranean," *San Francisco Chronicle*.

40. Poe, p. 241.

41. Same as above, p. 243.

42. Same as above, p. 253.

43. Van Sertima, p. 24.

44. Same as above, pp. 148-149.

45. Same as above, p. 153.

46. Same as above, p. 157.

47. Harris, p. 92.

48. Fran Alexander, ed., 1998, *Oxford Encyclopedia of World History* (New York: Oxford University Press), pp. 287-288.

49. Harris, p. 77.

50. Lerone Bennett, Jr., 1978, *Before The Mayflower: A History of the Negro in America, 1619-1964 (Revised Edition)* (USA: Johnson Publishing Company, Inc.), p. 16.

51. Diop, *African Origin*, p. 162.

52. Desroches-Noblecourt, p. 38.

53. Herodotus, p. 134.

54. Same as above.

55. Said Hamdun and Noël King, 1998, *Ibn Battuta In Black Africa* (Princeton: Markus Wierner Publishers), p. 38.

56. Diop, *Cultural Unity*, p. 195.

57. Diop, *African Origin*, p. 113.

58. Cheikh Anta Diop, 1987, *Precolonial Black Africa: A Comparative Study of the Political and Social Systems of Europe and Black Africa, from Antiquity to the Formation of Modern States* (Trenton: Lawrence Hill & Company, Africa World Press Edition), pp. 12-13.

59. Same as above, p. 103.

60. Roger Moody, ed.,1988, *The Indigenous Voice: Visions and Realities, Vol. I* (London: Zed Books Ltd.), p. 40.

61. Henri Pirenne, 1937, *Economic and Social History of Medieval Europe* (New York: Harcourt, Brace & World, Inc.), p. 21.

62. Poe, p. 6.

63. Same as above, p. 7.

64. Same as above, p. 14.

65. Soukhanov, ed., p. 458.

66. Sven Lindqvist, 1996, *"Exterminate All the Brutes": One Man's Odyssey into the Heart of Darkness and the Origins of European Genocide* (New York, The New Press), p. 7.

67. McEvedy, p. 24.

68. Jay Williams, 1962, *Knights of the Crusades* (New York: Harper & Row, Publishers, Incorporated), p. 46.

69. Same as above, p. 34.

70. Same as above, p. 35.

71. McEvedy, p. 88.

72. Same as above.

73. Poe, p. 207.

74. Williams, p. 63.

75. Wolfgang Schivelbusch, 1992, *Tastes of Paradise: A Social History of Spices, Stimulants, and Intoxicants* (New York: Vintage Books), p. 4.

76. Same as above, p. 9.

77. McEvedy, p. 90.
78. Stannard, p. 58.
79. Stannard, p. 59.
80. Schivelbusch, p. 22.
81. Stannard, pp. 59-61.
82. Same as above.
83. Brian Innes, 1998, *The History of Torture* (London: Brown Packaging Books Ltd.), p. 123.
84. Pirenne, p. 32.
85. McEvedy, p. 102.
86. Jaffe, p. 43.
87. Bennett, pp.16-19.
88. DuBois, p. 163.
89. Bennett, p. 43.
90. Jaffe, p. 44.
91. Paul Jacobs and Saul Landau with Eve Pell, 1971, *To Serve the Devil, Volume I: Native and Slaves* (New York: Random House), p. 42.
92. Stannard, p. 69.
93. Same as above, pp. 3-7.
94. Same as above.
95. Stannard, p. 76.
96. Same as above.
97. Same as above, p. 75.
98. Eduardo Galeano, 1973, *Open Veins of Latin America: Five Centuries of the Pillage of a Continent* (New York: Monthly Review Press), p. 29.
99. James W. Loewen, 1995, *Lies My Teacher Told Me: Everything Your American History Textbook Got Wrong* (New York: Touchstone), p. 90.
100. Galeano, p. 29.
101. Ward Churchill, 1997, *A Little Matter of Genocide: Holocaust and Denial in the Americas 1492 to the Present* (San Francisco: City Lights Books), p. 138.
102. Same as above.
103. Alexander, ed., p. 281.
104. Diop, *African Origin,* p. 24.
105. Churchill, p.105.
106. Stannard, p. 72.
107. Galeano, p. 49.
108. Diop, 1978, *Cultural Unity,* introduction by John Henrik Clarke, p. xii.
109. Jaffe, pp. 48-49.
110. Galeano, p. 47.
111. Same as above, p. 92.
112. Jaffe, p. 48.
113. Eric Williams, 1966, *Capitalism and Slavery* (New York: Capricorn Books), p. 35.
114. Hugh Thomas, p. 414.
115. Same as above, p. 412.
116. Same as above, p. 415.
117. Same as above, p. 424.
118. Same as above, p. 489.
119. Same as above, pp. 433-438.
120. Herbert Aptheker, 1984, "'We will be free': Advertisements for runaways and the reality of American slavery," Unpublished research paper, Ethnic Studies Program, University of Santa Clara, Santa Clara, CA.
121. Alfred W. McCoy, 1972, *The Politics of Heroin in Southeast Asia* (New York: Harper & Row), p. 59.

122. Karl Marx, 1979, *Capital: A Critique of Political Economy, Vol. 1* (New York: International Publishers), p. 751.
123. Jaffe, p. 57.
124. Omali Yeshitela, *Road to Socialism*, p. 139.
125. Omali Yeshitela, 1991, *Izwe Lethu i Afrika! (Africa Is Our Land)* (Oakland: Burning Spear Publications), p. 47.
126. Harris, p. 20.
127. Omali Yeshitela, 1997, "The Dialectics of Black Revolution: The Struggle to Defeat the Counterinsurgency in the U.S." (Oakland: Burning Spear Uhuru Publications), pp. 4-5.
128. G.V. Scammell, 1989, *The First Imperial Age: European Overseas Expansion c. 1400-1715* (London: Unwin Hyman, Ltd.), p. 213.
129. Same as above, p. 214.
130. Same as above.
131. Jaffe, p. 46.
132. DuBois, p. 149.
133. Williams, p. 61.
134. Schivelbusch, p. 51.
135. Williams, pp. 65-101.
136. Galeano, p. 94.
137. Same as above, p. 96.
138. W.E.B. DuBois, 1969, *The Suppression of the African Slave-Trade to the United States of America, 1638-1870* (New York: Shoken Books), p. 4.
139. Winthrop D. Jordan, 1968, *White Over Black: American Attitudes Toward the Negro, 1550-1812* (New York: W.W. Norton & Company, Inc.), p. 392.
140. Thomas, pp. 298-302.
141. Harris, p. 165.
142. Adam Hochschild, 1998, *King Leopold's Ghost: A Story of Greed, Terror, and Heroism in Colonial Africa* (New York: Houghton Mifflin Company), p. 124.
143. Chinweizu, 1975, *The West and the Rest of Us: White Predators, Black Slavers and the African Elite* (New York: Vintage Books), p. 64.
144. Hochschild, p. 124.
145. Same as above, p. 133.
146. Same as above, pp. 134-135.
147. Same as above, pp. 111-112.
148. Same as above, p. 231.
149. Same as above, p. 278.
150. Lindqvist, p. 54.
151. Hochschild, p. 67.
152. Lindqvist, p. 57.
153. Same as above, p. 17.
154. Poe, p. 340.
155. Horst Drechsler, 1966, *Let Us Die Fighting* (London: Zed Press), p. 144.
156. Same as above, pp. 150-167.
157. V.I. Lenin, 1975, *Imperialism, The Highest State of Capitalism*, (Peking: Foreign Language Press), pp. 93-94.
158. Morris, ed., p. 645.
159. V.I. Lenin, 1972, *Against Revisionism*, (Moscow: Progress Publishers), pp. 319, 320, 328, 330.
160. V.I. Lenin, 1976, *On Proletarian Internationalism* (Moscow: Progress Publishers), pp. 11-12.
161. Omali Yeshitela, 1987, "A Political and Economic Critique of Imperialism and Imperialist Opportunism" (Oakland: Burning Spear Publications), pp. 8-9.
162. Omali Yeshitela, February 1990, "We must push the pigs back at all cost," *The Burning Spear*, p. 25.
163. Stannard, p. 86.

Big Foot and 300 of his people were slaughtered by U.S. government forces in 1890. Their bodies were left to freeze in the snow. This photo is representative of the genocide of the indigenous peoples throughout U.S. history.
Credit: Smithsonian Institution

Burning of an African man in New York in 1740 after a militant uprising of the enslaved community. The lynching of Africans were as common in the North as they were in the South. Credit: Culver Pictures, Inc.

2

Broken Spears

There is an objective relationship between world slavery and U.S. affluence, and up until now the North American population, opportunistically and demagogically led by their stomachs, pocketbooks, and corrupt leadership have chosen the continued enslavement of the world.[1]

— *Omali Yeshitela*

By the end of the eighteenth century Europe was luxuriating in wealth and power and reveling in boundless optimism. Europe's "enlightenment" was reflected in its arts, architecture and philosophy.

The rest of the world, however, hardly had time to appreciate such lofty pursuits. Most of humanity was being victimized by the very lucrative European occupations of rape, theft, genocide and slavery, which provided the resources for Europe's newly found cultural awakening. With the slave trade generating incredible wealth, Europe was in a good mood. The violent and bloody process of "primitive accumulation of capital" that devastated Africa and the Americas, and destroyed world civilization, seemed to uplift Europe enormously.

In 1785, the German poet Friedrich von Schiller perhaps best summed up Europe's euphoria in his "Ode to Joy," which Beethoven set to music in his famous Ninth Symphony. Schiller's ode confidently proclaims in the first stanza that "all mankind will become brothers" and later professes much love for God and humanity:

> *You millions, I embrace you*
> *This kiss is for all the world!*

Brothers, above the starry canopy
There must dwell a loving Father.
Do you fall in worship, you millions?
World, do you know your Creator?
Seek Him in the heavens!
Above the stars he must dwell.[2]

In Mexico, however, an Aztec poet had written of his people's experience of the same process that brought joy to Europe:

Broken spears lie in the roads;
we have torn our hair in grief.
The houses are roofless now, and their walls are red with
*   blood.*
Worms are swarming in the streets and plazas,
and the walls are splattered with gore.
The water has turned red, as if it were dyed,
and when we drink it,
it has the taste of brine.
We have pounded our hands in despair
against the adobe walls,
for our inheritance, our city, is lost and dead.[3]

In Africa, the people expressed in song their hopes regarding the invading Europeans:

O mother, how unfortunate we are!...
But the sun will kill the white man,
But the moon will kill the white man,
But the sorcerer will kill the white man,
But the tiger will kill the white man,
But the crocodile will kill the white man,
But the elephant will kill the white man,
But the river will kill the white man.[4]

STOLEN DEMOCRACY

In France, the bourgeoisie, the rising capitalist class, enriched as elsewhere by the slave trade, was emboldened to overthrow the feudal aristocracy. The French fought in the American Revolution against the English and became intoxicated with newly gained notions of democracy. In 1793, the French Revolution followed the U.S. lead by less than 20 years with the cry of "liberty, fraternity, equality." Like the Americans, the French capitalists adopted the ideas that people had a right to take up arms against tyranny, which had long been the tradition in Europe. They believed that government should be based on republicanism rather than monarchy and that financial and social freedoms should be granted to all (white) men.

Democracy was historically alien to Europe, where the masses had long been voiceless pawns of the ruling elite. Like the land, the gold, and the potato, the concept of democracy was stolen and introduced into Europe after observation of African and indigenous American societies, even as these societies were being enslaved and exterminated. Democracy now became the "property" of Europeans, first of the bourgeois class and ultimately extending to the workers. The Europeans' search for "freedom" became the justification to enslave and eradicate those from whom they learned the idea.

Voltaire, Rousseau, Montesquieu and many of their eighteenth century contemporaries, whose writings form the basis for modern white concepts of democracy, became intrigued by the democratic societies of the Iroquois and other indigenous peoples of the Americas. Indigenous culture became chic in France. In characteristic European fashion, those white people are upheld today as great "philosophers" after annexing the ideas of the peoples whom Europe was oppressing and annihilating.

Voltaire, the French satirist and critic, advocated social systems that permitted "freedom of conscience."[5] The philosopher Rousseau "envisaged a city-state whose citizens assembled to deliberate on matters of common concern." The "general will" thus expressed would, Rousseau claimed, necessarily be just. These views had a powerful influence on the radical wing of the French Revolution. Montesquieu's call for governmental division of powers into "executive, judicial, and legislative" influenced the makers of the U.S. Constitution.

The ideas of these European savants, so foreign to the reality of European social organization, came directly from the constitution of the five-nation Iroquois League, made up of the Mohawk, Onondaga, Seneca, Oneida and Cayuga peoples. The French philosophers studied Iroquois society, arrogantly calling the people "noble savages."

The constitution of the Iroquois League was known as the Great Law of Peace, dating from about 1,000 A.D. Benjamin Franklin and Thomas Paine are said to have used the Great Law of Peace as the basis for the U.S. Constitution.

The Iroquois documents were far more just and equitable than any the United States adopted, wherein the indigenous peoples were denied the rights of citizenship and every enslaved African was defined as three-fifths of a person.

The word "caucus" is derived from an indigenous word and is indicative of the collective leadership style of the Iroquois nations. "Chief" is an English word, which was imposed on the native people to undermine their governmental power and suppress them.[6]

Bruce E. Johansen in *Forgotten Founders: How the American Indian Helped Shape Democracy,* writes:

> Politically, there was nothing in the empires and kingdoms of Europe in the fifteenth and sixteenth centuries to parallel the democratic constitution of the Iroquois Confederacy with its provisions for initiative, referendum and recall, and its suffrage for women as well as men.[7]

Under the Great Law of Peace, women held impeachment powers. Notably, both impeachment and democratic political power in the hands of women were unheard of in European systems of government. In the Iroquois system, if the conduct of any representative "appeared improper to the populace or if he lost the confidence of his electorate, the women of his clan impeached him and expelled him by official action, whereupon the women then chose a new sachem [representative]."[8] Johansen notes that,

> [M]any of the doctrines that played so crucial a role in the American Revolution were fashioned by European savants from observation of the New World and its inhabitants. These observations, packaged into theories, were exported, like the finished products made from raw materials that also traveled the Atlantic Ocean, back to America. The communication [sic] among American Indian cultures, Europe, and Euro-America thus seemed to involve a sort of intellectual mercantilism.[9]

"Intellectual mercantilism"? Intellectual parasitism is more apt.

Though the overall gist of the quote is correct, the genocidal attacks by Europeans against the Indians could hardly be called "communication." Again, the Europeans took a concept from those whom the white people were colonizing and suppressing, made it into a commodity and turned it into its opposite. "Democracy" became a tool empowering European capitalist men with the "freedom" to enslave, rape, ravage and murder everyone in sight in order to accumulate power and riches for themselves.

Under the Iroquois Great Law of Peace the standards for leadership were high, and these qualities were certainly never adopted by "democratic" heads of government in Europe or the United

States. Johansen quotes the Great Law, determining that, the leaders of

> ...the League of Five Nations shall be mentors of the people for all time. The thickness of their skins shall be seven spans, which is to say that they shall be proof against anger, offensive action and criticism. Their hearts shall be full of peace and good will and their minds filled with a yearning for the welfare of the people of the League. With endless patience, they shall carry out their duty. Their firmness shall be tempered with a tenderness for their people. Neither anger nor fury shall find lodging in their minds and all their words and actions shall be marked by calm deliberation.[10]

INVISIBLE HAND OF EXPLOITATION

While the American and French revolutions were taking place in the latter half of the eighteenth century, the Industrial Revolution was underway in England. The slave trade was flourishing and, despite its "breakaway colony" of America, England was poised to become the largest empire on the planet Earth. During this period, Adam Smith wrote *Wealth of Nations*, promoting the doctrine of "laissez faire," which justified an unregulated orgy of capitalist exploitation. Smith argued that an "invisible hand" would tend to the economic welfare of all.[11]

The mysterious "invisible hand," which bears a remarkable resemblance to Ronald Reagan's infamous "trickle down" theory of economics, was working well for the British. English business was booming. In *Capitalism and Slavery*, Eric Williams described the growing world capitalist economy:

> The triangular trade [between Africa, Europe and the Americas] thereby gave a triple stimulus to British indus-

try. The Negroes were purchased with British manufactures; transported to the plantations, they produced sugar, cotton, indigo, molasses and other tropical products, the processing of which created new industries in England; while the maintenance of the Negroes and their owners on the plantations provided another market for British industry, New England agriculture and the Newfoundland fisheries. By 1750 there was hardly a trading or a manufacturing town in England which was not in some way connected with the triangular or direct colonial trade. The profits obtained provided one of the main streams of that accumulation of capital in England which financed the Industrial Revolution.[12]

Not surprisingly, 1750 is the same year generally given as the beginning of the English Industrial Revolution.[13]

Liverpool, like Bristol and the other British beneficiaries of the stolen wealth, reveled in the spoils of the trade in human beings:

It was a common saying that several of the principal streets of Liverpool had been marked out by the chains, and the walls of the houses cemented by the blood of the African slaves, and one street was nicknamed "Negro Row." The red brick Customs House was blazoned with Negro heads. The story is told of an actor in the town, who, hissed by the audience for appearing before them, not for the first time, in a drunken condition, steadied himself and declared with offended majesty: "I have not come here to be insulted by a set of wretches, every brick in whose infernal town is cemented with an African's blood."[14]

MANIFESTO FOR WHITE WORKERS ONLY

Thus it was that the trade in African people and the rapine of most of the world brought an end to European feudalism and catapulted Europe into capitalism. As Chairman Omali Yeshitela has pointed out, the same process that created the immensely wealthy capitalists, who became the ruling class, also created the white working class. The slave trade, plunder and genocide created a pedestal upon which all white people sit, workers and rulers alike.

Serfs and peasants were tumultuously expelled from their farmlands so that the capitalists could transform them into urban industrial workers. Thousands of hands had become necessary to build the slave ships, mill the fabric, distill the rum, and refine the sugar, cotton and tobacco flowing to and from England in the triangular trade.

Early on, capitalist rulers drove white workers, including women and children, mercilessly in the factories and mines of Europe. Karl Marx defined these workers with a burgeoning class consciousness as the "proletariat," in effect the poorest, most oppressed sector of the working class, with the greatest stake in revolution.

But European workers quickly recognized their key role in powering the cogs that turned the wheels of the capitalist machine. They understood their power of leverage. Without the European workers, the raw materials from the colonies could not be turned into usable commodities and the industrialists could not reap their fortunes.

Moreover, the workers of Europe rapidly grasped their ability to use to their benefit the racist ideology that made up the ideological underpinnings of the capitalist system. They needed to prove to their bosses that they were not *slaves,* that indeed they too were white, thereby deserving to enjoy the benefits of life on the pedestal as well. By 1848, European workers were staging massive demonstrations and rebellions throughout the continent. If the capitalists wanted to have peace in Europe they were going to have to share some of the stolen loot and democracy.

Overturning the Culture of Violence

The Communist Manifesto, written by Karl Marx and Friederich Engels in 1847, is the famous proclamation which delineates the rights and aspirations of European workers. Incredibly, the document does not even mention the massive enslavement of African people, which was at its height and was being widely debated at the time. It was the slave trade that provided the impetus for the transformation of these former European serfs into workers.

The manifesto is conspicuously devoid of any mention of solidarity with the rights of enchained Africans, slaughtered Indians and other oppressed colonial subjects, even as Europe was openly raping Africa and most of the world with impunity.

Besides being the pinnacle of the slave trade, the 1840s saw the apex of the pervasive genocide against the indigenous peoples in the Americas. These things were no secret. Public campaigns of extermination were being sponsored by many states, backed by the U.S. government itself. In 1847, the United States was militarily attacking Mexico in order to steal its land. During this period every U.S. city was the scene of highly publicized terrorist attacks on African people by roving gangs of white workers almost daily.

Clearly, *The Communist Manifesto* was not talking about the plight of the majority of humanity. It was addressing the struggle of *white workers*, whom the manifesto designates as "civilized." Never mind that white workers were supporting and even participating in the slaughter and exploitation of the world's oppressed peoples so that capitalism could get the resources to pay white people more money.

The manifesto made no struggle with the majority of white communist workers in America who stood adamantly against the abolition of slavery. The document makes clear that participation in the communist struggle does not extend to those whom it designated as "barbarians." The manifesto puts forward the main goals of the white workers' struggle:

We have seen that the first step in the revolution by the working class is to raise the proletariat to the position of ruling class, to win the battle of democracy.

The proletariat will use its political supremacy to wrest, by degrees, all capital from the bourgeoisie, to central-ize all instruments of production in the hands of the state, i.e., of the proletariat organized as the ruling class, and to increase the total of productive forces as rapidly as possible.[15]

But the bourgeoisie's capital was (and is) stolen. By "wresting" the bourgeoisie's capital, then, the white "proletariat" would do nothing more than take over control of the slave trade and adminis-tration of the colonies; the white workers would oversee the geno-cide and supervise the exploitation of gold and other resources of Africa and the Americas.

Thus the "class" struggle of white workers as defined by *The Communist Manifesto* was not to destroy the pedestal of capitalism, but to change hands of the rulers of parasitic capitalism. White work-ers wanted a greater share of the gluttonous feast on the table of African enslavement. The bourgeoisie understood this quite well, as the quote by Cecil Rhodes in the previous chapter clearly shows.

The communists of the time were not able to understand what Omali Yeshitela has shown: "The real locus of the class contradiction in the real world exists in the contest between capitalism born as a world system, and the 'pedestal' upon which it rests."[16]

In other words, the true "proletariat" in the world is not made up of white people no matter how "poor" or "exploited" some may be. The proletariat of the world is the masses of African and other colo-nized workers who constitute the pedestal upon which the entire white population and the whole edifice of capitalism rests.

The struggle to overturn the capitalist system has always been and will continue to be led by African workers. White people must unite under that leadership in order to defeat the capitalist rulers.

Hosea Jaffe, in *A History of Africa,* remarks that "Africa cannot be seen correctly through 'European' eyes, however Marxist the spectacles used." Jaffe describes the conditions and struggle of those millions of Africans and others whom white communists called "barbarians," and who were "unhonored by international socialism and trade unionism." As Jaffe states,

> [African workers are]...without land or possessions, starving, half naked, unshod, unhoused, illiterate, unarmed, with no trade unions or civic or political rights, with nothing but their children and only their chains to lose, toiling under conditions worse than those in the factories and slums of the European Industrial Revolution, with lower wages, surrounded by an uncountable reserve army of unemployed. This last, combined with a system of European totalitarianism [against Africans], with army, police, concentration camps, executions and torture ever present, kept wages below their value [in the colonies] and thus generated the super-surplus value characteristic of imperialistic capital.[17]

OPPORTUNISM—WHITE WAY OF LIFE

Throughout the nineteenth century, the plundered wealth flowing into Europe was so great that white workers were very successful in winning greater and greater shares of the wealth accrued at the expense of millions of others around the world. Indeed, these economic gains have continued throughout the twentieth century. Marx and Engels were quite unprepared for the fattening conditions of European workers. Instead of the "growing emiseration" that Marx had predicted, sectors of white workers were in fact becoming quite affluent.

An opportunist is defined as a person who takes advantage of opportunities for "self-advancement, usually with no regard for principles or consequences."[18] Living on the pedestal of the enslavement and subjection of most of humanity, European workers were eager opportunists, and the communist movement was their vehicle for self-advancement. Marx, Engels and later Lenin were not able to understand the material basis of this opportunism, which Omali Yeshitela later exposed. In the process of studying this question, Chairman Yeshitela unearthed worried quotes by Engels that reveal his concern about the rampant opportunism of European workers. In a letter to Marx, dated October 7, 1858, Engels wrote:

> The English proletariat is actually becoming more and more bourgeois, so that this most bourgeois of all nations is apparently aiming ultimately at the possession of a bourgeois aristocracy and a bourgeois proletariat *alongside* the bourgeoisie.[19]

Thus, as Yeshitela has shown, the communist movement in particular and the white left in general have attempted to resolve contradictions between white workers and rulers *without disturbing the pedestal of African oppression.*

It is no surprise that even Marx, Engels and Lenin, the most advanced revolutionary thinkers of their times, were unable to see that colonized peoples would be the weak link in the imperialist chain. Born parasitic, capitalism's philosophical foundation and underlying ideology is racism. Sitting on the pedestal of slavery and genocide, the nineteenth and early twentieth century revolutionary leaders' vision was as limited by the material conditions in which they lived as that of anyone else.

Hosea Jaffe discusses the evolution of this concept of racism: "Before capitalist-colonialism there were no races; but now, suddenly and increasingly, there were races: once born, the myth grew into a 'reality.'"[20]

A Solution for European Workers

With the rapid rise of capitalism and industrialization in mid-nineteenth century Europe, workers were scrambling to win a piece of the loot of parasitic capitalism. Jobs were being created by plunder of the colonies, drawing increasing numbers of former serfs and peasants into the industrialized cities. But while millions of workers were beginning to enjoy some of the wealth and benefits of stolen capitalist resources, millions more impoverished laborers were joining the workforce.

Despite rebellions, many European workers were still "propertyless, largely illiterate, and entirely dependent upon wage earning for a living."[21] For the strata of still impoverished European workers, however, capitalism had begun to provide a new solution for quickly achieving a better life—a solution that was more attractive than the prospect of spending years in struggle with capitalist bosses throughout Europe.

Possibilities lay across the Atlantic Ocean, where on the backs of African and native people even the poorest white worker could climb up the ladder to affluence and "success." European workers poured into the United States in the mid-nineteenth century, looking for a share of the pot of gold that white people had been accumulating in North America for more than two hundred years.

In the early years of its colonial period, the "New World" was so rich from the "primitive accumulation" of slavery, genocide and land theft that it scarcely needed any white workers. Plantation owners and landed gentry, farmers, artisans and professionals typified the population.

Most, if not all, of the gentlemen farmers were slaveholders. Karl Marx noted,

> In the Northern States of the American Union, it may be doubted whether so many as a tenth of the people would fall under the description of hired laborers....In England...the laboring class compose the bulk of the people. Nay, the impulse to self-expropriation, on the part of laboring humanity, for the glory of capital, exists so little, that slavery...is the sole natural basis of colonial wealth.[22]

The original colonies in the United States were not enterprises of poor Englishmen seeking religious freedom and political ideals. These colonies were rather joint-stock companies in which British businessmen made investments and expected to make a fortune. Jamestown, Virginia, for example—the first English colony and the site where the first captive Africans were brought to labor inside U.S. borders—was financed by the Virginia Company of London.

King James I granted a charter to the group of London entrepreneurs in 1607 to establish the Virginia Company as a satellite English settlement in the Chesapeake region of North America. The King's instructions to the settlers were to "find gold and a water route to the Orient." According to a list published by Captain John Smith, "'gentlemen' made up about half of the group....The rest were artisans, craftsmen, and laborers."[23]

In other cases, the British crown simply "gave" huge grants of the native people's land to English aristocrats to develop as they chose. For example, what is today Maryland was given to Lord George Calvert, Lord Baltimore, and Pennsylvania to William Penn.[24]

LUST FOR WEALTH

North America was vast and fertile and rich with resources. By the time the land now known as Virginia was seized, millions of indigenous people had already been brutally killed at the hands of the Spanish in Central and South America and even into Florida, Georgia and South Carolina. But the English "gentlemen" needed slaves to do the work. So, in 1619, only 12 years after the establishment of the first British colony, the enslavement of Africans was instituted in North America.

Slavery, genocide and the ability to seize the land of the native people at will were intrinsic to the "American character," known for its bold and unashamed lust for wealth. The United States was also distinguished by the same propensity for slaughter and viciousness that had characterized Europe for thousands of years. The overwhelmingly brutal crimes of white people, including and especially white workers, however, cannot be understood without an understanding of Chairman Omali Yeshitela's insights into the material reality of parasitic capitalism. Yeshitela has written:

> Born as a parasitic social system which depended on the slave trade, the rape of Africa, Asia and Latin America for its emergence and maintenance, capitalism has continued to develop as a social system that is so structured as to require the enslavement of the entire black world as a prerequisite for North American and European wealth and well-being. It is a capitalist social system within which a handful of European nations live off the body of the rest of humanity—the black, brown, yellow and red peoples of the world.[25]

In *A Little Matter of Genocide,* Ward Churchill describes the white relationship to the indigenous people, exemplifying the class unity of white workers with the American parasitic social system described by Yeshitela. Churchill states:

Through most of the history of what has happened, the perpetrators, from aristocrats like Jeffrey Amherst to the lowliest private in his army, from the highest elected officials to the humblest of farmers, openly described America's indigenous peoples as vermin, launched literally hundreds of campaigns to effect their extermination, and then reveled in the carnage which resulted. [26]

Europe's Sugar Bowl

With the opportunities opened up by slavery and land theft, it took no time at all for Europeans to make money hand over fist in the "New World." The triangular trade tied the burgeoning North American economy to that of the British slave trade based in the Caribbean, which since the late eighteenth century, had spawned the incredibly lucrative sugar plantations there.

"It was," Eric Williams tells us in *Capitalism and Slavery,* "Negro slaves who made these sugar colonies the most precious colonies ever recorded in the whole annals of imperialism. Sugar was king," Williams affirms, "and the West Indian islands the sugar bowl of Europe." He continues:

> In this triangular trade England—France and Colonial America equally—supplied the exports and the ships; Africa the human merchandise; the plantations the colonial raw materials. The slave ship sailed from the home country with a cargo of manufactured goods. These were exchanged at a profit on the coast of Africa for Negroes, who were traded on the plantations, at another profit, in exchange for a cargo of colonial produce to be taken back to the home country.[27]

The Northeastern United States benefited as much as or more than the South from its early connection with the slave trade. As Williams tells us, "the West Indian colonies needed food....Thus did the North American colonies come to have a recognized place in imperial economy, as purveyors of the supplies needed by the sugar planters and their slaves."

In 1770, according to a scholar of the period quoted by Eric Williams, "It was the wealth accumulated from West Indian trade which more than anything else underlay the prosperity of New England and the Middle Colonies."[28]

All of Colonial America was economically tied to the trade in African bodies, not just the plantations of the South. It was wealth gained from the slave trade that created the economic basis for the American colonies to become independent from England.

INDIGENOUS HOSPITALITY

Expansive and magnificent, the Americas were far from empty, as the colonizers like to say. Writers of the white man's history have always fabricated the lie that the indigenous peoples lived in sparsely populated clusters. According to David Stannard, however, "such separate nations as the Mohawk, the Munsee, the Massachusetts, the Mohegan-Pequot, and others filled their territorial areas with as many or more residents per square mile as inhabit most western regions in the present-day United States."[29]

Stannard observes the "astounding diversity and multiformity among North America's aboriginal peoples." He notes,

> [S]ome communities were small, isolated, provincial, and poor, barely scraping subsistence from the soil. Others were huge urban and commercial centers where large numbers of people, entirely freed from the necessity of subsistence work, carried out other tasks of artistry, engineering, construction, religion and trade. And, between

these extremes, there were a rich variety of cultural organizations, a great diversity of social design.[30]

Despite their different cultures, Professor Stannard continues,

[O]ne characteristic of America's indigenous peoples that
does seem almost universal, transcending the great diversity of other cultural traits, was an extraordinary capacity
for hospitality....[I]n fact, the native people's affectionate
and fearless cordiality in greeting strangers was mentioned by almost all the earliest European explorers, from
Vespucci in South America in 1502, where the Indians
"swam out to receive us...with as much confidence as if
we had been friends for years," to Cartier in Canada in
1535, where the Indians "as freely and familiarly came to
our boats without any fear, as if we had ever been
brought up together."[31]

The European "gentlemen" colonizers arriving in Virginia, Massachusetts and New York were ignorant and indifferent to the basic
skills of survival. They would have starved without the help of the
indigenous people who willingly shared their own food supplies with
the white people. The Indians taught them where and how to fish
and how to plant and cultivate vegetables. According to Johansen:

During the years following the landing of the Pilgrims,
American Indians contributed many foods to the diet of a
growing number of Euro-Americans. By the twentieth
century, almost half the world's domesticated crops,
including the staples—corn and white potatoes—were
first cultivated by American Indians. Aside from turkey,
corn, and white potatoes, Indians contributed manioc,
sweet potatoes, squash, peanuts, peppers, pumpkins,
tomatoes, pineapples, the avocado, cacao (chocolate),

chicle (a constituent of chewing gum), several varieties of beans, and at least seventy other domesticated food plants. Almost all the cotton grown in the United States was derived from varieties originally cultivated by Indians. Rubber, too, was contributed by Native Americans.

Several American Indian medicines also came into use among Euro-Americans. These included quinine, laxatives, as well as several dozen other drugs and herbal medicines. Euro-Americans adapted to their own needs many Indian articles of clothing and other artifacts such as hammocks, kayaks, canoes, moccasins, smoking pipes, dog sleds, and parkas...[32]

GENOCIDE AS PUBLIC POLICY

The European response to such hospitality and generosity of spirit was genocide. Extermination of the native people was the open public policy of the white invaders. Indian women and children were sold as slaves as a means of financing the genocidal war against the native people as a whole. Biological warfare was waged against the native people, as is now well-known.

In 1763, Lord Jeffrey Amherst—for whom a town and university are named in Massachusetts—instructed one of his men, Colonel Henry Bouquet, to send smallpox-infected blankets to the Pontiac coalition who were defending their land near the Great Lakes against white aggressors. Ward Churchill quotes an account of this barbarous act:

> Amherst...wrote in a postscript of the letter to Bouquet that smallpox be sent among the disaffected tribes. Bouquet replied, also in a postscript, "I will try to [contaminate] them with some blankets that may fall into their hands, and take care not to get the disease myself."...To

Bouquet's postscript Amherst replied, "You will do well to [infect] the Indians by means of blankets as well as to try every other method that can serve to extirpate this [execrable] race." On June 24, Captain Ecuyer, of the Royal Americans, noted in his journal: "...we gave them two blankets and a handkerchief out of the smallpox hospital. I hope it will have the desired effect."[33]

Churchill notes that the resulting smallpox spread rapidly among the Ottawas, Mingos, Miamis, Lenni Lenapes (Delawares), and several other peoples. "By conservative estimate, the toll was over 100,000 dead, a matter which effectively broke the back of native resistance in what the United States would later call the 'Northwest Territory,' allowing its conquest less than thirty years later."[34]

The pleasure taken by the white people in inflicting direct anguish on the native people was remarkable. In New York, for example, where white nationalist mythology has it that the Dutch "bought" Manhattan island and much fur for a few baubles, the Dutch "ran their bayonets through men, women and children, hacked their bodies to pieces, and then leveled the villages with fire."[35] Chief Flying Hawk gave his account of this brutal massacre:

> The Indians had befriended the helpless adventurers when they came among them, and for their kindness the settlers attacked them one night and killed more than a hundred and twenty men, women and children while they were asleep in their wigwams....They ran their bayonets through the stomachs of little babies and flung them out into the river. They cut off the hands of the men and cut open the women with their swords. They went among them with a torch of fire and burned their homes until no Indians were left; and these all were friendly Indians who

sold the white people their island for needles, awls, and fishhooks, and brought the furs to them.[36]

DELIBERATE INFECTION WITH SMALLPOX

The long history of white people's atrocities against the native people in the Americas is well-documented in many easily accessible books, listed in the bibliography. They must be read for a full account of the slaughter. They show how ordinary white citizens participated enthusiastically in the orgies of genocide and often led them. Incredible cruelty, as in the examples cited above, are repeated over and over again.

Throughout U.S. history, newspapers openly discussed the "extermination" of the native people. For example Ward Churchill quotes a San Francisco newspaper article on the "Indian Question" from 1853: "people are…ready to knife them, shoot them, or inoculate them with smallpox—*all of which have been done* [Emphasis added]."

Churchill adds: "Thus, by the mid-nineteenth century, it appears that the eradication of Indians through *deliberate* infection with plague diseases had become so commonplace that it was no longer a military specialty. Rather, it had been adopted as a method of 'pest control' by average civilians."[37]

White people targeted indigenous women and children for murder in a manner that was "flatly and intentionally genocidal,"[38] says David Stannard. He adds,

> Observing the closeness of Indian parents and children, for example, and the extraordinary grief suffered by Indian mothers and fathers when separated from their offspring, [British colonizers] made it a practice to kidnap and hold hostage Indian children whenever they approached a native town.[39]

Most of us grew up watching an endless stream of movies and TV shows depicting white settlers firing on the native people. We were there in front of our TV sets rooting for the white people whose main task was kill the Indian and "settle" the land.

We never gave a thought to the fact that the indigenous people were defending their land against foreign invaders.

ARMY OF EXTERMINATORS

The white population constituted an armed militia, as was their "right" under the Second Amendment of the Constitution. The white settlers were deputized as "necessary to the security of a free State,"[40] and authorized to carry out summary executions of indigenous people at will.

The U.S. military, which assaulted the native people tirelessly, was made up of "irregular civilian militia,"[41] thousands of eager white volunteers anxious to play a role in the extermination. Clearly, the primary and most effective tool of genocide for the U.S. State was its armed white population.

As a young man, Abraham Lincoln, for example, signed up for the Indian-fighting army. Lincoln joined the U.S. forces in the Black Hawk War of 1832, infamous for its gruesome carnage. According to one history book, as the Black Hawk people were forced to retreat they made offers of peace, which the U.S. militia ignored. The native people were driven to the Mississippi River "where the men, women and children were mercilessly cut to pieces as they tried to cross."[42] The white soldiers had an "eight-hour frenzy of clubbing, stabbing, shooting [and] scalping."[43]

In typical Eurocentric fashion, the white left, in particular the Communist Party, has elevated Lincoln as the "great liberator."

While the young Lincoln was performing his genocidal duties as a foot soldier in the Black Hawk War, Andrew Jackson was the U.S. head of state. Jackson had swept into the presidency in 1828 on a populist platform enthusiastically backed by white working people. Revered as a vicious Indian killer, Jackson was also a slave trader, land speculator and merchant. Known as the "people's" president, Jackson spoke for "the humble members of [white] society—the farmer, mechanics and laborers..."

As such, Jackson was the "first president to master the liberal rhetoric, to speak for the common man."[44] So wrote Howard Zinn in his white apologist history book, *A People's History of the United States: 1492–Present*, which equates the carnage of African and indigenous peoples with the situation of white workers, absolving them of any responsibility for genocide.

Many people respect Zinn's historical outlook, but it is important to note that in his book, Zinn makes clear that he does not differentiate the genocide of the indigenous people and enslavement of African people from the opportunist "struggles," aspirations and even crimes of the white working class. His "people's history" equates the story of the oppressors with the struggle of the victims. Zinn states:

> Thus, in that inevitable taking of sides which comes from selection and emphasis in history, I prefer to try to tell the story of the discovery of America from the viewpoint of the Arawaks, of the Constitution from the standpoint of the slaves, of Andrew Jackson as seen by the Cherokees, of the Civil War as seen by the New York Irish, of the Mexican war as seen by the deserting soldiers of Scott's army, of the rise of industrialism as seen by young women in the textile mills of Lowell, of the Spanish-American war as seen by the Cubans, the conquest of the Philippines as seen by black soldiers on Luzon, the Guilded Age as seen by southern farmers, the First World War as seen by socialists, the Second World War as seen by pacifists, the New Deal as seen by blacks in Harlem, the postwar American empire as seen by peons in Latin America.[45]

But the participants in American history are not all one big happy, "diverse" family. The New York Irish were slaughtering African people in northern cities to get their jobs. They were furious when they were drafted into the Union Army, which promised to abolish the slave system, and in response, they intensified their attacks on Africans. White women in the textile mills of Lowell, Massachusetts had jobs making cloth from cotton grown by enslaved Africans. White farmers got their land by murdering the native people and seizing their territories, or by earning money brutally catching runaway slaves.

Zinn doesn't stop there. He not only absolves white people living and dead for our responsibility in these crimes and the resulting affluence we enjoy today, he actually goes on to *criminalize* African and other colonized people inside the U.S and blame them for their conditions:

> My point is not to grieve for the victims and denounce the executioners. Those tears, that anger, cast into the past, deplete our moral energy for the present. And the lines are not always clear. In the long run, the oppressor is also a victim. In the short run (and so far, human history has consisted only of short runs), the victims, themselves desperate and tainted with the culture that oppresses them, turn on other victims.[46]

Professor Zinn never quite explains how the "oppressor is also a victim," but we might ask him if he considers the Nazis "victims" when the target of slaughter was other Europeans. Or is the oppressor a victim only when the oppressed are not white?

Do victims "turn on other victims," or do the oppressors use the age-old European strategy of "divide and conquer" among the oppressed? The *true* victims of America could never begin to do anything to compare with the terror and violence imposed upon them by white power for the past 500 years.

The history of the United States is *not* the story of a succession of victims who became oppressors. It is the story of an oppressor nation enslaving and annihilating African, indigenous and other colonial subjects who are still oppressed and facing desperate conditions today. In the process, U.S. wealth and power were consolidated, and all white people, regardless of how poor and downtrodden, have had the opportunity to step up on the backs of African and other non-white peoples.

We beg to differ further with the good professor: we believe that it is rather the *failure* of white people to correctly sum up and take responsibility for the past that depletes our "moral energy for the present," and tries to keep African and other peoples enslaved for our benefit.

SHARP KNIFE

Andrew Jackson, the white working man's hero, set the precedent for the popular white people's democracy that characterizes America today. Jackson fought for all white workers to have the opportunity to sit comfortably on the pedestal of slavery and genocide. Many historians praise Jackson, and many schoolbooks still teach that he was an exemplary leader. One white-centered history book written by Henry Steele Commager, whose texts are commonly used in many high schools and colleges, extols Andrew Jackson's virtues:

> Jackson was one of the few Presidents whose heart and soul were completely with the plain people. He sympathized with and believed in them partly because he had always been one of them. He had been born in utter poverty...the boy, reared in hardship and insecurity,

dressed in the cheapest linsey-woolsey, and subject to a nervous disease, was probably humiliated again and again. A childhood sense of inferiority may help to explain his explosive temper, his keen sensitiveness, and his lifelong sympathy with the oppressed.[47]

These are the kinds of lies taught to our children. Andrew Jackson built his political career by killing indigenous people, who called him "Sharp Knife." Jackson oversaw and personally inflicted countless atrocities himself. In 1814, the future president

> ...supervised the mutilation of 800 or more Creek Indian corpses—the bodies of men, women and children that they had massacred—cutting off their noses to count and preserve a record of the dead, slicing long strips of flesh from their bodies to tan and turn into bridle reins.[48]

Jackson's attack on the Seminole people of Florida during the so-called Seminole War of 1818 in Florida cemented his political aspirations. However, the Seminoles—a union of African and indigenous exiles—were fierce fighters and gave Jackson a run for his money. William Loren Katz describes the Seminole society in his book *Black Indians:*

> Around the time African settlers arrived in Florida, refugees from the Creek Nation also settled there. This group called themselves "Seminoles" or runaways, and their Muskogee culture accepted a variety of Indian ethnic groups—Yuchi, Hitchiti, and Alabama...

> Africans proved far more familiar with Florida's tropical terrain than Spaniards or Seminoles. They transplanted a rice cultivation method practiced in Senegambia and Sierra Leone. Used to a more moderate climate, Semi-

noles began to learn how to survive in Florida from these ex-slaves. "From the beginning of Seminole colonization in Florida," writes Opala, "the Indian may have depended upon African farmers for their survival."

Georgia slaveholders were soon invading Florida, seeking their runaways, and were soon meeting a united resistance by red and black armed forces.[49]

Despite the Seminoles' reputation as powerful fighters, Jackson began bloody raids into Florida on the justification that it was a sanctuary for "escaped slaves and...marauding Indians." Using this genocidal campaign the United States pushed the Seminoles further and further south and seized their lands. Along the way, Jackson became quite rich as the governor of the Florida Territory.[50] The excellent Seminole fighters were never entirely conquered and "a sizable segment withdrew into the Everglades swamp country, from whence they were never dislodged."[51]

TRAIL OF TEARS

Andrew "Sharp Knife" Jackson proposed in his first message to Congress that all Indians would be forcibly removed to the west of the Mississippi in a genocidal death march which came to be known as the "Trail of Tears." The indigenous people were to be guaranteed "permanent Indian territory," in which supposedly no white person could settle. In 1830, the "Indian Removal Act" was passed into law, which legalized the "gradual relocation" of the native people.

In 1838, however, gold was found in the Appalachians and the Cherokee people were rounded up by the U.S. army and put in concentration camps. The Cherokee were forced to walk during the winter months across the U.S. plains. One in four people froze to death on the infamous "Trail of Tears."[52]

As Dee Brown relates in *Bury My Heart at Wounded Knee*:

The Choctaws, Chickasaws, Creeks, and Seminoles also gave up their homelands in the South. In the North, surviving remnants of the Shawnees, Miamis, Ottawas, Hurons, Delawares, and many other once mighty tribes walked or traveled by horseback and wagon beyond the Mississippi, carrying their shabby goods, their rusty farming tools, and bags of seed corn. All of them arrived as refugees, poor relations, in the country of the proud and free Plains Indians.[53]

Almost immediately the U.S. government broke its promise to respect sovereign Indian territory as thousands of white people, greedy for land, trekked west, slaughtering indigenous people along the way. "To justify these breaches of the 'permanent Indian frontier,'" explains Brown, "the policy makers in Washington invented Manifest Destiny, a term which lifted land hunger to a lofty plane. The Europeans and their descendants were ordained by destiny to rule all of America."[54]

In 1845, newspaper editor John O'Sullivan had coined the phrase taken up by the U.S. government and white America as a popular euphemism for genocide. O'Sullivan wrote, "Our manifest destiny [is] to overspread the continent allotted by Providence for the free development of our yearly multiplying millions."[55] "Manifest Destiny," was the rallying cry for violence which unleashed a bloodbath against the native people.

Scalping was a favorite pastime among the settlers, all the more so because it brought good money. An ancient European tradition introduced by the Spanish and the English into the Americas, scalping appalled the native people, who had never encountered such savagery.

All nationalities of European invaders offered attractive rewards to white people for the scalps of native people, including women, babies, even fetuses. The more famous the Indian warrior, the greater the reward—$100 or more.

Naturally, white people went wild for this new moneymaking scheme. Some in the "scalp trade had begun to identify themselves proudly by sporting breeches made of tanned Indian skin."[56] Scalping proved so lucrative that Englishmen, when they ran out of Indians to behead, started scalping other Europeans.[57]

One example of sheer carnage was the infamous massacre at Sand Creek, Colorado. This U.S. military attack on Cheyenne women and children in the 1860s was led by Colonel Chivington, whose goal was to kill all indigenous children because "nits make lice." One soldier who participated in the slaughter later wrote:

> In going over the battleground the next day, I did not see a body of man, woman, or child but was scalped, and in many instances their bodies were mutilated in the most horrible manner—men, women, and children's privates cut out, etc.; I heard one man say that he had cut the fingers off an Indian to get the rings on the hand....I heard of one instance of a child a few months old being thrown in the feedbox of a wagon, and after being carried some distance left on the ground to perish; I also heard of numerous instances in which men had cut out the private parts of females and stretched them over the saddle-bows and wore them over their hats while riding in the ranks.[58]

Another observer wrote of the murder of the Cheyenne people at Sand Creek:

> All manner of depredations were inflicted on their persons. They were scalped, their brains knocked out; the men used their knives, ripped open women, clubbed little children, knocked them in the head with their guns,

beat their brains out, mutilated their bodies in every sense of the word...worse mutilated than any I ever saw before...[C]hildren two or three months old; all lying there, from sucking infants up to warriors.[59]

GOLD RUSH AND GENOCIDE

In 1848, as white workers were massively rebelling in cities throughout Europe, Zachary Taylor was elected president of the United States. The battle between Northern and Southern capitalism over the system of slavery was heating up at the same time as the U.S. was waging a colonial war against the Mexican people to steal their land.

Boston Unitarian minister Theodore Parker, an outspoken anti-war "progressive" activist and opponent of the attack on Mexico, summed up the white liberal sentiment. He called Mexicans "'a wretched people; wretched in their origin, history and character," who should be exterminated as the Indians were. "Yes, the United States should expand," he said, "but not by war, rather by the power of her ideas, the pressure of her commerce, by the steady advance of a superior race, with superior ideas and a better civilization."[60]

In 1848 also, white people discovered gold in the California Sierra Nevada mountains. Conveniently it was just a few weeks after the United States signed the colonial Treaty of Guadeloupe Hidalgo which seized California, Nevada, Utah, Arizona, New Mexico and Colorado for the United States. Now the United States became the master of the continent, having stolen land from coast to coast. With California securely in the pocket of the United States, the gold rush precipitated yet another orgy of plunder and genocide by the "hungry swine" who lusted after this yellow metal. Today, California tourism celebrates the gold rush and thousands of visitors yearly tour the "gold country."

But the true story of the gold rush must be told. It is a paradigm of "primitive accumulation," and a model of flagrant genocide. White people went wild with slaughter and rapine, amassing fortunes great and small, and creating the economic foundation for one of the richest states in the United States today.

Before the white people arrived in California there were at least 400,000 indigenous people living there, a concentration higher than in any other part of what is currently the United States.

The native people of California, living in the lush and bountiful surroundings of California, "spent most of their time just having fun."[61] A slim volume called *Digger: The Tragic Fate of the California Indians from the Missions to the Gold Rush* by Jerry Stanley tells the horrifying story of the extermination.

Prior to the Europeans arrival, life in the lands now known as California had gone on for 12,000 years with the flow of nature. Stanley tells us that for the native people: "There was little difference between gathering acorns and swimming in a stream. Life was life."[62]

In 1542, the Spanish conquistador Juan Rodriguez Cabrillo disembarked onto California's shores at what is now San Diego, the land of the people whom the Spanish called the Diegueno. According to Stanley, when the Spanish men came ashore sporting beards and leather breastplates, exhibiting astoundingly rude behavior, without any women and emitting a foul body odor, the Diegueno were not sure "if they were humans, animals, or insects."[63] Typically, Cabrillo plopped down in the middle of the Diegueno's garden and stole their food supply.

By the 1760s swarms of Franciscan priests came from Spain to California, led by Father Junípero Serra. Their stated purpose was to "save the souls" of the Indians. Serra and his men built concentration camps—21 in all—called missions all along the Pacific coast where they impounded the native people and tortured and worked them to death. Their broken bodies were dumped into mass graves. Nearly

200 years later Adolph Hitler would model the German death camps after the Catholic missions of California.[64]

Today the Catholic Church is considering Father Junípero Serra, the master of organized torture and genocide, for sainthood and the missions have been restored to entice tourists to "Romantic California."

Thanks to the holy padres, by 1834 there were only 150,000 remaining of the 400,000 California Indians who were alive and thriving only 65 years earlier. In 1845, the white population of California was about 7,000. Six months after gold was discovered, there were 60,000. By 1850, California became the thirty-first state, with a white population of more than 150,000. Between 1849 and 1860, the height of the gold rush, one indigenous person was being killed every hour.[65]

HORROR UNPARALLELED

The invading whites called the native people "diggers," very close to the preferred name for African people. Of course, it was the white people who were digging—every inch of land they could get their bloody hands on in search of the gold. California governors John McDougall in 1850 and Peter Burnett in 1851 financed a popular war of public, intentional genocide against the native people. Stanley reports:

> The *San Francisco Chronicle,* one of the state's leading newspapers, said the California Indians "grazed in the fields like beasts and ate roots, snakes, and grasses like cattle, like pigs, like dogs...and like hungry wolves."...As early as April 1849, the newspaper *Alta California* predicted that in order for whites to mine gold "it will be absolutely necessary to exterminate the savages."

Stanley continues:

Early in 1849 white miners from Oregon entered a Maidu village, raped several women, and shot the men who tried to resist....In 1850, it hit them like a tidal wave. Whites overran their land by the thousands, and during the 1850s and 1860s the Indians were swept away like unwanted debris. Red Bluff, Marysville, and other towns offered bounties for Indian scalps, arms and hands, or other proof of a dead Indian...Whites formed unofficial militia units to kill Indians and submitted claims for expenses to the state. In 1851 and 1852 the state paid $1 million in such claims, and in 1857 issued $400,000 in bonds to pay the expenses of volunteers engaged in "the suppression of Indian hostilities."

Major Gabriel Raines, the commander at Fort Humboldt, wrote, "I have just been to Indian Island, the home of a band of friendly Indians, where I beheld a scene of atrocity and horror unparalleled not only in our own country, but even in history—babies with brains oozing out of their skulls, cut and hacked with axes, a two year old child with its ear and scalp torn from the side of its little head, and squaws exhibiting the most frightful wounds, their heads split in twain by axes."[66]

The California Indians fought fiercely against the white raiders who besieged villages, kidnapping native women and children, using and selling them as sex slaves. At least 5,000 indigenous children were kidnapped and sold as slaves and another 5,000 women and young girls as sex slaves. A hundred dollars or more was paid for indigenous girls under the age of ten.[67]

Between 1848 and 1860, more than $600 million worth of gold was extracted from the earth of California by white people, making the colonizers wealthy by the thousands. By 1860 only 35,000 native people in California remained: a people enslaved, their children raped, their land stolen, and their culture in ruins.

BRILLIANT INDIGENOUS RESISTANCE

The native people defended their lands and their people courageously, and their resistance was prolonged, causing the United States to suffer many military setbacks and spend millions of dollars on military reinforcement.

The Apache, whose lands encompassed both sides of the border with Mexico, were committed to defending themselves against both the Spanish and the North American invaders. One of the most outstanding Apache leaders and military strategists was Goyathlay, known to white people as Geronimo, who was never captured by any invader. In 1906, he proactively surrendered to the U.S. army following incessant deadly raids against his people.

Geronimo's whole family had been massacred by the Spanish colonial army of Mexico in 1858 near a town which the Apache called Kaskiyeh, and it was in response to this brutality that the young man's talents as a brilliant warrior were first revealed. Geronimo recalled:

> Late one afternoon when returning from town we were met by a few women and children who told us that Mexican troops from some other town had attacked our camp, killed all the warriors of the guard, captured all our ponies, secured our arms, destroyed our supplies, and killed many of our women and children....I found that my aged mother, my young wife, and my three small children were among the slain....I silently turned away and stood by the river. How long I stood there I do not know, but when I saw the warriors arranging for a council I took my place...

I arranged the Indians in a hollow circle near the river, and the Mexicans drew their infantry up in two lines, with the cavalry in reserve. We were in the timber, and they advanced until within about four hundred yards, when they halted and opened fire. Soon I led a charge against them, at the same time sending some braves to attack their rear. In all the battle I thought of my murdered mother, wife, and babies—of my father's grave and my vow of vengeance, and I fought with fury...

...Over the bloody field, covered with the bodies of Mexicans, rang the fierce Apache war whoop.[68]

All throughout the Civil War years, the U.S. government had a second front to defend: indigenous people struggling for their stolen land. In 1866, under the "political leadership of Red Cloud, the Oglalas, the largest of the seven groups of Lakota, forged a unified military response" to a U.S. military invasion of their lands, which was threatening the indigenous buffalo economy.

Ward Churchill tells us, "The Lakota had also consolidated a defensive alliance with the Arapaho and Northern Cheyenne, two other Indian nations whose 1851 treaty areas were violated by the U.S. offensive actions." All during 1866, this powerful confederation halted all traffic along the Bozeman trail, isolating and laying siege to the military posts along it, and wiping out the troops of Captain William C. Fetterman outside Fort Phil Kearney.[69]

The fierce defense led by Red Cloud forced the United States out of the Lakota homeland centering on the Black Hills of North and South Dakota. The U.S. Congress ratified a treaty in 1869, but treaties with the indigenous people have never meant anything to the American government, as we know. As soon as white people learned that there were precious mineral deposits in the Black Hills, the U.S. cavalry was attacking again.

Tesunke Witko, known as Crazy Horse, and Tantanka Yotanka, known as Sitting Bull, were other incredible guerrilla tacticians and fighters who defended the sacred Lakota land. As a Cheyenne, Crazy Horse fought along with the Oglala in the ongoing defense of their territory in June 1876. One account describes Crazy Horse's military genius:

> When [U.S. General] Crook sent his pony soldiers in mounted charges, instead of rushing forward into the fire of their carbines, the Sioux* faded off to their flanks and struck weak places in their lines. Crazy Horse kept his warriors mounted and always moving from one place to another. By the time the sun was in the top of the sky he had the soldiers all mixed up in three separate fights. The Bluecoats were accustomed to forming skirmish lines and strong fronts, and when Crazy Horse prevented them from fighting like that they were thrown into confusion. By making many darting charges on their swift ponies, the Sioux kept the soldiers apart and always on the defensive. When the Bluecoats' fire grew too hot, the Sioux would draw away, tantalize a few soldiers into pursuit, and then turn on them with a fury.[70]

A few days later on June 25, the Lakota and the Cheyenne wiped out the U.S. army battalion led by General George Armstrong Custer at Little Big Horn. Much to the surprise of the arrogant invading "bluecoat" general, nearly 10,000 indigenous people were camping in the valley. Custer had aspirations of running for president, like Andrew Jackson before him, based on his fame as an "Indian killer." As we know, Custer's ambitions were dashed by powerful Indian resistance:

---

* The Lakota and Oglala have rejected the European name "Sioux." This quote from *Bury My Heart at Wounded Knee* predates that decision.

"The smoke of the shooting and the dust of the horses shut out the hill," Pte-San-Waste-Win said, "and the soldiers fired many shots, but the Sioux shot straight and the soldiers fell dead. The women crossed the river after the men of our village, and when we came to the hill there were no soldiers living and Long Hair (Custer) lay dead among the rest....The blood of the people was hot and their hearts bad, and they took no prisoners that day."[71]

"THE WHITE MAN WILL NEVER BE ALONE"

Many other indigenous fighters waged successful insurgencies for years against the United States. But the U.S. motto that "the only good Indian is a dead Indian"—enthusiastically backed by the vast majority of white citizens—prevailed. By the second half of the nineteenth century just about all the surviving indigenous people were trapped on impoverished concentration camps known as "reservations," their great civilizations destroyed.

Today the million and a half or so native people who exist as captives on their own land have a life expectancy of 45 years[72]—as compared to more than 75 years for white people. Thus, even our long life span is stolen.

When Europeans first invaded this land the indigenous peoples lived long, healthy lives while white people in the filthy, disease-ridden cities of Europe expected to live only into their thirties. At the end of the twentieth century native people have an infant mortality rate nine times that of white babies, while in Europe during Columbus' time, about half the children died before reaching the age of ten.[73]

In 1855, Chief Stealth, also known as Seattle, perhaps envisioning the day of reckoning for white power and the rising up of oppressed peoples, made this haunting prediction:

We are two distinct races with separate origins and separate destinies. There is little in common between us....But why should I mourn at the untimely fate of my people? Tribe follows tribe, and nation follows nation, and regret is useless. Your time of decay may be distant, but it will surely come, for even the white man....cannot be exempt from the common destiny. We may be brothers after all. We will see.

And when the last red man shall have perished, and the memory of my tribe shall have become a myth among the white men, these shores will swarm with invisible dead of my tribe, and when your children's children think themselves alone in the field, the store, the shop, upon the highway, or in the silence of the pathless woods, they will not be alone....At night when the streets of your cities and villages are silent and you think them deserted, they will throng with the returning hosts that once filled and still love this beautiful land. The white man will never be alone.[74]

Chief Stealth was right: white people are indeed forever haunted by our past and present relationship to the genocide against the native and African peoples. Could it be that the inherited weight of these crimes on the shoulders of white youth plays itself out in the epidemic of violence against their parents, teachers and schoolmates?

It is perhaps no coincidence that one of the most brutal in the rash of school shootings by white students took place in Littleton, Colorado in 1999, so near to the Sand Creek massacre only 140 years earlier. The terror that stalked the primarily white youth in Columbine High School, and which was described at length in every newspaper for weeks, was the *every day reality* for indigenous and African peoples at the hands of white attackers for hundreds of years.

North American youth are simply turning back on white society what has historically been our normal and consistent behavior towards the majority of other peoples on the planet.

Torture and genocide have neither shamed nor repulsed white people, and so it follows that violence is the cornerstone of our whole entertainment industry today. There is hardly a movie, TV show or novel that is not riddled with senseless violence, which has become increasingly grotesque in order to continue to titillate North Americans. The mass murder, mutilation, dismemberment, sex with corpses—acts perpetrated by serial killers that we read about in the daily papers—should be no surprise when we discover our true history. We are witnessing an implosion of the culture of violence.

AFRICAN FIGHTBACK

Inflicting war and violence on oppressed people was part of life for white America during the formative years of the country and throughout the nineteenth century. While slaughtering native people in the West, white people were suppressing and killing African people in the rural South as well as in the northern cities. Like the native people, and sometimes together with them, enslaved Africans were in a constant state of resistance and rebellion.

All classes of white people stood together in their attack on African people. No matter that a white person was too poor to own a slave; he could always get a loan to rent one. Barring that, he could become a foreman on a plantation or a bounty hunter for escaped Africans.

Like scalping, slave catching was a brutal and lucrative job for many white people. In *Runaway Slaves: Rebels on the Plantation*, John Hope Franklin and Loren Schweninger describe the slave catcher's profession:

Among this group were men who specialized in tracking slaves. They sometimes owned or could secure dogs and were willing to expend substantial effort to find their prey. They were hired by planters who could not spare their overseers, plantation managers, or other whites on the plantation to go on the frequent expeditions that might last for days, sometimes weeks. Charging by the day and mile, they were often illiterate, nonslaveholding whites who could earn what was for them a sizable amount—ten to fifty dollars—for bringing back a runaway.

A few "professionals" worked for higher stakes. Employed by slaveholder John Seaton of Loudoun County, Virginia, John Upp of Middleburg set out in late February 1817 to pursue a runaway. The experienced Upp journeyed east into Fairfax County, then toward the District of Columbia. He apprehended the slave after only two weeks, put him in the Alexandria jail, then carried him back to Middleburg to claim his $150 reward.[75]

African people exhibited their ardent desire to be free from the bonds of slavery and these endless attacks. African resistance and attempts at escape were tireless. Franklin's book gives such accounts:

At times [Africans] gathered together in bands of runaways wreaking havoc on plantations and farms. Living in isolated, heavily wooded, or swampy areas, some of these groups maintained their cohesiveness for many years, a few for more than a generation. Most, however, found it difficult to sustain themselves without being constantly on the move. Members of fugitive gangs made forays into populated farming sections for food, clothing, livestock, and trading items. Sometimes they bartered with free blacks, plantation slaves, and nonslaveholding whites....In virtually every state, there were gangs of ten to twenty outlying slaves....Despite their ephemeral nature, runaway gangs were a constant source of fear and anxiety for whites.[76]

The courageous rebellion led by Nat Turner in August 1831, during Andrew Jackson's presidency, certainly struck terror into the hearts of North Americans. According to one account:

These six slaves, then, started out, in the evening of August 21, 1831, on their crusade against bondage. Their first blow—delivered by Turner himself—struck against person and family of Turner's master, Joseph Travis, who were killed. Some arms and horses were taken, the rebels pushed on, and everywhere slaves flocked to their standard; a result which Turner, starting out with but a handful of followers, must have had excellent reasons to anticipate. Within 24 hours approximately 70 slaves were actively aiding in the rebellion. By the morning of August 23rd, at least 57 whites— men, women, and children—had been killed, and the rebels had covered about twenty miles.[77]

One Virginia "gentleman" wrote of Turner's rebellion:

These insurrections have alarmed my wife so as really to endanger her health, and I have not slept without anxiety in three months. Our nights are sometimes spent in listening to noises. A corn song, or a hog call, has often been the subject of nervous terror, and a cat, in the dining room, will banish sleep for the night. There has been and still is a *panic* in all this country...[78]

There were many other under-reported and less well-known rebellions, as well as acts of resistance and sabotage, including escape, feigned illness, strikes, poisonings and burning of the planters' land and property. Slave owners never rested easy:

> Slaves pulled down fences, sabotaged farm equipment, broke implements, damaged boats, vandalized wagons, ruined clothing, and committed various other destructive acts. They set fires to outbuildings, barns, and stables; mistreated horses mules, cattle, and other livestock...[79]

The fabrication of the idyllic Southern plantation with the kind masters and the contented, well-treated slaves is ridiculous. The conditions enforced after the kidnapping of a whole people from their land were miserable and resistance was part and parcel of every day life. The historian Herbert Apetheker notes at least 250 organized African uprisings aimed at freedom and land ownership in which at least 10 people were involved.

In Maryland, an African woman was executed in 1766 because she had burned down the slave owner's home, tobacco house and outhouses.

Between 1830 and 1860 as many as 60,000 African people escaped to the North through the Underground Railroad. Escape had become so common that slave owners paid $300 for one bloodhound during this period. According to one report, "Individual attempts at assassination or property damage by gun, knife, club, axe, poison, or fire were so numerous that undertaking an enumeration of all would be a well-nigh impossible task."[80]

NO SUCH THING AS BENIGN SLAVERY

Forced to live in tiny huts with few or no windows, sleeping on dirt floors and allowed to eat only the least nutritious leftovers of the planter's table, Africans sought any and every means to resist or escape. The main pastime of white people seems to have been con-cocting sadistic tortures for African people. As in the West, all classes of Southerners constituted a white citizen's militia: their mission was to capture and torture escaping Africans and return them to servi-tude. Franklin states:

> Many thousands of white southerners served in these companies. Some of them, like Hugh F. Grant, were prominent members of their communities, but others were propertyless whites who joined merely for the plea-sure of the hunt.[81]

Contrary to prevailing white fantasy, there were no "benign" slave masters, regardless of how "nice" the white people were to each other. Brutal behavior against African people was the norm across the board even by non-slave owning whites. African women were regularly used as sex slaves by the white plantation owners, including the slave-owning "founding fathers" of the United States.

DNA testing has recently proved what the African community has long known about Thomas Jefferson, who so loved "democ-racy." The author of the U.S. Declaration of Independence was a rapist who fathered up to five children by Sally Hemings, his wife Martha's personal slave and illegitimate half-sister whose mother had been raped by Martha Jefferson's father. Jefferson's rape of Sally began when Hemings was but a young teenager.

An article in *U.S. News and World Report* from November 1998 relates how guided tours of Jefferson's plantation, Monticello, are now forced to give a truer picture of Jefferson than the one in the schoolbooks:

> "Thomas Jefferson said that all men were created equal," [the tour guide] is telling about a dozen listeners...."Yet he owned 200 slaves....Jefferson said the slaves didn't have

the same moral standards as we." [The guide] proceeds to catalog behavior not usually associated with the author of the Declaration of Independence: how Jefferson built a 10-foot fence around his famous garden to keep slaves from stealing his vegetables.* How he opposed teaching them to write because he feared they might forge passes to leave his plantation. How he employed cruel foremen who whipped the slaves. How it bothered him when the sounds of fiddling and laughing drifted from the slave quarters in the evenings because he felt they should be resting up for the next day's labors. As for reports of Jefferson's [rape of] Sally Hemings, [the tour guide] observes: "That sort of thing happened all the time with slave owners. Blacks had no rights."[82]

Indeed it did. Now the descendants of the enslaved African woman known as Venus are attempting to use DNA testing to prove their family's long oral tradition that it was slave master George Washington who raped her and fathered a son.[83]

TORTURE OF AFRICANS

As the nineteenth century progressed, many thousands of Africans escaped enslavement, making the slave system increasingly untenable. While Africans were courageously fighting for their freedom, no real solidarity was forthcoming from white people, including those who voiced support for abolition. Few, if any, white people helped out on the Underground Railroad for which Harriet Tubman and other Africans risked their lives daily. According to John Hope Franklin, white assistance was extremely rare and generally only hap-

---

* Known to be a devoted vegetarian and an environmentalist, Jefferson's vegetable gardens were world renowned. While in Paris he once met with the Vietnamese ambassador to try to obtain rice for cultivation in the U.S. Source: (John Kennedy, Jr., November 1998, "The Master Mind," *George*, p. 92.)

pened when white people had their own self-interest in mind: "Whatever the actual circumstance, it was rare that whites did not have ulterior motives. They sought a partner in crime, payment for counterfeit papers, assistance in their own escapes from jail or debt."[84]

Scholars have compiled eighteenth century runaway slave advertisements listed in U.S. newspapers, producing enormous volumes of plantation owners' ads searching for their escaped "property."[85]

Professor Herbert Apetheker cites some of the tortures revealed in these ads, including:

> "[H]e has been severely whipped, from which he bears intolerable marks all over his body; severe whippings which his back will show..." or "[she] has many scars about her neck and breast, her back will prove her to be an old offender...has lost a piece of one of her ears;" or "...this one fled despite seven or eight pound clogs on his legs; this one had his nose slitted and both ears cropped;" and "this one had an iron hoop around her eighteen year old neck;" and "this one carries the full name of the owner branded between her breasts;" and "this one had fled despite a fourteen pound clog of iron on one leg."[86]

The advertisements also show the powerful stance of resistance of African people:

> Joshua Eden of Charles Town, South Carolina, reported the flight on November 4, 1775 of his slave...and..."though he is my Property, he has the audacity to tell me, he will be free, that he will serve no Man, and that he will be conquered or governed by no Man."[87]

> Joseph Weatherly of Ogeechee, Georgia, announced that in 1774, five of his slaves, including one woman, seized a boat; in an attempt to "look for their own country."[88]

NORTHERN WHITE VIOLENCE

White violence against Africans and Indians was universal, despite the myth that Northerners were somehow more concerned about social justice. All throughout the nineteenth century, white workers in the northern cities waged unceasing terrorist attacks on the African communities there. Prior to the Civil War, Northern white workers, including and especially white communists and socialists, were unanimously united against the abolition of the slave system. As in Europe, every movement of white workers in the United States has sought to obtain a greater portion of the enormous wealth exploding from the enslavement of African people and the theft of the indigenous people's land.

As the United States was independent from England, wave after wave of European workers by the tens of thousands began to flood the United States from across the Atlantic. The wealth from African enslavement was transforming the United States economy from the agrarianism of the eighteenth century to the industrial system, which characterized the nineteenth century. Each nationality found its own niche, its own particular means of stepping on the backs of African people in order to climb the ladder to middle class "success."

The English and Dutch who long had secured their positions in white society were not about to open up their jobs and occupations to the newcomers. Thus each new surge of Europeans had to prove their "whiteness" in order to get a foot up on the pedestal of parasitic capitalism. "No Irish need apply" signs were posted everywhere as thousands arrived seeking gold in the streets only to be discriminated against in the job market by other white people.

White workers who had been in the United States for more than a generation formed terrorist organizations called "Native American clubs," which were the counterpart of the Southern Ku Klux Klan and Knights of the White Camelia. The target of their terror was African people, but the clubs were also used to exclude the Irish from employment.

The response of the cowardly Irish, like other Europeans, was not to struggle against the capitalist bosses or even to fight those longer-established white workers who were sealing off their sectors of employment. The Irish instead viciously attacked African people, who, of course, never had done anything to oppress any white people.

Through sheer terror, the Irish seized the meager service jobs held by Africans who had escaped to the north. As Irish women took over the domestic jobs previously held by African women, they demanded to be called "help" rather than servants.

"Free" Africans in the North were allowed absolutely no civil rights and very few jobs although as a whole they were highly skilled; their "single accepted public role [was] that of the victim of rioters."[89]

W.E.B. DuBois wrote describing some of the violence perpetrated by white workers:

> For three days in Cincinnati in 1829, a mob of whites wounded and killed free Negroes and fugitive slaves and destroyed property. Most of the black population numbering over two thousand, left the city and trekked to Canada. In Philadelphia, 1828-1840, a series of riots took place which thereafter extended until after the Civil War. The riot of 1834 took the dimensions of a pitched battle and lasted for three days. Thirty-one houses and two churches were destroyed. Other riots took place in 1835 and 1838, and a two days' riot in 1842 caused the calling out of the militia with artillery.[90]

White workers also attacked any manifestation of African cultural independence in the North. In towns where more and more Africans were gathering, they began celebrating their traditional holidays and festivals with "spectacular African dancing, the building of beautiful arbors and the crowning of a Black king."[91] In 1821, African people in New York City had established the African Grove Theater, featuring talented black actors and playwrights. These institutions were short-lived however; they were targeted and eradicated both by white workers' attacks and by the government, which outlawed them.[92]

Once the African festivals were destroyed, white people began the practice of blackening their faces to perform in minstrel shows, which became immensely popular during the Andrew Jackson era, emerging as America's favored cultural pastime. The minstrels continued on with Al Jolson and others well into the twentieth century, until the Black Power Movement of the '60s put an end to the degrading practice.

The minstrels were clearly political forms of entertainment—white promoted attacks on and suppression of African people. Additionally the minstrels built support for major United States government campaigns of genocide, such as the war on Mexico to steal the land. Minstrel audiences were often young white workers who themselves painted their faces black. At these white supremacist shows, white workers could "find solace and even joy,"[93] according to one apologist book. After the show, white people in black face would then go out in gangs and brutalize African people.

In 1842, Irish and other white workers attacked a demonstration by an African temperance society which "began a parade through the streets of south Philadelphia intending to wind up on the banks of the Schuylkill for a celebration of Jamaican Emancipation Day...." A white crowd attacked the parade and chased the Africans back to their community where Africans fought back. White gangs then "contented themselves with chasing and beating with sticks, staves, and iron bars any...Negro who had the misfortune to come into the district...."[94]

WHITE ATROCITIES JUSTIFIED

Today, many books by white leftists dealing with lynching, "racism" or labor justify and dismiss the atrocities carried out by white workers against African people. They cite the "poverty" or "economic hardships," of white people, or offer the theory that white workers were "duped" with racism and "divided" from Africans by the capitalist rulers. According to these books, white workers are the only people in history who do not have to take responsibility for their actions!

Are we to say that white workers raped, killed, lynched, burned, mutilated and tortured African and indigenous people on a daily basis for 400 years because the white rulers and bosses were duping them?

The Irish attacked African people tirelessly for decades and "mutilated the corpses of the free Blacks they lynched." David R. Roediger's Eurocentric book, *The Wages of Whiteness*, justifies the Irish assault. He says,

> [L]ife was hard for the Irish in America because the anxieties and the desires resulting from a loss of a relationship with nature were particularly acute...no antebellum European immigrant group experienced the wrenching move from the preindustrial countryside to full confrontation with industrial capitalism in an urban setting with anything like the intensity of Irish Catholics.[95]

And what about the anxieties and the desires of African and indigenous people? What about *their* wrenching move from the "preindustrial" countryside to full confrontation with industrial capitalism? If "a loss of a relationship with nature" was reason for genocide, Africans should have slaughtered white workers by the millions.

In any case, despite their "particularly acute" loss of a "relationship with nature," the brutality of the Irish toward African people was quite typical of all white people in America, whether they came from urban or rural environments.

The question is, why didn't the Irish attack the English and other whites who *actually* controlled the job market, not to mention the capitalists themselves? The opportunity to get jobs by attacking African people was a convenient, if vicious, solution used not only for the Irish but for all European immigrants.

Philip Foner, long associated with the American Communist Party, describes some of the carnage in his book *Organized Labor and the Black Worker 1619-1973:*

> Before the 1840s and 1850s, black workers in many northern cities had monopolized the occupations of longshoremen, hod-carriers, white washers, coachmen, stablemen, porters, bootblacks, barbers, and waiters in hotels and restaurants. A huge influx of white foreigners, particularly after the Irish famine in 1846, caused a radical change. The unskilled Irish, in particular, pushed the Negroes out of these occupations, depriving many blacks of employment.[96]

No Africans then killed the Irish and mutilated their bodies.

Like Roediger, Foner then goes on to justify the Irish violence against African people when Africans took jobs while white people were striking for higher wages. Foner states that "struggling for economic survival, blacks were forced to become scabs." Calling African workers "scabs" is just another anti-black attack. African people were simply attempting to work in the only jobs available to them.

Foner already said that white people blatantly terrorized and pushed African people out of all employment into a situation so desperately poor that often the only working person in the family was the mother, who was a washerwoman. Foner also remarks in another part of his book that when Africans did strike along with white workers' unions, they still would not "open up their unions to blacks."[97]

Foner gives an account of the "revenge" with which the white people responded to the Africans' attempt to feed their families by seizing an opportunity to work while whites were on strike. He justifies the violence and lets the white workers off the hook:

> The white workers retaliated not only by attacking the strikebreakers but by invading Negro ghettos, assaulting and killing black people, and destroying homes and churches in an attempt to force blacks to leave the city. Unskilled Irish workmen, themselves victims of nativist riots and anti-foreign and anti-Catholic elements, could usually be counted upon to join an anti-Negro mob. While competition for jobs between the Irish and blacks, both poverty-stricken, was a major cause of many anti-Negro riots, the mobs were often organized—and sometimes even led—by "scions of old and socially prominent Northern families" who had close economic and social links with the South, and who exploited fear of black competition to combat the Abolitionists.[98]

Again the ruling class supposedly incited these atrocities, and the poor white workers were not responsible for their actions. Those pitiful Irish henchmen were once again duped!

Overall, Northern workers were unanimous on the question of the suppression of African people. The French historian Alexis de Tocqueville observed on his tour of the United States in the 1830s that anti-African fervor was stronger in the North than in the South.[99]

In addition to the Irish, German immigrants were flooding into the United States on the heels of the workers' uprisings in Europe.

Those who considered themselves communists and socialists numbered greatly in the ranks of the new immigrants. Among them were people who knew Karl Marx personally and who participated in the heady days of the European workers movement in the 1840s, which had produced *The Communist Manifesto*. These radicals and revolutionaries had no interest in uniting with the Africans for their freedom. Hermann Kriege, who preached land reform and free soil, stated clearly in 1846:

> That we see in the slavery question a property question which cannot be settled by itself alone. That we should declare ourselves in favor of the abolitionist movement if it were our intention to throw the Republic into a state of anarchy, to extend the competition of the "free working-men" beyond all measure, and to depress labor itself to the last extremity....That we feel constrained, therefore, to oppose Abolition with all our might, despite all the importunities of sentimental philistines and despite all the poetical effusions of liberty-intoxicated ladies.[100]

CIVIL WAR TO MAINTAIN WHITE POWER

African resistance played a key role in deepening the contradictions between Northern and Southern white people, which would ripen into internal warfare in 1861. As the Civil War neared, at least half a million Africans lived outside of slavery. There was little freedom for African people in the North, as we have seen. Besides being assaulted by white workers daily and kept unemployed, they were denied civil rights.

In 1857, the Supreme Court delivered the Dred Scott decision, which stated that African people were inferior to whites, that they could not become U.S. citizens and that they "had no rights which a white man was bound to respect."

Chief Justice Roger B. Taney issued the majority position, which was based firmly on the pro-slavery clauses of the U.S. Constitution. Taney argued that "under the Constitution slaves were property, just like any other property, and that consequently the Constitution permitted no distinction between them and property in general."[101] The Dred Scott decision was instrumental in the growing polarization of interests between the North and the South.

There were material reasons rather than moral sentiments behind the abolition movement in the United States and Europe. African resistance was increasingly terrifying to white slave owners, industry was becoming far more lucrative than agriculture, and direct colonialism in Africa was proving more useful to capitalism than shipping human cargo halfway across the world.

When the Republican Abraham Lincoln was elected president in 1860, seven Southern states seceded from the Union. This happened despite the fact that Lincoln was not committed to abolishing the institution of slavery. Lincoln represented the emerging white middle class, the former white worker who now sat comfortably on the pedestal of slavery and genocide.

As one historian put it, Lincoln "spoke for those millions of Americans who had begun their lives as hired workers...and had passed into the ranks of landed farmers, prosperous grocers, lawyers, merchants, physicians and politicians."[102] As such, Lincoln embodied the burgeoning new face of business and industry, which recognized the increasingly archaic character of the agrarian slave system.

Abraham Lincoln was as much a political opportunist as any other U.S. president. His threat to emancipate enslaved Africans was a tactical move to attempt to force the South to end the war. Lincoln himself certainly did not see African people as "equal" to whites, and he often proposed sending the former slaves back to Africa. When speaking to Northern liberals, Lincoln sometimes called for white people to end "this quibbling about this man and the other man, this race and that race and the other race being inferior...."[103] But when addressing small-town Midwestern whites he made his feelings on the question quite clear. This is Lincoln's statement made in Charleston, Illinois, as he was campaigning for president in 1858:

> I will say then, that I am not nor ever have been in favor of bringing about in any way, the social and political equality of the white and black races [applause], that I am not, nor ever have been in favor of making voters of the negroes, or jurors, or qualifying them to hold office, or having them to marry with white people. I will say in addition, that there is a physical difference between the white and black races, which I suppose, will forever forbid the two races living together upon terms of social and political equality, and inasmuch as they cannot so live, that while they do remain together, there must be the position of superior and inferior, that I as much as any other man am in favor of the superior position being assigned to the white man.[104]

Northern workers ardently supported the enslavement of Africans. When it was clear that they would be drafted into the Union army during the war, white workers rioted massively. Typically, the objects of their rebellions were not U.S. government federal or military offices, however. In New York, white rioters tortured, killed and mutilated every African they could get their hands on. The pro-slavery Copperhead movement of Northerners who supported the South during the Civil War had a tremendous base north of the Mason-Dixon Line.

White workers deserted the ranks of the Union army in droves rather than fight on the side of the North, with its threat of ending slavery. DuBois reports that "more than 2,500 deserters from the Union army were returned to the ranks from Indianapolis alone during a single month in 1862; the total desertions in the North must have been several hundred thousands."[105]

An official report on the conditions faced by Africans as a result of the white anti-black violence at the onset of the Civil War states:

> Driven by the fear of death at the hands of the mob, who the week previous had, as you remember, brutally murdered by hanging on trees and lampposts, several of their number, and cruelly beaten and robbed many others, burning and sacking their houses, and driving nearly all from the street and alleys and docks upon which they had previously obtained an honest though humble living, these people had been forced to take refuge on Blackwell's Island, at police stations, on the outskirts of the city in the swamps and woods...and in the barns and outhouses of the farmers of Long Island and Morrisania. At these places were scattered some 5,000 homeless men, women and children.[106]

One African in Detroit described what he saw when white people rioted against the draft: "a mob, with kegs of beer on wagons, armed with clubs and bricks, marching through the city, attacking black men, women and children."[107] He heard the white mobsters say that they were going to kill every African in town.

On January 1, 1863, when Lincoln issued the Emancipation Proclamation, he was clearly moving with political expediency. When he entered into the Civil War his foremost intention was to "preserve the Union," with all its enormous wealth and resources, at all costs. "If I could save the Union without freeing *any* slave I would do it;" Lincoln stated, "and if I could save it by freeing *all* the slaves I would do it; and if I could save it by freeing some and leaving others alone I would also do that."[108]

Two years into the war Lincoln needed the Emancipation Proc-lamation to bring the South to its knees. Under the proclamation, which was far from universal, Africans were to be freed in only those states still fighting against the Union. Nothing was said about enslaved Africans elsewhere. The *London Spectator* wrote: "The prin-ciple is not that a human being cannot justly own another, but that he cannot own him unless he is loyal to the United States."[109]

After emancipation, African people joined the Union Army in great numbers, bolstering its strength with courage and military skill. The influx of thousands of African soldiers into the Union Army forced Confederate General Robert E. Lee to surrender in April 1865, thus ending an incredibly bloody conflict that left 600,000 dead.

African people fought powerfully. W.E.B. DuBois tells us that African men were "repeatedly and deliberately used as shock troops, where there was little or no hope of success. In February 1863, Colo-nel Thomas Wentworth Higginson led black troops into Florida, and declared: 'It would have been madness to attempt with the bravest white troops what successfully accomplished with black ones.'"[110]

With the end of the war, the Thirteenth Amendment was passed in 1865, reversing the Dred Scott decision and stating that neither "slavery nor involuntary servitude, except as a punishment for a crime whereof the party shall have been duly convicted, shall exist within the United States, or any place subject to their jurisdiction."

The clause "except as a punishment for a crime" has proven useful today with the massive imprisonment of African people, most of whom are forced into near slave labor for the government or private industry.

RECONSTRUCTION AND BLACK POWER

For the brief period known as Reconstruction following the Civil War, African people were able to exercise power in the South. Congress passed a number of laws in the late 1860s and early '70s making it a crime to deprive African people of their rights as well as granting them the ability to enter into legal contracts and buy property. Federal officials were required to enforce these rights, and U.S. troops occupied the South supposedly to make sure that these laws were enforced.

Faced with political power, African people, after centuries of unspeakable oppression, began to organize quickly, confidently and brilliantly, building a society based on social justice and freedom. It was an exercise of Black Power. The former slaves began "immediately asserting their independence of whites, forming their own churches, becoming politically active, strengthening their family ties," and building freedom schools.

Within a year, black voters elected two African senators and twenty African congressmen.[111] African people organized trade unions, established newspapers, held conventions and mass meetings and circulated petitions to win full enjoyment of their democratic rights. They bought guns and dogs to defend themselves, which they were previously prohibited from doing. One historian has summed up:

> These Reconstruction governments erected public school systems. They democratized local and county units. They gave fair representation in state legislatures to the back country districts. They tried to free the judiciary from the executive. They established more equitable tax structures. They created public social services…institutions for the blind, insane, orphaned. With state funds they began to build railroads.[112]

During this period, African people pooled their own meager resources to create schools for children and adults. They enacted voluntary taxes to purchase land, construct buildings and hire teachers for the freedom schools. The first African colleges were built during the Reconstruction years, including Fisk University in Tennessee, Hampton Institute in Virginia and Howard University in Washington, D.C. By 1869, only four years after the end of the slave system, African men and women outnumbered white people in the teaching profession throughout the Southern states.[113]

Africans in the South were clear on their demand for economic power. According to one report:

> The desire for autonomy...shaped African-Americans' economic definition of freedom. Blacks wished to take control of the conditions under which they labored, and carve out the greatest degree of economic independence. Most refused to work any longer in gangs under the direction of an overseer, and generally preferred renting land to working for wages. Above all, economic freedom meant owning land of their own.

> In the aftermath of the Civil War, many former slaves insisted that through their unpaid labor, they had acquired a right to a portion of their owners' land. "The property which they hold," declared an Alabama black convention, "was nearly all earned by the sweat of our brows." In 1865, in some parts of the South, blacks seized abandoned land or refused to leave plantations, insisting that the property belonged to them. On the property of a Tennessee planter, former slaves not only claimed to be "joint heirs" to the estate but also, the owner complained, took up residence "in the rooms of my house." Others, citing the Freedmen's Bureau Act and the land distribution policy announced by General Sherman, expected the federal government to guarantee them access to land.[114]

WHITE TERROR GROUPS

Despite the federal occupation of the South during Reconstruction, countless white terrorist groups proliferated, waging a relentless campaign of murder and assault against African people to keep them from exercising their power. In 1865, the Ku Klux Klan was formed in Pulaski, Tennessee,[115] one of many white terror groups that killed thousands—perhaps tens of thousands—of African people in the years following the war. One account stresses:

> The victims included pregnant women and old people, black workers whose only offense was to be hired for a job desired by whites, blacks of all ages whose crime was to have acted "uppity," and white and black schoolteachers [in the black freedom schools]...The terrorists gave first priority to destroying the power of blacks to offer armed resistance....[116]

In May 1866, white workers in Memphis took 46 Africans from their homes and lynched them, and 45 Africans were killed that year in New Orleans in the same manner.[117]

Two years later, during the Louisiana elections of 1868, it is estimated that 2,000 Africans were murdered.

> In Shreveport a gang of Italian fishermen and market vendors called "The Innocents" roamed the streets for ten days before the elections, literally killing every African they could find. Some 297 Africans were murdered in New Orleans. In Bossier Parish, "One hundred and twenty corpses were found in the woods or were taken out of the Red River after a 'Negro hunt.'"[118]

In 1871, 100 Africans were lynched in Kentucky alone.[119] In Grants Parish, Louisiana, in 1873 more than a hundred white men attacked a large group of African people who had erected defensive fortifications in the town of Colfax. The Africans sought safety in the courthouse, which the white terrorists quickly burned to the ground. Africans who attempted to surrender were shot; others bolted from the fire and ran into the woods. The white terrorists went out into the woods and murdered the Africans, killing more than 200 people.[120]

There were at least 33 major white mob attacks on African people in which at least one person was killed in the South during this period. Forty-two percent of these incidents occurred in cities with populations greater than 5,000.

Post Civil War assaults on Africans were not confined to the South. White violence in the North continued and intensified, especially against Africans attempting to exercise their right to vote. On election day in Philadelphia in 1871, at least four Africans were killed, including a schoolteacher and rising leader of the African community, Octavius V. Catto.[121]

U.S. army and federal officials assigned to the South did nothing, of course, to stop this anti-African violence. No more than 10 percent of Klansmen were ever brought to trial. When several KKK terrorists were convicted in South Carolina in 1871, President Ulysses S. Grant pardoned them within months.[122]

The United States has always taken away any rights it grants to African people, and in 1877 federal troops were withdrawn from the South and Reconstruction was ended following the Tilden-Hayes Compromise. In only 12 years and in the face of unremitting white terror, Africans had built a formidable society. Now robbed of any political power, Africans were pushed back to poverty, government-condoned terror, oppression and disenfranchisement of "any rights the white man has to respect."

The Tilden-Hayes Compromise made it explicitly clear that real freedom and political power for African people were never to be found within the U.S. governmental system.

In the election of 1876, a tie was cast between Rutherford B. Hayes, an Ohio Republican, and the New York Democrat Samuel J. Tilden who represented Southern interests and demanded full autonomy for the Southern states. Congress was designated to resolve the vote and the election was given to Hayes in a compromise agreement that called for the withdrawal of federal troops from the South.

As the troops pulled out, an exodus of thousands of African people left the South, setting up towns and collective farms in Kansas, Oklahoma and other areas west of the Mississippi, as well as in Canada and Cuba. Martin Delaney led this powerful migration movement, which struggled for genuine political independence for Africans.[123]

VIOLENCE INTENSIFIES

As the U.S. army was removed to the North in 1877, an unmitigated reign of terror was unleashed against black people as Southern whites continued to perfect the atrocity of lynching. Jim Crow laws were enacted and African people were subjected to the oppressive sharecropping system, which was very similar to slavery itself. If Africans dared to exercise their right to vote, they did so at the risk of their lives. Nevertheless, African people fought for their rights and at the turn of the century in North Carolina alone there were nearly 1,000 African people holding elected office.[124]

After Reconstruction, terror was the order of the day. If white attacks on Africans in the North took the form of relentless warfare, in the South they took on the character of a sadistic ritualistic performance. One book notes:

> The lynchers, characteristically, were not content merely
> to kill the victim; the act of lynching was often trans-
> formed into a public spectacle, and sometimes hundreds

or thousands of whites from the surrounding countryside would come to town to observe the event. The mob inflicted death, death that was the result of extraordinary, sadistic cruelty. Before death came the victim was tortured, tormented by having limbs or sexual organs amputated, by being slowly roasted over a fire. Before or after death the body might be riddled with bullets and dragged along the ground. After death pieces of the charred remains would often be distributed as souvenirs to the mob whose members desired a keepsake as a remembrance of the notable happening.[125]

No doubt many of these "keepsakes" have been passed down from generation to generation.

The lynchings of African people were enormous and festive occasions. Photographs reveal the gala spirit. White women and men cheerfully posed for snapshots, grinning from ear to ear, nicely clad in suits and dresses behind the smoldering ashes of an African who is being burnt at the stake. Lynchings lasted for days; they were a family affair.

From the photos and from newspaper accounts of the time, children, grandmothers and pregnant women loved to participate in the slaughter. Lunches were packed, bands played so the white people could dance, and vendors sold their wares.

Like the many white leftist books that purport to apologize for Northern white workers' violence against African people, books by liberals and leftists also justify and defend the Southern white workers' atrocities.

A Festival of Violence: An Analysis of Southern Lynchings, 1882-1930 by Stewart E. Tolnay and E.M. Beck is one such book, which puts the blame for lynchings on the white ruling class or the Ku Klux Klan. White workers, the predators and perpetrators of the crimes, are again portrayed as "victims" and "dupes" of a ruling class that supposedly blinded them.

In reality, of course, white workers were not duped. They simply had exactly the same worldview in relation to African people as the ruling class. White workers all over the country were striving to rise to the middle class on the backs of African people.

These white leftist writers generally separate the Ku Klux Klan from white workers in general, as if the Klan was not made up of masses of white working people. They treat the Klan as something apart, an aberration, which it was not. There were literally hundreds of groups that were included under the name "Klan," including the Knights of the White Camelia, Knights of the White Rose, Pale Faces, Red Jackets, Knights of the Black Cross, White Brotherhood, Constitutional Guards, among many others.[126] The Klan defended the white labor unions and one of its main goals was to protect the white job market. The book, *A Festival of Violence,* justifies white violence in putting forth its thesis:

> We suspect that whites lynched African-Americans when they felt threatened in some way—economically, politically, or socially. Further complicating the situation was the peculiar Southern caste system that helped shape the white community's expectations of its position in the social hierarchy with regard to that of blacks. It would be naive to claim that whites commiserated over their poor fortune and then decided to organize a mob to go out and lynch a black. Rather our assumption is that competitive relations between the races, and the caste system, were capable of poisoning the social environment within which the two races coexisted. Within that environment whites were then predisposed to react violently to even the slightest provocation—or to invent provocative acts where none existed....[127]

The problem is that African people were not threatening white people "economically, politically or socially." It was quite the other way around. Why is it African people were not "predisposed to react violently to even the slightest provocation"? If they had, would these liberals have defended them?

The book *White Violence and Black Response from Reconstruction to Montgomery* by Herbert Shapiro is another leftist document that sums up these atrocities against African people by taking the responsibility away from white workers. Like Tolnay and Beck, Shapiro also holds the "white rulers" for the attacks. Shapiro states:

> The political violence of the Reconstruction era and that of the Populist years were connected by the willingness of the white rulers of the south to employ whatever means were necessary to destroy the unity of blacks and whites....Although the phenomenon of lynching ante-dated the Civil War, in the post-Reconstruction period the killing of blacks by white mobs, either individually or in groups, became an occurrence of increasing frequency. This violence...was generated...by a general social crisis, in which the steep economic depression of the period was a key element.[128]

What unity of blacks and whites is he talking about? Is there any historical documentation of Southern whites standing in solidarity with African people? Note that once again, Shapiro blames the lynchings on the "white rulers" and the "economic depression of the period."

ROPES AND PYRES

One of the clearest, most disturbing documentations of the lynching of African people is to be found in Ralph Ginzburg's *100 Years of Lynchings,* in which he simply chronicles newspaper articles' descriptions of the lynchings of the time. Helpfully, Ginzburg attempts no analysis of the sadistic white violence, since the "facts in this book speak too eloquently for themselves."[129]

One account from the Vicksburg, Mississippi, *Evening Post* of February 8, 1904, reports that,

> When the two Negroes were captured, they were tied to trees and while the funeral pyres were being prepared, they were forced to hold out their hands while one finger at a time was chopped off. The fingers were distributed as souvenirs. The ears of the murderers [sic] were cut off. Holbert was beaten severely, his skull was fractured and one of his eyes, knocked out with a stick, hung by a shred from the socket.

> Some of the mob used a large corkscrew to bore into the flesh of the man and woman. It was applied to their arms, legs and body, then pulled out the spirals, tearing out big pieces of raw, quivering flesh every time it was withdrawn.[130]

Newspaper accounts of lynchings reveal the courage and resistance of Africans in the face of unspeakable atrocity. From Arkansas:

> Inch by inch the Negro was fairly cooked to death. Lowry retained consciousness for forty minutes. Not once did he whimper or beg for mercy.[131]

From Georgia:

> The Negro was unsexed and made to eat a portion of his anatomy which had been cut away...The Negro was taken to a grove, where each one of more than five hundred people, in Ku Klux ceremonial, had placed a pine

knot around a stump, making a pyramid to the height of ten feet. The Negro was chained to the stump and asked if had anything to say. Castrated and in indescribable torture, the Negro asked for a cigarette, lit it and blew the smoke in the face of his tormentors.[132]

One story of a Georgia lynching published in the *Washington Eagle* in July 1921 tells of the festive attitude of the crowd. It also shows how these activities have continued on into this century:

The pyre was lit and a hundred men and women, old and young, grandmothers among them, joined hands and danced around while the Negro burned. A big dance was held in a barn nearby that evening in celebration of the burning, many people coming by automobile from nearby cities to the gala event.[133]

White women played an especially important role in instigating these festivals of sadism. At least a third of all lynchings were based on a supposed rape. White women repeatedly made this charge, usually to cover up their own crimes or to keep from their husbands liaisons with other men, as is depicted in the film *Rosewood*.

Of course, it was not necessary for a white woman to go so far as to charge rape; she could and did become the catalyst for lynchings by just saying that an African man spoke to or even looked at her. With a single word or gesture a white woman held the power of life and death over any African man who could be brutally assaulted by a vicious white mob and executed without trial or legal recourse.

The feminine role in the lynchings exemplifies clearly that white women sit on the pedestal of African slavery along with white men. Even as victims of male abuse, oppression and discrimination, white women are still active members of the oppressor nation. Like the white labor movement, the feminist movement has historically sought more power for white women inside of the parasitic capitalist system.

Statistics show that most white women are raped by men whom they know.* We can be sure that thousands of white women have falsely sentenced Africans to a horrible death throughout the history of the U.S. with the rape charge and still do. In 1994, Susan Smith drowned her own babies in a lake in South Carolina. Her classic alibi: a black man did it. Omali Yeshitela explains,

> Feminism is a product of oppressor nation ideology. It's biological analysis is a reflection of the historically-based intra-class contest within North American and European society for women to have a greater independent right to and share of imperialist plunder. It covers up the crimes of imperialism that have impoverished and brutalized the majority of the peoples on the planet.[134]

White women were key to the whole lynch mob spirit. One account reports:

> Women figured prominently in a number of outbreaks [of lynchings]. After a woman at Sherman had found the men unwilling to go into the courtroom and get the accused, she got a group of boys to tear an American flag from the wall of the courthouse corridor and parade through the courthouse and grounds, to incite the men to do their "manly duty."...At Marion, several women were close in with the men who knocked down the jailhouse door and seized the accused Negroes. In several instances, mothers with children in arms were in the midst of the mob. Expectant mothers were also in evidence...At Darien,

---

* According to the National Center for Victim's Rights (www.nvc.org), 78 percent of rape victims know their attacker.

Ocilla and Thomasville the part played by the women seemingly inspired the mobs to greater brutalities.[135]

Nowhere was the women's movement of the nineteenth century speaking out against these atrocities. That is not surprising since, like the white left, the women's movement has been a white rights movement contributing to maintain the oppression of African people. While the white women's movement opportunistically hooked up with the abolition movement and used some strong, outspoken African women, like Sojourner Truth, for their own advantage, the movement was still staunchly white nationalist. Elizabeth Cady Stanton, upheld by white women today as one of the heroines of women's liberation, stated that she could not endorse the vote for African men because,

> I would not trust him with my rights; degraded, oppressed himself, he would be more despotic with the governing power than ever our Saxon rulers are...If women are still to be represented by men, then I say let only the highest type of manhood stand at the helm of State.[136]

White women in the South were put forward as virginal, unattainable and cold, yet enticing, examples of womanhood. They were part of the slave master's property and African men would be killed for just looking.

In fact, rape and oppression of women was a white man's custom, its origins dating far back into Europe's shadowy past. White plantation owners raped African women every day, as the examples of Thomas Jefferson and George Washington show. They literally kept harems of African women. Massive and widespread white rape and sexual abuse of indigenous women and girls was part of the genocidal violence against the whole people.

With our history of systematic rape of African women by slave owners, it is no surprise that the sexual practices of many white people today intertwine violence and suppression with sexual pleasure. Sadomasochism, for example, quite popular in white society, including the gay community, plays out this white sexual fantasy of the "master-slave relationship" with whips, handcuffs and other torture devices.

WHITE ALIENATION

What was everyday life like for white people in the orgy of violence of the nineteenth century? Was it really the pleasant, slow-moving good old days so romanticized in novels and film? At the same time our ancestors were inflicting wanton carnage on African, indigenous and other peoples, could life on the hearth of white America possibly have been so idyllic?

As we can see, it is the pedestal of slavery and genocide that has given white people our affluence, our assumptions of superiority, our experience of democracy, our enjoyment of every possible "advancement" of technology. But the veneer of civilization, stolen from others, has never really covered up the raw culture of violence, hatred and barbarism, which has characterized European society since the dawn of human activity there.

Winthrop Jordan in his book, *White Over Black*, notes that the white man "sought his own peace at the cost of others and accordingly found none."[137]

A parasitic society could hardly be healthy. The violent and pervasive crisis internal to white society—historically and today—makes that clear. The wholesale slaughter of Africans and indigenous people scarcely made white society more inviting.

Ironically, at the same time that our forefathers were massively exterminating the indigenous people, thousands of white people went to live with the Indians. Perhaps this was a form of protest against the genocide; more likely it was simply that life was superior among the native people. Benjamin Franklin commented that no white person who had gone to live with the indigenous people "can afterwards bear to live in our societies." Franklin explained, "All their government is by Counsel of the Sages. There is no force; there are no Prisons, no officers to compel Obedience, or inflict Punishment."[138]

Franklin was surely not surprised by the desertions from his hometown. Philadelphia, the so-called city of brotherly love, the scene of so much white terror against African people, was a place of squalor, lawlessness and violence. "Crime arrived with the first ships," writes one commentator:

> A year after William Penn established his "Holy Experiment" in 1682, he found it necessary to set up a whipping post. Six years later, the benevolent founder wrote in despair of the drunkenness, prostitution, gambling and crime that reigned on the riverfront....

> Lawlessness and mayhem reached a crescendo during the middle decades of the nineteenth century. Criminal gangs ruled entire neighborhoods. Some volunteer fire companies were little more than warring gangs. Anti-Catholic...riots in the summer of 1844 left two Catholic churches and several blocks of homes in ashes and at least a dozen dead. At one point, rioters and the militia blasted away at each other with cannons. Major anti-black riots erupted every few years during the same period.[139]

Another account of a study of white life in Philadelphia observed the overwhelmingly violent character of white workers:

In the 1840s, 1850s, consumption of alcohol was at an all-time high. Drinking correlates highly with violent behavior...And the most murderous group was...the Irish....

Street fights were so common it was almost a form of recreation. Bricks were known as Irish confetti...Among the many gangs were the Schuylkill Rangers, who were practically river pirates...

[In Philadelphia]...infanticide was one category of murder that rose catastrophically in the second half of the century. During one four-year period in the late 1860s, 483 dead infants were found on the city's streets, lots and cesspools.[140]

Throughout the nineteenth century alcoholism was rampant, as was drug addiction in white society. Opium, heroin and cocaine were used on a mass scale all across the U.S. With the triangular trade, sugar and coffee were introduced to the North American diet to produce energy for the workday. Narcotics were used to relax. In *The Politics of Heroin,* Alfred McCoy states that in the mid- to late-1800s patent medicine manufacturers produced legal drugs to assist every bodily function and induce any desired state of mind.

There were cocaine-based drugs to overcome fatigue, morphine remedies to soothe worn nerves and heroin medications to calm the agitated mind or respiratory system. Paralleling the increase in sugar and coffee use, Americans' annual consumption of opium rose fourfold from 12 grains per person in the 1840s to 52 grains in the 1890s.[141]

Life for the Southern poor whites was no less depraved than that in the northern cities. W.E.B. DuBois quotes Frederick Law Olmsted on their conditions:

I saw as much close packing, filth and squalor, in certain blocks inhabited by laboring whites in Charleston, as I have witnessed in any Northern town of its size; and greater evidences of brutality and ruffianly character, than I have ever happened to see, among an equal population of this class, before.[142]

And so the picture emerges: Europeans brought their violence with them to the Americas. They used it to try to make a life for themselves by assaulting and killing others. Catholics, Protestants, Jews; Irish, German, Italian—all made the decision to pay any human price to get a piece of stolen bounty for themselves. Regardless of how poor or downtrodden they were, at no time did they seek to unite with the struggle of African people in overturning white power and building a just society.

Indeed, the poorer and more oppressed whites were, the more they attacked African and native people. The culture arising out of such conditions could only be cold, competitive, morally impoverished and isolated from humanity and the human spirit.

Break With White Power

We North Americans, the white population, are haunted by the millions of human beings whose deaths paid for our lifestyle, whose enslavement bought our prosperity, whose terror and despair financed our children's aspirations. The specter of genocide is manifest in the violence and alienation being expressed by our youth, by our society's massive need for Prozac, alcohol and other drugs. We have amassed enormous stolen wealth from people whose babies were killed so that we can shop in concrete malls every week. We are so removed from true human relationships that we weep en masse at the deaths of parasitic media creations such as Princess Diana or John Kennedy Jr., who did absolutely nothing in their lives but spend money expropriated from the suffering of others and pose for photographers.

Many of us today are looking for an opportunity to change our lives and find meaning in our society. But the essential questions must be answered and the fundamental contradictions must be solved before we can find peace of mind for ourselves and our children. Our relationship to African people and the majority of the peoples on the planet must be rectified for genuine change to occur. How can we find honest solutions to our problems while sitting on the pedestal of oppressed humanity?

Until the formation of the African People's Solidarity Committee by the African People's Socialist Party, there has never been a principled way that white people could approach African and colonized peoples and break with their long-established relationship with white power. There has been an occasional moral stand by an individual white person in history—although the examples are few and far between. But there has never before been a principled organization formed by the liberation movement of African workers themselves that enables us to take responsibility for the atrocities and parasitism of the white population as a whole.

This relationship calls on us to go back into white society to build an honest solidarity for the struggle of African people as they work to build a system that can provide a human solution for all the world's people.

The existence of the African People's Solidarity Committee lets white people find our genuine human interests by responding to the leadership of African workers and playing a part in building a New World for humanity. The African People's Solidarity Committee gives white people a future.

Chairman Omali Yeshitela best sums up what has been presented in this chapter:

We believe that if white people would become a part of humanity and end their separation from the human family, they have an ability to unite with the struggle of African people around whom every freedom, every material resource they have revolves. Everything they have came from us. They have the ability to end their self-imposed isolation and join with the other peoples around the world. They can unite with African people in the struggle for independence. We're not saying that we like you or don't like you because of race or because you're this color or some nonsense like that.

If white women suffer oppression, white power is the basis of it. If white homosexuals suffer oppression, white power is the basis of it. If white workers suffer exploitation, white power is the basis of it. Just like white power caused the misery of the people of Nicaragua, Viet Nam, Asia, Africa and the black community, white power is the reason for the contradictions facing white people. If you want to be free, then you join with the Black Revolution, overthrow white power and become a part of humanity.[143]

Overturning the Culture of Violence

1. Omali Yeshitela, 1991, *Izwe Lethu i Afrika! (Africa is Our Land)* (Oakland: Burning Spear Publications), p. 98.
2. Frederick Von Schiller, "Ode to Joy," (www.well.com/user/eob/poetry/Ode_To_Joy).
3. David E. Stannard, 1992, *American Holocaust: The Conquest of the New World* (New York: Oxford Press), p. 86.
4. Adam Hochschild, 1998, *King Leopold's Ghost: A Story of Greed, Terror, and Heroism in Colonial Africa* (New York: Houghton Mifflin Company), p. 138.
5. Fran Alexander, ed., 1998, *Oxford Encyclopedia of World History* (New York: Oxford University Press), p. 710.
6. Jack Weatherford, 1998, *Indian Givers: How the Indians Transformed the World* (New York: Ballantine Books), p. 142-145.
7. Bruce E. Johansen, 1982, *Forgotten Founders: How the American Indian Helped Shape Democracy* (Boston: The Harvard Common Press), p. 14.
8. Weatherford, pp. 138-139.
9. Johansen, p. 14.
10. Same as above, p. 27.
11. Henry W. Littlefield, 1957, *History of Europe Since 1815* (New York: Barnes & Noble Inc.), p. 11.
12. Eric Williams, 1966, *Capitalism and Slavery* (New York: Capricorn Books), p. 52.
13. Alexander, ed., p. 327.
14. Williams, p. 63.
15. Karl Marx and Frederick Engels, 1988, *The Communist Manifesto* (New York: Pathfinders), p. 33.
16. Yeshitela, *Izwe Lethu*, p. 50.
17. Hosea Jaffe, 1988, *A History of Africa* (London, Zed Books Ltd), pp. 76-77.
18. William Morris, ed., 1982, *The American Heritage Dictionary, Second College Edition* (Boston: Houghton Mifflin Company), p. 872.
19. V.I. Lenin, 1972, *Against Revisionism* (Moscow: Progress Publishers), pp. 325-326.
20. Jaffe, p. 46.
21. Littlefield, p. 8.
22. Karl Marx, 1979, *Capital: A Critique of Political Economy, Vol. 1* (New York: International Publishers), pp. 768.
23. "A Brief History of Jamestown," Jamestown Rediscovery (www.apva.org/history/index).
24. Peter N. Carroll and David W. Noble, 1988, *The Free and the Unfree: A New History of the United States* (New York: Penguin Books), pp. 57-58.
25. Omali Yeshitela, 1987, *The Road to Socialism is Painted Black: Selected Theoretical Works* (Oakland: Burning Spear Publications), p. 178.
26. Ward Churchill, 1987, *A Little Matter of Genocide: Holocaust and Denial in the Americas 1492 to the Present* (San Francisco: City Lights Books), p. 2.
27. Williams, pp. 52-108
28. Same as above, pp. 108-110.
29. Stannard, p. 28.
30. Same as above, pp. 31-32.
31. Same as above, p. 52.
32. Johansen, pp. 4-5.
33. Churchill, *Little Matter*, p. 154.
34. Same as above.
35. Dee Brown, 1971, *Bury My Heart at Wounded Knee: An Indian History of the American West* (New York: Holt, Rinehart and Winston), p. 4.
36. Paul Jacobs and Saul Landau with Eve Pell, 1971, *To Serve the Devil, Vol. I: Natives and Slaves* (New York: Vintage Books), p. 44.
37. Churchill, *Little Matter*, p. 156.
38. Stannard, p. 119.

39. Same as above, pp. 104-105.
40. Mort Gerberg, 1987, *The U.S. Constitution for Everyone* (New York: Perigee Books), p. 40.
41. Brown, p. 411.
42. Alan Nevins and Henry Steele Commager with Jeffery Morris, 1986, *A Pocket History of the Unites States* (New York: First Washington Square Press), p. 180.
43. Churchill, *Little Matter*, p. 218.
44. Howard Zinn, 1995, *A People's History of the United States 1492-Present* (New York: Harper Collins Publishers), p. 212.
45. Same as above, p. 10.
46. Same as above.
47. Nevins, Commager, Morris, p. 165.
48. Churchill, *Little Matter*, p. 186.
49. William Loren Katz, 1997, *Black Indians: A Hidden Heritage* (New York: First Aladdin Paperbacks), p. 50.
50. Zinn, p. 128.
51. Churchill, *Little Matter*, p. 217.
52. Brown, pp. 6-7.
53. Same as above.
54. Same as above, p. 8.
55. Zinn, p. 149.
56. Churchill, *Little Matter*, p. 185.
57. Same as above, p. 184.
58. Brown, p. 90.
59. Churchill, *Little Matter*, p. 234.
60. Zinn, p. 154.
61. Jerry Stanley, 1997, *Digger: The Tragic Fate of the California Indians from the Missions to the Gold Rush* (New York: Crown Publishers, Inc.), p. 16.
62. Same as above, p. 17.
63. Same as above, p. 27.
64. James W. Loewen, 1995, *Lies My Teacher Told Me: Everything Your American History Textbook Got Wrong* (New York: Touchstone), p. 126.
65. Stanley, pp. 75-79.
66. Same as above, pp. 66-69.
67. Same as above, pp. 66-71.
68. Frederick Turner, ed., 1996, *Geronimo: His Own Story* (New York: Penguin Books), pp. 77-83.
69. Ward Churchill and Jim Vander Wall, 1988, *Agents of Repression: The FBI's Secret Wars Against the Black Panther Party and the American Indian Movement* (Boston, South End Press), pp. 103-104.
70. Brown, pp. 289-290.
71. Same as above, p. 296.
72. "Clinton Visits Heart of Indian Poverty," July 9, 1999, *San Francisco Chronicle.*
73. Stannard, p. 60.
74. Jacobs and Landau, p. 67.
75. John Hope Franklin and Loren Schweninger, 1999, *Runaway Slaves: Rebels on the Plantations* (New York: Oxford University Press), pp. 156-157.
76. Same as above, p. 86.
77. Herbert Aptheker, 1987, *American Negro Slave Revolts* (New York: International Publishers), p. 298.
78. Same as above, p. 307.
79. Franklin and Schweninger, p. 2.
80. Aptheker, pp. 140-163.
81. Franklin and Schweninger, p. 154.

82. Lynn Rosellini, November 9, 1998, "At Monticello: Cutting the Great Man Down to Size," *U.S. News & World Report*, p. 66.
83. Nicholas Wade, July 7, 1999, "Descendants of slave's son contend that his father was George Washington," *The New York Times*.
84. Franklin and Schweninger, p. 31.
85. Herbert Aptheker, 1984, "We will be free: Advertisements for runaways and the reality of American slavery," unpublished research paper, Ethnic Studies Program, University of Santa Clara, Santa Clara, California, p. 7.
86. Same as above, p. 15.
87. Same as above, p. 6.
88. Same as above, pp. 18-19.
89. David R. Roediger, 1999, *The Wages of Whiteness: Race and the Making of the American Working Class* (New York: Verso), p. 56.
90. W.E.B. DuBois, 1972, *Black Reconstruction in America 1860-1880* (New York: Antheneum Press), p. 18.
91. Roediger, p. 102.
92. Same as above, p. 103.
93. Same as above, p. 116.
94. Sam Bass Warner, Jr., 1971, *The Private City* (Philadelphia: University of Pennsylvania Press), p. 140.
95. Roediger, p. 151.
96. Philip S. Foner, 1976, *Organized Labor & The Black Worker 1619-1973* (New York: International Publishers), p. 6.
97. Same as above, p. 7.
98. Same as above.
99. Same as above, pp. 6-17.
100. DuBois, *Black Reconstruction*, p. 18.
101. William Z. Foster, 1976, *The Negro People in American History* (New York: International Publishers), p. 174.
102. Zinn, p. 184, quoting Richard Hofstadter.
103. Same as above, p. 183.
104. Howard Holzer, ed., 1994, *The Lincoln-Douglass Debates* (New York: Harper Collins Publishers, Inc.), p. 189.
105. DuBois, *Black Reconstruction*, p. 103.
106. Same as above, pp. 103-104.
107. Zinn, p. 187.
108. Carroll and Noble, p. 217.
109. Zinn, p. 187, quoting Richard Hofstadter.
110. DuBois, *Black Reconstruction*, p.107.
111. Zinn, p. 195.
112. Foster, p. 317, quoting Louis M. Hacker.
113. Eric Foner and Olivia Mahoney, 1995, *America's Reconstruction: People and Politics after the Civil War* (Baton Rouge: Louisiana State University Press), pp. 44-48.
114. Same as above.
115. Foster, p. 327.
116. Herbert Shapiro, 1988, *White Violence and Black Response: From Reconstruction to Montgomery* (Amherst: The University of Massachusetts Press), pp. 10-11.
117. Richard O. Boyer and Herbert M. Morais, 1973, *Labor's Untold Story* (New York: United Electrical, Radio & Machine Workers), pp. 11-37.
118. Sakai, p. 41.
119. Boyer and Morais, p. 37.
120. Stewart E. Tolnay and E. M. Beck, 1992, *A Festival of Violence: An Analysis of Southern Lynchings, 1882-1930* (Chicago: University of Illinois Press), pp. 5-6.

121. Shapiro, pp. 16-17.
122. Same as above, p. 15.
123. Foster, pp. 336-364.
124. Same as above, p. 362.
125. Shapiro, p. 31.
126. Foster, p. 327.
127. Tolnay and Beck, p. 3.
128. Shapiro, p. 30.
129. Ralph Ginzburg, 1988, *100 Years of Lynchings* (Baltimore: Black Classic Press), p. 5.
130. Same as above, p. 63.
131. Same as above, p. 145.
132. Same as above, p. 153.
133. Same as above.
134. Omali Yeshitela, March 1991, "International Women's Day: African women in the lead," *The Burning Spear*, p. 2.
135. Arthur F. Raper, 1970, *The Tragedy of Lynching* (New York: Dover Publications), p. 12.
136. Allen, p. 146.
137. Winthrop Jordan, 1968, *White Over Black: American Attitudes Toward the Negro, 1550-1812*, (New York: W.W. Norton & Company), p. 582.
138. Loewen, p. 109.
139. Ron Avery, 1997, *City of Brotherly Mayhem: Philadelphia Crimes & Criminals* (Philadelphia: Otis Books), p. 4.
140. Ron Avery, November 5, 1990, "Crime of the century," *The Philadelphia Daily News*.
141. Alfred W. McCoy, 1991, *The Politics of Heroin: CIA Complicity in the Global Drug Trade* (New York: Lawrence Hill Books), p. 7-8.
142. DuBois, *Black Reconstruction*, p. 26.
143. Omali Yeshitela, 1996, "Resistance of African People: Crisis of Imperialism," (National People's Democratic Uhuru Movement), pp.22-23.

Marcus Garvey, leader of a movement for black power in the 1920s.

Malcolm X, leader of the Black Power Movement of the 1960s. Credit: Archive Photos.

Hundreds rally in Oakland, California when, after international protests, Black Panther Party leader Huey P. Newton is freed from prison in 1970.

3

Black Power and the
White Man's Game

*The history of our relationship with the United States
is documented in blood, gore and humiliation. This
is a history that has seen us forcibly removed from
Africa, our Mother Country, and subjected to a brutal existence in the United States as slaves and colonial subjects. This has taken place on land stolen
from the indigenous population that has barely survived the continuing genocidal attacks upon it. The
history of African people in the United States is also a
history of struggle and resistance against the brutal
conditions of existence imposed upon us by an alien
and foreign power whose only interest in our people
has been our capacity to provide wealth and profits
for our oppressors.*[1]

— *Omali Yeshitela*

By the year 1900, the majority of all human beings on the planet were enchained by the bonds of European colonialism. Those who had survived the massive, all-encompassing campaigns of genocide, that is. The British cracked their whip over a hundred nations across the globe, including small island nations in the Caribbean and the South Pacific, a huge section of Africa running from Cairo to Cape Town, and several countries in Asia, among them India, Pakistan, Iraq and Kuwait.

Under the dour Queen Victoria (who called herself the "Empress of India"[2]), middle class Englishmen decorated their houses with Persian rugs, Indian prints, African masks and baubles, knickknacks and loot from around the globe. Tea from Ceylon and India, coffee from Kenya, diamonds from South Africa, rum and sugar from the Caribbean, tobacco and cocaine from the Americas and opium from Asia enriched their proper little lives.

Nestled cozily in the British Isles, their pedestal seemed so secure that English policemen rode about on bicycles, unarmed. British citizens fantasized that their blood-soaked colonial system had produced a United Kingdom upon which "the sun never set."

Little did the British realize that the slave was awakening and shattering his chains. Tremors were beginning to rumble from deep within imperialism's pedestal. More than anything else, the twentieth century would be distinguished by African Revolution, and by wave after wave of struggles for national liberation around the world.

Other European countries were scrambling for colonial leftovers from Britain's feast on the body of mankind. France held parts of Africa, as well as Southeast Asian drug colonies that they called "French Indochina." In Viet Nam, Cambodia and Laos, the French planted 1,512 legal opium dens and 3,098 retail opium shops. With more than 20 percent of the brutalized colonial populations addicted, France was raking in the drug money. No need to launder it. A third of all France's colonial revenue was generated by its legal opium trade in Asia; it was perfectly acceptable.[3]

Early in the new century, the great African leader Marcus Garvey was able to articulate, perhaps better than anyone else at the time, the reality of parasitic capitalism and the essence of the African struggle. His poem, "The White Man's Game: His Vanity Fair," quoted here in part, tells a story that is as true today as it was then. It expresses the brutal actuality as well as irrepressible confidence in the future for African people:

> *Lying and stealing is the whiteman's game;*
> *For rights of God nor man he has no shame*
> *(A practice of his throughout the whole world)*
> *At all, great thunderbolts he has hurled;*
> *He has stolen everywhere—land and sea;*
> *A buccaneer and pirate he must be,*
> *Killing all, as he roams from place to place,*
> *Leaving disease, mongrels—moral disgrace...*
>
> *American Indian tribes were free,*
> *Sporting, dancing, and happy as could be;*
> *Asia's hordes lived then a life their own,*

To civilization they would have grown;
Africa's millions laughed with the sun,
In the cycle of man a course to run;
In stepped the white man, bloody and grim,
The light of these people's freedom to dim...

Out of cold old Europe these white men came,
From caves, dens and holes, without any frame,
Eating their dead's flesh and sucking their blood,
Relics of the Mediterranean flood;
Literature, science and art they stole,
After Africa had measured each pole,
Asia taught them what great learning was,
Now they frown upon what the Coolie does...

Out of the clear of God's Eternity
Shall rise a kingdom of Black Fraternity;
There shall be conquests o'er militant forces;
For as man proposes, God disposes.
Signs of retribution are on every hand:
Be ready, black men, like Gideon's band.
They may scoff and mock at you to-day,
But get you ready for the awful fray...[4]

PARASITIC AMERICA

Across the Atlantic, the United States was flexing its muscles, grabbing up everything in sight. By the end of the nineteenth century, the United States extended from coast to coast, its wind-swept plains and mountains now eerily desolate from the extermination of the native people and their buffalo. America's murderous destiny was indeed manifest. The haunting photograph of "Big Foot in death," whose body lay frozen in the snow after being shot by U.S. soldiers at the massacre at Wounded Knee in 1890 tells the story.

Hakiktawin, a young woman who barely survived that massacre related her experience of the slaughter:

> I was running away from the place and followed those who were running away. My grandfather and grand-mother and brother were killed as we crossed the ravine, and then I was shot on the right hip clear through and on my right wrist...I did not go any further as I was not able to walk....[5]

Big Foot and 300 of his people—men, women, children, elderly and babies—were annihilated on that day, December 29, 1890. Their bodies were left where they had fallen until after a blizzard, which froze them into grotesque shapes.[6] Earlier that same year, the U.S. Bureau of the Census had officially declared that the "internal frontier was closed,"[7] reporting less than 250,000 indigenous people, whose population had once ranged in the tens of millions. Ward Churchill observes,

> Although the literature of the day confidently predicted, whether with purported sadness or with open jubilation, that North American Indians would be completely extinct within a generation, two at the most, the true magnitude of the underlying demographic catastrophe has always been officially denied in both the United States and Canada.[8]

At the end of the nineteenth and the beginning of the twentieth centuries, new waves of workers from Europe flooded the shores of the United States. They were Italians, Jews and other Eastern Europeans hungry for a chance to feast on the blood of African and indigenous people. During this period, ostentatious displays of wealth were flaunted by members of the ruling class, including John D. Rockefeller, J.P. Morgan and Andrew Carnegie, some of whom had started out in poverty. As the saying ran in Europe, "the streets of New York were paved with gold." Thus the American dream—the possibility of going from "rags to riches" by stepping on the backs of colonized peoples—was sought after by millions of European immigrants who were pouring off the boats.

Following in the footsteps of the Irish, Germans and English before them, the new wave of European immigrants quickly found their niches on the pedestal, continuing the tradition of becoming "white" by exploiting black people. Italians soon began importing drugs to sell in the African community, setting up gambling rackets, and creating prostitution rings that often used African women. The Italian Mafia was later glamorized in an endless stream of movies. Certainly it is arguable that the dealings of the Mafia were no "dirtier" or more parasitic than capitalist business as a whole.

Like just about every other sector of white business, the key to Italian wealth lay in exploiting black people. Many Mafia turf wars were fought over who would exploit the colonies inside U.S. borders. The government sees the Mafia as a threat possibly because, operating outside of the established perimeters of business, the "Godfathers" pay little in taxes. To paraphrase the Frank Sinatra song, the Mafia bosses do it "their way."

In African communities throughout the country, the Jewish immigrants tended to find their place by opening highly exploitative furniture and dry goods stores where they extended high-interest "credit" to African people.

In *Crisis of the Negro Intellectual*, Harold Cruse notes that white-owned businesses in Harlem (most of which were Jewish-owned) did not hire any African workers until they were forced to do so by militant black organizations as late as the 1930s and 1940s.[9] Many Jewish businessmen, backed by white leftists, then labeled this African community struggle against exploitation as "anti-semitic." Cruse quotes an activist of the period who exposed how Jewish members of the Communist Party USA called the 1935 rebellions in Harlem "a hoodlum-led Negro pogrom against the Jewish shopkeepers of Harlem."[10]

Within one generation, Italians and Jews had made enough money to send their children to college. Jews, in particular, rapidly entered the "professional" class of doctors, lawyers and college professors. Cruse remarks that

> [F]or all practical purposes (political, economic and cultural) as far as Negroes are concerned, Jews have not suffered in the United States. They have, in fact, done exceptionally well on every level of endeavor, from a nationalist premise or on an assimilated status.[11]

Certainly, even before the wave of immigration that brought thousands of Eastern European Jews to Ellis Island, many Jewish people had already made their fortunes in the slave economy of the South. "The highest social and governmental circles of the Confederacy included aristocratic Jewish clans," states one report. Many were slave plantation owners and officers in the Confederate Army, and some held posts in Jefferson Davis' cabinet. After the Civil War, Jews in the South concentrated on becoming merchants and shopkeepers like many of those who were to follow.[12]

Thus America's parasitic traditions proved beneficial to generation after generation of European workers.

TASTE OF EMPIRE; TASTE OF BLOOD

In 1893, the United States attacked Hawaii, which had been described by U.S. officials as "a ripe pear ready to be plucked." In 1894, the United States invaded Nicaragua "to protect American interests."[13] By 1898, the United States was ready for full-scale aggression, whereby President William McKinley launched the blatantly imperialist Spanish-American War. A *Washington Post* editorial on the eve of this aggression exposed America's true mission:

A new consciousness seems to have come upon us—the consciousness of strength—and with it a new appetite, the yearning to show our strength....Ambition, interest, land hunger, pride, the mere joy of fighting, whatever it may be, we are animated by a new sensation. We are face to face with a strange destiny. The taste of Empire is in the mouth of the people even as the taste of blood in the jungle.[14]

The United States seized Guam, Puerto Rico, the Philippines, Hawaii and, for all practical purposes, Cuba as a result of this colonial attack. John Hay, the U.S. Secretary of State called the Spanish-American aggression "a splendid little war."[15] One history book rhapsodized: "It seemed an ideal war. Its casualty lists were short, it cost no great debt, it raised American prestige abroad, and the nation emerged with its pockets full of booty."[16]

Under the leadership of Toussaint L'Ouverture, Haiti had waged a successful anti-colonial revolution against the French in 1798, setting up an independent African island-state in the Caribbean. Winston Churchill had cautioned the United States about the dangers of Cuba, which could follow in the footsteps of Africans in Haiti.

In 1895, José Martí led a heroic insurgency of the Cuban people against Spanish colonialism. The next year, Churchill wrote concerning Cuba in the American magazine, *Saturday Review*:

A grave danger represents itself. Two-fifths of the insurgents in the field are Negroes. These men...would, in the event of success, demand a predominant share in the government of the country...the result being, after years of fighting, another black republic.[17]

In the Philippines, the United States was carrying out its usual objective: genocide against the Filipino people who were fighting a conscious war of national liberation. In November 1901, a correspondent from the Philadelphia Ledger wrote from Manila:

> The present war is no bloodless...engagement; our men have been relentless, have killed to exterminate men, women, children, prisoners and captives, active insurgents and suspected people from lads of ten up, the idea prevailing that the Filipino as such was little better than a dog.[18]

In 1900, the *San Francisco Argonaut* probably better reflected American public opinion regarding the genocidal war against the Filipino people when it wrote:

> We do not want the Filipinos. We want the Philippines. The islands are enormously rich but, unfortunately they are infested by Filipinos. There are many millions there and it is to be feared their extinction will be slow.[19]

Many African people in the United States opposed the Spanish-American War, including Bishop Henry M. Turner of the African Methodist Episcopal Church. Turner called the U.S. attack "an unholy war of conquest." Four African regiments were sent to the Philippines where an "unusually large number" of black troops deserted, some of whom joined the Filipino resistance. David Fagan was an African soldier who deserted the U.S. infantry and accepted a commission in the Filipino resistance army. For two years, he led a fierce attack on the U.S. army.[20]

Like the Vietnamese some 70 years later, the Filipino resistance movement made a special appeal toward African soldiers, putting up posters calling for solidarity. One African soldier, William Simms, wrote from the Philippines:

I was struck by a question a little Filipino boy asked me, that ran about this way: "Why does the American Negro come...to fight us where we are much a friend to him and have not done anything to him. He is all the same as me and me all the same as you. Why don't you fight those people in America who burn Negroes, that make a beast of you...?"[21]

Indeed, some African soldiers of the Spanish-American War were fighting those inside the United States who tried to make a beast of them. In Lakeland, Florida, during this period, African servicemen pistol-whipped a drugstore owner when he refused to serve one of them. Fighting off a white crowd who was defending the store owner, the Africans then killed a white person. Around the same time, African soldiers rose up and fought courageously in the streets of Tampa after a white soldier used an African child for target practice.[22]

FIRST IMPERIALIST WORLD WAR

In 1901, Theodore Roosevelt became president after building his career by leading the attack on San Juan, Puerto Rico during the Spanish-American War. Roosevelt was known as an imperialist, a nature lover, conservationist and champion of the "strenuous life."

With his motto, "speak softly and carry a big stick," Roosevelt was excellent at preserving the environment—simply by getting rid of its natural human inhabitants. By sending in the Cavalry to forcibly remove the native people who had lived here for thousands of years, he designated hundreds of thousands of acres of land for parks—including Yosemite in California.

Roosevelt built the Panama Canal at the expense of thousands of African lives in the Canal Zone, after blatantly fomenting a revolt and seizing the isthmus from Colombia in 1903. He had sent in the

Marines without agreement from Congress, bragging, "I took the Canal Zone and let Congress debate, and while the debate goes on the canal does also."[23] He was vicious in his colonial treachery in Latin America, adding the Roosevelt corollary to the Monroe Doctrine in 1904 under which the U.S. government gave itself the right to collect "bad debts" from Latin America.[24]

Roosevelt was popular among white workers and was closely aligned with the Progressive Movement, eventually forming his own Progressive Party. Roosevelt represented the emerging new U.S. power that was beginning to challenge England and the rest of Europe for hegemony over world capitalist domination.

By the end of Roosevelt's second term, war was on the horizon. Much of Europe was out prowling to find a way to redivide the colonial spoils and snatch more loot for themselves. In 1914, World War I —Omali Yeshitela calls it the first imperialist world war—broke out. The conflagration was triggered when Archduke Francis Ferdinand, heir to the empire of Austria-Hungary, was assassinated in Sarajevo, Bosnia-Herzegovina, where fratricidal violence and "ethnic cleansing" continue to this day. The 1914 incident was only one of a long series of hostilities between European nations that were lining up in two opposing camps like packs of feral dogs ready for the kill. Their real prey was Africa.

The United States entered the fray in 1917, it claimed, to make the world "safe for democracy." A year later, the United States emerged the victor of the war and a major imperialist world power.

In November 1917, as the imperialist world war was raging, the Bolshevik Revolution seized power in Russia under the leadership of V.I. Lenin. With the creation of the Soviet Union, the first socialist state was born.

THE NEW AFRICAN

African soldiers returning to the United States from World War I found not only a changed world; many had undergone a tremendous transformation themselves. A new urban, proletarianized, internationalist consciousness was developing in the black community, and resistance was in the air.

It had been four decades since the betrayal of the promise of Reconstruction with the withdrawal of United States troops from the South in 1877. During those years, African people, now supposedly "free," had endured an endless tide of lynchings, gang attacks, Jim Crow laws, substandard housing, denial of democratic rights, as well as exclusion from employment by bosses and unions alike. Prisons that scarcely existed before 1865 were now bursting with Africans.

Chain gangs and work camps provided a wealth of unpaid labor for the Southern states and former slave owners. Forced out of jobs by the Ku Klux Klan and the white unions, unemployed Africans were imprisoned and sent to chain gangs by means of the vagrancy laws that were enacted after Reconstruction. In Mississippi, penal laws effectively reenslaved black people, turning them over as free labor to farmers and plantation owners. The 1866 law stated:

If any freedman, free Negro, or mulatto convicted of any of the misdemeanors provided against in this act, shall fail or refuse for the space of five days, after conviction, to pay the fine and costs imposed, such person shall be hired out by the sheriff or other officer, at public outcry, to any white person who will pay said fine and all costs, and take said convict for the shortest time.[25]

Returning to these conditions after fighting for American "democracy" abroad was intolerable. The mood of African people was angry and they militantly demanded to be guaranteed their democratic and human rights in the United States. The movement led by the brilliant Marcus Garvey spoke to this militancy, uniting and organizing millions of African people worldwide. Garvey's appeal was especially felt by the growing African working class as tens of thousands fled the South, hoping to find work and a taste of democracy in the Northern cities.

Garvey said of African people's relationship to the first imperialist world war:

> The New Negro has fought the last battle for the white man, and he is now getting ready to fight for the redemption of Africa. With mob laws and lynching bees fresh in our memories, we shall turn a deaf ear to the white man....Let every Negro all over the world prepare for the new emancipation...in the end there shall be a crowning victory for the soldiers of Ethiopia on the African battleground.[26]

Garvey's stand of resistance was echoed by many African people. One African ex-serviceman said,

> I done my part and I'm going to fight right here till Uncle Sam does his. I can shoot as good as the next one, and nobody better start anything. I ain't looking for trouble, but if it comes my way I ain't dodging.[27]

But the terror continued. In 1918 there was a "lynching orgy"— 63 authenticated murders of African people by whites, 19 in Georgia alone. Five of the victims were women. Two African men were burned at the stake before death and four after death. In Texas, an African mother and her five children were lynched by white predators, the mother shot as she attempted to drag the bodies of her sons from their burning cabin.[28]

In Georgia, following a severe whipping by a white farmer, an African man, in a stand of courageous resistance, returned to the farm and fired a gun through the farmhouse window, killing the farmer and wounding his wife. The African then escaped. White people gathered, seizing eleven African people at random, including a woman who was close to her full term of pregnancy. A British writer, Stephan Graham, traveling through Georgia at the time, described the hideous pleasure taken by white people in the orgy of violence directed toward the pregnant African woman and her unborn child.

> They tied her upside down by her ankles to a tree, poured petrol on her clothing and burned her to death. [She]...was in her eighth month with child. The mob around her was not angry or insensate, but hysterical with brutal pleasure. The clothes burned off her body. Her child, prematurely born was kicked to and fro by the mob.[29]

MATCHING FIRE WITH HELLFIRE

As many African soldiers returned from the war, they became targets for white atrocities. The incidents from the state of Georgia provide examples for the ubiquitous attacks on African soldiers: one veteran was beaten to death for "wearing his uniform too long." Another was burned to death. An African soldier was shot for "refusing to yield the road," while another was hanged for discussing the rebellions in Chicago in 1919. An African soldier was lynched at Pope City for "firing a gun." At Ocmulgee, whites accused Africans of plotting an uprising and then burned an African man at the stake.[30] And on and on.

At a rally protesting similar white atrocities against African people in Omaha in 1919, and supporting the courageous African resistance, Garvey pronounced:

> The best thing the Negro of all countries can do is to prepare to match fire with hellfire. No African is going to allow the Caucasian to trample eternally upon his rights.

We have allowed it for five hundred years and we have now struck.[31]

During the Red Summer of 1919, as it was called, Africans did indeed match fire with "hellfire." Armed African insurrections shook the country. During those months, African communities across the United States organized insurgencies that were as sophisticated, organized and well armed as any that have ever taken place before or since.

White predators faced trained African fire power, and white people began to have to pay a price for their mass murder of African people carried out for so long with impunity.

One of the best known armed insurrections took place in Chicago after white people stoned a young African man to death while he was swimming in Lake Michigan on July 27. Africans gathered at the scene, accusing a white man of the murder. Typically, the police refused to arrest the white murderer and attempted to arrest an African man instead. This incident sparked armed rebellion on the south side of Chicago where Africans defended their community well from the violence of a rioting crowd of reactionary white people.

The African community was so well organized that for seven days no white person was able to cross the boundaries into the south side. In the face of armed resistance, and unable to penetrate the lines of African defense, white people resorted to cowardly methods similar to those used against the Apaches and others who have defended themselves against white power. Since most black people were employed outside their community, whites gathered at streetcar transfer points on the North side to attack African people going to and from work. Of the 23 Africans killed during the week of insurrection, most were killed in this manner.[32] Thus, the rebellion was weakened only by vicious white violence against noncombatant members of the African community. Fifteen white people also died in that uprising.

One African eyewitness applauded his community's readiness for armed combat, estimating that the community possessed at least 1,000 rifles "and enough ammunition to last for years if used in guerrilla warfare."[33]

According to well-known Chicago journalist, Mike Royko, the Daley Machine that has ruled Chicago for decades* was quite probably instrumental in that assault on the African community. Daley was the long-time president of the Hamburg Social and Athletic Club, members of which were acknowledged participants in the attack.[34]

The thuggish Hamburg club put Daley and other politicians into office in Chicago, where they remain in power today."[35] Clearly, the notorious Daley Machine and the brutal Chicago Police Department have been built and maintained on a tradition of anti-black violence.

ATTACKS BY WHITE WORKERS DEFENDED

In addition to the Chicago uprising, powerful African community rebellions also shook many other cities during the summer of 1919. Africans rose up in Omaha, Knoxville, Washington, D.C., Tulsa, Charleston, as well as smaller towns such as Elaine, Arkansas, Longview, Texas and Waukegan, Illinois.[36] In every instance these just insurrections were attacked by white workers, not supported by them.

Again, we see how history books by white leftists dealing with the insurrections of 1919 *defend* the white marauders. Herbert Shapiro's *White Violence and Black Response* lets the white perpetrators off the hook and equates African resistance with white slaughter by using terms like "racial hostilities." Again, Shapiro uses economics to justify white anti-black brutality during the Red Summer of 1919.

Shapiro says:

---

* Richard J. Daley was mayor from 1955 - 1976. He died in office. Richard M. Daley, his son, was elected in 1989, after serving as State Attorney. The young Daley was mayor until 1993.

> This episode [the white stoning of an African at Lake
> Michigan] served as the provocation that brought to the
> surface the racial hostility existing in Chicago. The hatred
> stemming from a constricting job market and the efforts
> by blacks to secure adequate housing by moving into
> previously all-white neighborhoods had reached an
> intensity where any incident in that a black refused to
> accept racial subordination could touch off a massive
> assault upon the black community.[37]

Shapiro seems to be saying that a "constricting job market" and
moving into a given neighborhood constitute a sound justification
for terror, hatred and "massive assault upon the black community."
Is he assuming that this is "normal" human behavior? If that were
the case we would see the African community in a permanent state
of violence against white people in response to a job market that is
always "constricting." We would see attacks in neighborhoods that
are perennially invaded by white people who want to gentrify the
African community.

African people are not responsible for the constricting job market for white workers. We have yet to see a white crowd stoning to
death the owner of a corporation or factory as he is swimming in
Lake Michigan. And while African resistance to being excluded from
decent jobs and housing by white power is in fact justified, we have
yet to see mobs of African people lynching whites for any reason
whatsoever, despite the history of atrocities against them.

In *Organized Labor & the Black Worker*, put out by International
Publishers, a Communist Party publishing house, Philip Foner also
equates the actions of both African and white people. Foner goes so
far as to actually *blame* African people for the white attacks:

> Discriminatory practices by labor unions and the conse-
> quent strike breaking by Negroes were also factors in the

terrible Chicago race riots of 1919, although clashes over the housing situation there contributed significantly to the bitter animosity between the races. Disgusted with the treatment they had received during the stockyards organizing campaign of 1918 and by the fact that the unions barred them from all but menial jobs, black workers frequently replaced striking whites in the stockyards during the summer of 1919. *Black strikebreaking, in turn, helped produce the bloody 1919 race riot.* [Emphasis added.] [38]

So, if African people had just accepted their oppression quietly, things would have been fine, according to Foner. If they had not taken their only opportunity to put food on their tables after being barred from jobs by white workers, there would have been no "race riot." What Foner refers to as "clashes over the housing situation" was in fact African people attempting to find something beyond the high-rent, rat- and roach-infested shacks usually allocated to the African community. Foner's "animosity between the races," implies mutual dislike between racial groups, as opposed to members of the white oppressor nation assaulting an oppressed people that is increasingly prepared to resist.

In addition to blaming African people for white predatory attacks, these leftist writers repeatedly use the phrase "white mob," an offensive cover-up. The term implies a situation in which no person is responsible for his or her actions, having lost their brains in the motion of a nameless crowd. Murder is murder, whether perpetrated by a single killer or a large group. We make our choices and should bear the responsibility.

REBELLION IN TULSA

The commitment of African people to resist white violence continued to grow. In 1921 the African community brilliantly defended itself in Tulsa, Oklahoma. Since the Reconstruction period African people had thrived there, attaining perhaps the highest level of economic and political independence of any black community in the United States.

On May 30th of that year, a white girl named Sarah Page, falsely accused an African man, Dick Rowland, of assaulting her. Some say that Rowland accidentally stepped on her foot, although, as we know, it is quite possible that Rowland never had any contact with Page at all. White women have had thousands of African men lynched for no reason whatsoever. In any case, Page never pressed charges. One account tells us:

> That evening...a crowd of some 400 whites gathered outside the jail at nine o'clock, and by ten-thirty the throng numbered some 1,500 to 2,000 persons. Given the situation and Tulsa's historical record it was reasonable to assume that the crowd intended to seize Rowland and lynch him. Black Resistance, however, intervened. Word of the white crowd reached the black community, "Little Africa," and some 75 armed black men went to the jail set on assuring the prisoner's safety. The blacks were persuaded by the police to return home, but as they were about to leave a white man attempted to disarm one of the blacks, a shot was fired and then many shots, and when the clash was broken off about midnight two blacks were dead along with ten whites.[39]

The next morning, 10,000 white people descended on the African community armed with machine guns. White people flew airplanes over the community, launching the first military aerial bombing in the Western Hemisphere, a precursor of the deadly bombing of the African MOVE collective in Philadelphia in 1985. Homes of African people were set on fire, and the death toll in Tulsa has been estimated to be as high as 300. African people defended themselves courageously and were empowered by their resistance. According to John Hope Franklin, after the upheaval, "The self-confidence of Tulsa's Negroes soared, their businesses prospered, their institutions flourished, and they simply had no fear of whites."[40] Today, African survivors of the attack have brought their case for reparations before the Oklahoma Legislature.

In 1923, Fannie Taylor, a white woman in Sumner, Florida used the same vicious story to launch an attack on the flourishing town of Rosewood, Florida. After her white lover roughed her up, she claimed that a black man broke into her house and beat her while her husband was away. A drunken white posse was quickly formed, and before it was over they wiped out the black town of Rosewood. By all reports, Rosewood was a village of successful African businesses and homes; an oasis of cultural and economic self-reliance, in sharp contrast to the desolate white company town of Sumner. The townspeople fought back courageously. A newspaper story gives the gruesome account:

> A group of whites confronted Sam Carter, a black man they believed helped the attacker flee. When he did not confess, Carter was tortured and his body was riddled with bullets and then hanged from a tree...

> By the next day, a mob estimated at 400 to 500 had descended upon Rosewood. They split up to search the hamlet. Violence worsened two days later when a group of whites approached a house with about 15 to 25 blacks inside.[41]

Eight people died in the violence, including two white attackers. The entire town was burned to the ground. Those who survived the horror lost every thing they owned. In 1994, African survivors of the Rosewood attack won reparations from the state of Florida.

MARCUS GARVEY

It is no coincidence that African people courageously defended themselves in this period following World War I; they were well organized and they had a powerful leader as their voice. In the 1910s and '20s, the magnificent movement led by Marcus Mosiah Garvey captured the imagination and the loyalty of the masses of African people not only inside the United States, but around the world.

There has never been a movement before or since that equaled the size and scope of Garvey's United Negro Improvement Association and African Communities League, known as the UNIA. Nevertheless, the Garvey Movement has been wiped out of history books by both the United States power structure and the white leftists. It is estimated that Garvey had three to five million followers, and more than 800 branches of the UNIA existed around the world.[42]

Garvey's famous slogan, "Africa for the Africans, those at home and those abroad," encapsulated the understanding that African people were one people no matter where they had ended up after being kidnapped and enslaved by Europeans. It was Garvey who invented the red, black and green African flag. Garvey's vision of a united and liberated Africa influenced many African revolutionaries, including the Black Panthers of the 1960s and the outstanding African revolutionary leader from Ghana, Kwame Nkrumah. Some 35 years after the Garvey Movement, Nkrumah called for one, united socialist African government.

Marcus Garvey was born in Jamaica on August 17, 1887. He is said to have been descended from the Maroons, Africans who escaped from enslavement and who had "governed a virtually independent black nation in the mountains of Jamaica from 1664 to 1795," according to Ted Vincent's *Black Power and the Garvey Movement.*[43]

Garvey believed that independent political and economic power was necessary for the freedom of African people and that the liberation of Africa was the first priority. In 1920, a year after the Red Summer, 2,000 African people from all over the world participated in the UNIA convention in New York. Garvey's newspaper, *Negro World*, circulated worldwide, played an important role in bringing together so many African people. At this convention delegates ratified the "Declaration of Rights for the Negro People of the World."

Genuine economic development was central to the Garvey Movement, and movement businesses and financial institutions sprang up in large cities and small towns alike all over the United States. The Black Star Steamship Line was perhaps the UNIA's most renowned political and economic institution. Its goal was not only to be self-sustaining; it was to ferry Africans back and forth from the African continent. In addition, by 1920 the Chicago division of the UNIA had established a moving firm, a laundry and a hat factory. Ted Vincent describes the incredible breadth of the organization and its "framework for a future world government for black people."[44] Vincent continues:

> Pittsburgh had moving vans and a short-lived publishing company. Many Association-run businesses were opened in Cleveland and Cincinnati....New York City was the home office for Universal Restaurants and Universal Chain Store groceries, that had branches in Philadelphia, Newark, and other cities....The New York division also owned a millinery, a chain of laundries, and a record company that produced a speech by Garvey and recordings of the UNIA orchestra and musical personalities in the Association....
>
> While black socialists talked of building socialism, Garveyites created a working model. Insofar as the UNIA was a "nation" it was a nation with a collectivist economy.[45]

The UNIA had its own civil service, and nearly every branch had large Liberty Halls for political and social events. There was a UNIA court system which held trials. The organization even issued passports. The larger U.S. divisions had memberships of five to ten thousand people.[46]

The UNIA was the most profoundly internationalist movement of its time. Vincent surmises that Garvey had greater connections around the world than the Communist International itself. The Garvey Movement had a heavy influence on the revolution in Nicaragua at the time and some 50 years later. It was the *Negro World* that published reports from Augusto Sandino who was leading the Nicaraguan people's insurgency against U.S. invasion in the 1920s.[47] At the same time, the *Negro World* had a Chinese columnist, Paul Weng, who kept Africans updated on the people's revolution of China.

Ho Chi Minh, the great leader of the Vietnamese revolution that defeated U.S. imperialism in 1975, visited Garvey Movement meetings at Liberty Hall in New York when he was a merchant seaman in the '20s.[48]

An undercover police report on Garvey from 1919 reflects the international character of the movement:

> Garvey's office on 135th Street is sort of a clearing house for all international radical agitators, including Mexicans, South Americans, Spaniards, in fact blacks and yellows from all parts of the world...radiate around Garvey...[49]

GARVEY MOVEMENT CRUSHED

Marcus Garvey brought African people worldwide to the brink of a true national liberation struggle against U.S. and Western imperialism. In the ensuing years, no other movement has yet come close to building such an international infrastructure of state power for

African people. Had he been successful, Garvey could have changed the course of history by liberating Africa and African people everywhere early in the twentieth century. With so many millions in the ranks of the UNIA this scenario was very possible.

The Garvey Movement did not die a natural death or fail to meet its objectives through any internal weaknesses of its own, however. Like the Black Power Movement 40 years later, it was brought down by undercover operations of the U.S. government. J. Edgar Hoover launched his long, insidious career as head of the FBI by engineering the attack on Marcus Garvey and his movement, using this attack as the prototype for the later COINTELPRO against the Black Panther Party and the Black Power Movement of the 1960s.

The attack on the Garvey Movement had the support of a neocolonial sector of the African petty bourgeoisie that was threatened by the strength of the Garvey Movement for Black Power and a liberated Africa. A. Philip Randolph and his magazine the *Messenger* waged a "Garvey Must Go" campaign. In January, 1923, a "committee of eight," made up of some of Randolph's closest African neocolonial allies, penned a letter to the U.S. Attorney General calling out the government to "disband and extirpate this vicious movement." The letter stated in part:

> As the chief law enforcement officer of the nation, we wish to call your attention...certain Negro criminals and potential murderers, both foreign and American born, who are moved and actuated by intense hatred of the white race....
>
> The movement known as the Universal Negro Improvement Association has done much to stimulate the violent temper of this dangerous movement. Its President and moving spirit is one Marcus Garvey, an unscrupulous demagogue...[50]

J. Edgar Hoover and the U.S. government worked quickly, using this letter to derail Garvey and the UNIA that the government had long perceived as a threat. By May of that same year, Garvey was on trial for mail fraud and was sentenced to five years' imprisonment. He spent three months in the Tombs Prison in New York until he was released on bail. In 1925, Garvey was incarcerated in the Atlanta Federal Prison and in 1927, he was deported. He was only 40 years old, having been only in his thirties at the height of his movement.

For all practical purposes his organization was destroyed. The Black Star Steamship Line was soon dissolved and the New York Liberty Hall mortgaged. Garvey died in London in 1940.[51]

Despite the destruction of his movement, Garvey never ceased to have confidence that the liberation of African people is inevitable. As he was being deported he spoke these inspiring words:

> Day by day we hear the cry of "Africa for the Africans." This cry has become a positive, determined one. It is a cry raised simultaneously the world over, because of the universal oppression that affects the Negro.
>
> No one knows when the hour of Africa's redemption cometh. It is in the wind, it is coming. One day, like a storm, it will be here. When that day comes, all Africa will stand together...
>
> The more I remember the suffering of my forefathers, the more I remember the lynchings and burnings in the Southern States of America, the more I will fight on even though the battle seems doubtful. Tell me that I must turn back, and I laugh you to scorn. Go on! Go on! Climb ye the heights of liberty and cease not in well doing until you have planted the banner of the Red, the Black and the Green on the hilltops of Africa.[52]

The influence of Marcus Garvey on the future of African people and parasitic capitalism itself is embedded in stone. Despite the fact that his history has been blotted out by the white power system, Garvey's legacy lives on in the African People's Socialist Party and the Uhuru Movement. Though both the U.S. government and the white left believed that they had disposed of Garvey and African Revolution, only 15 years after Garvey's death the seeds of a new revolutionary movement of African people would begin to take shape in the United States.

GARVEY VS. WHITE COMMUNISTS

The white-led Communist Party USA (CPUSA) was in complete unity with the U.S. government's program to destroy the Garvey Movement, having itself waged a concerted campaign to undermine Garvey's black community base for years.

In the 1920s, at the height of the Garvey Movement, the party had unsuccessfully attempted to recruit Africans into its ranks, reportedly with hundreds of thousands of dollars of funding from the COMINTERN, the international organization of Communist parties.[53]

While the Garvey Movement had millions of African members, the CP had almost none. The white left could not bear to see Africans banding together with their sisters and brothers around the world, organizing a movement to reclaim their stolen land, wealth and civilization. Such a movement truly challenged capitalism at its very foundation. It exposed the opportunism of a white workers movement, that aimed to keep the pedestal of black oppression intact, and that functioned as nothing more than the left wing of the Democratic Party. The CP used the motion of the black movement to build itself, and never addressed the needs or aspirations of the African masses, as Harold Cruse exposes in *The Crisis of the Negro Intellectual*:

There was a lengthy stretch during the early 1920s when the newly-formed Communist factions were so busy trying to cash in on Garvey's movement that little, if any, theoretical work was done on the broad Negro question. But after the Communists failed either to win Garvey over or undermine him, they tried to win Negro support through the Labor movement.[54]

The CPUSA consistently intervened destructively in the internal affairs and debates of the African movement. It funded a contending organization, the African Blood Brotherhood, led by black integrationists who had joined the Communist Party, and who never had a base in the African community. Among the leaders of the African Blood Brotherhood was Cyril Briggs who had "emerged from A. Philip Randolph's Messenger group."[55] The African Blood Brotherhood was used by the CPUSA as a tool to try to undermine Garvey and his powerful black nationalist movement that was embodied in the "Africa for the Africans" slogan.

The Garvey Movement was a model of socialist internationalism, as Ted Vincent noted, but the white communists could not support a socialism led by African people. With the white left slogan "black and white unite and fight," communists wanted Africans to integrate into a white-led movement that aspired to do nothing more than change hands of the rulers of white power from the white bosses to white workers.

Garvey understood well the treachery and opportunism of the white left and its apology for the terror waged against African people. Garvey exhibits a healthy aversion to the white communists:

> Communism is a white man's creation, to solve his own [p]olitical and economic problems.
>
> It suggests the enthronement of the white working class over the capitalistic class of the race....

It was never conceived and originally intended for the economic or political emancipation of the blacks, but rather to raise the earning capacity of the lowest class of white workers....

The scheme, therefore, to make Negroes Communists, is a vile and wicked one, as coming from the white communists.

All wars in Africa, the colonies where the natives have been shot down and punished, were carried out by the common white man in the ranks. In the lynchings that have occurred in the Southern section of the United States of America, the mob has always been made up of the lowest class of the white race...The mob has always been made up of the common, ignorant people from whom Communists are made up and whom the party is intended to give political power or economic advantages.[56]

Garvey was clear that when the white left "inveigle(s) darker peoples into Communism, they are only endeavoring to use [Africans] to gain a greater advantage in the economic scale."[57]

ARROGANT PATERNALISM

The same white left pundits who apologize for the lynchings of and attacks on African people by white workers, also attack the Garvey Movement. Books by white leftists treat Garvey in a condescending manner. Shapiro's *White Violence and Black Response* sums up Garvey with pathetic lies and almost comical sour grapes:

Garvey had captured the imagination of blacks with a grand design of international struggle for black liberation. But he never had the capacity to unify black people everywhere behind his leadership [sic!] and at no point did he formulate a strategy and tactics oriented to the situation of blacks in the United States. Short of depending upon a universal black revolution, he formulated no conception of how victories could be wrested from American racism on its home ground....[58]

Apparently, eight million members were not enough to convince Mr. Shapiro of Garvey's "capacity to unify black people everywhere behind his leadership." An enormous system of collective businesses bringing community-controlled economic development to the black community in the United States and around the world was not a good enough strategy for Mr. Shapiro. True, Garvey was not so interested in "racism." Like the Uhuru Movement today, Garvey was intent on building political power for African people. Then, whether white people like Africans or not becomes irrelevant. With power in their own hands, African people can prevent whites from acting out our racism. Moreover, wresting victories from American racism, i.e., changing the ideas in the heads of white people, is our job, not the work of Africans.

Shapiro's sentiments reflect the stance of the Communist Party towards Garvey. During the Garvey Movement, the CPUSA attempted to counterorganize African people into its ranks. Not surprisingly, despite all its efforts, the CP never did attract the masses of African workers even after the destruction of the Garvey Movement. It is almost laughable to try to imagine a scenario in which African people would abandon a future painted by Marcus Garvey for one that would transfer white power into the hands of white workers. One account shows that the

> ...FBI concluded that the Communist Party never had much success in its campaign to "sway the Negro" despite an "inordinate" investment of "time, funds, propaganda and personnel," including Comintern subsidies as high as

$300,000 and dating from 1922 [the height of the Garvey Movement]. The Bureau would not even credit the party with attracting a significant minority of black members. In 1928 the CPUSA claimed 50 Negro members, though some of the comrades, according to FBI sources, estimated the total number of black recruits could be "counted on the fingers of one's hand." If the party did better in the 1930s and 1940s, [after the Garvey Movement was crushed] it probably never had more than 4,000 active, disciplined, dues-paying Negro members. By 1956 total black membership dropped to less than 1,400.[59]

To the corrupt and opportunist white communists, the life and death struggle of African people was nothing more than a mechanism to build their organization politically and financially. In *Crisis of the Negro Intellectual*, Harold Cruse raises the suspicion that the CP literally stole thousands of dollars from African people who sent in contributions to the Communist Party-led campaign in the 1930s defending nine young African men who had been framed up on a rape charge by two white women. These men were condescendingly called the Scottsboro "Boys" by the CPUSA, and the campaign was used as a recruitment tool into the party.

African people responded to the Scottsboro defense by sending donations to the CP's New York offices. As Cruse recounts, at exactly the same time, the party installed magnificent new printing presses for their paper *The Daily World*. "More than one Harlem leader hinted broadly that the presses had been paid for by the Negro donations intended to help the Scottsboro defense," Cruse relates.[60]

In the face of the history of treachery of the Communist Party and the white left, Yeshitela has concluded:

The response of the North American left was never to follow the leadership of this vital, dynamic movement....Instead its efforts went toward controlling it and historically when this has failed, to destroy it.[61]

CRISIS OF CAPITALISM

In 1929 the U.S. stock market crashed and the global "Depression" meant a reorganization of the world capitalist economy. The capitalist system was facing one of its most serious crises in many years. It was this same crisis that brought about "fascism" in Europe and the "New Deal" in the United States. These two responses of white power were interestingly similar, especially in relation to colonized peoples.

While the capitalist ruling class used the Depression to build larger and larger corporate entities of colonial extraction, white workers everywhere fought for and successfully won a far greater share of colonial power and wealth than ever before. The Nazis in Germany were "national socialists" appealing to the working class. U.S. President Franklin Roosevelt's New Deal also was a national socialistic program benefiting white workers.

For African people, whether inside the United States or as colonial subjects in Africa, the crisis of imperialism meant little. "Fascism" with white terror, genocide, martial law, an absence of democratic rights and blinding poverty had always existed for Africans and colonized peoples everywhere.

The 1930s "labor struggles" that old white leftists wax nostalgic about, were campaigns for white rights. They bolstered imperialism's power with the promise of greater unity from white workers in exchange for greater material benefits. In the '30s, as political analyst J. Sakai notes, all sectors of white workers

> became full citizens of the U.S. empire, and...won rights and privileges both inside and outside the factories. In return, as U.S. imperialism launched its drive for world

hegemony, it could depend upon the armies of solidly united settlers serving imperialism at home and on the battlefield.[62]

Throughout this period of white workers' struggles, lynchings and other violent attacks on African people increased. A study published by the "U.S. Commission on Interracial Cooperation" in 1933 made note of the particularly "sadistic tendencies among the lynchers":

> The desire merely to kill was not enough to explain the lynching of James Irwin at Ocilla, Georgia, in which the victim was jabbed in the mouth with a sharp pole, his toes and fingers removed joint by joint, and his teeth extracted by wire pullers; following these tortures and "further unmentionable atrocities' Irwin's still living body was saturated with gasoline and a match applied, where-upon hundreds of shots were fired into the body....A double lynching at Scooba, Mississippi, was reportedly organized by two men prominently identified with church, school and other community activities.[63]

During the Depression years, government and white citizen attacks inside the United States intensified against Mexican people, who had been terrorized, lynched, beaten and branded since their land had been stolen in 1848. In the 1930s half a million Mexican people were brutally deported to Mexico, often ripped apart from families and loved ones. One report from the period sums up the attacks on Mexicans by white workers and the silence of the white left:

> When Mexican sheep-shearers went on strike in West Texas in 1934, one of the sheepmen made a speech in that he said: "We are a pretty poor bunch of white men if

we are going to sit here and let a bunch of Mexicans tell us what to do."

With scarcely an exception, every strike in which Mexicans participated in the borderlands in the thirties was broken by the use of violence and was followed by deportations. In most of these strikes, Mexican workers stood alone; that is, they were not supported by organized labor, for their organizations, for the most part, were affiliated neither with the CIO nor the AFL.[64]

Rodolfo Acuña writes in *Occupied America: A History of Chicanos*:

Intended to reorganize capitalism and head off rebellion, the New Deal also provided the illusion that the workers had a friend in the White House. And although Franklin Roosevelt was immensely popular among Mexicans, most did not benefit from his programs. They were noncitizens and/or agriculture laborers—two sectors generally excluded from New Deal programs. Mexicans who were U.S. citizens also had the burden of proving themselves "Americans."[65]

Acuña tells us that in the '30's Mexican farmworkers were making about 16 cents an hour. Thus:

Conditions forced Mexicans, whom growers had previously considered docile, to become angry strikers. An all-out war erupted in which growers relied on the Immigration Service to deport leaders, pressured state and federal agencies to deny Mexicans relief, used local and state authorities to terrorize workers, killed and imprisoned strikers, and made a sham of any semblance of human rights.[66]

AFRICAN APATHY FOR WAR

With unabated violence against African and other oppressed peoples inside its borders, the United States entered the second imperialist world war after Pearl Harbor was bombed by the Japanese in 1941. Some say that U.S. President Franklin Roosevelt knew about the attack on the Hawaiian port in advance, or even provoked it as a means of mobilizing white people to fight in the war. But while North Americans did indeed become enthusiastic to fight, Africans remained uninterested in the white man's battles. "The Negro is...angry, resentful, and utterly apathetic about the war," wrote an African journalist.[67]

Lynchings, police brutality and Northern white citizen violence were as relentless as ever. In response, African people rose up in powerful rebellions in Harlem in 1935 and in Detroit and Harlem in 1943. In addition, African soldiers drafted to fight in World War II defended themselves courageously against attack and even murder by white servicemen. At Fort Dix, New Jersey, for example, "A fifteen minute battle ensued involving white and black soldiers and several military police who had been called out."[68]

Many African soldiers were also savagely prosecuted on falsified rape charges, for which they could be given the death penalty. According to one report, a white commander of a black regiment posted a notice on a Pennsylvania military base: "Any cases between white and colored males and females, whether voluntary or not, is considered rape and during time of war the penalty is death." In response, a near insurrection from the African soldiers lasted for months on that base. In Memphis, Tennessee in 1944, African soldiers were beaten to death.[69]

But Africans resisted fiercely. At Brookley Field, Alabama, black soldiers drove out MPs and a white civilian who started to search the black soldiers' quarters; as many as a thousand shots were fired. In Louisiana, African soldiers seized weapons and began firing after a rumor spread that police had shot and killed a black soldier. In 1944, in Ft. Lawton, Washington, African soldiers attacked a barracks of Italian prisoners of war in reprisal for the fact that the army treated the white prisoners better than the African soldiers.[70]

During the war, the March on Washington Movement led by the neocolonialist A. Philip Randolph, who had set up the government attack on Marcus Garvey, threatened to draw 100,000 Africans into the Capitol to demand equal rights in hiring by the defense industry. Horrified at the thought of so many Africans converging on the District of Columbia, U.S. President Roosevelt quickly created the Fair Employment Practices Committee (FEPC) to avert the demonstration. The FEPC supposedly ended the discriminatory hiring policies.[71]

But as African workers began to force the U.S. government to actually carry out its commitment to "fair" hiring practices, white left and Communist Party-dominated trade unions all over the country began a rash of "hate strikes" in an attempt to keep African workers out of the jobs.

In Philadelphia, for example, in 1944, a hate strike was called by white streetcar workers when eight Africans were hired as motor-men. The strike blocked public transportation for six days until the government and 5,000 government troops were sent in.[72]

The prevailing sentiment of the African community ran passionately against participation in the second imperialist war. Why would Africans want to fight a U.S. war against Hitler when the same conditions existed inside the United States for them?

Many black neocolonial leaders of the time tried in vain to win the African community to support the war. Their appeal to stand "shoulder to shoulder" with white fellow citizens fell on deaf ears in the African community, however. An interesting and, in spite of itself, rather humorous incident in a white leftist book illustrates the futility of the NAACP in trying to mobilize black people to fight for the United States:

> Walter White, then executive secretary of the NAACP, told of his horror at hearing from a teacher in a well-known Negro college in the South of the attitude of his students to the war. One of the students, "with infinite bitterness," exclaimed in a discussion of the war, "I hope Hitler wins!" The teacher...argued that "conditions would be even worse under Hitler." The student...replied:

> "They can't possibly be any worse than they are for Negroes in the South right now. The Army jim-crows us. The Navy lets us serve only as messmen. The Red Cross refuses our blood. Employers and labor unions shut us out. Lynchings continue. We are disenfranchised, jim-crowed, spat upon. What more could Hitler do than that?"

> But White was to be even more horrified later on, when addressing a Midwestern audience:

> "I told the story of the Southern student as an illustration of the kind of dangerous, shortsighted thinking that Negro Americans had to guard zealously against. To my surprise and dismay, the audience burst into such applause that it took me some thirty or forty seconds to quiet it. Though I went into as detailed an explanation of the fallacy of such thinking as I could, I left the meeting with a feeling of depression born of the conviction that I had not convinced all of my audience that Hitlerism could and would be worse."[73]

NEW TOP DOG OF IMPERIALISM

The United States emerged from the second imperialist world war as the unopposed leader of the world capitalist system. But as the United States was taking over as the number one oppressor nation, peoples in the colonies were increasingly struggling for independence. In the face of rising national liberation movements around the world, the United States relied on the system of "neocolonialism," as opposed to the direct colonial rule previously favored by the European powers.

Under neocolonialism, imperialist powers set up puppet leaders from the colonized nations to do the bidding of the U.S. government, while giving the appearance of national independence. The strategy was used abroad as well as in the African community inside the United States.

As the new top dog of imperialism, the United States began to experience an unparalleled economic boom. The 1950s were characterized by the Cold War, during which "anti-communist" sentiment was used as a cover to attack anti-colonial struggles around the world.

Inside the United States, as African people continued to catch hell, massive housing tracts with split-level homes were being built in the suburbs so that the white population could escape the largely African populated cities, and experience the new burst of wealth flowing into the United States.

By the end of World War II, the economic gains of white workers were so great that the Communist Party disintegrated simply because it was no longer needed as a tool for white workers to be able to share a greater portion of colonial power and wealth. While the CPUSA maintains that U.S. government "repression" led by Senator Joseph McCarthy in the 1950s destroyed their organization, in fact it is clear that the CP fell apart of its own accord. In his booklet *The Mythology of the White Proletariat*, J. Sakai tells us:

> The false view that the CPUSA was crushed by "McCarthyite repression" not only serves to conceal the mass shift away from class consciousness on the part of settler masses, but also helped U.S. imperialism to conceal the violent colonial struggles of that period.[74]

In 1949, approximately 114 Communist Party members were arrested by the government, 29 of whom were given two-to-five year sentences. While CP members claimed that government repression "almost obliterated" the party, in fact, as Sakai points out, the government issued a series of warnings and reproaches to frighten white communists "back into line with imperialist policy against the USSR. There were no death squads, no shoot-outs, no long prison sentences—the CPUSA wasn't even outlawed, and published its newspaper and held activities throughout this period."[75]

In 1953, the federal execution of Julius and Ethel Rosenberg for allegedly being "atom bomb spies" sent many CP members scurrying to the anonymous white suburbs where they made bonfires of their communist books. In 1956, revelations that some of the rumors of Stalin's excesses were possibly true created another mass exodus from the CP rosters, leaving its membership depleted. Whatever the excuse, the real reason for the desertion of the members of the CP was economic. White workers, by and large, had gotten what they wanted, and were now fat and comfortable.

The white left still refers to the 1950s as a period in which government repression drove out all left response in this country. But, while white leftists were hiding out "underground," African people were openly in the throes of a militant new movement that was going to rock this system to its very foundations. Despite the defeat of the Garvey Movement, the domestic colony inside the belly of the beast was again rising up in what became a conscious national liberation movement.

Sit-ins, Marches and Freedom Rides

In 1955, Mrs. Rosa Parks refused to give up her seat on a Montgomery, Alabama bus to a white man. In doing so, she effectively unleashed a mass movement of African people so powerful that it would define life in America for the next 15 years, and dictate U.S. policy for years to come. Mrs. Parks, a 43 year old seamstress at the time, explained why she decided to sit down in the "white" section of the bus:

> Well, in the first place, I had been working all day on the job. I was quite tired after spending a full day working. I handle and work on clothing that white people wear. That didn't come in my mind but this is what I wanted to know: when and how would we ever determine our rights as human beings?...It just happened that the driver made a demand and I just didn't feel like obeying his demand. He called a policeman and I was arrested and placed in jail....[76]

The Montgomery bus boycott was on. Civil rights leaders, including the 27 year old minister Dr. Martin Luther King, converged on the town, organizing sit-ins and protests for which a hundred African people were indicted and many were sent to jail. African churches were bombed by white people and shotgun fire blasted through the home of Dr. King. But African people continued to struggle, and in November 1956 the Supreme Court was forced to outlaw segregation on local bus lines.[77]

By 1957, with the struggle for African children to attend the all-white Little Rock, Arkansas schools, the sterile colonialist assumptions of white society had been permanently shattered. The movement for African democratic rights—called the Civil Rights Movement—took this country by storm. A powerful and beautiful expression of the will of African people to be free, the movement was characterized by mass political awakening by Africans of all ages: children, youth, middle aged and elderly African people took part in the exuberant activism of the time.

It was a movement of fearless school children standing up before the vicious dogs, mace and fire hoses of the U.S. government. There were marches, sit-ins, freedom rides and mass rallies in churches packed with grandmothers in hats and heels and proper dresses. The movement was typified by jail cells full of young people singing freedom songs.

It was the poor and oppressed African masses in the South coming alive, riding the irrefutable moral high ground of the struggle for justice. A sense of the inevitability of victory was in the air, and a determination of African people to keep their "eyes on the prize" was felt by millions. Many songs gave voice to the spirit of this movement, for example:

Ain't gonna let nobody turn me 'round
turn me 'round, turn me 'round,
Ain't gonna let nobody turn me 'round,
I'm gonna keep on walkin', keep on talkin'
Marching up to freedom land. [78]

People made great by their courage and commitment rose up from among the impoverished sharecroppers and descendants of the slaves—Fannie Lou Hamer, Ella Baker, Willie Ricks, along with countless now-nameless heroes, led their people in local and national struggles.

Despite its mass character, the Civil Rights Movement of the 1950s and early '60s was led by the black middle class, the petty bourgeoisie. Black undertakers, professors and preachers led the Southern struggle, not for national liberation and self determination as Garvey's movement had thirty years earlier. The rising African petty bourgeoisie was interested in achieving full civil rights for themselves and integration with white people, aspirations very different from those of the vast African working class.

The liberal white ruling class had its own interests in seeing limited gains for the Southern Civil Rights Movement. This is why Robert Kennedy and other white ruling class liberals of the time directly intervened and participated in the movement.

CLASS BASIS OF CIVIL RIGHTS MOVEMENT

Chairman Omali Yeshitela of the African People's Socialist Party has developed an incisive and brilliant analysis of the material conditions that brought about the rise of the 1950s Civil Rights Movement, and ultimately the full-scale Black Revolution of the 1960s. Yeshitela summed up in a speech reprinted in the pamphlet "Dialectics of Black Revolution":

> There was a historical basis for the Black Revolution inside this country. The impetus for our Revolution was material....What happened after the second imperialist war was that Europe and the United States changed places. Now the United States was becoming the central imperialist force controlling the world economy.

> Before the second imperialist war, Europe, collectively, was the central force controlling the world economy. Europe controlled Africa, Asia and even portions of Latin America.

> As a consequence of the second imperialist world war, great resources began to flow into the United States. Thus we saw a requirement for more workers to transform the raw materials coming from Africa, Asia and Latin America into finished products. Workers were no

longer available from what was called Eastern Europe as they had been in the past...because Eastern Europe was a part of the so-called Soviet Bloc.

So in order to get workers they went down South where they had to destroy the relations of production that were based on labor-intensive capitalist production.

We had a situation in which the liberal sector of the bourgeoisie then acquired its definition as "liberal" based solely on the fact that it needed black workers in the factories. It had to break up the traditional relations of production.

To do that required struggle, and it required black people to have the ability to go to school. To participate in capital-intensive production you've got to know how to operate the machines, function in factories, and have a minimum level of literacy.

Therefore you see the emergence of white liberals championing the needs and the rights of black people. They were struggling to stop the exploitation in the South so that we could be exploited in the North as well as in the factories that were going to develop in the South itself.[79]

As Yeshitela shows, because the white ruling class liberals backed the black middle class, the goals of the leaders of the Civil Rights Movement could only be a limited legal "revolution." The aim was not to transfer control of state power into the hands of African people. The philosophy of nonviolence, therefore, was key to this movement. In the process, however, this black middle class movement awakened the masses of African workers who were coming to some very different conclusions about the nature of the struggle.

As the leading spokesman of the African petty bourgeoisie, Martin Luther King articulated a philosophy of nonviolence. King attempted to keep the lid on the deeper revolutionary struggle for real political power that was simmering just under the surface. King insisted—as Yeshitela has pointed out—that a "philosophical commitment to nonviolence was morally cleansing and empowering."

After centuries of genocidal white violence, African people were being told to "turn the other cheek," not only during Civil Rights marches and demonstrations when attacked by white civilian or government forces, which might have been tactically justifiable. Africans were also being told not to fight back in general. As we see from the long history of African resistance, this was something African workers by and large were not willing to do. It was around this and other questions that the essence of the struggle between the black middle class and the working class revolved.

Many African workers had long been armed, and they had to be. As we have shown in this book, violence perpetrated against the African population has always been a daily reality in this country. A nonviolent response to the terror African people face is something that serves the interests of white people and the U.S. State in maintaining the pedestal of African exploitation. For these reasons, the white left and liberals arrogantly call for nonviolence for African people in the United States. When it comes to Cuba or Viet Nam or Nicaragua or other struggles outside of U.S. borders, they make no such demand.

By the early 1960s, the voice of African workers, who were becoming clear that they were waging an anticolonial struggle, increasingly began to supersede the middle class call for nonviolence. The photograph of Malcolm X standing at the window armed with a semi-automatic rifle became the symbol of African working class resistance.

In the late 1950s, Robert Williams, then the head of the NAACP branch in Monroe, North Carolina, became known throughout the country and the world for arming himself in response to the regular Ku Klux Klan forays that terrorized the African community. One series of Klan attacks took place after Africans led a struggle for their children to have the right to use the local swimming pool.

Williams' friend, Dr. Perry was threatened during these Klan attacks, and Williams' armed forces defended Perry and his family:

> In August, somebody called my house when I wasn't home and told my wife that the Klan had met that night and they were gonna get me tomorrow night. Well, they didn't get me then or after that....The Klan paraded around my house a couple of times....But then we met gunfire with gunfire.[80]

YOUTHFUL ENERGY, PHYSICAL COURAGE

It was the bold, young Student Nonviolent Coordinating Committee (SNCC) that best characterized the black movement of the early '60s. In many ways, SNCC was the vehicle for the transition from the Civil Rights Movement to the militant Black Power Movement.

In February 1960, a small group of black students at the predominately black North Carolina Agricultural and Technical College in Greensboro held a sit-in at the lunch counter of the downtown Woolworth store. Their actions generated enthusiastic support from others and the next morning 30 students joined the original four. Two days later, hundreds of students filled the Woolworth's, and soon black students throughout the South were holding similar protests. That year, more than 50,000 people participated in various demonstrations in a hundred cities. Over 3,600 people were put in jail.[81]

A year later the Congress of Racial Equality (CORE) organized "freedom rides" in which Africans and white people rode together on buses from the North to the South in violation of Southern segregation of interstate travel. This segregation had long been illegal but never enforced by the federal government. In May of 1961, two buses left from Washington, D.C. headed for New Orleans. The buses never arrived at their destination. According to one report,

> In South Carolina, riders were beaten. In Alabama, a bus was set afire. Freedom Riders were attacked with fists and iron bars. The Southern police did not interfere with any of this violence, nor did the federal government....[82]

April 16 through 18, 1960, the great African organizer Ella Baker called the founding conference of the Student Nonviolent Coordinating Committee to give leadership to struggling African students all over the South who had been thrust into the leadership of a rising new movement.

SNCC quickly evolved beyond a student organization, however, and its own title became an anomaly. Its goals and tactics grew by leaps and bounds into the broader realms of struggle around the life and death questions facing the African masses. SNCC distinguished itself by having organizers who went out into the rural African communities, living and working with the people. It was this practice, rather than a commitment to nonviolence, that determined the character of SNCC.

It was the people who radicalized the members of SNCC rather than the other way around, for the masses of impoverished African people had interests that lay far beyond the integration of a lunch counter. Yeshitela explains:

> SNCC was not only distinguished within the liberal African petty bourgeoisie-led Black Liberation Movement by its youthful energy and physical courage. It was also distinguished by its deep connection to the masses of oppressed African toilers with whom SNCC members lived and organized, suffering the same oppressive fate that the masses suffered themselves.

This connection with the people was the primary basis for SNCC's growing radicalization. The growing relationship that SNCC was developing with the Nation of Islam through its most influential and working class oriented revolutionary leader, Malcolm X, increasingly fused a revolutionary character onto the mass Black Liberation Movement. This relationship enhanced its development from a defensive movement for civil or democratic rights to an offensive movement for national liberation that was generally and broadly conscious of its aims.[83]

MISSISSIPPI SUMMER

SNCC's Mississippi Summer Project of 1964 was one of its most pivotal campaigns of the period. Thousands of white students came from the North into Mississippi where the ground was soaked with the blood of African people. The summer project occurred during the time that SNCC was building the Mississippi Freedom Democratic Party to demand that the upcoming Democratic convention seat black Mississippi delegates. It was the summer project that had the most profound effect on the consciousness of white students and brought the immediacy of the struggle of African people into white suburban America.

In James Forman's *The Making of Black Revolutionaries*, the SNCC leader wrote of the organization's strategy for the Mississippi Summer Project:

> In SNCC we had often wondered, How do you make more people in this country share our experiences, understand what it is to look in the face of death because you're black, feel hatred for the federal government that always makes excuses for the brutality of Southern cops and state troopers?

> We often wondered: How can we find the strength to continue our work in the face of the poverty of the people, to do everything that shouts to be done in the absence of so many resources?
>
> The Mississippi Summer Project was an attempt to answer those questions....
>
> It is a highly dramatic story of black people in Mississippi and how almost a thousand volunteers—mostly white students—came to the state to help work on voter registration, the building of the new Mississippi Freedom Democratic Party, the setting up of "freedom schools."[84]

As Forman said, hundreds of Northerners responded to SNCC's call to come to Mississippi to participate in its freedom campaigns that summer. They were mostly upper middle class white students, since it was necessary to have a thousand dollars for bail, transportation and expenses in order to participate. They came generally from the lush, liberal Northern suburbs of New York City, hoping to experience the world their maids and housekeepers lived in, to look at the face of colonialism.

As it turned out, the spotlight of national attention was immediately focused on the summer project. On the first day of the project, three of the civil rights workers turned up missing. They were Andrew Goodman, a college student from Queens College in New York, 24 year old Michael Schwerner from Brooklyn, both white, and Congress of Racial Equality (CORE) worker James Chaney, a 21 year old African man. It wasn't until August that their bodies were found near Philadelphia, Mississippi. They had been shot to death by white terrorists, and Chaney, the African victim, had been brutally beaten, his skull totally crushed in.

For the first time, America's spotlight was on Mississippi. In a press conference called by SNCC, Rita Schwerner, Michael's young widow, was moved to express a principled statement of solidarity with African people in discussing the murder of her husband:

> It's tragic that white Northerners have to be caught up into the machinery of injustice and indifference in the South before the American people register concern. I personally suspect that if Mr. Chaney, who is a [black] native Mississippian, had been alone at the time of the disappearance, that this case, like so many others...would have gone unnoticed.[85]

WHITES RADICALIZED BY BLACK MOVEMENT

It was SNCC, and the tremendous motion of African people in the Civil Rights Movement, that sparked the white student radicalism of the 1960s. Many white activists from that period refuse to acknowledge this. They prefer to believe that we miraculously emerged out of the comfortable white suburbs and hundreds of years of deeply ingrained white nationalist complacency into "revolution" on our own. The fact was, the movement of African workers and peasants challenged the deepest assumptions of a generation of white middle class youth who were growing increasingly alienated from the expectations of their lifestyle, but who never questioned giving up life on the pedestal of African colonialism.

In the early '60s, with the Communist Party pretty much out of the picture, a "New Left" grew up, inspired by the militancy and internationalism of the Black Movement. No longer revolving around the white rights labor struggles of the thirties, the new white left was perhaps best characterized by the Students for a Democratic Society (SDS) that was sparked by the black student movement.

The founding statement of SDS expressed the growing alienation of a generation of privileged whites: "We are people of this generation, bred in at least modest comfort, housed now in universities, looking uncomfortably to the world we inherit."[86]

Despite obvious honest respect for the courage of the masses of struggling African people, the standpoint of middle class white students in the 1960s was self-centered, subjective and Eurocentric, unable to conceive of genuine solidarity with African people in the United States and colonized peoples around the world. Chairman Yeshitela has clarified that because of our dominant relationship to the parasitic world economy, white people continue to define the world based on our own needs. We define the struggles particular to us within the minority European and North American oppressor nations as international.

Early in the history of SNCC, several SDS members and other white students joined or participated in the campaigns of the black-led organization. For a while, the Southern black struggle was the "happening" thing for white students whose revolutionary attention span was never long. Many white students who went down South did nothing more than attempt to imitate SNCC's militant style while rejecting the essence of the political questions that a movement of colonized people would necessarily pose for members of the oppressor nation.

For example, after the SNCC-led Mississippi Summer Project of 1964, the hundreds of white students returned to their college campuses having been educated in methods of waging struggle. At the University of California, Berkeley, contention broke out with the university when the returning students were not permitted to set up tables with information about SNCC and other Civil Rights organizations.

Mario Savio was a Friends of SNCC organizer at Berkeley who had participated in the Mississippi Summer Project of 1964. The refusal of the administration to let students express their support for the struggle of African people led Savio to organize the Berkeley Free Speech movement. Militant student rebellions and the burning of a

police car on the campus ensued. As a result, the free speech propo-
nents quickly won their objectives and the university administration
backed down.

However, the white students seeking free speech never went
ahead, then, and built solidarity with the militant movement of African people led by SNCC. They seemed to forget all about the struggle of African people, who were catching as much hell in
neighboring Oakland as they were in the Southern states. The struggle for "free speech" turned into a white rights movement for students to be allowed to curse, run around naked and otherwise
"express themselves" on the college campus.

CHANGE IN THE AIR

The Mississippi Summer Project was one of the great turning
points in the transformation of the Civil Rights Movement into the
Black Power Movement. It marked the moment that African working
class and poor people had begun to seize the leadership of their
struggle, wrenching it out of the hands of the African petty bourgeois preachers and students who were backed by white liberals. By
the end of the summer of 1964, 80,000 Africans had joined the Mississippi Freedom Democratic Party, freedom schools had been established, thousands had been arrested during mass struggle, and
national and international media turned their attention on the Southern black movement.

Fannie Lou Hamer, the daughter of a sharecropper, rose up out
of SNCC to lead the confrontation with the white power structure at
the national Democratic Party convention at the end of August in
Atlantic City. She led the delegation in walking out when they were
granted only two nonvoting seats by the national Democratic Party.
The Democrats had also refused to evict the murderous all-white
Mississippi Democratic Party from the convention.

Change was in the wind, and the atmosphere in the United States was electric with the rising power of the motion of black people. When Fannie Lou Hamer walked out of the Democratic Convention of 1964, she took with her whatever was left of the belief on the part of the African masses that change would come through the white power system. Consciousness was growing among African workers that their movement was much greater than a quest for democratic and voting rights. It was a movement for power.

During the March on Washington in 1963, which was sponsored by liberal sectors of the white ruling class and government, Martin Luther King gave his now famous "I have a dream" speech. Thousands of African people from all over the country poured into Washington for the demonstration. The U.S. government was forced to pass the Civil Rights Bill in 1964, followed the next year by the Voting Rights Act, a full century after the abolition of the slave system.

Nevertheless, it was at this juncture that the movement of African people developed into a revolutionary anticolonial movement. Omali Yeshitela explains:

> It's interesting because the 1963 March on Washington resulted in the passage of the Civil Rights Bill in 1964. Then in 1965 the Voting Rights Act was passed. That was supposed to mean that the struggle was over because that's what it was supposed to have been about—civil rights and voting rights. But in 1966, when it should have been over, the Black Power demand was put forward, saying, "Civil rights won't do. It's about black power, having our own power."[87]

The same year that the Voting Rights Act was passed, Malcolm X, the Northern militant and the voice of urban African workers, was brutally assassinated in Harlem. Armed uprisings and rebellions began to sweep cities across the country.

THE BALLOT OR THE BULLET

Malcolm X was born on May 19, 1925 to Louise and Earl Little, active participants in the Marcus Garvey Movement. He was born in Omaha, Nebraska, only six years after the Red Summer of 1919, when the African community of Omaha rose up in rebellion. Malcolm was raised in East Lansing, Michigan where his father was killed in 1931 by white terrorists from a Klan-type organization. Later, while in prison, Malcolm X converted to the Islamic teachings of Elijah Muhammad that played a role in his developing political awareness.

By the early '60s, Malcolm X represented the growing conscious-ness of the African working class in the Northern cities. In 1964 he left the Nation of Islam, and attempted to build the Organization of Afro-American Unity that called for political independence for Afri-can people and black control of the political and economic life of the African community.[88] He played a key role in transforming the African liberation struggle into a genuine threat to the U.S. govern-ment for the first time since the Garvey Movement.

A brilliant speaker, Malcolm X summed up the conditions and aspirations of the African working class. While Martin Luther King was exuding, "I have a dream," Malcolm X was talking about the "American nightmare." He had no patience for philosophical nonvio-lence and the politics of "waiting" for freedom. In his famous speech called "The Ballot or the Bullet" delivered in Cleveland in April, 1964, Malcolm X stated:

> And now you're facing a situation where the young Negro's coming up. They don't want to hear that "turn the other cheek" stuff, no. In Jacksonville, those were teenagers, they were throwing Molotov cocktails. Negroes have never done that before. But it shows you there's a new deal coming in. There's new thinking com-ing in. There's new strategy coming in. It'll be Molotov

cocktails this month, hand grenades next month, and something else next month. It'll be ballots, or it'll be bullets. It'll be liberty, or it will be death. The only difference about this kind of death—it'll be reciprocal....

The economic philosophy of black nationalism is pure and simple. It only means that we should control the economy of our community. Why should white people be running all the stores in our community? Why should white people be running the banks of our community? Why should the economy of our community be in the hands of the white man?[89]

The masses of African people heard Malcolm's message well. As Yeshitela says, "There was always an undercurrent of resistance to the philosophical idealism, tactics, strategies and political objectives of the liberal African primitive petty bourgeoisie from within the broad perimeter of the Black Liberation Movement."[90]

On February 21, 1965, an assassin gunned down Malcolm X as he was speaking at the Audubon Ballroom in Harlem, New York. He had recently returned from his trip to Africa and was working for "the successful linking together of our problem with the African problem, or making our problem a world problem."[91]

In his book, *Agents of Repression*, Ward Churchill notes that "it has been convincingly argued that the Bureau [FBI] was involved in the orchestration of the assassination of Malcolm X."[92] The FBI memorandum on COINTELPRO makes clear that the U.S. government kept massive files on Malcolm X and considered him one of the contenders for the role of "black messiah."[93]

Chairman Omali Yeshitela, speaking at a Malcolm X commemoration event, emphasized the continued importance of the ideas of Malcolm X for African people today:

To believe in Malcolm X, to honor and extol the ideas of Malcolm X is to believe in ourselves, our history, and our future...To honor and extol the ideas of Malcolm X is to struggle for the liberation of Africa and the unity of all African people.[94]

BLACK POWER

In 1966, Willie "Mukassa" Ricks, the brilliant SNCC organizer and unsung hero of the Civil Rights Movement, raised the slogan "Black Power" during the Meredith March in Mississippi. The call for black power instantly ignited the imaginations of the African working class everywhere. It was a slogan that resounded throughout the United States and around the world. James Forman wrote:

Those two words electrified the nation and the world. Black people wanted power, the words said. Only power could change our condition....We had moved to the level of verbalizing our drive for power—not merely for the vote, not for some vague kind of freedom, not for legal rights, but for the basic force in any society—power. Power for black people, black power.[95]

The leadership of the black petty bourgeoisie and its alliance with the liberal white ruling class was being cast off by the masses of African people. Black workers were now defining the aims of their movement. The liberal bourgeois notion of philosophical nonviolence was being replaced by militant revolutionary strategies and tactics. Watts, Detroit, and countless other cities were burning in the flames of Black Revolution. Yeshitela explains:

The growing independent participation of the masses in the struggle against U.S. colonial white power broke all the boundaries imposed by the alliance between the liberal white ruling class and the liberal African primitive petty bourgeoisie throughout the United States....Spontaneous rebellions by colonized African masses were leaving their mark in the smoldering embers of city after city.

By 1965 rebellion had occurred in the African community of Watts in Los Angeles. It was clear the liberal African petty bourgeoisie was losing its hegemonic hold on the people. Dr. Martin Luther King Jr....was brought to Watts by the white ruling class to pacify the rebelling masses. The chief proponent and most outstanding leader of the liberal alliance, King was booed off the speaker's platform by militant Africans.

In 1966 the Student Nonviolent Coordinating Committee raised the slogan-demand for Black Power that crystallized the transformation of our movement. The Black Power demand indicated the loss of political hegemony by the liberal African petty bourgeoisie, as African workers began to speak for ourselves in our own interest....

The growing independent involvement of the masses of oppressed African working people, both employed and unemployed, within the Black Liberation Movement was primarily responsible for the split that developed within the liberal front of the Black Liberation Movement. This was expressed by SNCC's Black Power slogan and demand...Increasingly SNCC's worldview was also reflecting the same independence from the liberals that had been assumed by the African masses.[96]

In 1967, Africans rose up in the greatest number of rebellions in U.S. history. The U.S. National Advisory Committee on Urban Disorders reported,

[E]ight major uprisings, 33 "serious but not major" out-breaks, and 123 "minor" disorders. Eighty-three died of gunfire, mostly in Newark and Detroit. The "typical rioter" was "proud of his race, extremely hostile to both whites and middle class Negroes and, although informed about politics, highly distrustful of the political system."[97]

WHITES EVICTED FROM SNCC

The Student Nonviolent Coordinating Committee-initiated demand for Black Power brought to the foreground many pressing philosophical and political questions, including the relationship of race to class and the relationship of white people to the black movement. The fact that white people had been members of SNCC since its founding in 1960 was an issue that had long been the subject of debate. African SNCC members found themselves needing to wage seemingly endless struggles with the white members. The late Kwame Toure, then known as Stokely Carmichael, stated in regard to the opportunist, self-absorbed stance of white people in and around SNCC at the time:

> I have said that most liberal whites react to "black power" with the question, What about me?, rather than saying: Tell me what you want and I'll see if I can do it...One of the most disturbing things about almost all white supporters of the movement has been that they are afraid to go into their own communities—that is where the racism exists—and work to get rid of it. They want to run from Berkeley and tell us what to do in Mississippi; let them look instead at Berkeley. They admonish blacks to be nonviolent; let them preach nonviolence in the white community. They come to teach me Negro history; let them go to the suburbs and

open freedom schools for whites. Let them work to stop America's racist foreign policy.[98]

In 1966, the Atlanta Office of SNCC, based in the black community of Vine City, wrote a paper calling for the ouster of white people from the organization. The paper pointed out that the white members had their own agenda, steering every debate dealing with the African community off the subject by bringing up idealistic notions of "brotherhood" and "love." The paper stated:

> When we view the masses of white people we view the overall reality of America, we view the racism, the bigotry, and the distortion of personality, we view man's inhumanity to man; we view in reality 180 million racists.[99]

The authors of the Vine City paper correctly charged that most white radicals and SNCC members

> sought to escape the horrible reality of America by going into the black community and attempting to organize black people while neglecting the organization of their own people's racist communities. How can one clean up someone else's yard when one's own yard is untidy?

The authors declared that white people should try to raise themselves to the "humanistic level" of African people:

> We are not, after all, the ones who are responsible for a genocidal war in Viet Nam; we are not the ones who are responsible for neocolonialism in Africa and Latin America; we are not the ones who held a people in animalistic bondage for over 400 years.[100]

In response to the paper, SNCC voted at the Atlanta conference of 1966 to expel its white staff and members, stating that they should "work in the white communities against racism and repression."[101] James Forman wrote that:

> [A] whole new rhetoric and a new set of attitudes as well as policies emerged at this time. The phrase "civil rights movement," long moribund, died forever with the birth of Black Power. At the same time, recognition of the need for black people to organize themselves and conduct their own struggle—together with the need for whites to fight racism in white communities—led to an increasing emphasis on all-blackness in SNCC as well as other militant groups.[102]

In our typical self-centered fashion, white people did not unite with SNCC's decision to send North Americans back home to take on our work inside the belly of the beast. Instead, the whites reacted subjectively. After the vote was taken for SNCC to expel its white members, all the North Americans got up and angrily walked out.

The SNCC decision to evict white people also posed a real problem for SDS, which had enjoyed its insider relationship with SNCC and its ability to make forays into the African colony at will, rather like missionaries or peace corps members. These white people were quite challenged by SNCC's decision since they had so long basked in the glow of the genuine militancy of the revolutionized African community. SNCC's call to struggle inside the white community created for SDS a real crisis, a "malaise at the national level."[103] The white-centered book, *SDS*, states that,

> [SNCC] announced a new policy of "black power" that specifically sought to exclude whites from organizing in black communities. It was the official pronouncement of

the death of the dream, which of course was known to be dying, of multiracial organizing in multiracial communities for multiracial justice. And with it the generation of SDS leadership that had grown up inextricably entwined with SNCC and the Civil Rights Movement....The generation that had achieved its political consciousness through integration, found its past, like a rug in an old vaudeville routine, ripped from under its feet.[104]

But SDS recovered quite quickly from its crisis. During the summer of 1966, as the struggle of African people in the United States heightened to revolutionary levels and the Vietnamese people were struggling against U.S. colonial aggression, the national SDS conference returned to a blatant white rights agenda. Their priorities now included the student movement, lifestyle questions, youth culture, dress, drugs and rights within the university system, according to the documents of SDS at the time.[105]

Now freed from any obligation to the black movement, SDS became an organization of political stars, the golden children of the affluent petty bourgeoisie, no longer tied to the serious political leadership of the African masses. The white radicals were now funded by rich liberals and surrounded by well-known, media-loving supporters like Philip Berrigan, Paul Goodman, William Kunstler, Herbert Marcuse and others.

Soon SDS would discover Viet Nam, a question on which many white political careers would be built. Opposition to this war gained greater urgency as more and more young white men returned from Southeast Asia in body bags. Though it was the Civil Rights and Black Power Movement that had made radicalism fashionable, the agenda of the New Left was to remain firmly white-centered, just like the CP-dominated "old left" from which it professed to distinguish itself.

BLACK PANTHERS ON THE RISE

In 1966, African communities were electrified by the emergence of the Black Panther Party (BPP) in Oakland, California under the leadership of Huey P. Newton. Distinguishing themselves from earlier movements based in nonviolence, their original title was the Black Panther Party for Self Defense, until its name was shortened. Omali Yeshitela describes the rise of the BPP:

> The Black Panther Party represented a fusion of the independent resistance of the rebelling African masses who were in many ways influenced by SNCC, and the anti-colonialist ideology of economic independence and revolutionary self-determination as exemplified in the unfinished philosophy of Malcolm X....For all practical purposes the Black Panther Party became the revolutionary center within the U.S.[106]

The Black Panther Party and the movement for Black Power gripped the masses, elevating the movement to the level of anti-colonial struggle. Organizing the people under the discipline of revolutionary formations, the movement now became a real threat to white power.

The youthful Panthers put forward revolutionary ideology and programs, promoted women to leadership positions, and trained militarily. Their uniforms of black leather jackets and berets were emulated by African people all over the United States and the world. They put revolutionary institutions on the ground, including free clinics and breakfast for children programs, sickle cell anemia testing centers, free shoe programs and freedom schools. The Panther movement quickly became a real base for revolutionary dual power. Huey Newton stated that,

Black Power is really people's power. The Black Panther Program, Panther Power as we call it, will implement this people's power. We have respect for all of humanity and we realize that the people should rule and determine their destiny....To have Black Power doesn't humble or subjugate anyone to slavery or oppression. Black Power is giving power to people who have not had power to determine their destiny. This is regardless of color. The Vietnamese say Viet Nam should be able to determine its own destiny. Power to the Vietnamese people....We in the black colony in America want to be able to have power over our destiny and that's Black Power.[107]

Besides the Black Panther Party, other similar revolutionary organizations rose up out of this period. These included the Southern-based Junta of Militant Organizations (JOMO), led by Omali Yeshitela (then known as Joseph Waller), then a SNCC organizer based in St. Petersburg, Florida. The introduction to the pamphlet "Social Justice and Economic Development for the African Community: Why I Became a Revolutionary," by Omali Yeshitela tells of his early introduction to the struggle of African people:

On December 26, 1966, 25 year old Joseph Waller led a group of young African people into the City Hall of St. Petersburg, Florida. Without uttering a word, Waller ripped down an offensive, demeaning, racist mural that had hung for years on the first landing of the stairs in full view of every visitor to the building.

Depicting African people in vicious caricature playing musical instruments while white people partied on the beach, the mural made a clear statement. It revealed the subservient position that African people were forced to have in this Florida town built on tourism and retirement industries catering to white people.[108]

Yeshitela's actions sparked the Southern Black Power movement. For tearing down the mural, Yeshitela was charged with 11 counts and sentenced to five years in prison. He became the undisputed leader of African people in Florida and much of the South. Spending most of the late '60s in and out of prison as a result of the mural conviction, Yeshitela formed the Junta of Militant Organizations (JOMO) from behind bars in 1966. JOMO was a militant working class organization similar to the Black Panther Party. It also chose the Black Panther as its symbol—a symbol that had been initiated originally by the Lowndes County Freedom Organization that SNCC had formed in Alabama in 1964. Yeshitela's JOMO was the root of today's Uhuru Movement.

Black is Beautiful

As the 1960s drew to a close, white America was reeling from the explosion of the Black Power Movement, and the victories of the Vietnamese people against the U.S. Army. Black Power was on everyone's lips and the stunning new generation of African revolutionaries set the tone for everything from internationalism and anti-imperialism to popular soul music, dance and fashion. James Brown's song with the words "Say it loud; I'm black and I'm proud" reverberated across the United States. Even the conservative *Life*, *Time* and *Newsweek* magazines shouted "Black is Beautiful" from their covers.

Despite the deadly U.S. government counterinsurgent retaliation against the movement that was to come, African people would never again be pushed back to a former position of expected servility to white people. The white population now had to pay a price in blood on the streets of America for 400 years of unspeakable violence against African people. A page had turned in U.S. history, and many long held white assumptions were permanently shattered. Omali Yeshitela summed up the impact of the '60s:

> The consequences of raising the Black Power slogan transformed everything. It immediately separated from the concept of civil rights and the idea that the solution was to integrate into America. Instead it put the struggle on an anti-colonial plane....Now we were saying we're not trying to integrate—we want our own power. We want Black Power!

> You walked down to the corner and all the young bloods who were never interested in the movement before knew what Black Power meant. You saw people struggling to acquire it all over the country.

> People began to fight back. It took the struggle away from that nonviolent "love your enemy" stuff.

> The Black Power demand transformed things almost overnight. All over the world, African people were chanting "Black Power."[109]

Overturning the Culture of Violence

1. Omali Yeshitela, 1987, *The Road to Socialism is Painted Black: Selected Theoretical Works* (Oakland: Burning Spear Publications), p. 13.
2. William Morris, ed., 1982, *The American Heritage Dictionary: Second College Edition* (Boston: Houghton Mifflin Company), p. 1462.
3. Alfred W. McCoy, 1991, *The Politics of Heroin: CIA Complicity in the Global Drug Trade* (New York: Lawrence Hill Books), p. 110.
4. Robert A. Hill and Barbara Bair, eds., 1987, *Marcus Garvey: Life and Lessons* (Berkeley: University of California Press), p. 119-139.
5. Dee Brown, 1971, *Bury My Heart at Wounded Knee: An Indian History of the American West* (New York: Holt, Rinehart & Winston), p. 444.
6. Same as above, p. 445.
7. Howard Zinn, 1995, *A People's History of the United States: 1492- Present* (New York: Harper Perennial), p. 290.
8. Ward Churchill, 1997, *A Little Matter of Genocide: Holocaust and Denial in the Americas: 1492-Present* (San Francisco: City Lights Books), pp. 129-130.
9. Harold Cruse, 1971, *The Crisis of the Negro Intellectual: From Its Origins to the Present* (New York: William Morrow & Company, Inc.), p. 496.
10. Same as above, p. 52.
11. Same as above, p. 483.
12. Diane Roberts, December 6, 1999, "Jews' Southern roots run deep," *St. Petersburg Times*.
13. Zinn, p. 291.
14. Same as above, p. 292.
15. Same as above, pp. 302-305.
16. Alan Nevins and Henry Steele Commager with Jeffrey Morris, 1986, *A Pocket History of the United States* (New York: Washington Square Press), p. 365.
17. Zinn, p. 296.
18. Same as above, p. 308.
19. William L. Patterson, ed., 1971, *We Charge Genocide: The Crime of Government Against the Negro People* (New York: International Publishers), p. 26.
20. Zinn, p. 311.
21. Same as above.
22. Same as above, p. 310.
23. Nevins and Commager, p. 372.
24. Fran Alexander, ed., 1988, *Oxford Encyclopedia of World History* (New York: Oxford University Press Inc.), p. 575.
25. Joanne Grant, ed., 1968, *Black Protest: History, Documents & Analysis 1619 to Present* (New York: Fawcett Premier), p. 154.
26. Ted Vincent, 1988, *Black Power & the Garvey Movement* (Oakland: Nzinga Publishing House), p. 56-57.
27. Herbert Shapiro, 1988, *White Violence and Black Response: From Reconstruction to Montgomery* (Amherst: The University of Massachusetts Press), p. 176.
28. Same as above, p. 146.
29. Same as above, pp. 145-146.
30. Same as above, p. 147.
31. Vincent, p. 56.
32. Shapiro, pp. 150-151.
33. Same as above, p. 151.
34. Mike Royko, 1971, *Boss, Richard J. Daley of Chicago.*(New York: E.P. Dutton & Co.), pp. 36-38.
35. March 17, 1996, *Chicago Sun Times*.
36. Vincent, p. 49.
37. Shapiro, p. 150.

38. Philip S. Foner, 1976, *Organized Labor & the Black Worker 1619-1973* (New York: International Publishers), p. 145.

39. Shapiro, p. 183.

40. Same as above, p. 185.

41. "Florida remembers mob terror of 1923," January 29, 1994, *San Francisco Chronicle*.

42. Vincent, p. 8.

43. Same as above, p. 100.

44. Same as above, p. 27.

45. Same as above, pp. 162-163.

46. Same as above.

47. Same as above, p. 5-6.

48. Bernard B. Fall, ed., 1968, *Ho Chi Minh On Revolution: Selected Writings, 1920-66* (New York: The New American Library, Inc.), p. 51.

49. Vincent, p. 7.

50. J. Sakai, 1983, *The Mythology of the White Proletariat: A Short Course In Understanding Babylon* (Chicago: Morningstar Press), p. 116.

51. Hill and Bair, eds., p. 196-298

52. Amy Jacques-Garvey, ed., 1971, *Philosophy & Opinions of Marcus Garvey* (New York: Atheneum), p. 10.

53. Kenneth O'Reilly, 1989, *"Racial Matters": The FBI's Secret File on Black America 1960-1972* (New York: The Free Press), p. 44.

54. Cruse, p. 135.

55. Shapiro, p. 208.

56. Hill and Bair, eds., pp. 296-298.

57. Vincent, p. 41.

58. Shapiro, p. 169.

59. O'Reilly, p. 44.

60. Cruse, p. 311, quoting Quentin Reynolds.

61. Yeshitela, *Road to Socialism*, p. 109.

62. Sakai, p. 76.

63. Shapiro, p. 206.

64. Sakai, p. 84, quoting Carey McWilliams.

65. Rodolfo Acuña, 1988, *Occupied America: A History of Chicanos* (New York: Harper Collins Publishers), p. 199.

66. Same as above, p. 209.

67. Zinn, p. 410.

68. Shapiro, p. 306.

69. Same as above, p. 307.

70. Same as above, p. 308

71. Foner, *Organized Labor*, p. 241.

72. Same as above, p. 265.

73. Robert C. Twombly, 1971, *Blacks in White America Since 1865* (New York: David McKay Company, Inc.), p. 305.

74. Sakai, p. 128.

75. Same as above, p. 129.

76. Zinn, p. 442.

77. Same as above.

78. Clayborne Carson, 1981, *In Struggle: SNCC and the Black Awakening of the 1960's* (Massachusetts: Harvard University Press), p. 64.

79. Omali Yeshitela, 1997, "The Dialectics of Black Revolution: The Struggle to Defeat the Counterinsurgency in the U.S." (Oakland: Burning Spear Uhuru Publications), pp. 12-14.

80. James Forman, 1985, *The Making of Black Revolutionaries* (Washington, D.C.: Open Hand Publishing, Inc.), p. 166.

81. Zinn, p. 444.

82. Same as above, p. 145.

83. Omali Yeshitela, 1991, *Izwe Lethu i Afrika! (Africa is Our Land)* (Oakland: Burning Spear Publications), p. 7.

84. Forman, p. 372.

85. Juan Williams, 1987, *Eyes on the Prize: America's Civil Rights Years, 1954-1965* (New York: Viking Penguin, Inc.), p. 231.

86. Teodori Massimo, 1968, *The New Left: A Documentary History* (New York: Viking Penguin, Inc.), p. 164.

87. Yeshitela, "Dialectics of Black Revolution", p. 19.

88. Clayborne Carson, 1991, *Malcolm X: The FBI File* (New York: Carroll & Graf Publishers, Inc.), p. 24.

89. George Breitman, ed., 1990, *Malcolm X Speaks: Selected Speeches and Statements* (New York: Grove Weidenfeld), pp. 31-39.

90. Yeshitela, *Izwe Lethu*, p. 6.

91. Carson, *In Struggle*, p. 135.

92. Ward Churchill and Jim Vander Wall, *The Cointelpro Papers: Documents from the FBI's Secret Wars Against Dissent in the United States* (Boston: South End Press), Chapter 6.

93. Carson, *Malcolm X*, pp. 1-30.

94. Omali Yeshitela, 1982, *Not One Step Backwards!: The Black Liberation Movement from 1971 to 1982* (Oakland: Burning Spear Publications), p. 36.

95. Forman, p. 457.

96. Yeshitela, *Izwe Lethu*, pp. 7-9.

97. Zinn, pp. 451-452.

98. Churchill and Vander Wall.

99. Carson, *In Struggle*, p. 197.

100. Same as above.

101. Forman, p. 452.

102. Same as above, p. 458.

103. Kirkpatrick Sale, 1973, *SDS* (New York: Random House), p. 277.

104. Same as above, p. 276.

105. Same as above.

106. Yeshitela, *Izwe Lethu*, pp. 12-13.

107. Philip S. Foner, ed., 1970, *The Black Panthers Speak: The Manifesto of the Party: The First Complete Documentary Record of the Panthers' Program* (Philadelphia: J.B. Lippincott Company), p. 61.

108. Omali Yeshitela, 1997, "Social Justice and Economic Development for the African Community: Why I Became a Revolutionary" (Oakland: Burning Spear Uhuru Publications), p. i.

109. Yeshitela, "Dialectics of Black Revolution," p. 18.

The U.S. counterinsurgency against the Vietnamese people and their liberation movement during the 1960s.
Credit: Bettmen/Corbis.

The U.S. counterinsurgency against the Black Liberation Movement in the U.S. during the 1960s: the brutal assassination of beloved Black Panther leader, Fred Hampton, 1969.

4

Counterinsurgency:

War Against Oppressed Peoples

The people rose up to lead our own movement in the '60s and that movement was crushed. We were tired of seeing our mamas going out to take care of somebody else's children while our own children went without anybody being able to take care of them...People just wanted to be free. That's all Africans wanted. We had youngsters like Fred Hampton who was just 21 years old when he was murdered. We are talking about children like Huey P. Newton was at the time...We are talking about young men like Malcolm X who stood so tall and showed us the full stature that the African can assume...

— Omali Yeshitela

The Universal Declaration of Human Rights is an inspiring document, upholding the ideals of a world without oppression and slavery, war and genocide. The declaration affirms that the "recognition of the inherent dignity and of the equal and inalienable rights of all members of the human family is the foundation of freedom, justice and peace in the world."[1]

In the mid-1960s, with pressure from the emerging national liberation movements around the world, the United Nations passed the International Covenant on Civil and Political Rights. The covenant reflects the optimistic spirit of the period when revolution against imperialism was the main trend across the Earth.

The articles of the covenant assert that, "All peoples have the right of self-determination. By virtue of that right they freely determine their political status and freely pursue their economic, social and cultural development. All peoples may, for their own ends, freely dispose of their natural wealth and resources....In no case may a people be deprived of its own means of subsistence."[2]

As Chairman Omali simply said of the right to self-determination for oppressed peoples: "Anything less goes against human nature."[3]

The will of oppressed peoples of the world to express their cultures, to uphold their histories, to forge their destinies and enjoy their resources in amicable relationship with others on this planet—this is the driving force of the movements for national liberation.

To live in dignity, without interference, subjection, violence and exploitation is the inalienable right of all members of the human family and the only basis of peace on Earth. Isn't this a world that all rational people would wish to inhabit?

VICTORY AND COUNTEROFFENSIVE

During the 1960s, the peoples of Viet Nam, Cuba, Angola, Mozambique, Namibia, as well as African and others inside this country and internationally, courageously challenged U.S. imperialism for their freedom. Despite the fact that some of these revolutions later succumbed to years of both covert and open assault by the United States, these struggles for self-determination have irretrievably weakened imperialist power. As a result, there are no more days of unchallenged world "peace" brought about by the "big stick" of American repression.

The confident swaggering American style is now broken, even as imperialist aggression continues to terrorize the majority of humanity. For many years now, the victories of oppressed peoples have weakened imperialism, and a weakened imperialism has lashed out in counterattack. It has been this struggle between the oppressed and the oppressors that characterized both the foreign and domestic policies of twentieth century America.

The brutality of the reactionary backlash of imperialism has no limits. White power strikes with genocidal blows from every possible front—military, political, ideological, cultural and economic. The United States mutilates babies, bombs civilians, abrogates oppressed people's rights, slanders their beliefs, suppresses their

235

cultures and starves them to death—all in the name of defending "U.S. national interests."

Such a posture by the United States is one of frailty, however, and hatred for Yankee imperialism around the world is unbounded. If a nuclear bomb annihilated the United States today we can be sure, there would be dancing in the streets throughout Africa, Asia and Latin America tomorrow.

One of the defining blows to U.S. imperial power in the '60s was the victory of the Vietnamese revolution. Both the United States and France are still licking their wounds from resounding defeats by this courageous Southeast Asian people who had endured more than a hundred years of devastating French colonialism. After routing the French aggressors in 1954, the war-weary Vietnamese people, on the brink of starvation, rose to fight for another two decades, vanquishing the U.S. colonial aggressors as well.

Because of the U.S. imperialist debacle at the hands of the Vietnamese people, American pundits still talk about the "Viet Nam syndrome," a widespread psychological malady in the United States that prevails even today. Omali Yeshitela defines this disorder as the fear of waging an aggression where it is likely that U.S. soldiers would be sent home in body bags. Today, the United States relies on bombs and infrared technology to make nighttime air attacks on civilian populations. Notably, it has yet to launch another ground war in which U.S. troops must face an adversary eye to eye.

In 1985, Gabriel Kolko summed up in his book *Anatomy of a War: Viet Nam, the United States and the Modern Experience*:

> All that the United States has the ability to accomplish today is to impose immeasurable suffering on people whose fates its arms and money cannot control. To do so once more would also demand from the American public a price it eventually refused to pay in Viet Nam and is even less likely to give willingly in the future.[4]

Counterinsurgency: War Against Oppressed Peoples

The United States is still reeling from its *internal* challenges of the 1960s as well. During that time, the struggle for self-determination raged on the streets of every city and town. For this reason, the pangs of another affliction, the "Black Power syndrome," are still felt inside the belly of the beast today. The central focus of the U.S. domestic policy is currently based on fears that a black liberation movement would rebuild in this country. White power continues to be haunted by a struggle in which 25 percent of the African population at large, and 43 percent of the African population under the age of 22 considered themselves part of the Black Revolution, as was the case in the late 1960s.[5]

At home and abroad, the U.S. is trying to put the genie back into the bottle, to re-enchain the mass of humanity, to stomp oppressed peoples into submission—to recreate the days of easy imperialist peace. Internationally, U.S. war generally takes place against the so-called "Third World" of Africa, Asia and Latin America. Inside the United States, the domestic policy targets the same victims: African, Mexican, indigenous and Puerto Rican peoples.

The methods the United States uses against subjected peoples everywhere are strikingly similar: police containment, chemical warfare, massive imprisonment, economic embargo, deepening exploitation and criminalization. Genocide. Whether at home or abroad, these policies of suppression are enthusiastically supported by most of us, the white population, nearly across the board—liberals and right-wingers alike. But, despite the popularity of U.S. aggression, the same dialectic is at work. The suppression of whole peoples promotes fear, vigilance and the need for white power to watch its back at all times.

Ahead of us, in the twenty-first century, lies the unfolding human drama, still to be completed. Imperialism is in crisis. It is dying, but not yet dead. Hundreds of millions of imperialism's subjects refuse to lie down quietly inside the pedestal of white power any longer. An objective look at the world informs us that eventually the oppressed peoples of the Earth will indeed tilt the scales onto the side of victory for the great plurality of humanity, and the white power capitalist system will be destroyed.

This inexorable march towards the liberation of oppressed nations will, without doubt, one day fulfill its historic destiny. As African people say, "What goes around comes around." It's just a matter of time. For now, the struggle between the oppressed and the oppressor continues.

PRIMARY U.S. POLICY

For nearly three decades, the African People's Socialist Party has probed relentlessly the nature of the harsh conditions facing African people in the United States in the years since the Black Revolution of the '60s. Many of those who participated in that movement never knew what hit them. They were either shot down in the blink of an eye, framed up and imprisoned by a web of lies and deceptions, or forced to back down politically, perhaps without even realizing it. But with an organization based in the African working class and a clear political theory, the African People's Socialist Party has been able to survive and sum up the government's military assault in the '60s.

Omali Yeshitela himself was imprisoned for two and a half years. His sentence resulted from government repression following his removal of a racist painting that hung in the lobby of the City Hall in St. Petersburg, Florida, his hometown. While in prison in the late '60s, he formed the Junta of Militant Organizations (JOMO), an organization with similarities to the Black Panther Party (BPP).

In 1972, JOMO and two other African organizations merged to form the African People's Socialist Party. Over the years, Yeshitela and the APSP have developed theoretically, politically and organizationally. Yeshitela has demonstrated a brilliant ability to rise to the demands of each new period of struggle. Despite continued government attack and the changing political climate brought about by white power's repression, he and the APSP have survived.

From the vantage point of seasoned veterans in the struggle, the Party was able to conclude that the Black Revolution didn't just die out or lose popularity. It was attacked with the full force of the U.S. State. It was crushed by what the military calls *counterinsurgency*, a war waged against colonized peoples who are rising up for their freedom against U.S. imperialism.

Since the 1960s, counterinsurgency—also known as "unconventional" warfare—has been the main focus of the U.S. military. Indeed, the United States no longer anticipates conventional war, in which it would face fully equipped European armies on large, open battlefields. The U.S. Marines are now trained to land in the mountains of Mexico, the rain forests of the Congo or the streets of inner city Oakland, as the "Urban Warrior" mock invasions of predominately African U.S. cities in 1999 showed.[6]

One source uses the military's own definition in exposing the all-encompassing nature of counterinsurgency:

> Rather than acknowledge the counterrevolutionary nature of its operations in the Third World, the Pentagon has chosen the clinical term "counterinsurgency" to describe its response to movements for national liberation...[7]

> The official Pentagon definition of counterinsurgency, as provided in the *Dictionary of United States Military Terms for Joint Usage,* is: "Those military, paramilitary, political, economic, psychological, and civic actions taken by a government to defeat subversive insurgency." Insurgency is defined as a "condition resulting from a revolt or insurrection against a constituted government that falls short of civil war."[8]

Robert Taber in *The War of the Flea: How Guerrilla Fighters Could Win the World!* puts counterinsurgency in a more human context:

> When we speak of the guerrilla fighter we are speaking of the *political partisan*, an armed civilian whose principal weapon is not his rifle or his machete but his relationship to the community, the nation, in and for which he fights.
>
> Insurgency, or guerrilla war, is the agency of radical social or political change; it is the face and the right arm of revolution. Counterinsurgency is a form of counter-revolution, the process by which revolution is resisted. The two are opposite sides of the coin, and it will not do to confuse them or their agents, despite superficial similarities.[9]

In real terms, insurgency is simply the movement of colonized peoples to free themselves from an oppressive, alien power. It is the fight for self-determination and control of their destinies and resources. Insurgency—resistance to oppression—is as old as the parasitic system of capitalism itself; and so is imperialist counterinsurgency. But not until the United States faced anti-colonial revolution around the world and inside its own borders was counterinsurgency elevated to the primary U.S. military policy both domestically and internationally.

"EXPOSE, DISRUPT, NEUTRALIZE"

Chairman Omali Yeshitela emphasizes:

> In the 1960s, we saw black revolution in this country. I mean that literally....There was real revolution that came close to overturning U.S. imperialism...African people, starting from 1954 or '55, and lasting through 1969 or '70, fought U.S. imperialism tooth and nail almost by

ourselves. There was not a day in more than 14 years in this country that they had peace from social instability caused by the true pedestal upon which this whole rotten edifice rests.[10]

The U.S. government was very clear that the center of revolution inside the United States was African, thus the government was intent on destroying the Black Power Movement. FBI Director J. Edgar Hoover, who had launched his career some 40 years earlier in attacking the Garvey Movement, went on record as saying that the Black Panther Party represented the "greatest threat to the internal security of the country."[11]

No serious long-term challenge to the status quo was found emanating from the rowdy, anarchistic white students who were demonstrating on college campuses. The government knew that once the revolutionary articulations of Black Power were silenced, white students would return to their cozy lives in the suburbs.

Without the leadership of the Black Revolution, white radicals could be diverted easily. Psychedelic drugs, lifestyle issues and the fear that the price of their activism might be their lives—as it was for African militants—would take care of white anti-imperialism in the 1960s. And so it was that only a few years into the '70s, white radicals had "turned on, tuned in and dropped out," or simply cut their hair, bathed and returned to college.

By 1965, the government had already assassinated Malcolm X, just as he was building a militant organization of African workers. In 1966, the government used the FBI to coordinate an official counterinsurgent program against the Black Revolution that was as covert, deadly and sophisticated as anything it was doing against revolutionary movements in Africa, Asia or South America. That program was called COINTELPRO, an acronym for counterintelligence program. It was headed up by FBI operative William Sullivan, under J. Edgar Hoover's tutelage.

Revealed in the 1970s through documents released by the Freedom of Information Act, the goals of COINTELPRO were precise and succinct: "expose, disrupt, misdirect, discredit, or otherwise neutralize the activities of black nationalist, hate-type organizations and groupings, their leadership, spokesmen, membership and supporters...."[12]

The meaning of "neutralize" in U.S. counterinsurgency-speak needs no explanation. Typically, groups that were standing up for the aspirations of impoverished and oppressed African people were labeled "hate-type organizations."

The stated objectives of COINTELPRO were to:

> ...prevent the coalition of militant black nationalist groups; prevent the rise of a messiah who could unify and electrify the militant black nationalist movement; prevent violence on the part of black nationalist groups; prevent militant black nationalist groups and leaders from gaining respectability; and prevent the long-range growth of militant black nationalist organizations especially among the youth.[13]

COINTELPRO documents speculated about who such a "black messiah" might be, noting that:

> Malcomb [sic] X might have been such a "messiah;" he is the martyr of the movement today. Martin Luther King, Stokely Carmichael and Elijah Muhammed all aspire to this position. Elijah Muhammed is less of a threat because of his age. King could be a very real contender for this position should he abandon his supposed "obedience" to "white liberal doctrines" [nonviolence] and embrace black nationalism.[14]

Martin Luther King was, in fact, killed in 1968 almost immediately after he began to "abandon his allegiance to white liberal doctrines."

With the cry of "Black Power" raised in 1966, the African masses had begun to articulate their own aims for political power, rather than look to those expressed by the liberal black petty bourgeoisie and the white liberals for integration. African workers seized control of a movement that people like King had tried to limit to "civil rights." As Omali Yeshitela tells us, the legitimacy of the preachers and black middle class had declined in the eyes of an African working class intent on gaining power in its own hands.

In 1965 King, with his pacifist message, had been booed off the stage by African people at a rally in Will Rogers Park during the Watts rebellion in Los Angeles. Because of this, King was pulled toward the demands of the revolutionary African working class, a move necessary if he was to maintain his position of leadership and, indeed, his place in history.

Martin Luther King was shot down in Memphis, Tennessee on April 4, 1968, as he was about to address a militant sanitation workers strike. This march represented a turning point in his political career: he had begun to support the demands of African workers on their own terms, as opposed to nonviolent civil rights marches that upheld the agenda of the black middle class.

Prior to his assassination, King had spoken at Riverside Church in New York where he questioned whether he could continue to advocate nonviolence for African people in face of the violence being perpetrated by the U.S. government against the Vietnamese people. Fatefully, the prerequisite conditions for his "neutralization" under COINTELPRO had come about.

Ironically, King's assassination, which sparked a renewed wave of angry rebellions by African workers in city after city, helped to further galvanize African people towards the Black Revolution.

Thirty years later Coretta Scott King and her children filed a civil lawsuit in Memphis against Loyd Jowers after he claimed publicly that he had hired an unidentified killer to assassinate the civil rights leader. In June 1997, King's son, Dexter Scott King, declared in a televised interview that he and his family believed that James Earl Ray was not guilty of the murder of his father. He asserted that "President Lyndon B. Johnson must have been part of a military and governmental conspiracy to kill Rev. King."[15]

The King family filed the suit with the belief that it would expose that James Earl Ray was only a pawn in a larger conspiracy to murder Martin Luther King. In December 1999 a jury of six whites and six Africans ruled that the assassination "was not the work of James Earl Ray—a petty thief convicted of the murder—but the heinous product of a conspiracy masterminded and covered up by organized crime and by government agencies."

The jury found that Jowers, 73, who owned Jim's Grill a floor below the rooming house from which Ray allegedly shot King on April 4, 1968, helped "others, including government agencies" assassinate King and frame Ray. During his closing arguments, William Pepper, the lawyer for the King family, stated that "the U.S. Army had a sniper squad poised to shoot King if the Mafia operative failed. He said the FBI, CIA, Army intelligence and Memphis police helped to cover up the conspiracy."[16]

MURDERS, SURVEILLANCE AND FRAMEUPS

COINTELPRO went on to unleash a fury against the African Movement. In Oakland, California, 17 year old "Li'l" Bobby Hutton, a beloved young member of the Black Panther Party—he is said to be the Panther's first recruit—was shot down by the Oakland Police Department on April 6, 1968, just two days after the King's assassination. In 1969 alone, at least twenty-eight members of the Black Panther Party were killed by this undeclared war against the black community struggle for happiness and political independence. James Forman, former leader of the Student Nonviolent Coordinating Committee (SNCC) elaborates on the casualties in *The Making of Black Revolutionaries,*

> Fred Hampton, Huey P. Newton, Morton Sostre...are well-known names of black people victimized by the repression of the United States. In the case of H. Rap Brown, we can see the government at work with its full arsenal of tools for repression. Rap was kept under house arrest, not allowed to leave New York City, from 1967 to 1970. Then, in March of 1970, Rap was supposed to stand trial in Belair, Maryland, for his alleged crimes in Cambridge. Ralph Featherstone and 'Che' Payne Robinson, as staff members of the Black Economic Development Conference, went to Belair to make arrangements for Rap's arrival. They were both killed in their car by an explosion of dynamite, almost surely planted by some government agency....
>
> There are also many other lesser known people, such as the five brothers murdered in Augusta and two more in Jackson, Mississippi; Carl Hampton killed in Houston; the De Soto brothers in Chicago; Brother Melvin X in California. There is Lee Otis Johnson, a SNCC political activist in Texas now serving thirty years on trumped-up charges of possession of marijuana; Donald P. Stone and ten other SNCC people serving three years for allegedly destroying government property during an anti-war demonstration in Atlanta.[17]

In addition to assassination, COINTELPRO tactics included eavesdropping, attacks on movement offices, frame-ups and false imprisonment. Geronimo Pratt, set up by the FBI, was imprisoned for more than 20 years and only released by political pressure in 1997. Sundiata Acoli, a Black Panther from New Jersey, is still incarcerated today. U.S. government agents and informants were planted in organizations. Disinformation, lies and slander were disseminated. Evidence was fabricated and letters from one group to another were forged with inflammatory contents.

In 1967, the FBI launched the Ghetto Informant Program that enlisted a "grass roots network" of snitches in the African community. These included employees and owners of taverns and liquor stores, drugstores and pawnshops, barber shops, apartment building janitors, etc. By the summer of 1968 more than 3,000 people had been recruited to these tasks.[18]

YOUNG FRED HAMPTON ASSASSINATED

As the '60s came to a close, the rampant COINTELPRO terrorist tactics continued to horrify, but no longer surprise, African people. One of the most brutal government counterinsurgent assaults was the December 4, 1969 premeditated government murder of brilliant young Fred Hampton, Chairman of the Chicago branch of the Black Panther Party.

Hampton's death squad-style execution is the only assassination of a Black Power Movement leader that the U.S. government has actually acknowledged to date. This admission came about as a result of a lawsuit against the government filed years later by the families of Hampton and Mark Clark, a Panther leader from Peoria, who was also killed in the assault. Documents exposed during the trial show that the Chicago Police reported their plans to assassinate Hampton in a memo directly to J. Edgar Hoover on the day before the attack.[19]

Only 21 years old at the time of his assassination, Fred Hampton was considered one of the rising national leaders of the Black Panther Party. A powerful orator, Hampton had built the strongest on-the-ground "survival" programs of any Panther organization in the country. The thriving free breakfast for children program fed more than 3,000 meals weekly in Chicago. Under Chairman Fred's leadership, the Chicago Panthers had organized doctors and other medical workers to donate their time to a successful free clinic that began to put control of health care into the hands of African workers.

Loved by the African community—Hampton's memory is still deeply cherished by African people in Chicago today—Chairman Fred was known for his ability to unite all sectors of black people, including members of rival "gangs." It is possible that Chairman Fred Hampton also may have begun to fit the U.S. government's profile for a new black "messiah."

By late 1969, every other major Panther leader around the country was either framed up and in prison, awaiting trial, in exile or already assassinated. Fred's leadership abilities and his capacity to strengthen the organization must have been apparent to the FBI.[20] Clearly the U.S. government wanted him "neutralized." Fred's death effectively broke the back of the Illinois Black Panther Party, and ultimately the entire organization.

Fred Hampton seemed to anticipate his own assassination, and his famous statement is still quoted by the movement today: "You can kill a revolutionary, but you can't kill the revolution." Nevertheless, no one was prepared for the exceptionally brutal assault that was waged against him and his comrades.

In the bitter, cold early morning hours of December 4, 1969, an army of police descended on Hampton's tiny apartment on Monroe Street on Chicago's West Side in the pre-planned assault. A number of Panthers from around the state, in Chicago for a Party conference, had spent the night and were sleeping in the pre-dawn hours when the police invaded. Hampton had been drugged by the cowardly FBI agent provocateur William O'Neal, who had put Seconal into Kool Aid that Fred drank before he went to bed. O'Neal had also earlier sketched the floor plan of Fred's apartment for the police.*

Ward Churchill describes the vicious attack in his book *Agents of Repression:*

> At about 4:30 [the police] launched an outright assault upon the Panthers, and promptly shot Mark Clark point blank in the chest with a .30 caliber M-1 carbine. Clark, who had apparently nodded off in a front room with a shotgun across his lap, barely had time to stand up before being killed more-or-less instantly. His reflexive response to being shot discharged the shotgun. It was the only round fired by the Panthers during the raid.
>
> [Chicago Policeman "Gloves"] Davis immediately proceeded to pump a bullet into eighteen-year-old Brenda Harris, who was lying (unarmed) in a front room bed; [CPD Daniel] Groth hit her with a second round. [CPD Joseph] Gorman, joined by Davis and his carbine, then began spraying automatic fire from his .45 caliber Thompson submachinegun through a wall into the bedrooms. All forty-two shots fired by the pair converged on the head of Hampton's bed, pinpointed in O'Neal's floor plan; one of the slugs fired by Davis, struck Hampton in the left shoulder, seriously wounding him as he slept. While this was going on, the second subteam, firing as they came, crashed through the back door. This was followed by a brief lull in the shooting, during which [CPD Edward] Carmody and another (unidentified) raider entered Hampton's bedroom. They were heard to have

---

* O'Neal later confessed to his role and, in 1990, committed suicide by running in front of a speeding car on Lakeshore Drive in Chicago.

the following exchange: "That's Fred Hampton...Is he dead?...Bring him out. He's barely alive; he'll make it."

Two shots were then heard, both of which were fired point blank into Hampton's head as he lay prone, followed by Carmody's voice stating, "He's good and dead now." The chairman's body was then dragged by the wrist from the bed to the bedroom doorway, and left lying in a spreading pool of blood.[21]

Fred Hampton's wife, Akua Njeri (then known as Deborah Johnson) miraculously survived that attack. A remarkable and courageous woman, Njeri was eight and half months pregnant as she slept beside her husband when the assault began. Their son, Fred Hampton Jr., was born three weeks later. Unlike others who survived the '60s, Njeri has never ceased to struggle for the freedom of African people. Today, Akua Njeri is the national President of the National People's Democratic Uhuru Movement, an organization dedicated to exposing and defeating the counterinsurgency that killed her husband and that plagues the African community today.

Akua Njeri expresses in her own moving words the trauma of the 1969 assault that killed her husband and Mark Clark and wounded her comrades:

> I saw sparks of light going across the entranceway to the rear bedroom. I saw what appeared to be a million pigs converge at the door. Fred Hampton raised his head up real slowly. It was the slowest movement I've ever seen from Fred Hampton. He had clearly been drugged. He raised his head and laid it back down in that same position and closed his eyes. The mattress vibrated from bullets going into it. The plaster was flying...
>
> I was very pregnant. That was December 4th. Our son was born December 29....One of the pigs pulled open my

robe and said, "What do you know. We have a broad here." He grabbed me by the hair and flung me into the kitchen area. I stayed in the kitchen area and the shooting continued.

A voice that was unfamiliar to me said, "He's barely alive. He'll barely make it." Some more single shots rang out and a voice again unfamiliar to me said, "He's good and dead now." I knew they were talking about Fred Hampton. I felt that at that point they had murdered Fred Hampton.[22]

Despite the terror she lived through, Njeri raised her son, Fred Hampton Jr., to continue in the struggle for which his father had given his life. Fred Jr. took up the mantle of his father's legacy and became a local organizer for the Uhuru Movement. Manifesting many of the same leadership qualities of his father, Fred Hampton Jr. was himself sent to prison by a government frame-up in 1993.

The cold blooded murder of Fred Hampton went without response from the very active white left and "anti-imperialists" of the time.

WAR AGAINST BLACK POWER

The COINTELPRO assault on the movement of African people in the '60s involved many—perhaps all—agencies of the U.S. government as well as many sectors of white society. Omali Yeshitela gives a sense of the depth of this counteroffensive:

The U.S. counterinsurgency against the U.S.-based African Revolution was extensive. Several U.S. presidents and lesser political figures, from governors, senators and local mayors, were involved as well as various agencies and levels of the U.S. government including federal and state legislatures. This also included the draft board, the Internal Revenue Service, judges, grand juries, local military police organizations and all branches of the U.S. military and the Central Intelligence Agency, as well as the National Security Agency.

University, college and high school campus officials, prison wardens and jail officials as well as nearly all of the white media and much of the African primitive petty bourgeoisie-owned media became a part of the counterinsurgency against our movement, along with the general population of generally hostile North Americans, or white people. This last group included religious representatives of almost very belief and denomination.[23]

By late 1969, little more than three years after the founding of the Black Panther Party in Oakland, California, COINTELPRO had effectively decimated the Black Revolution inside the United States. With Panther leaders murdered or in prison, Panther offices firebombed, black revolutionaries slandered, organizations divided by provocateurs, the goals of COINTELPRO had essentially been met.

Although the Black Panther Party as an organization would continue to exist for a few more years, the essence of the movement from deep within the heart of the African working class was shattered as the new decade dawned. African people were reeling from the defeat of their short-lived but magnificent movement—one that had posed the most significant internal challenge to U.S. imperialism ever.

The Black Panther Party had risen up out of the streets of the inner cities, attracting young and dazzling representatives of the African working class. For a moment, African workers and poor people had experienced a taste of power. The Black Panther Party was recognized by revolutionary and progressive forces throughout the world as the legitimate representative of the anti-colonial movement of African people inside the United States. Panther leaders had been welcomed to Cuba and Algeria. Later, Huey Newton was invited to Viet Nam where he was greeted as an unofficial ambassador from African people in the United States.

It was the black movement of the 1960s that brought about every positive change of that era. The motion of African people ignited the massive anti-war movement among white people of the time. The Black Movement "brought white women out of the kitchen and white homosexuals out of the closet," as Omali Yeshitela says. The white women's and gay "liberation" movements borrowed revolutionary vocabulary and tactics from African people. Never facing the ravages of a COINTELPRO assault, however, the women's and gay movements survived and prospered as imperialism's loyal opposition—white rights movements struggling for an equal share of white power.

The Black Power Movement also inspired revolutionary aspirations among the Puerto Rican, Mexican and indigenous populations in the United States. The Puerto Rican Young Lords, American Indian Movement and the Mexican Brown Berets were examples of popular organizations that sprung up with revolutionary politics and platforms similar to that of the Black Panther Party.

ANTI-COLONIAL MOVEMENTS ATTACKED

As the black movement was being silenced, the United States moved to defeat the movements of other struggling colonized peoples within its borders as well.

Based in New York and Chicago, the Puerto Rican Young Lords mobilized their people on the mainland United States to demand independence for the island colony. Led by Enrique "Cha Cha" Jimenez, the Young Lords, like the Panthers whom they emulated, were targeted by COINTELPRO. The government slapped Jimenez with a spurious kidnapping charge, of which he was convicted in 1969. He was later acquitted on appeal after "government misconduct" was found to be involved in the charge.[24]

Throughout the Southwest, Mexican workers were organizing for their liberation and the return of their stolen land. This new generation of urban, proletarianized Mexican people inside the United States called themselves Chicanos. Like the African working class and other colonized peoples in this country, the masses of Mexican workers had always been terrorized at the hands of the government and white people alike. As Rodolfo Acuña tells us in *Occupied America*:

> The counterpart of the Black Panthers and the Puerto Rican Young Lords was the Brown Berets. In 1967 the Young Citizens for Community Action formed in East Los Angeles. The group was sponsored by an interfaith church organization. In time, the organization evolved from a community service club to an "alert patrol" that set as its goal the "defense" of the *barrio*.

COINTELPRO methods were used against the Brown Berets almost immediately. Acuña relates how the police and sheriff's deputies

> ...raided the Berets, infiltrated them, libeled and slandered them, and even encouraged countergroups to attack members. The objective was to destroy the Berets and to invalidate the membership in the eyes of the Anglo and Chicano communities.[25]

When the Mexican students of East Los Angeles organized school walkouts protesting the brutal colonial education conditions, members of the Brown Berets were targeted as "outside agitators." Thirteen Mexican people, including seven Brown Beret members were indicted by a grand jury for the walkouts. "The defendants appealed and the case was declared unconstitutional, but only after years of legal harassment."[26]

Despite the government repression, masses of Mexican people organized under the demand for liberation. Like the Panthers, the Brown Berets dealt with the basic issues of the people, revolving around food, housing, unemployment and education in the *barrios*.

On August 29, 1970, more than 10,000 Mexican people marched in Los Angeles in opposition to the U.S. war against the Vietnamese people. The militant but peaceful march, sponsored by the Chicano Moratorium, united around slogans such as *"Raza sí, guerra no!"* A squad of 1,200 police occupied the park, attacking the demonstrators with teargas and guns. The police killed three people, including a 15 year old youth and the respected journalist Rubén Salazar.

> Mass arrests followed. Prisoners were kept chained in fours, in two buses at the East Los Angeles substation. Sheriff's deputies did not allow them to drink water or go to the bathroom for about four hours. Deputies maced the chained prisoners at least three times... [and] man-handled a pregnant girl.[27]

As African, Mexican and Puerto Rican people were building their anti-colonial movements, the indigenous people were rising up in a renewed fight for their land and self-determination. Struggles were taking place around the country—led in Florida by the Seminoles, in New York by the Mohawks and in Arizona by the Yaquis, to name a few.[28]

In the early '70s, a powerful defense erupted once again in the Black Hills region that indigenous people had so long fought to protect from seizure by white power. This struggle centered on Wounded Knee, the sight of the slaughter of Big Foot and his Minneconjou people by the U.S. army in 1890. It is now part of the Pine Ridge Reservation in South Dakota. This is the area that was won by the victory of Red Cloud in 1869 and defended by the crushing defeat of General Armstrong Custer in 1876 at the hands of the indigenous military leaders known as Crazy Horse and Sitting Bull. These Lakota lands have always been sacred to the Indian people.

An account by Ward Churchill explains the indigenous movement that emerged in the late '60s: "[P]aralleling the SNCC demands for Black Power articulated by Stokely Carmichael and H. Rap Brown, [the] National Indian Youth Council (NIYC) pushed 'Red Power' through its newspaper, *ABC: Americans Before Columbus.*"

In 1968 the American Indian Movement (AIM) was born, "self-consciously patterned after the Black Panther Party's community self-defense model pioneered by Huey P. Newton and Bobby Seale two years previously in Oakland."[29]

In January 1972, a 51-year-old Oglala man, Raymond Yellow Thunder, was murdered in typical white-man style in Gordon, Nebraska. Two white men drove "the Indian around in their car, beat him, abused him, tortured him, and threw him naked into an American Legion dance hall where he was further taunted. He was found dead a week later in the trunk of a car." Angry and this time organized, indigenous people rose up. AIM leaders stated that "if justice is not immediately forthcoming, we'll be back to take Gordon *off the* map."[30]

In response to the growing militancy on Pine Ridge, as well as the fact that uranium was found on the reservation about the same time, the U.S. government once again raided the area. This was no small operation. In February 1973, writes Ward Churchill,

> [T]he Pentagon invaded Wounded Knee with 17 armored personnel carriers, 130,000 rounds of M-16 ammunition, 41,000 rounds of M-1 ammunition, 24,000 flares, 12 M-79 grenade launchers, 600 cases of C-S gas, 100 rounds of M-40 explosives, helicopters, Phantom jets, and personnel, all under the direction of General Alexander Haig.[31]

The Oglala people courageously fought the U.S. government for three years until 1976. During this period, 69 AIM members and supporters were killed by the armed FBI squads and more than 300 native people were wounded. The rate of political assassination on Pine Ridge during this three-year period was, according to Churchill, "almost equivalent to that in Chile during the three years after a military coup supported by the United States deposed and killed President Salvador Allende."[32]

Again the white left was silent.

SMASHING THE SPIRIT OF THE PEOPLE

The Black Power Movement was an electric current connecting the peoples of the world. The spirit of African internationalism, which Marcus Garvey had so effectively demonstrated 40 years earlier, once again united African people on the streets of Detroit and Chicago with their brothers and sisters throughout Africa and the diaspora.

This internationalism extended to all oppressed peoples struggling against colonialism, peasants in Bolivia, combatants in Viet Nam, workers in China, *campesinos* in Mexico. New leaders were embraced by millions as the people's heroes: Che Guevara, Fidel Castro, Ho Chi Minh, Mao Zedong, Kwame Nkrumah, Huey Newton, Patrice Lumumba.

The promise of Black Revolution ignited the spirit of African people everywhere. Those captured inside the belly of the monster had risen up in a movement so powerful that it shook the very foundations of a system that was the enemy of the peoples of the world. The children of the slaves, destitute sharecroppers, housing project residents, children of the ghettos raised on streets strewn with broken glass, walked tall in a struggle that sent shock waves throughout the world.

Grandfathers and toddlers, mothers and youth—the poorest, most slandered, most exploited people on the planet were suddenly the makers and movers of human destiny, the driving force behind world events. Their vision was self-determination in a world without oppressors and oppressed. Together, colonized peoples had the power to bring down the beast, which had kept the majority of humanity in bondage for so long.

Revolution is exuberant, transformational and optimistic. It fills people with the understanding of the infinite possibilities for the future. Revolution takes the moral high ground, creating the "New Man and New Woman" that Che described.

Revolution inspires people to actions and talents, courage and ingenuity they never knew they had. No task or goal is impossible; the revolution lets the oppressed find a way with only a "rifle, some sneakers and a bowl of rice" as Malcolm X said.[33] Revolution is the heady and confident power of the people.

Counterinsurgency, on the other hand, has no higher ideals. It does nothing more than protect an oppressive and dying status quo by smashing the people's movement and their spirit. It is embodied in the classic U.S. military statement: "We had to destroy the town in order to save it." One analyst discusses counterinsurgency:

> The purpose of the counter-revolutionary is negative and defensive. It is to restore order, to protect property, to preserve existing forms and interests by force of arms, where persuasion has already failed....[P]rimarily the counterinsurgent's task must be to destroy the revolution by destroying its promise—that means by proving militarily, that it cannot and will not succeed.
>
> That military victory against true guerrillas is possible seems doubtful on the basis of modern experience barring the use of methods approaching genocide...[34]

COINTELPRO, the counterinsurgency against the Black Revolution of the 60s, took place within this context of U.S. counterinsurgency against revolutionary upheavals of colonized peoples throughout the whole world. It was during these upheavals of the 1960s that counterinsurgency became the main military focus of the U.S. government. The CIA, FBI and many other agencies of U.S. State power were put to work developing and carrying out programs to destroy revolution.

KENNEDY'S NEW KIND OF STRATEGY

The move to usher in counterinsurgency as the major U.S. military policy was engineered by none other than President John F. Kennedy, the darling of white liberals. In 1962, Kennedy made a speech at West Point Military Academy in which he stated:

> Subversive insurgency is another type of war, new in its intensity, ancient in its origins—war by guerrillas, subversives, insurgents, assassins; war by ambush instead of by combat; by infiltration instead of aggression, seeking victory by eroding and exhausting the enemy instead of engaging him....It requires in those situations where we must counter it....a whole new kind of strategy, a wholly different kind of force and therefore a new and wholly different kind of training.[35]

Knowing that the U.S. military was no match for disciplined, politicized anti-colonial armed forces, Kennedy studied books on guerrilla warfare by Mao Zedong and Che Guevara. He read about the ancient dialectical approach to people's warfare put forward in China by Sun Tzu in *The Art of War,* written more than 2,000 years ago:

> When they are fulfilled be prepared against [the enemy]; when they are strong, avoid them. Use anger to throw

them into disarray. Use humility to make them haughty. Tire them by flight. Cause division among them. Attack when they are unprepared, make your move when they do not expect it.[36]

Guerrilla warfare is the resistance of oppressed peoples in organized form. Insurgent guerrilla warfare had been used brilliantly by Queen Nzinga against the Portuguese in the fifteenth century, Chaka Zulu against the British in the nineteenth century and by Geronimo, Crazy Horse and Sitting Bull against the European invaders. By the time of Kennedy's presidency the United States was facing insurgent revolutionary struggles in the colonies of Korea and Viet Nam, among others.

The stunning victory of the Vietnamese over the French in 1954 was a wake-up call to U.S. imperialism that Kennedy was able to pick up. He recognized that the major threat faced by the U.S. military was not in Europe but from colonized peoples everywhere.

Kennedy forced thousands of Pentagon and State Department officials to take special courses in counterinsurgency that included a study of the works of Mao and Che.[37]

It was Kennedy who formed the Green Berets and who personally supervised the arming and training of the "Special Forces." Michael Klare explains in his book, *War Without End: American Planning for the Next Viet Nams*:

> When he discovered that the military establishment was not disposed to move quickly in the area of guerrilla warfare, Kennedy used his authority as Commander-in-Chief to get new programs started. The American counter-guerrilla effort was sadly lacking in ingenuity and leadership, former White House aide Theodore Sorensen recalled in 1965 that the President, "far more than any of his generals

or even [then Secretary of Defense Robert S.] McNamara, supplied that leadership."

Kennedy ordered a fivefold increase in Special Forces strength and directed that they wear the green beret.. Kennedy personally supervised the selection of new jungle equipment, and ordered more helicopters, light-weight field radios, and high-powered rifles for the Special Forces.[38]

Kennedy instituted the International Police Academy that trained brutal counterinsurgent policemen from around the world. He upgraded the School of the Americas where the death squads and torturers of Latin America are still trained today. Thanks in large part to Kennedy's efforts, nearly 60,000 military personnel and civilians from North and South America have been trained in torture, assassination and other counterinsurgent methods at the School of the Americans over the past 50 years.[39]

Famous graduates of the School of the Americas include the late Salvadoran death-squad boss Roberto D'Aubisson, Guatemalan secret police chief Col. Julio Roberto Alpirez, deposed Haitian torturer Col. Michel François and imprisoned former Panamanian President Manuel Noriega.

In his book, Michael Klare elaborates on the U.S. military shift from conventional to unconventional methods of warfare:

> A *conventional war* is fought with non-nuclear weapons by the regular armed forces of a nation; such a war may be limited or…entail the total mobilization of the belligerents' warmaking capabilities. *Unconventional warfare* usually connotes operations conducted by irregular military units (guerrillas, commandos, intelligence operatives, etc.) with light arms or…outlawed weapons such as chemical or biological agents…Typical unconventional

operations include sabotage, assassination, ambushes, hit and run attacks on isolated outposts, and clandestine propaganda campaigns. When performed by a nation technically at peace, such operations are usually covert and are conducted by secret or semisecret organizations. In the United States, unconventional warfare activities are usually called special operations, and various 'special' units have been formed to conduct them.[40]

In other words, conventional warfare is when Europeans fight other European imperialist powers. Conventional warfare is governed by United Nations rules and terms regulating everything from the treatment of prisoners to the prohibition of bombing civilians. Unconventional warfare is when the imperialists fight African or other non-white colonized peoples. It is counterinsurgency. As Robert Taber noted in *The War of the Flea*, counterinsurgent methods generally approach genocide.

INSTRUMENT OF COERCION

Counterinsurgency is carried out by the U.S. State apparatus; it is not the work of any aberrant or wayward U.S. agency. It is not something bad that the CIA or J. Edgar Hoover once did, nor is it some renegade act or the result of some "rotten apple" in the police department.

Counterinsurgency is the main military policy of the U.S. State. Thus the CIA, FBI, police departments and other agencies are doing what they were created to do. They are attempting to suppress by any means whatsoever oppressed peoples inside the United States and around the world in order to maintain the status quo.

The State is an instrument of restraint that defends the interests and stolen resources of the capitalist white ruling class and the white population as a whole. Based on earlier definitions by the Russian revolutionary V.I. Lenin, Omali Yeshitela has brilliantly put forward an understanding of the State that is key to comprehending the counterinsurgency against African people. As the Chairman explains:

> The State is an organization that is comprised of the bureaucrats and other instruments of coercion like the police department, the army, the navy, the prisons and the court system. The State is simply organized coercion. It is something that will make somebody do something against his will.

> The State exists anytime a society is split between those who have and those who don't have, between slaves and slave masters....

> If you don't have a State apparatus, the people who have nothing, who are ripped off by those who have everything, will take the oppressors' heads off and take back everything that's been stolen from them. So the State is necessary to keep the society itself from exploding into disarray. The police department is a function of the State.

> What is it that stands between a homeless person and an abandoned house sitting in the community? What separates a hungry person from grocery stores with their shelves overflowing with food except the police? It's the State.[41]

It is the State that carries out and administers the counterinsurgency against African people in this country.

BIOLOGICAL AND CHEMICAL WARFARE

One form of the counterinsurgent attacks used against African people has been biological and chemical warfare, a central focus of the CIA in its counteroffensives against oppressed peoples of the world as well. Like other forms of counterinsurgency, biological and chemical weapons are not new. One of the first notorious cases of biological warfare was when the British gave smallpox-infested blankets to the native people.

In the twentieth century, investigation into the activities of the "CIA and the organizations from which it sprang reveals an intense preoccupation with the development of techniques of behavior control, brainwashing, and covert medical and psychic experimentation on unwitting subjects," asserts Alexander Cockburn in his book *Whiteout.*[42]

The well-known Tuskeegee Experiment carried out for 40 years between 1932 and 1972 is an example of biological warfare used against African people. Six hundred African men from rural Alabama were selected for a "study" by the U.S. Public Health Service. Four hundred of the men had syphilis while 200 unaffected men were the "control group." The men with the disease were given no medical treatment, even after penicillin was developed as a cure in 1943, since the government wanted to "study the natural progress of the venereal disease."[43]

Never informed they had syphilis, the African men were told they were being treated for "bad blood," and were given "medicine" that was nothing more than aspirin and an iron supplement.

The atrocity of Tuskeegee was only one example of U.S. government biological and chemical "experimentation." In 1989 the *San Francisco Examiner* ran a full-page article, "Test-tube warfare: Biological weaponry revives in '80s." The army's top secret germ warfare tests in the 1950s and 1960s included subjecting a Pennsylvania-Virginia "naval supply line to a non-lethal simulant of a fungus that is 10 time more lethal to blacks than whites, noting that 'within this system are employed...many Negroes.'"[44]

In the 1950s, the CIA launched its MK-ULTRA project that used LSD, heroin and other drugs on unsuspecting subjects as a form of mind control. One suspected victim of MK-ULTRA was the African singer, actor and political activist associated with the Communist Party, Paul Robeson, according to allegations made by his son Paul Robeson Jr. In the spring of 1961, Robeson was apparently drugged by CIA agents in Moscow on the eve of a planned trip to Cuba to visit with Che Guevara and Fidel Castro. One report explains:

> The trip never came off because Robeson fell ill in Moscow, where he had gone to give several lectures and concerts. At the time it was reported that Robeson had suffered a heart attack. But in fact Robeson had slashed his wrists in a suicide attempt after suffering hallucinations and severe depression. The symptoms came on following a surprise party thrown for him at this Moscow hotel.
>
> Robeson's son...has investigated his father's illness for more than 30 years. He believes that his father was slipped a synthetic hallucinogen called BZ by U.S. intelligence operatives at the party in Moscow. The party was hosted by anti-Soviet dissidents funded by the CIA....
>
> Robeson left Moscow for London, where he was...turned over to psychiatrists who forced him to endure 54 electro-shock treatments. At the time, electro-shock, in combination with psycho-active drugs, was a favored technique of CIA behavior modification. It turned out that the doctors treating Robeson in London and, later, in New York were CIA contractors....[45]

BLUEPRINT FOR COUNTERINSURGENCY

The counterinsurgent attacks on African people in the United States have followed the guidelines of the general U.S. military policy. Under John F. Kennedy, the U.S. military developed tactics for counterinsurgency upon which the strategy for COINTELPRO was clearly based. Michael Klare's *War Without End* lays out this blue-print for war against oppressed peoples included the following four points:

1. **Rapid deployment**—the rapid response capability. Klare states that "in order to be successful a counterinsurgency effort must destroy the guerrilla organization before it gains widespread popular support." The fact that the Black Panther Party was destroyed after only four years of existence, effectively breaking the back of the Black Power movement, indicates that "rapid response" was a guiding factor in the COINTELPRO strategy.

2. **The electronic battlefield**. This is based on necessity since guerrilla fighters are excellent on the ground, while United States and Western militaries are not. In Malaya, for example, British counterinsurgent forces required 260,000 troops in order to defeat 8,000 guerrillas in 1960—a ratio of 33 to 1. The electronic battlefield, then, gives the imperialists a technological advantage through the use of a wide range of computerized surveillance devices, infiltration alarms and the infrared detection systems. Envisioned as "space age" technology in the 1960s, infrared technology is a reality used so brutally against the Iraqis and others today. In addition, all forms of electronic surveillance and wire tapping were—and still are—used against the Black Power Movement. Today phone tapping is about to be legalized as one of the provisions of the Juvenile Crime Bill which targets African children as young as 14 years old.

3. **The mercenary apparatus**—the use of indigenous or neighboring forces to fight the revolutionary army. The Meo tribesmen were used against the Vietnamese and, of

course, the contras against the Sandinista revolution in Nicaragua. Inside the United States, African traitor police, along with neocolonial politicians and bureaucrats are used brutally against the black community.

4. **Social systems engineering**—nonmilitary attacks on the people, psychological warfare and supposed "economic assistance" ostensibly to meet the needs of the people, which ends up in the pockets of traitors, police and administrators. In addition, social systems engineering includes "resources control" which restrains the movement of people and resources in and out of a "target zone" in order to undermine the insurgents' administrative infrastructure.[46]

"Social systems engineering" includes federal programs such as Weed and Seed, that have been put in more than a hundred African and other colonized communities around the country. The Uhuru Movement has successfully exposed and politically defeated the devious Weed and Seed program in St. Petersburg, Florida.

A counterinsurgent program made from the pattern used throughout the colonized countries, Weed and Seed creates a target area in African or other oppressed communities. In the case of St. Petersburg, the "target area" was designated as the area around the Uhuru House organizing center. The government promises to give "seed" money for economic development within the Weed and Seed target area. These resources never materialize. First it has to "weed" out the "undesirable elements" by carrying out massive sweeps and arrests throughout the community, a process that never ends.

Weed and Seed imposes a racist two-tiered law on the community, with those arrested in the target zone facing federal or otherwise stiffer penalties than those in other parts of town arrested on the same charges. Although some members of the community may initially be duped into supporting this program out of fears of drugs and crime, in fact the "weed" aspect of the program never decreases drugs in the community.

Under Weed and Seed, the police create a system of snitches and give them drugs to deal in order to entrap customers. Those caught buying the drugs are then offered the choice of serving hard time or themselves becoming informants who provide the police with information about the "movement of goods and people" in and out of the target zone.[47] Soon there are more drugs flowing through the community than ever before.

PHOENIX PROGRAM

U.S. counterinsurgent methods are similar regardless of which colonial subjects are the targets. At the same time that the government was waging COINTELPRO against African people in the United States, it was carrying out a sinister sister program against the struggling people of Viet Nam. That program was called Operation Phoenix, the "other war" against Viet Nam.

Like COINTELPRO, the goal of the Phoenix Program was to "identify and neutralize" the revolutionary leaders and organizational apparatus of the National Liberation Front (NLF), the revolutionary forces of Viet Nam which was led by the Vietnamese Workers Party. The Phoenix program was headed by CIA agent William Colby with Theodore Shackley playing a leadership role—names which also come up in the unraveling of the deadly counterinsurgency against African people inside the United States over the past three decades.

Despite the tens of thousands of people killed, the Vietnamese, with their 2000-year history of fighting to defend their nation, defeated the Phoenix Program. Neither the French nor the Americans were a match for the military abilities of the Vietnamese, which by the mid-twentieth century had coupled a strong national unity with communist and anti-imperialist principles. Having a written history dating from 200 B.C., the Vietnamese upheld the

Trung sisters who in 39 A.D. had successfully led an army in fighting off Chinese invaders.

Like the peoples of so many other cultures in Africa and the Americas who have had to fight the brutal European invasions and terror, the Vietnamese people have a rich, collectivist culture. The book *Giap: The Victor in Viet Nam* by Peter Macdonald describes traditional life in Viet Nam:

> There were thousands of villages in the nation, some of them consisting of several hamlets grouped together. The village council, consisting of the most prominent citizens, such as landowners and retired mandarins, dealt with all purely local affairs, including law enforcement, the assessment and levying of taxes, and the provision of labor on a communal basis. Nearly every village had a mutual-aid society, which people paid into to cover the expense of funerals. There were also guilds, of metal workers, carpenters, stonemasons—which monitored standards of craftsmanship—and the elderly women's Buddhist association, open to women over fifty and sometimes to widows in their forties.
>
> Also, every village had an emergency relief organization, a concept that began in the Red River delta. Farmers gave an agreed amount of their rice, depending on how much land they had, to create a stockpile. Any surplus was sold off and the profit shared by the poor. In the event of a crop failure the rice was distributed equally to everyone in the village. There were also associations for people interested in leisure activities such as cockfighting, wrestling and fishing. Economically and socially the village was a self-contained entity.[48]

Counterinsurgency: War Against Oppressed Peoples

In 1858, the French seized Danang and by the 1870s all of Viet Nam was a French colony, whose major colonial commodity was opium, bringing France untold millions of dollars in profits. In 1946, Ho Chi Minh launched the revolutionary war to oust French imperialism. By 1954, the Vietnamese had broken the back of French colonial rule. "Although the bulk of the 500,000-man French Expeditionary Corps remained intact (172,000 casualties in eight years of fighting)," relates Robert Taber, "its spirit was broken, and the political compromise that followed failed to disguise the fact that French arms had met ignominious defeat in the field, at the hands of what had been considered a rag-tag native army that could be smashed in ten weeks."[49]

Led by the ingenious General Vo Nguyen Giap, the Vietnamese military tactics baffled and mystified the French who failed to realize initially that,

> [A]lthough they controlled the roads, they were fighting an enemy that had no need of roads, being without transport or heavy artillery to move. They seized strong points, but these strong points commanded nothing, since the enemy was not stationary but fluid and offered no contest for strong points or for territory.
>
> The French controlled the roads. The guerrillas passed safely in the jungle and rice paddies on either side at a distance of one hundred yards, unseen. The French held the towns. The enemy had no design on the towns. For where the French were fighting to control the national territory...the guerrillas were interested only in winning its population.[50]

After the resounding defeat of the brutal French colonizers, who were routed out of North Viet Nam, the United States attempted to recolonize Viet Nam by funding South Vietnamese neocolonial dictator Ngo Dinh Diem, and sending in military forces. In December of 1960, there were 900 U.S. troops in Viet Nam, a number that escalated to hundreds of thousands in the next few years. In January 1968, the Viet Minh launched the Tet offensive which effectively defeated U.S. aggression. By April 30, 1975, the United States, like the French, left the Southeast Asian country running. Viet Nam was once again unified.

Facing such a formidable force, the United States waged two wars, the overt and the covert. It spared no viciousness, using Agent Orange and other forms of chemical warfare and massively bombing the Vietnamese countryside. In its usual ridiculous manner, the U.S. government thought it could win "the hearts and the minds" of the Vietnamese by torturing and killing the people, especially attempting to make examples of those who participated in the revolutionary organizations. About the Phoenix Program, William Colby testified that:

> [I]n 1969 a total of 19,534 suspected VCI (Viet Cong Infrastructure)* agents had been "neutralized"—of this number 6,187 had been killed, 8,515 arrested, and 4,832 persuaded to join the Saigon side. By May 1971, 20,587 people had been killed under the Phoenix program.[51]

As reported in *The New York Times* on August 3, 1997, during Congressional hearings on the Phoenix program testimony was presented that:

> Vietnamese civilians were indiscriminately rounded up, tortured and murdered by Americans in the effort to eliminate Viet Cong cadres. K. Barton Osborn, a former pri-

---

* "Viet Cong" was a derogatory term coined by the U.S. government denoting the revolutionary Vietnamese revolutionary army. The people themselves called the army the Viet Minh, followers of Ho Chi Minh.

vate in Viet Nam and part-time employee of the CIA, told the committee that he knew of hundreds of murders committed during his first fifteen months in Viet Nam in 1967 and 1968. None of the Vietnamese prisoners he had seen detained for questioning, Osborn reported, had ever lived through their interrogations.[52]

BE LIKE CHE!

Even as it was waging the COINTELPRO and Phoenix programs, the United States was making countless other counterinsurgent attacks on revolutionary movements around the world. Patrice Lumumba was killed by the CIA in the Congo. Liberation movements in the Dominican Republic were crushed. The U.S. was constantly attempting to assassinate Fidel Castro in Cuba, and so on.

Argentine-born Ernesto "Che" Guevara, upheld and loved by oppressed and freedom-loving peoples all around the world even today, was one of the victims of U.S. counterinsurgency. Guevara participated as a leader not only in the Cuban Revolution with Fidel Castro, but fought with revolutionary armies in Africa and throughout Latin America against U.S. imperialism. Guevara's book, *Guerrilla Warfare,* widely read by revolutionaries around the world, confidently asserted that the people's revolution *can* win a war against the imperialist army.

In 1967, as the Black Panther Party was building inside the United States, Che was leading a liberation struggle in Bolivia against the U.S.-backed Barrientos regime. The United States sent both the CIA and the Green Berets to Bolivia to defeat the revolution and "neutralize" Che. Along with his band of guerrillas, Che was captured in the mountains, having been betrayed by the white leftist Regis DeBray who revealed to the Bolivian authorities where Guevara was hiding out. On October 9, 1967 Che was executed at the hand of U.S. CIA agent Felix Rodriguez. A Cuban *gusano,* drug trafficker and vile counterinsurgency expert, Rodriguez later surfaced in the late 1980s as a participant in the Iran-contra affair and the key pointman for Oliver North in providing aid to the contras to attack the Nicaraguan Revolution.[53] Rodriguez is said to claim to still wear Guevara's watch taken from the revolutionary's corpse after he was assassinated.

In response to the assassination of Che Guevara, Fidel Castro paid an emotional tribute to his comrade before a crowd of nearly a million people in Havana about 10 days after Che's murder:

> If we want the...model of a human being who does not belong to our time but to the future, I say from the depths of my heart that such a model, without a single stain on his conduct, without a single stain on his behavior, is Che! If we wish to express what we want our children to be, we must say from our very hearts as ardent revolutionaries: we want them to be like Che![54]

WAR AGAINST AFRICAN POPULATION

Inside the United States, by the end of the '60s, the Black Power Movement was being immobilized by some of the same methods, same agencies and same government officials that were launching covert attacks on oppressed peoples around the world.

Michael Klare's book, *War Without End,* written a long time ago when the memory of the Black Revolution of the '60s was still fresh, compares the attack on African people in the United States to the counterinsurgencies against external nations:

> In studying the U.S. Public Safety Program [counterinsurgent police program] abroad, one is sooner or later struck by the extent to which the goals, doctrines, and practices of this program have been adopted by authorities in the United States as an answer to our own internal difficulties...Among the specific recommendations made by

[Public Safety Director Byron] Engle for the control of urban disorders were the massive use of chemical munitions, stringently enforced curfews, and the establishment of special tactical police units available on a twenty-four hour standby basis. Precisely the same recommendations were made to President Johnson by former Pentagon aide Cyrus Vance and were later put into effect in Washington, D.C. when rioting broke out following the death of Martin Luther King Jr. in April 1968.[55]

The "recommendations" pointed out by Klare were indeed implemented, not only against the Black Power Movement but against the entire African population of the United States. For African people, counterinsurgency did not end with the defeat of their movement of the '60s; it had barely begun. Once the destruction of the Black Power Movement was complete, the U.S. government began to wage a proactive counterinsurgency to make sure African people would never organize and rise up again. Omali Yeshitela explains:

The counterinsurgency which had begun in the sixties with the explicit aim of destroying our independent anti-colonial organizations and leaders had now been turned against the whole people just as in the days of Jim Crow, prior to the success of the Civil Rights movement.[56]

It is this counterinsurgency that defines the conditions of life for the entire African community today.

With the Black Revolution defeated, thousands of black elected officials appeared on the scene as traitorous agents of white power. These neocolonialists were key to the success of the U.S. counteroffensive. As the next three decades unfolded, conditions for African workers would intensify so greatly that they would spark massive rebellions if carried out by white officials. Omali Yeshitela describes the human face of this intensification:

> Today the consequences of the defeat of the Black Revolution are glaring for all to see. The black working class suffers as never before. Millions of us do not even have the benefit of working for the slave wages in the back-breaking jobs usually reserved for us.
>
> Unemployment stalks our community with the viciousness of a white lynch mob.
>
> Especially battered are black women who carry the burden of the colonial contradiction to the gestapo social agencies, such as food stamp and welfare offices; to the hospital delivery rooms, where they are three times more likely to die during childbirth than are white women; to their empty apartments, where too many raise their children alone, those who are not among the one in forty who will see her baby die in its first year of life.
>
> Throughout the United States the destruction of the Black Revolution of the Sixties can be seen in the growing numbers of white mob and police attacks on unorganized black working class communities, resulting in death and terror.
>
> The prisons in the United States are bursting at the seams with our sisters and brothers, among whom are some of the finest leaders of the Black Revolution of the Sixties. Many of them hang on to life by the thinnest thread as conditions and the reactionary ideologies of the administrators contribute to ever-growing violence, and the Supreme Court Justices and other colonialist public officials clamor for speedier use of the death penalty.

> At the same time, the white ruling class is becoming increasingly successful in "criminalizing" the entire black community, winning more and more white solidarity to itself against the general, oppressed and colonized black community through its orchestrated uproar about crime in the streets.[57]

Today, counterinsurgency is the essence of U.S. foreign policy that is popularly supported by the white population, eliciting only an occasional qualified protest from the left. The North American public is so enthusiastic about U.S. genocidal attacks on the Iraqi people that, as we know, President William Jefferson Clinton was able to use the bombing of the Middle Eastern country to boost his ratings during his impeachment hearings. The murder of thousands of Iraqi children was all it took for white people to forgive Clinton for his escapade with Monica Lewinsky.

The counterinsurgency being carried out *inside* the United States, however, is not directly acknowledged by the government. Nevertheless, taking the form of a "war on crime" and a "war on drugs," its popularity among white voters is also immense. Counterinsurgency against the black community is the central domestic platform of both the Democrats and the Republicans. Blatantly genocidal in character, the war against African people right here goes by without a squeak of protest from the white left.

Currently, African people make up over half of the 2 million people in the U.S. prison system. Most of those incarcerated are young and impoverished, convicted of drug-related charges despite proof of the government's culpability as the source of the narcotics. Day after day, hour after hour, young African people of childbearing age are swept away to the concentration camps that are proliferating like flies throughout the countryside. Africans are shot down by the police, forced out of their housing, their babies are stolen from them through the foster care system. These are the "disappeared" of America. Similar conditions in El Salvador or Chile have produced massive demonstrations by liberals in Berkeley or New York.

Just as he bombs Iraq, Clinton intensifies the attack on the African community as a method of increasing his popularity. Pass the Crime Bill or, even better, the Juvenile Crime Bill, cut off welfare, tear down housing projects, put one hundred thousand new police on the streets to shoot more Africans—Clinton's ratings soar. The white left is too busy saving the redwoods (but not the indigenous people), winning gay rights in the military or union organizing for higher wages to notice the "little matter of genocide" before its very eyes.

The Uhuru Movement, led by the African People's Socialist Party and representing the interests of African workers and poor people, has run very much against the wind when it campaigns against the U.S. counterinsurgency inside its borders. Generally organizations from the Mexican, indigenous and Filipino communities, where people face similar conditions, have united with the effort to stop this war.

The white left has ignored and united with the counterinsurgency, placing the blame for conditions in the African community on the victims themselves. Or, the left liquidates the obvious reality by saying that "everyone"—including white people—is targeted by the conditions of counterinsurgency.

White left slogans like "The war on drugs is a war on poor people," or statements denouncing the "criminalization of a whole generation," fly in the face of reality. The world we see around us tells us that not all "poor" communities are under assault; it is African and other nonwhite communities who live under the gun. White neighborhoods do not have helicopters flying overhead day and night; police and Special Weapons forces do not patrol our streets and break down our doors. Our children are not massively hauled off to prison or shot down by police daily, even though statistics show white people use more than three quarters of the illegal drugs in the United States.

In addition to the clear empirical knowledge, available if we but open our eyes, the U.S. government's own statistics prove that the only war being waged inside U.S. borders is one to suppress African and other colonized peoples. J. Edgar Hoover summed it up far better than any white leftist. The U.S. government is indeed waging an attack against its own "greatest internal threat."

UNCLE SAM, THE PUSHERMAN

On October 8, 1998, President Clinton, faced with impeachment, released Volume II of the CIA's investigative report on its own drug dealing. Known as the Hitz Report, this document was used by the CIA to clear itself of charges of pushing narcotics, which arose following Gary Webb's newspaper series, *The Dark Alliance* in 1996. In spite of its efforts to cover up the truth, however, Volume II of the Hitz report is an *admission* of guilt by the CIA. A *Consortium for Independent Journalism* article clarifies:

> CIA Inspector General Frederick Hitz confirmed long-standing allegations of cocaine trafficking by contra forces. Hitz identified more than 50 contras and contra-related entities implicated in the drug trade.
>
> Hitz detailed, too, how the Reagan administration protected these drug operations and frustrated federal investigations which threatened to expose these crimes in the mid-1980s.
>
> In perhaps the most stunning disclosure, Hitz published evidence that drug trafficking and money laundering tracked directly into Reagan's National Security Council where Lt. Col. Oliver L. North oversaw contra operations....
>
> In the lengthy report—Volume Two of a two-volume set on contra drug allegations—Hitz continues to

> defend the CIA on one narrow point: that the CIA did not conspire with the contras to raise money through cocaine trafficking.
>
> But Hitz made clear that the contra war took precedence over law enforcement...[58]

The CIA, of course, would never disclose the entirety of its own crimes in its own reports, but increasingly the evidence overwhelmingly proves what the African community has long known: the U.S. government is responsible for the deadly drugs flooding their streets.

Thus, the key weapon in the counterinsurgency against the African community has been the "massive use of chemical munitions"—chemical warfare in the form of drugs. This method of chemical warfare has been convenient, lucrative and nearly unparalleled for its genocidal results.

As a result of the government-imposed drugs, more than three million African people are tied to the prison system. Police and drug related violence is rampant. Families and communities have been devastated through drugs engineered for rapid addiction. It is no coincidence that deadly drugs appeared massively in the African community as the Black Power Movement was being attacked.

Searching through microfilms of any newspaper from the later '60s, one invariably finds a section dealing with news about the struggles of the Black Movement on local and national levels. Wedged in among the articles on black political activities is an item about the increase of heroin addiction in the African community. Prior to the '60s, as Chairman Omali says, a few African artists and musicians were known to use marijuana and occasionally heroin, but generally drug use was rare in the African community.

By the late '60s and early '70s, as the CIA and other military and government forces were importing heroin from Southeast Asia, the drug began to flood the streets of the African community. By 1970 there was even a heroin addiction rate of up to 20 percent inside of nearly every unit of the U.S. military stationed in Viet Nam.[59] At the same time, it is estimated that there were more than 150,000 addicts in New York City, and more than a half million throughout the United States.[60] The numbers were rapidly rising.

In the late '70s, the government shifted the focus of its foreign military intervention from Southeast Asia to Central America. After the Vietnamese routed the United States, the victory of the revolutionary Sandinista government in Nicaragua in 1979 drew North American attention there. In Central and South America the United States found a new wealth of narcotics in the form of cocaine.

Long the favored drug of the rich and elite, cocaine had potential to be useful on the home front. After the powder was cooked into rocks to be smoked, it was sold cheaper, creating a more popular addiction for the masses. By the early 1980s the crack epidemic was sweeping West Coast African communities.

During this period, the headquarters of the African People's Socialist Party—the leadership of the Uhuru Movement—was located in Oakland, California. Observing the drug infestation in the city that had been the birthplace of the Black Panther Party a decade and a half earlier, the Uhuru Movement single-handedly began to expose the drug-dealing role of the U.S. government. The Uhuru Movement organized forums, wrote articles in *The Burning Spear* and other newspapers, and held demonstrations chanting, "Who's the real dope pusher in the world today? The government, the government, the CIA."

Countless posters were put up stating that, "The White House is the crack house! Uncle Sam is the pusher man," and "The war on drugs is a war on the black community!" The Uhuru Movement was clear that crack was the latest front of the government's counterinsurgency against African people.

As far back as 1985, Chairman Omali asserted that African people do not have "the planes and the ships to bring in the drugs," a statement that has subsequently been echoed through the grapevine of African communities throughout the United States.

DARK ALLIANCE

It is no surprise that after a decade of Uhuru-led campaigns, Gary Webb would have first published his *Dark Alliance* series in the *San Jose Mercury News*. San Jose is a city in the greater San Francisco Bay Area, about 45 minutes south of Oakland. Webb's articles—now a book—represent the first bourgeois media source to substantiate the Uhuru Movement's allegation that the CIA and U.S. government are responsible for the profusion of crack on the streets of the African community.

Webb's expose, however, is limited in scope and fails to register the genocidal social devastation the African community has experienced—and continues to experience—as a result of the drugs. Webb actually relieves the U.S. government of any responsibility, denying that the imposition of drugs in African communities was U.S. *policy*. Nor does Webb call for any price to be paid by the U.S. government, the CIA *or* the white population that stood by and did nothing but vote in more stringent anti-African legislation, while enjoying the wealth that is pumped into the white economy from drug profits.

As a result of the organizing, analysis and political campaigns of the Uhuru Movement, African people around the country were clear about the source of crack for years before Webb's series. As early as 1990, a *New York Times* polls showed that more than 45 percent of the U.S. African population believed that the government was responsible for drugs coming into the African community. An article in the *San Jose Mercury News* some six years before Webb's series revealed that:

> In neighborhoods from Harlem to Anacostia in Washing-
> ton, D.C., to Watts, many blacks believe that the white

establishment has intentionally allowed narcotics to devastate their communities, even encouraged drug abuse as a form of genocide.

"It's almost an accepted fact," said Andrew Cooper, publisher of the *City Sun*, a Brooklyn-based black weekly. "It is a deep-seated suspicion. I believe it....

"But there's just too much money in narcotics. People really believe they are being victimized by The Man. If the government wanted to stop it, it could stop it..."

The article continues:

"There's an element that finds this a beautiful aspect of the genocidal attitude toward African-American youth," said the Rev. Lawrence Lucas, a Harlem priest known for his acerbic criticism of the white establishment. "You're killing them with drugs. You're killing them with the crime connected with drugs. You send them to jail and eliminate African-American males as fathers.

"White middle class Americans are the ones who make the money on the billions spent on law enforcement necessary to keep feeding black and Hispanic youths through the jail mill. It's a little too coincidental not to believe this was orchestrated by a group of people for other purposes."[61]

WAR ON DRUGS

Along with the drugs, the "wars on drugs" has been a key counterinsurgent tool used by imperial powers against their colonies for hundreds of years—all the way back to what Karl Marx ironically called the "rosy dawn" of capitalism.

Some white people are shocked at the charge that the U.S. government would purposefully put drugs in the African community. Why would this be shocking? Imperialists have attempted to addict their colonial subjects to drugs for hundreds of years. They enslaved African people for 250 years, orchestrated genocide against the native people, colonized and brutalized nearly the whole world. Why *wouldn't* they inflict drugs on the African community?

As a commodity, drugs are and always have been incredibly profitable to the overall colonial economy. We have already discussed some of what the French did with opium in Viet Nam, but the scope was much larger than that. Alfred McCoy's *The Politics of Heroin in Southeast Asia* reports that Portuguese merchants introduced opium smoking to Asia in the 1500s.

Karl Marx counted the British-imposed opium trade and opium war against China as a part of the "primitive accumulation of capital" along with the enslavement of African people and the theft of the land and resources of the indigenous people.

McCoy's book reveals that by 1838 the British were exporting over 2,400 tons of opium a year to China from its colony of India where it cultivated the opium poppy. When opium spread rapidly throughout China, the emperor banned the drug, an act which the vicious British colonizers refused to respect. China's defiance of the British imperialists was the justification for England's "Opium War." McCoy states that the British used Chinese immigrants throughout Southeast Asia to help spread the opium trade. McCoy writes:

> By the late nineteenth century, the government opium den was as common as the pith helmet, and every nation and colony in Southeast Asia—from North Borneo to Burma—had a state-regulated opium monopoly. The indigenous population gradually picked up the habit, too, thus fostering a substantial—and growing—consumer market for opium among the Thais, Burmese, Vietnamese

and Malayans. While the health and vitality of the local population literally went up in smoke, the colonial government thrived: opium sales proved as much as 40 percent of colonial revenues and financed the building of many Gothic edifices, railways, and canals that remain as the hallmark of the colonial era.

McCoy also notes a century-old prototype for the cheaper smokable derivative of cocaine called crack. He describes a French factory built in Saigon in the 1890s to process raw Indian resin in a new form to target a more "popular" base of drug users:

> The new factory devised a special mixture of prepared opium that burned quickly, thus encouraging the smoker to consume more opium than he might use ordinarily....More dens and shops were opened to meet expanded consumer demand (in 1918 there were 1,512 dens and 3,098 retail shops). Business boomed.

> As [French colonial] governor-general Doumer himself had proudly reported, these reforms increased opium revenues by 50 percent during his four years in office, accounting for over one-third of all colonial revenues.[62]

The French colonizers in Viet Nam also set a precedent for an effective and lucrative "war on drugs" in Viet Nam. It was a model the United States would implement against African people as it took over Southeast Asia's opium trade after the French were defeated by the Vietnamese.

Under the French-imposed colonial opium trade, large numbers of

> ...plantation workers, miners, and urban laborers spent their entire salaries in the opium dens. The strenuous work, combined with the debilitating effect of the drug

and lack of food, produced some extremely emaciated laborers, who could only be described as walking skeletons. Workers often died of starvation, or more likely their families did.[63]

By the 1940s, the Vietnamese revolutionary forces built anti-opium campaigns that gained international support, forcing the French to wage a so-called "war on opium" inside of Viet Nam. This supposed anti-opium campaign was called "Operation X," a true precedent for "just say no" and other counterinsurgency operations that the U.S. government and its CIA use today.

McCoy reports that when the French invaded Viet Nam in 1946 that the "counterinsurgency efforts were continually plagued by a lack of money...." Therefore, in a fashion similar to that being constantly exposed in the U.S., the French transferred the opium trade into the hands of its secret intelligence division which is the French counterpart of the CIA:

> The solution was Operation X, a clandestine narcotics traffic so secret that only high-ranking French and Vietnamese officials even knew of its existence. The anti-opium drive that began in 1946 had received scant support from the "Indochina hands;" customs officials continued to purchase raw opium from the Hmong, and the opium smoking dens, cosmetically renamed "detoxification clinics," continued to sell unlimited quantities of opium....
>
> [T]he opium trade remained essentially unchanged. The only real differences were that the government, having abandoned opium as a source of revenue, now faced serious budgetary problems; and the French intelligence community, having secretly taken over the opium trade,

had solved theirs. The opium monopoly had gone underground to become Operation X.[64]

MAJOR COMMODITY ON THE WORLD MARKET

Imperialists are still fighting all over the drug-rich Golden Triangle of Southeast Asia. The United States inherited control of much of the world drug trade when it stepped in to Viet Nam after the French were routed. American imperialism had long attempted to usurp the drug trade from the British and the French as part of the mantle of world imperialist power.

In the late 1940s, Marseilles, France was the postwar heroin center for Europe and the United States. The drug kingpins of this Mediterranean city were backed by "CIA arms, money, and disinformation."[65] The online journal *Foreign Policy in Focus* notes that in the early 1950s the

> Nationalist Chinese army, organized by the CIA to wage war against Communist China, became the opium baron of The Golden Triangle (parts of Burma, Thailand, and Laos), the world's largest source of opium and heroin. Air America, the CIA's principal proprietary airline, flew the drugs all over Southeast Asia.
>
> A laboratory built at CIA headquarters in Northern Laos was used to refine heroin. After a decade of American military intervention, Southeast Asia had become the source of 70 percent of the world's illicit opium and the major supplier of raw materials for American's booming heroin market.[66]

From 1973 to 1980, the Nugan Hand Bank of Sydney, Australia was one of the major undercover CIA financial institutions used to fund drug trafficking, money laundering and international arms dealing. "Among its officers were a network of U.S. generals, admirals and CIA men, including former CIA Director William Colby, who was also one of its lawyers."[67] The bank had branches in Saudi Arabia, Europe, Southeast Asia, South America and the United States.

In the 1980s, the United States began funding the counterinsurgent contras to overthrow the revolutionary Sandinista government in Nicaragua. As part of this effort, it began using contras and their supporters to import drugs and sell them in the United States. According to *Foreign Policy in Focus*:

> [Gary Webb's] *San Jose Mercury News* series documents just one thread of the interwoven operations linking the CIA, the contras, and the cocaine cartels....In 1989, the Senate Subcommittee on Terrorism, Narcotics, and International Operations (the Kerry committee) concluded a three-year investigation by stating: "There was substantial evidence of drug smuggling through the war zones on the part of individual contras, contra suppliers, contra pilots, mercenaries who worked with the contras, and contra supporters throughout the region....In each case, one or another agency of the U.S. government had information regarding the involvement either while it was occurring, or immediately thereafter...."[68]

At the same time in Costa Rica, there were several CIA-contra networks involved in drug trafficking, including one involving CIA operative John Hull's farm along the Nicaraguan border. Anti-Castro Cuban-Americans in Costa Rica employed by the CIA as military trainers for the contras also trafficked drugs. A Miami accountant for Colombia's Medellin cocaine cartel testified that he

> ...funneled nearly $10 million to Nicaraguan contras through long-time CIA operative Felix Rodriquez [respon-

sible for assassinating Che Guevara], who was based at Ilopango Air Force Base in El Salvador. Cocaine-laden planes flew to Florida, Texas, Louisiana, and other locations including several military bases. Designated as 'Contra Craft,' planes carrying these shipments were not to be inspected. When some authority wasn't apprised and made an arrest, powerful strings were pulled to result in dropping the case, acquittal, reduced sentence, or deportation.[69]

COCAINE: COLONIAL COMMODITY

For many years, Colombia has been the world's leading cocaine producer, putting out 772 metric tons a year, roughly half the world supply, as estimated by the United Nations.[70] The DEA estimates that 80 percent of the cocaine in the United States comes from Colombia through Mexico, a pipeline that the United States obviously controls or attempts to control.[71]

In the 1980s Colombian drug traffickers based in the city of Medellin were high-profile, violent "cocaine cowboys." This was an inconvenience to the United States, which hypocritically denounces illegal drug use while making billions of dollars on it. The Medellin cartel was therefore militarily destroyed by United States and Colombian forces in dramatic fashion in the early '90s.

Immediately the Cali cartel rose up. The drug kingpins of Cali were a more genteel breed, wearing pinstripe suits and holding afternoon teas with their families on the lawns of their mansions. After exposure in the late '80s in the U.S. media by such programs as the "Frontline" series of the Public Broadcasting System, the United States demanded that Colombia also arrest leaders of the Cali cartel.

The Colombian government, having long been financially backed by drug cartels, resented U.S. intrusion into its internal affairs. Nevertheless, in an apparent move to keep U.S. military aid and drug markets, Colombia did arrest Cali cartel leaders, giving them light sentences.

At the moment, according to internet reports, a third generation of Colombian drug traffickers has emerged, again concentrated in Medellin but this time in much smaller, quieter high-tech drug organizations rather than huge "cartels."

One article reports that the new Colombian drug traffickers are discreet, difficult to infiltrate and are "mostly people between the ages of 25 and 40 who have no criminal records and work through legitimate small businesses." They are "internet savvy, have a keen grasp of global finance and are deft money launderers."[72] This new breed of drug dealers is apparently something the U.S. government can live with for the moment.

In any case, the flow of more than 772 tons of cocaine each year out of Colombia continues unabated, regardless of which style cartel is in vogue. Estimates are that Colombian repatriated drug profits vary between $4.5 and 10 billion a year. This is a relatively low amount considering the $400 to 500 billion dollar yearly world drug profit; but with drugs, like any colonial crop, most profits are made inside the colonizing countries. U.S. and European distributors make 10 to 20 times the price paid for cocaine in the "Third World" country of origin.

Recently a newspaper article revealed that Colombia "has begun to include income earned from growing illegal drugs in the way it calculates the size of the nation's economy....

"For the moment," the article notes, "the new accounting system does not include the much larger sums of money earned from the processing or trafficking of cocaine, marijuana and heroin, only the growing of the raw materials."[73]

Traffickers in Colombia get $950 to $1,235 a kilo for cocaine that is sold for $10,500 to $36,000 in the United States. A kilo of heroin gets $3,000 in the underdeveloped producing country, while it fetches a wholesale price of $95,000 to $210,000 in the United States.[74]

United Nations statistics estimate drug profits worldwide to be about $440 billion a year, or 8 percent of all international trade, and the majority of all laundered money in the world, a figure that seems incredibly conservative.

When William Jefferson Clinton spoke before the United Nations in 1998, he stated that "Up to $500 billion in criminal proceeds every single year—more than the GNP of most nations—is laundered, disguised as legitimate revenue, and much of it moves across our borders."[75]

To the world capitalist economy, drugs are but another colonial commodity, whose prices are controlled by Wall Street and the World Bank, no less than oil from Kuwait or diamonds from South Africa. With cocaine and heroin bringing in far better prices than coffee and tea, or even oil, countless impoverished colonized countries, starved by the United States and genocidal International Monetary Fund policies, are waiting in the wings for a chance to jump into the drug market.

DRUG ECONOMY

The on-line research journal *Foreign Policy in Focus* estimates that about $100 billion a year flows into the U.S. financial system from drugs,[76] but others have estimated this amount to be as high as $250 billion. Even this is probably an underestimation. As the leader of the world capitalist economy, the United States is said to control about 80 percent of the world oil reserves. It seems unlikely that it would be happy with any thing less than the majority of the world drug profits.

The United States today is waging a vicious "war on drugs" counterinsurgency inside of Colombia in order to *maintain* Colombia's capitalist drug economy. The United States has "certified"

Colombia as a drug fighting nation, making it eligible for even more massive military aid. The United States is attempting to keep Colombia out of the hands of the insurgent guerrilla movement led by the Revolutionary Armed Forces of Colombia (FARC) that controls nearly half of Colombia's countryside.[77]

Similar to the situation inside the United States, the so-called war on drugs in Colombia never eradicates drugs. The only things wiped out by the $500 million U.S.-backed military assault are the indigenous peasants who are the military targets in the countryside. Nevertheless, the indigenous people are fighting a very successful armed struggle, which will undoubtedly draw the United States deeper and deeper into another armed quagmire.

In 1997, the United States also "certified" Mexico as a drug-fighting ally. Mexico is second only to Colombia in cocaine trafficking and production. New revelations appear daily in the newspapers about the depth of the violence, intrigue, money laundering and drug involvement on the highest levels of President Ernesto Zedillo's government. As a certified country, Mexico receives at least $37 million dollars in U.S. helicopters and surveillance aircraft, and an additional $10 million for command-and-control electronics.

Like Colombia, Mexico is the scene of powerful, armed insurgencies led by the oppressed peasants. In addition to the well-known movement in Chiapas, headed up by the Zapatista National Liberation Army (EZLN), the states of Guerrero and Oaxaca are centers of support for the Popular Revolutionary Army (EPR). Organized armed resistance to U.S. imperialism and its narco-puppets in Mexico is growing throughout the country. As in Colombia, it is the revolutionary forces, the peasants and oppressed workers who feel the brunt of the U.S. government's Mexican "war on drugs," which serves to keep the narcotics moving smoothly across the U.S. border.

In addition to Colombia and Mexico, drug cartels and organizations are popping up worldwide in impoverished countries. In Bangkok, Hong Kong, Ankara, Moscow, Palermo and Lagos, drug trafficking organizations are competing for the world drug market, especially the ravenous one inside the United States.

Newspapers report that crack and cocaine are now "on the wane" and heroin is on the rise. Interestingly these reports appeared just as the United States was involved in the former Yugoslavia amid allegations that the thuggish U.S.-backed Kosovo Liberation Army (KLA) is tied to major heroin trafficking in Europe. One account explains:

> The supply route for arming KLA "freedom fighters" are the rugged mountainous borders of Albania with Kosovo and Macedonia....A recent intelligence report by Germany's Federal Criminal Agency suggests that: "Ethnic Albanians are now the most prominent group in the distribution of heroin in Western consumer countries."[78]

As the leader of world capitalist economy, the United States surely controls or attempts to control the bulk of the international drug trade. Inside the United States, those drugs are aimed at the African and other oppressed communities. They are a key component of the counterinsurgency inside this country.

DEFEAT THE COUNTERINSURGENCY!

And as we can see, the war against African people here in the United States takes place in the context of U.S. counterinsurgency against colonized peoples worldwide.

As Chairman Omali Yeshitela eloquently asserted in his closing statement of the International Tribunal on Reparations for African People in the U.S. held in Brooklyn, New York in 1982, where he acted as People's Advocate:

> Our movement was attacked viciously...It was a method that the CIA had first attempted in Viet Nam, but failed. It

was a method that in South Viet Nam was called the Phoenix Program. The idea of the Phoenix Program was to decapitate the leadership of the revolutionary movement in South Viet Nam. The CIA murdered, assassinated...39,000 cadres of the National Liberation Front in South Viet Nam in an attempt to decapitate that movement, to crush the people's struggle to be free.

In the United States of America, the United States government used that same Phoenix Program. It decapitated the Black Liberation Movement. Everywhere you looked, black people who stood on the side of freedom and justice and socialist democracy for black people found themselves either in prison all over this country, dead, or underground.[79]

In 1991, the African People's Socialist Party founded the National People's Democratic Uhuru Movement (NPDUM), a national organization, open to people of all nationalities, to expose and defeat the counterinsurgency being waged against African people in the U.S. At the founding convention of NPDUM, Chairman Omali Yeshitela called for the new organization to work to build mass support to end this counterinsurgency against African people. The Chairman stated:

> Comrades, Sisters and Brothers, there are millions of African people within this North American hell who are looking for leadership out of this permanent state of wretchedness our enemies have apparently affixed to our destiny. These are the Africans: locked in the housing projects which daily look more like prisons; pursued through the desolate trash-littered streets of the African colony by homelessness, death, and special police thugs; humiliated by welfare and welfare agents who act like parole officers; and generally afflicted with all the symp-

toms of modern slavery. These are the Africans, millions and millions of them, who have awaited this convention and who now await our return to our communities where we will join them and take up the struggle to complete the Black Revolution of the Sixties.[80]

Overturning the Culture of Violence

1. Universal Declaration of Human Rights, December 10, 1948, adopted by the United Nations General Assembly.
2. International Covenant on Civil and Political Rights, December 16, 1966, adopted by the United Nations General Assembly.
3. Susan Eastman, May 20-26, 1999, "Emerging alliances," *Weekly Planet*, p. 20.
4. Gabriel Kolko, 1997, *Anatomy of a War: Viet Nam, the United States, and the Modern Historical Experience* (New York: The New Press), p. 558.
5. Ward Churchill and Jim Vander Wall, 1988, *Agents of Repression: The FBI's Secret Wars Against the Black Panther Party and the American Indian Movement* (Boston: South End Press), p. 63, quoting Noam Chomsky.
6. Bill Staggs, March 13, 1999, "Mock invasion takes a detour above sea life," *The New York Times*.
7. Michael T. Klare, 1972, *War Without End: American Planning for the Next Viet Nams* (New York: Vantage Books), p. 44.
8. Same as above, 44n.
9. Robert Taber, 1970, *The War of the Flea: A Study of Guerrilla Warfare Theory and Practice* (New York: The Citadel Press), p. 21.
10. Omali Yeshitela, 1997, "The Dialectics of Black Revolution: The Struggle to Defeat the Counterinsurgency in the U.S." (St. Petersburg: Burning Spear Uhuru Publications), p. 11.
11. Churchill and Vander Wall, p. 77.
12. Same as above, p. 58.
13. Philip S. Foner, 1970, *The Black Panthers Speak: The Manifesto of the Party: The First Complete Documentary Record of the Panther's Program* (Philadelphia: J. B. Lippincott Company), p. xxvi.
14. Churchill and Vander Wall, p. 58.
15. "King son says LBJ in on conspiracy," June 20, 1997, *San Francisco Chronicle*.
16. "Jury verdict changes little in King case," December 10, 1999, *St. Petersburg Times*.
17. James Forman, 1985, *The Making of Black Revolutionaries* (Washington, D.C.: Open Hand Publishing Inc.), p. 542.
18. Kenneth O'Reilly, 1989, *"Racial Matters:" The FBI's Secret File on Black America, 1960-1972* (New York: The Free Press), p. 161.
19. Churchill and Vander Wall, p. 70.
20. Same as above, p. 401.
21. Same as above, p. 73.
22. Akua Njeri, 1991, "My Life with the Black Panther Party" (Oakland: Burning Spear Publications), p. 37-38.
23. Omali Yeshitela, 1991, *Izwe Lethu i Afrika! (Africa Is Our Land)* (Oakland: Burning Spear Publications), p.15.
24. Churchill and Vander Wall, p. 398n.
25. Rodolfo Acuña, 1988, *Occupied America: A History of Chicanos* (New York: Harper Collins Publishers, Inc.), p. 337.
26. Same as above, p. 338.
27. Same as above, p. 338-348.
28. Churchill and Vander Wall, p. 119.
29. Same as above, pp. 118-119.
30. Same as above, pp. 119-122.
31. Same as above, p. 144.
32. Same as above, p. 175, quoting Roberto Maestas and Bruce Johansen.
33. George Breitman, ed., 1990, *Malcolm X Speaks: Selected Speeches and Statements* (New York: Grove Weidenfield), p. 37.
34. Taber, p. 23.
35. Klare, p. 39.
36. Sun Tzu, 1991, *The Art of War* (Boston: Shambhala Publications), pp. 6-7.

37. Klare, p. 39.

38. Same as above, p. 40.

39. School of the Americas Watch, (www.soaw.org).

40. Klare, p. 34.

41. Omali Yeshitela, "A Lynching in Jasper Texas: Thousands of Legal Lynchings Across the U.S.," (St. Petersburg: Burning Spear Uhuru Publications), p. 6.

42. Alexander Cockburn and Jeffrey St. Clair, 1998, *Whiteout: The CIA, Drugs and the Press* (New York: Verso), p. 145.

43. Same as above, p. 66.

44. Vicki Haddock, March 5, 1989, "Test-tube warfare," *San Francisco Examiner.*

45. Jeffrey St. Clare, April 28, 1999, "Did the CIA poison Paul Robeson?," *Anderson Valley Advertiser.*

46. Klare, pp. 45-47.

47. "A Call To Reject the Federal Weed and Seed Program in Los Angeles," 1992, The Urban Strategies Group: A Project of the Labor/Community Strategy Center.

48. Peter Macdonald, 1993, *Giap: The Victor In Viet Nam* (New York: W.W. Norton Company, Inc.), p. 42.

49. Taber, p. 60.

50. Same as above, p. 62.

51. Klare, p. 265.

52. Same as above.

53. Jon Lee Anderson, 1997, *Che Guevara: A Revolutionary Life* (New York: Grove Press), p. 750.

54. Same as above, p. 741.

55. Klare, p. 268.

56. Omali Yeshitela, 1993, "Defeat the Counterinsurgency: Main Resolution to the Founding Convention of the National People's Democratic Uhuru Movement" (Chicago: National People's Democratic Uhuru Movement), p. 8.

57. Omali Yeshitela, 1987, "Complete the Black Revolution of the Sixties" (Oakland: Marcus Garvey Club), p. 9.

58. Robert Perry, October 15, 1995, "CIA's Drug Confession," *The Consortium of Independent Journalism* (www.consortiumnews.com).

59. Alfred W. McCoy, 1991, *The Politics of Heroin: CIA Complicity in the Global Drug Trade* (New York: Lawrence Hill Books), p. 390.

60. Same as above, p. 438.

61. Howard Kurtz, no date available, "Many blacks blame drug woes on conspiracy among whites," *San Jose Mercury News.*

62. Alfred McCoy, 1972, *The Politics of Heroin In Southeast Asia* (New York: Harper & Row), pp. 58-87.

63. McCoy, *CIA Complicity*, p. 112.

64. Same as above, p. 133.

65. William Blum, November 1996, "In Focus: the CIA, contras, gangs and crack," *Foreign Policy in Focus, Vol. 1, No. 1*, p. 2. (www.foreignpolicy-infocus.org/briefs/vol1/cia)

66. Same as above.

67. Same as above.

68. Same as above.

69. Same as above.

70. Larry Rohter, June 27, 1999, "Colombia to adjust GDP to include drugs," *San Jose Mercury News.*

71. Harold D. Wankel, May 15, 1999, IDEA Special Agent Testimony by "Money laundering by drug trafficking organizations," House Banking and Financial Committee, (www.alternatives.com/crimes/DEAMONEY).

72. Steve Macko, July 17, 1998, "Colombia's New Breed of Drug Traffickers," *ERRI Daily Intelligence Report, Vol. 4,* (www.emergency.com/clmbdea).

73. Rohter, June 27, 1999.

74. Scott Ehlers, June 1998, "In focus: drug trafficking and money laundering," *Foreign Policy in Focus, Vol. 3, No. 16,* p. 1. (www.foreign-infocus.org/briefs/vol3/v3n16lau).

75. Same as above.

76. Same as above.

77. "U.S. military intervenes in Colombia," July-August 1997, *The Burning Spear,* p. 4.

78. Michel Chossudovsky, April 7, 1999, "Kosovo freedom fighters' financed by organized crime," *Antifa Info-Bulletin.*

79. Omali Yeshitela, 1983, *Reparations Now! Abbreviated Report from the International Tribunal on Reparations for Black People in the U.S.* (Oakland: Burning Spear Publications), p. 114.

80. Yeshitela, *Defeat the Counterinsurgency,* p. 23.

Of the two million people in prison in the United States in the year 2000, half of them are African.
Credit: Photodisc.com

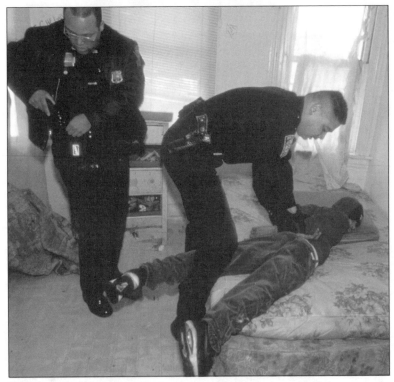

Martial law in the African community.
Credit: Imageworks.

5

Genocide in Modern Form

*The so-called "war on drugs" represents another criti-
cal component of the U.S. counterinsurgency against
our struggle. The war on drugs is actually the U.S.
military response to the drug economy that the U.S.
white rulers have imposed on our starving community. The illegal drug economy, which employs millions of youthful African workers as penny ante
players in a $100 billion white-controlled economy, is
headed up by the same white rulers who head up the
legal white controlled capitalist economy. The idea
that some African youths, living in a state of animal-
like colonial existence in the housing projects, control
a $100 billion economy should be laughable.* [1]

— *Omali Yeshitela*

O ne of the oldest, longest standing, most distinguished and decorated Euro-American traditions is the practice of genocide. Political careers have been built on it, fortunes amassed by it, the American dream realized by it. Western art, science and national identity are the result of it. Genocide is as American as apple pie, and as popular.

In 1946, the United Nations General Assembly passed a resolution defining this practice:

> Genocide is the denial of the right of existence to entire human groups, as homicide is the denial of the right to live of individual human beings; such denial of the right of existence shocks the conscience of mankind, results in great losses to humanity in the form of cultural and other contributions represented by these groups, and is contrary to moral law and to the spirit and aims of the United Nations. Many instances of such crimes of genocide have occurred, when racial, religious, political and other groups have been destroyed, entirely or in part. The punishment of the crime of genocide is a matter of interna-

tional concern. The General Assembly therefore, affirms that genocide is a crime under international law that the civilized world condemns, and for the commission of which principals and accomplices—whether private individuals, public officials or statesmen, and whether the crime is committed on religious, racial, political or any other grounds—are punishable.[2]

This proclamation was passed after the Jews were killed in Nazi Germany, an act that, as Omali Yeshitela has pointed out, may more correctly be termed fratricide. This resolution and the subsequent United Nations Convention on the Prevention and Punishment of the Crime of Genocide came about through tremendous pressure from the liberal white community.

But Adolph Hitler devised his concentration and slave labor camps based on the centuries-old treatment of African and indigenous peoples by European colonizers. For hundreds of years, countless Africans and Indians had been enslaved and colonized—tortured, worked to death, slaughtered, their bodies mutilated and dumped into mass graves. There was no outcry from most Europeans, including Jews. The genocide of hundreds of millions of people to build and maintain capitalism elicited no shame or remorse from the white world.

With no name and no stigma attached to it, genocide was simply "manifest destiny" and "progress"—the necessary, if "unfortunate," process of obtaining land, gold and labor for white society.

Until Europeans did to other Europeans what they had been doing to African and indigenous peoples for centuries, the annihilation of whole peoples was never questioned. No secret, the mass slaughter of black and brown peoples was taken for granted.

For Europeans and North Americans, the practice of genocide was even fun, exhilarating and sporting. Genocide is so titillating for white people that popular sado-masochistic sexual practices are based on its methods: torture, bondage, domination and enslavement.

In *American Holocaust,* David Stannard tells us that following the malicious and genocidal U.S. massacre of indigenous men, women, children and babies at Sand Creek, Colorado in 1864, led by Colonel John Chivington:

> There was exultation in the land. "Cheyenne scalps are getting as thick here now as toads in Egypt," joked the *Rocky Mountain News.* "Everybody has got one and is anxious to get another to send east."

A concerned senator, however, traveled from Washington to Colorado to "confront Colorado's governor and Colonel Chivington openly on the matter." The senator invited the general public to a town hall meeting at the Denver Opera House to discuss the Sand Creek slaughter. Stannard tells us:

> During the course of the discussion and debate someone raised a question: Would it be best, henceforward, to try to "civilize" the Indians or simply to exterminate them? Whereupon, the senator wrote in a letter to a friend, "there suddenly arose such a shout as is never heard unless upon some battlefield—a shout almost loud enough to raise the roof of the opera house—"EXTERMINATE THEM! EXTERMINATE THEM!"[3]

This anecdote is perhaps a good indicator of the popularity of genocide throughout American history. It informs us of the initiative taken by the general white populace in the annihilation of the indigenous people.

Such enthusiasm for genocide is not just to be found in the dusty annals of our past, however. It continues on in the conditions inflicted upon African people today—conditions voted in by the majority of white people. After all, counterinsurgency is genocide carried out by the institutions of the State—the police, the prisons, the education and welfare systems.

WITH INTENT TO DESTROY

The Convention on the Prevention and Punishment of the Crime of Genocide, passed by the United Nations in 1948, reads in part:

> Genocide means any of the following acts committed with intent to destroy, in whole or in part, a national, ethnical, racial or religious group, as such:
>
> a) Killing members of the group;
>
> b) Causing serious bodily or mental harm to members of the group;
>
> c) Deliberately inflicting on the group conditions of life calculated to bring about its physical destruction in whole or in part;
>
> d) Imposing measures intended to prevent births within the group;
>
> e) Forcibly transferring children of the group to another group.[4]

When the convention was finally ratified by the United States, 40 years after its passage, some wondered whether Congress had put off signing it for so long for "fear that it might be held responsible, retrospectively, for the annihilation of Indians in the United States, or its role in the slave trade, or its contemporary support for tyrannical governments engaging in mass murder."[5]

Indeed, the United States *must* be held retroactively accountable for its past genocide. Genocide is not something simply to be acknowledged regretfully many years later. Hundreds of millions of African and indigenous human beings were wiped out in a process that brought an almost incomprehensible amount of wealth into the United States. This wealth, soaked in the blood of oppressed peoples, continues to compound in value for us today.

Inevitably the day of reckoning will come. Justice does not care if our great-grandfathers or our children's children stand for the crime. A price will be paid. Retribution will be exacted one day.

Still, it is easier to acknowledge the transgressions of the past than to admit the reality of today. The true human challenge before us, then, is to not only take responsibility for our history, but to have the courage also to take a stand to end genocide as it is happening right now.

The Genocide Convention was ratified by the United States in 1988 under President Ronald Reagan, even as he was tightening the bloody death grip of counterinsurgency on African, indigenous and other oppressed peoples living in this country right now.

Look at the provisions of the convention. Is there any part of this internationally accepted definition of genocide that does *not* fit the conditions imposed on the African community today? Can any one of us in the white community *honestly* say we don't know that week by week, day by day, hour by hour, African people are facing a situation *deliberately inflicted to bring about their physical destruction in whole or in part*?

Yet now that there is a name and definition for genocide, its current application to African people in this country today is denied.

The information in these chapters is readily available in the mass media—in books, newspapers, and magazines, on television newscasts every day. No government commits genocide in secret. Support from the citizenry is essential. We vote in thousands of new laws for more and more police that kill and cause serious bodily harm to African people in large numbers. We enthusiastically support legislation to lock up African people for life, measures *intended* to prevent births in the population. We are indifferent as African children are forcibly transferred from their parents to white people through the foster care system or sent to prison at the age of 14 under juvenile crime bills.

There are no leftist marches demanding an end to this modern-day genocide. Yet genocide is the foundation of our current economic boom. The beneficiaries of these crimes are not only the CEOs on Wall Street, the bankers, or transnational corporations; it is white people ourselves. All of us.

Counterinsurgency—the suppression of a people's ability to be free—goes hand in hand with genocide. Robert Taber comments in *War of the Flea*, that there "is only one means of defeating an insurgent people who will not surrender, and that is extermination."[6] This has always been the European solution.

Take off the rose-colored glasses and look at the American dream in the light of day. You will see the bleached bones of millions of slaughtered human beings stretching from coast to coast. And you will see, this very day, locked up in prisons, on the streets of the inner cities, on the reservations, in the *barrios*, in the colonial schools, under the gun of the police, millions of living people, suffering humanity, fodder for the U.S. genocide machine.

JUST SAY NO

Slander of an entire population is essential to any effective genocide campaign. "Nits make lice," they said of indigenous babies as they impaled them with bayonets, laughing. "Kill the gooks" they said as they napalmed villages full of children and mothers and the elderly in Southeast Asia. "Spics," "wetbacks," "niggers"—these dehumanizing names have served to incite every atrocity known to man. Slander is particularly important for counterinsurgency. And so it continues.

In the 1980s, the U.S. government launched its "Just Say No," campaign under the leadership of Nancy Reagan after crack began to inadvertently seep into the white population. The campaign was a cover-up for the fact that Nancy's husband was responsible for the proliferation of street drugs in the United States; cocaine was everywhere.

Part of the overall counterinsurgency, "Just Say No" had a two-fold goal. It would wean white people away from drug use—especially cocaine. White people were massively anesthetizing themselves with the white powder that the U.S. government, under Ronald Reagan's regime, was importing by the mega-ton.

More importantly, however, "Just Say No" was effective in criminalizing African people and laying the basis for an overwhelmingly massive intensification of the attack against them. As a result of Reagan's program, well funded, easily accessible drug treatment programs and Narcotics Anonymous groups began to swell in the white communities. Meanwhile, the African community was given the jacket of the "crack nation"—a drug-crazed, violent and criminal population.

Only a few years earlier, it was known throughout the world that African people were oppressed and struggling in the United States. Now, according to white power, they were suddenly incorrigible felons, violent assassins, implacable junkies and unreformable drug sellers.

It was during this period that the U.S. government and media began introducing new labels that rendered our usual names for African and oppressed people obsolete. Now they were the "unredeemable underclass." White people could save themselves from drugs; Africans were condemned to eternal addiction. Wayward white kids were "misunderstood;" African children became "superpredators," who must be jailed when barely out of diapers.

African women were portrayed as "welfare queens" who would defraud poor, unsuspecting white taxpayers at every turn. African youth in housing projects with not enough money in their pockets to take a bus across town were suddenly "drug kingpins." Their mug shots filled the daily papers.

This slander against the African community justifies any and all atrocities inflicted by the law, the courts, the police and the prisons. In 1988, Jerry Adler, writing in *Newsweek* magazine, viciously expressed the government's line criminalizing the African population:

> There are two Americas. No other line you can draw is as trenchant as this. On one side, people of normal human appetites, for food and sex and creature comforts; on the other those who crave only the roar and crackle of their own neurons, whipped into a frenzy of synthetic euphoria. The Crack Nation. It is in our midst, but not part of us....[7]

The "people of normal human appetites, for food and sex and creature comforts" are hungry for genocide. Omali Yeshitela's excellent statement comes to mind: "There is an objective relationship between world slavery and U.S. affluence, and up until now the North American population, opportunistically and demagogically led by their stomachs, pocketbooks, and corrupt leadership, have chosen the continued enslavement of the world."[8]

DEVASTATION OF CRACK

By the time that Gary Webb's "Dark Alliance" series appeared in the *San Jose Mercury News* in 1996, African people were angry. They had already spent years enduring slander, chemical warfare and drug-related violence. Life in black communities was a living hell. In October following the appearance of Webb's articles, CIA Director John M. Deutch was forced to make a rare appearance before a sizable audience in Los Angeles' South Central community. The *Los Angeles Times* reported the event:

> Fighting off hecklers during a 90-minute town hall-style meeting...Deutch denied charges that his agency helped

or turned a blind eye to Latin American cocaine dealers. The gathering of 800 at Locke High School quickly deteriorated into a shouting match. Many in the audience said they arrived feeling angry—wanting answers to the disturbing allegations—and left even angrier, convinced that the answers would never materialize. Even the congresswoman who invited Deutch (Rep. Juanita Millender-McDonald) was condemned by some during the meeting for giving the CIA too comfortable a platform....Many who came to Friday's hearing had been touched, directly or indirectly, by the way crack has ravaged families in the black community. They placed little faith in the CIA director's promise of a complete inquiry. "Nothing is going to come out of it," said Dwight Vaughn, a former addict who now runs a rehabilitation program....[9]

Similarly, an article in *The Oakland Tribune* reflected the disdain held by the African community for the U.S. government's role in the drugs. The article stated that,

In dozens of interviews, blacks from nearly every walk of life—from workaday wage earners to police, from emergency room doctors to drug counselors and preachers—said they believe the federal government played a role in the deadly crack trade.

"If not the CIA, somebody that has boats and airplanes...had to have been involved," said the Rev. Kenneth Chambers of the West Side Missionary Baptist Church.

Even if a full-fledged government investigation turns up no evidence of CIA complicity, many Oaklanders say they will regard that as a cover-up. "If the government brought it here, there won't be any evidence," said Tonya Carr, a food service worker who lives in East Oakland.

Patrick Connell, a clinical attending physician in the Highland Hospital emergency room, has overseen the treatment of thousands of crack victims. Considering how widespread the crack trade is, he said, he "absolutely" believes it involves the U.S. government.[10]

No one was surprised when the CIA officially cleared itself of any wrong doing in the Hitz Report.

In Oakland and Los Angeles, African people today are lodging a class action suit against the CIA, alleging that the "agency's decision not to report drug smuggling to other authorities in the 1980s caused the crack epidemic to spread in inner city communities."[11]

At a black community tribunal, held at the Uhuru House in Oakland, on June 6, 1999, Olivia Woods, one of the plaintiffs in the suit, testified quite movingly of her experience and why she is suing the CIA:

I'm a grandmother and a great-grandmother. I have raised my son's two children for the last twelve or thirteen years. He died from an overdose of crack cocaine in '87, and the children's mother at that time was also addicted, so she had no means or ways to take care of her own children.

I took them into my home and I've had the responsibility of them ever since. I'm 71 years old and my life has changed. I've become a nurturer, a mother figure. I've given up any life that I might have had for myself to donate to my grandchildren who no longer have the love and support of their father, nor their mother. Even though she is still alive, she is unable to provide any kind of care for them.

I've had a grandson also die from crack cocaine, two grandsons in prison, one because he is what they consider a "revolving door criminal." He gets out of jail, and he hasn't done anything, but he can't stay clean. He has no support in the community. There is no place he can go where he can get any kind of support and help, so he falls back into the trap. He begins meeting with the same people he was with before, and if he can't test clean, or if out of fear he doesn't report, he's sent back to prison. This has been going on for the last 10 years. He has not spent more than 6 months out of prison during that time. It's basically because he's addicted to crack cocaine.

He doesn't grow it; he didn't import it. If for whatever reason, he is unable to break the cycle, the habit of it, he's still incarcerated. My main concern, even though this has happened to me and my grandchildren and to other grandmothers and mothers and the whole community at large, is for the children.[12]

PENNY ANTE DRUG TRADE

Inside the African community, the United States government has created a dependent low-scale illegal drug economy, which Yeshitela calls the "penny ante drug trade." With massive unemployment and economic embargo by white power in the African community, the small-time colonial drug economy is sometimes the only way to put food on the table.

Omali Yeshitela sums up the illegal drug trade that is used to criminalize African people:

Some young African thinks that he went into business on his own, thinks that he thought of the idea of selling dope. He doesn't know anything about political economy or the forces that control the resources that come into his community. He doesn't know that a dependent, colonized population can't build its own houses, can't grow the food that it eats, can't make the clothing that it wears....

He thinks that it was his idea to sell dope, when the reality is that there is nothing in our community that white power and the imperialists don't want there. That's why you can't find a hospital there. That's why you can't find a job there. That's why you can't even find a supermarket in your community. If they don't want it there, you won't have it there. That's the reality.

Dealing drugs wasn't his idea. If it had been possible for him to have a job building houses, he would have taken a job building houses, repairing cars, paving streets, growing food, selling insurance even. But it wasn't possible. The only option was the option that white power imperialism put into the community, and that was the dope.

The reality is that the guy out there selling the drugs didn't understand that he was a government employee. The biggest employer in the community is Uncle Sam. Uncle Sam is pushing the dope in the community and a whole bunch of African people are tied to it.[13]

While the African community is forced into the low-scale drug economy, criminalized and slandered in the process, the real drug money is in the white community. The Chairman has pointed out:

You don't find Africans out there making $300 or $400 a day selling drugs in the black community....The reality is those Africans who sell drugs wear everything they own. Those rings you see on their fingers, that gold around their necks, those cars they drive—that's it. When they get ready, the police are going to come and take all of that away from them. They are going to take their mama's house too and say it was bought with drugs.[14]

An article from the *Milwaukee Journal Sentinel* by Jack Norman, titled "View Drug Dealing as Work, Study Says," backs up Chairman Omali's allegations. It cites a study entitled, "The Business of Drug Dealing in Milwaukee," released June 15, 1998. The article states:

Drug dealing is often "an innovative, entrepreneurial, small business venture' that employs more than 10 percent of the young men in many central city neighborhoods, according to a new study....

"Much of what we call 'crime' is actually work," writes John Hagedorn, a longtime researcher into Milwaukee's gang culture who is an assistant professor of criminal science at the University of Illinois at Chicago.

"Most drug entrepreneurs are hard working, but not super-rich," wrote Hagedorn in his report, prepared for the Wisconsin Policy Research Institute and released today. "Most drug entrepreneurs aren't particularly violent."

Hagedorn's work was based on surveys and interviews with drug dealers in two Milwaukee neighborhoods.

In the two neighborhoods, Hagedorn turned up 28 distinct drug "firms" employing 191 people. At least 10 percent of the Latino or African-American men ages 18 to 29 in the neighborhoods were employed at least part time in the drug business, he reported.

One-third of the businesses had gross monthly revenues of less than $1,000, and only four of the 28 exceeded $5,000 monthly....[15]

FIRST LINE OF OFFENSE

Tyranny is a necessary component of counterinsurgency and genocide. No one would vote for his or her own demise. For colonized peoples around the world and inside the United States, there have never been any rights that the oppressor felt bound to respect. The specter of fascism that white liberals so fear has been the order of the day for African people in this country, whether enslaved or "free."

In the 1960s, the powerful struggle of African people won some measure of civil and democratic rights for the first time. Although Africans had been "emancipated" for a century, the right to vote was only granted to them in 1965 with the passage of the Voting Rights Act.

But by 1967, the United States was already passing laws to deny freedom of speech and association for black people. Congress enacted, for example, the H. Rap Brown Bill that made it a crime to cross state lines in order to "incite a riot." More correctly it became illegal for African people to openly express their political views. As a result of this bill, Brown was restrained in New York for 3 years. In Florida a similar bill, the Inciting to Riot Act, also known as the "Joe Waller Bill" was enacted.

In 1968, in the wake of rebellions after the assassination of Martin Luther King, Congress passed the Omnibus Crime Control and Safe Streets Act. This bill nationalized police forces, granting federal subsidization of the training, arming, and modernization of local police forces.[16] The police were now out of the hands of local authorities and became more of a National Guard, as used in U.S.-backed colonial dictatorships throughout the "third world."

In the early 1970s, with heroin landing in CIA planes and flooding the African communities, the United States instituted its oppressive early forerunners of the "war on drugs" legislation. In 1972 President Richard Nixon established the Office of Drug Abuse Law Enforcement (ODALE), a precursor of the Drug Enforcement Administration (DEA). ODALE was empowered by presidential order to requisition agents into the oppressed communities from other federal agencies, including the Bureau of Narcotics and Dangerous Drugs, the Bureau of Customs, the Internal Revenue Service, and the Bureau of Alcohol, Tobacco and Firearms.[17]

The various ODALE forces could use

> ...court authorized wiretaps and no-knock warrants, as well as "search incidental to arrest" procedures. This unique office could also feed the names of suspects to a target-selection committee in the Internal Revenue Service, which would then initiate its own audits and investigations. The office received most of its funds not from congressional appropriations but from the Law Enforcement Assistance Administration (LEAA), an appendage of the Justice Department created by Congress in 1968 for the purpose of financially assisting state and local law enforcement units....Most of its operations were financed by funneling grants from the LEAA to local law enforcement units that participated with ODALE in its raids against narcotics suspects.[18]

Backed by ODALE with LEAA money, Special Weapons and Tactics teams (SWAT) and camouflage-wearing militarized police forces began to be deployed against African communities all over the United States.

In addition, between 1963 and 1972, 200 FBI agents per year received Army riot control training at a special Army seminar conducted at Fort Belvoir, Virginia. The course "was designed to transfer the military philosophy of civil disturbance suppression to the civil law enforcement arena."[19]

Following the mandate of the Omnibus Crime Control and Safe Streets Act of 1968, the U.S. government began using the U.S. police in the same way that it had been using police forces in colonized countries since the 1950s—as the first line of defense against anti-colonial movements.

A British counterinsurgency expert, Sir Robert Thompson, had once extolled the value of the police as a suppressive force. Thompson stated:

> The best organization to be responsible for all internal security intelligence is the special branch [i.e., counter-subversive unit] of the police force rather than any other organization. The police force is a state organization reaching out into every corner of the country and will have had long experience of close contact with the population.[20]

POLICE CONTAINMENT

Thus evolved the public policy of police containment of the African community. Specific counterinsurgent functions became the central focus of policing as it takes place in oppressed communities.

In *War Without End*, Michael Klare notes four factors which play a role in counterinsurgent police work universally. These factors are designed specifically to crush movements of oppressed peoples and to keep them from rising up again. They are resources control, identification, surveillance, and pacification.

Resources control works to stop the flow of selected resources, both human and material, into communities and revolutionary movements of oppressed peoples. This program is designed to crush financial and political support for political organizing in these communities and to diffuse any popular revolutionary base. The police often attempt to infiltrate any genuine organization or form vigilante groups which they control, such as "crime watch."

Identification is a key part of population and resources control; in Viet Nam everyone 15 years and older was required to register with the Saigon government and carry ID cards. In the United States, the widespread use of "pro-active policing" gets the data and fingerprints of African people into police computers regardless of whether the police have had any run-ins with them or not. Today, we see this practice extended even to routine fingerprinting of children in elementary schools.

The *surveillance* function is obvious, including wiretapping, the use of listening devices, and the employment of infiltrators and spies in movement organizations. Surveillance has been used since the defeat of the revolutionary black movement in this country to frame up and intimidate African people. Significantly, surveillance will be legalized under the Juvenile Crime Bill legislation.

The function of *pacification* is deceptive and in fact the most deadly. While the name brings to mind "goodwill" projects in impoverished communities, in fact "the paramount task of the U.S. pacification effort is the identification and neutralization" of revolutionary forces. The Phoenix Program in Viet Nam, discussed above, and COINTELPRO were "pacification" programs.[21]

Understanding that an oppressed African community is potentially revolutionary at any given time, police departments continue to use all four of these counterinsurgent factors in African communities.

"Community policing," currently in place in most cities, is one of the programs that implements these factors, especially identification and surveillance. Klare notes that after the 1968 rebellions following the assassination of Martin Luther King, "U.S. government subsidization of the training, arming and modernization of local police forces ...became an established mechanism for domestic law enforcement."[22]

With all of this in mind, the massive police brutality that is raging against African people today should not be surprising. Police murders are not the work of just a few "rotten apples"; the police are doing what they were trained to do whether they act as "nice" policemen or killer cops. The police are agents of the U.S. State; their work is to suppress the colonized African community.

As Chairman Omali urges,

> We must organize, not just to stop a police killing, because that's not enough. The police are instruments of State power and they are fighting to keep things just as they are. So that Mexico continues to be called California, Texas, Colorado, Arizona and New Mexico. So that the indigenous people are still kept in concentration camps that they call reservations. So that the Africans are still denied even basic assumptions of humanity.[23]

POLICE STATE

Year after year, the counterinsurgency continues, dispensing the drugs, filling the prisons, beating down African people, taking away democratic rights. First Amendment rights guaranteeing freedom of speech, religion, the press, along with the right of assembly are denied African people by more and more Supreme Court decisions. The Fourth Amendment, which supposedly protects against unreasonable searches and seizures, is under particular assault when it comes to black people.

In 1980, the warrantless arrest and seizure of stolen items from vehicles of people stopped for traffic violations was ruled not in violation of the Fourth Amendment. In 1984, the Supreme Court ruled that prison inmates were not entitled to Fourth Amendment protection against unreasonable searches and seizures in their individual cells. In 1987, search warrants were held valid under the Fourth

Amendment despite ambiguous description of the place to be searched. The resulting search of a wrong apartment by police was held reasonable and not in violation of Fourth Amendment.

In 1989, excessive force used by police was upheld under "objective reasonableness" of the Fourth Amendment. By end of the '80s, a Washington Post/ABC News poll reported that 62 percent of North Americans were even willing to forfeit some of their *own* democratic rights to support the war on drugs, the code word for the attack on the African community.[24]

A warrantless protective sweep of a house in conjunction with an arrest was held permissible under the Fourth Amendment in 1990 if a policeman reasonably believes that the area to be swept harbors individuals posing danger to the police.[25]

All welfare recipients in Michigan are currently being forced to undergo drug testing across the board, according to a *Washington Post* article. The federal "Welfare Reform" law of 1996 allowed states to test all candidates for welfare, and Michigan is the first to do so. The state of Michigan is "saying that if you want money for food and shelter, you have to give up the Fourth Amendment rights that others have." Refusal to submit to testing or to enter treatment if found positive results in the loss of welfare in a system that only grants benefits to families with children under 18.[26]

In addition to these and so many other attacks on civil rights, the ability to vote has virtually been taken away from African people. The Sentencing Project, a nonprofit organization that advocates alternatives to prison sentences, reports that today because of felony convictions,

> [A]bout 1.46 million black men of total voting-age population of 10.4 million have lost their right to vote....Laws in 13 states bar 510,000 black men from voting because of felony convictions. An additional 950,000 are ineligible

to vote because of laws regarding felony offenders in prison, on parole or on probation in 46 states.[27]

With 13 percent of African men disenfranchised, African people are in much the same situation that existed before the 1965 Voting Rights Act was passed. They have suffrage in theory, but in reality cannot vote. One article gives some startling facts:

> In seven states—Alabama, Florida, Iowa, Mississippi, New Mexico, Virginia, and Wyoming—fully a quarter of all black men are permanently ineligible to vote. In Florida alone, 204,600 black men, and in Texas 156,600 black men, have lost the vote.
>
> In some cities in the states in which convicted felons are permanently disenfranchised, as older, pre-prison-boom blacks die out, the proportion of black men of all ages who lack the right to vote will rise to about one third by 2020. In certain parts of some Southern cities—Houston, Memphis, Miami, and New Orleans, for example—it may be as many as half. Conceivably, an overwhelmingly black town could have an electoral register dominated by a white minority.[28]

Furthermore, under conditions imposed by the counterinsurgency, African people have no right to assemble. Like the vagrancy laws of old, many states have passed laws calling for the arrest of more than two people gathered in one place in African communities. In Philadelphia, a law was passed that calls for the arrest of anyone sitting on the sidewalk for more than 20 minutes.

AMERICA'S DISAPPEARED

In Berkeley and other cities, thousands of white people have marched at different times to denounce the victims of Latin America's death squads that sweep people off the streets, subjecting them to torture, brutal imprisonment and murder. These victims of imperialist terror are called the "disappeared" by their people. It's not necessary to leap over the inner cities of the United States to go all the way to El Salvador or Chile, however, to protest the missing. They are right here. The counterinsurgency against the African community regularly sweeps away thousands and thousands of African people.

The brutal "Operation Hammer" in the late 1980s in Los Angeles exemplified such sweeps. A description of the attack follows:

> More than 1,400 people—mostly young black men— were arrested and booked in mobile processing centers on charges ranging from illegal weapons to old parking tickets. Or they were picked up for violating curfews that applied only in poor black and Hispanic neighborhoods. Hundreds who weren't arrested had their names recorded in the LAPD's gang roster for further surveillance...[29]

By 1990, the counterinsurgent assault was so obvious that a *Los Angeles Times* article was forced to echo the chants long heard at Uhuru-led demonstrations and rallies. It asserted that:

> ...the nation's war on drugs has in effect become a war on black people...

> As America's cities and towns, led by President Bush and drug czar William J. Bennett, have intensified the battle against drugs—particularly cocaine—these authorities say, the efforts have been disproportionately concentrated in black communities.

For one thing, law officers and judges say, although it is clear that whites sell most of the nation's cocaine and account for 80 percent of its consumers, it is black and other minorities who continue to fill up America's courtrooms and jails....

Across the nation, blacks—and some Latinos—complain that their neighborhoods are barricaded, that roadblocks are set up for identification checks, that they are routed from their apartments without warrants, that police target them with "shoot on sight" policies and that they are disproportionately arrested in "sweep" operations for minor misdemeanors and traffic violations that have nothing to do with the drug war....

Consequently, police, judges and attorneys say, under the nation's current approach, black America is being criminalized at an astounding rate. According to an analysis by the Sentencing Project in Washington, D.C., one in four black men in their twenties in the United States is either in jail, in prison, on parole or on probation. By contrast, the study found only 6 percent of white men in their 20s—or about one in every 17—fell into the same categories. Women's prisons, once hardly used, are filling to capacity with black faces.

Separate studies by the FBI and National Institute for Drug Abuse in 1988 came to the identical conclusion that blacks make up only 12 percent of the nation's drug users. Studies of those who consume drugs, in fact, show slightly lower percentages of blacks and Latinos than whites in every age category.[30]

CRIME BILL

In 1994, President William Jefferson Clinton passed the Violent Crime Control and Law Enforcement Act, known as the Crime Bill, another of the lethal legal weapons in the counterinsurgency against African people. The Crime Bill allocates $30.2 billion to implement the following provisions:

- "Three Strikes, You're Out" on the federal level. Under this provision, third-time felons are sent to prison for life. Most people prosecuted on a three strikes law have been African.
- Children tried as adults. This includes youth as young as 13 years old who will be sent to adult prisons where they will be abused and brutalized.
- $9.7 billion for prison building. This includes $1.8 billion to reimburse states for incarcerating Mexican people.
- Sixty new categories that impose the federal death penalty.
- 100,000 new police in cities throughout the country. President Clinton boasted about carrying out this provision, which coincides with the rash of police murders and atrocities across the country.

In order to qualify for Crime Bill funds and to get some of the 100,000 new police, cities and counties must set up and implement community policing programs. Far from being a gentler form of law enforcement, "community policing" is a counterinsurgent program long used to carry out the goals of resource control, identification, surveillance and pacification, cited above.

In addition to implementing community policing in order to qualify for Crime Bill funds, states must also enforce the "truth in sentencing" laws. This means that individuals convicted of 'violent' crimes must serve at least 85 percent of their sentences, as opposed to the previous average of 55 percent.[31]

POLICE BRUTALITY

"Blacks' dissatisfaction with police is more than twice that of whites' in Chicago and New York, and is nearly as high elsewhere, a Justice Department survey of 12 cities found," reported *The Wall Street Journal,* in June 1999.[32]

No wonder. Police murders and brutality against African people are everyday occurrences, the result of the policy of police containment.

Today it is estimated that 89 percent of police departments have paramilitary units. Forty-six percent have been trained by active duty armed forces, in violation, incidentally, of the Posse Comitatus Act of 1878, which made it illegal for the military to act as police on U.S. territory or waters.[33] With such an occupying army patrolling the streets of the African community, fatalities, casualties and "collateral damage" are to be expected.

Just how many thousands of African people are in fact brutalized and killed by the police every year? All reports on police brutality point out that national statistics are nearly impossible to find. They are covered up from department to department, and no comprehensive U.S. government statistics are kept on these crimes. Nevertheless the headlines scream the reality almost daily. Cops are killing and brutalizing Africans in every city, every town, every rural community.

Some statistics float to the surface through groups like Amnesty International or Human Rights Watch. In New York City between 1990 and 1993, 117 people were killed by the police and an additional 271 were wounded.[34] In 1998 the city of New York paid out a record $40 million to resolve 739 claims and lawsuits that accused police of brutality. During that year, 2,324 claims seeking damages from the city in police brutality cases were filed.[35] In California, in 1995, 122 people were killed by the police and 33 people killed by police use of pepper spray. [36]

We can look to police brutality complaints filed with the Justice Department to give us some idea of the depth of this violence. In fiscal year 1996, 11,721 complaints of police brutality were received by the Justice Department's civil rights division, according to watchdog groups. Of these complaints, only thirty-seven cases were presented to a grand jury, with a total of only twenty-nine convictions or pleas.[37]

Occasionally cases of police violence or murder are so blatant that they are picked up by the national news, making the victims' names household words. The video of Rodney King being brutally beaten in Los Angeles was widely shown on TV. Abner Louima, tortured with a plunger in the rectum, and Amadou Diallo, 22, murdered with 19 bullets out of 41 shot at him, sparked movements in New York.

In Riverside, California, 19 year old Tyisha Miller was murdered by police after being shot at least two dozen times as she lay asleep in her car. The assassination of TyRon Lewis, 18, killed by three shots from police while his hands were raised in St. Petersburg, Florida, generated community rebellions and Uhuru Movement campaigns.

Donta Dawson, 19, shot in the back of the head as he sat in his car in Philadelphia, was the basis of community pressure led by the Uhuru Movement in that city. These police executions gained broader notoriety because of expressions of outrage by the African community.

Most of the thousands and thousands of victims of police brutality, however, get no more attention than small articles in the back pages of the daily papers that heap slander on the name of the deceased. Only their devastated families and loved ones are aware of the truth about the victim.

For example, these articles, clipped from the *Oakland Tribune* in 1997 and 1998, do everything possible to justify police murders:

- "Man Killed After Traffic Stop: No warrants but wearing a bulletproof vest," headlined an article describing how cops gunned down 23 year old Charles Williams. Apparently it is understood that both warrants and bulletproof vests constitute justification for police execution.[38]

- "Police officer kills suspect flashing 'gun,'" refers to the police murder of 24 year old Bill Vaughn Jr. who is incorrectly described as a drug dealer. The article casually mentions that— oops!—Vaughn's "weapon" turned out to be a toy gun. The family denies even that. Many in the African community charge that the police plant a real or imitation gun every time they kill an African person.[39]

- "Woman killed during struggle with policeman," relates the story of the police murder of Venus Beaird, 37. A beloved and well-known union member from Oakland, Beaird was killed by police in her own home, in front of her 17 year old daughter after attempting to refuse police entrance to her apartment. [40] Such headlines are all too common in every city.

DEATH SQUADS

By 1999, the existence of death squads in the Ramparts Division of the Los Angeles Police Department was coming to light. On August 19 of that year, an item in the English *Guardian,* reported:

> An elite group of detectives in the Los Angeles police force, known as the "death squad" is under investigation by the FBI after officers killed two unarmed robbers by shooting them in the back... The dead men, Jose Rafael Figueroa, 24, and Mario Guerrero, 23, were each killed by a single shotgun blast...

> [C]ritics of the squad, officially called the special investigations section (SIS), point to its long history of shooting suspects in almost identical circumstances.

Lawyer Steven Yagman has taken on the [most recent] case as his 14th lawsuit against the SIS since 1990. He claims that the "death squad," as he called the SIS in court hearings, has now killed 59 suspects in more than 50 shootings since 1977 and in all but one case the dead were shot in the back.[41]

As this book goes to press, the LAPD scandal continues to unfold, exposing police, prosecutors and judges on the highest level. More than 10,000 convictions could be overturned and Los Angeles will pay at least $500 million or more in damages.

At the West Coast Conference Against Police Brutality held at the Uhuru House in Oakland in 1997, Chairman Omali Yeshitela explained this deadly plague by identifying the police as an effective tool of the U.S. State apparatus:

> Our communities have been so demonized, so criminal-ized, that the system doesn't have to offer up real expla-nations any more. What they do, of course, is offer a rap sheet and a mug shot, saying, "You know he did have a criminal record," as if he gave it to himself....
>
> It's important for us to see the families of the victims. We must recognize that the boy did have a mama and a sister and a cousin, and they care and they hurt because of what has happened....There's so much pain in our com-munities as a result of police violence, but we have to go beyond the pain, and organize. Why is it that we hear the same story over and over all over this country?
>
> It's because of the rape and pillage and slavery that resulted in our impoverishment and the destruction of whole civilizations, and built the U.S. capitalist system. In the process of this rip-off the State emerged....We're talk-ing about a whole system based on parasitism. We're

talking about a blood-sucking system that is like a parasite. In order for them to maintain this relationship, it's necessary for them to have the State and the police.[42]

DRUG-DEALING POLICE

The police have been exposed for playing a direct role in bringing the drugs into the African community. It makes sense that the police would be one of the government's main vehicles for trafficking. They are the first line of defense in a counterinsurgency that uses deadly drugs as one of its main tools. Tied to their narcotics trafficking, the police attack, murder and steal from countless African people. Many are too intimidated by the gestapo tactics to even file a complaint. Some of the more notorious of these cases have taken place in major U.S. cities:

- *New Orleans*—In October 1994, a 32 year old African woman, Kim Groves, was murdered by the police for filing a brutality complaint against Officer Len Davis. Groves had witnessed Davis pistol-whipping a teenager. Davis and eight other policemen were exposed and indicted on charges of conspiracy to distribute cocaine. At least 30 other New Orleans policemen have been charged with armed robbery, kidnapping, battery, bribery, extortion, rape and murder between 1992 and 1996.[43]
- *Philadelphia*—In 1995, more than 2,000 criminal cases had to be reopened and more than 100 convictions were overturned because several squads of police were involved in planting evidence in drug cases, shaking down drug suspects, pocketing the money, and making false arrests.[44]
  One cop, Jack Baird, admitted stealing over $100,000 from dozens of people. Baird, who was highly praised by his supervisors for his police work, was a vicious and brutal animal, according to reports. He and others routinely broke into the homes of African people, beat them mercilessly, and stole their

money. Bessie Sharpe is one Northside Philadelphia resident who was brutally vandalized by Baird and others. They tore up her whole house and stole $3,000 of hard earned cash that was stuffed under her mattress.[45]

In 1994, the Pennsylvania police union refused to let cops participate in a survey to measure their exposure to, and opinions of, official misconduct. According to *The New York Times:*

> The National Institute of Justice, part of the Department of Justice, surveyed 700 Ohio officers and found 10 percent had seen fellow officers perform an illegal search for drugs. In Illinois, the survey, which excluded Chicago, found one-quarter of 1,200 officers questioned had seen such an improper search.[46]

- *New York*—In 1992, Michael Dowd and five other New York City police officers were arrested for stealing cocaine from dealers, selling it off the dashboards of their squad cars and raking in hundreds of thousands of dollars a week. Two years later, another police gang, "The Morgue Boys," rampaged though their precinct, raiding drug houses, beating up dealers and reselling cocaine. The gang was fond of firing off their guns while partying on-duty. More than 30 cops were indicted. Settlements to victims of this case cost the city over $10 million.[47]
- *Washington, D.C.*—In 1996, members of the "Dirty Dozen" police gang were exposed as working for what they thought was a major cocaine organization in an FBI sting. The lead cop, Nygel M. Brown, recruited 11 other policemen to work for an FBI "drug ring."[48]

The police criminality cited here is not a result of "corruption." It is simply an example of how the police function as agents of the U.S. State in the war against black people. It's not a matter of good cops or bad cops. The police work for the State in carrying out their assigned duties in the war against the African community. The police are no different than Air Force pilots who drop bombs on the victims of U.S. aggression abroad; it doesn't matter if they are mean and brutal bombers or if they are really nice guys. The people on the ground are still dead.

The counterinsurgent policy of police containment of African communities is the status quo in this country. Efforts to make the police "nicer" are ridiculous and irrelevant. New York's laughable attempt to clean up the force as a result of much protest from African people illustrates this. After the numerous cases of police torture and murder of African and Puerto Rican people in New York City, Mayor Rudolph Guiliani promised to make the NYPD act "more respectfully." They will be required to respond to people with "Yes, sir" and "No, sir" or "Yes, ma'am" and "No, ma'am." BBC News reported, "Undercover politeness officers will make random checks to ensure police are keeping to the standards."[49]

So now, monitored by the undercover politeness agents, New York cops will ask an African victim, "Sir, would you prefer 40 shots to your chest or just a plunger up your rectum?"

It is no wonder that cops are hated and feared by the African community. A 1999 poll in New York City is representative: "Nearly 9 out of 10 black residents questioned in the survey said they thought the police often engaged in brutality against blacks, and almost two-thirds said police brutality against members of minority groups is widespread."[50]

"THREE STRIKES, YOU'RE OUT"

Since 1994, California and many other states have passed their own "three strikes" laws. On the ballot as Proposition 184, the Three Strikes, You're Out initiative passed overwhelmingly in California, including in San Francisco and Berkeley, home of "progressive" white voters. On the same California ballot was the anti-Mexican

Proposition 187, which took away rights from the Mexican population in California. Some white liberals supported the just Mexican-led
effort to defeat Prop. 187, but united with "Three Strikes," which was
going to massively incarcerate Mexican and African people in a state
that boasts of the third highest prison population in the world.

"Three Strikes" not only mandates 25 years to life for a third felony, it doubles sentences for second felonies. Judges and courts can
upgrade misdemeanors to felonies at will. Thousands of Africans
have been stopped for "driving while black." If a person responds to
this injustice—saying something the policeman doesn't like—he can
be arrested for "resisting arrest," which can be levied as a felony
charge. Strike one. And so it continues. By the time an African is 18,
he often has two "strikes."

A classic example of "Three Strikes" sentencing was the case of
Michael Garcia of Los Angeles who was given 25 years to life in
prison for shoplifting a package of meat valued at $5.62. California's
law, one of the most stringent in the United States, provides that the
first two strikes must be serious or violent and the third can be any
felony. In reality, 70 percent of all second and third strike cases filed
in California in 1994 were "non violent and nonserious offenses."[51]

By 1996, two years after the "Three Strikes" legislation passed,
the headlines of the *San Francisco Chronicle* already asserted the
predictable: "Huge Racial Disparity in '3 Strikes' Sentences: Rate for
blacks is lopsided, study says." The article read:

> African Americans are being sent to prison under the 2
> year old "Three Strikes" law 13 times more often than
> whites, according to an analysis of state correction statis-
> tics released this week.
>
> The study...says that last year 43 percent of inmates
> imprisoned for a third "strike" under the new law were
> African Americans, even though blacks represent only 7

percent of the total state population and one-fifth of all Californians arrested for felonies.

At the same time, whites who make up 53 percent of the state population and account for a third of all felony arrests—constitute less than 25 percent of the inmates serving prison terms for 'third strike' convictions.

'Not since the days of the all-white juries and state-sponsored discrimination under Jim Crow laws has the United States seen such a dramatic display of systematic overrepresentation in its public policies,' the study says. 'Three Strikes and You're Out' can truly be said to be California's Apartheid."[52]

The report cited in the above article, compiled by the San Francisco-based Center on Juvenile and Criminal Justice, exposed that Africans and whites used drugs at about the same rate, yet African people were arrested for drug offenses at roughly five times the rate of whites during the height of the drug war in 1989. An *Oakland Tribune* article on the same report revealed:

The study showed that whites fare better in the criminal justice system than do members of other ethnic groups. One-third of white first offenders had their charges reduced while only one-fourth of African Americans and Latinos were given the same benefit of the doubt.

Other statistics from the report:

- Five times as many young black men are in jail or on parole in California as there are African men of all ages enrolled in four-year college degree programs.
- White first offenders receive rehabilitative placements in the community at twice the rate of blacks or Mexicans.

- Mexicans go to prison for drug offenses at twice the rate of whites. Africans receive prison sentences one-third more frequently than whites."[53]

Not surprisingly, California's "Three Strikes" law was strongly backed by the Prisons Guards Union, which put $100,000 into the proposition that has swelled California's 50 prisons beyond capacity.[54]

JUVENILE CRIME BILL

One of the most disturbing fronts of the counterinsurgency is the popular move to imprison African children. Currently, an extension of the Crime Bill, the Juvenile Crime Control Act, is pending in Congress. At the same time, the Juvenile Justice Initiative is on the ballot in California. These bills put youth under the jurisdiction of federal courts with harsher sentences and fewer rights. The Juvenile Crime Bill targets children as young as 13 by sending them to adult prisons where they will be brutalized and raped. It also lowers the age of the death penalty from 18 to 16.

This legislation was not made for white youth who are arming themselves in a nationwide rampage of violence and murder against schoolmates, teachers and parents. The goal of the Juvenile Crime Bill, like its adult counterpart, is to jail black people.

An article in the *San Francisco Chronicle* pointed out that:

> According to national crime statistics...in 1995 less than one half of one percent of all U.S. children between the ages of 10 and 17 were arrested in cases involving serious or violent crimes.....James Bell, a staff attorney for the Youth Law Center in San Francisco, said dire conditions for juveniles in detention are only going to get worse—especially for disproportionately represented minority youth—if the federal bills pass.[55]

In the 1980s, the state of Florida began giving prosecutors, rather than judges, total discretion as to whether to try a child as an adult. Thus, "two hundred percent more children have been locked up in adult Florida prisons since the law went into effect." New York has followed this same trend. A 14 year old arrested for a violent crime is automatically tried as an adult there and a 16 year old arrested for *any* felony faces adult prosecution.[56]

PRISONS PACKED WITH AFRICAN PEOPLE

Prison rates are soaring so fast that it is hard to keep track of them. As of February 2000, the U.S. prison population topped two million, and the numbers are rising. The United States, with less than five percent of the world's population, has a quarter of the world's prison inmates.[57] "Crime" has nothing to do with it since the national crime rate has dropped every year since 1992. An article in the *San Francisco Chronicle* shows that in 1998 the largest decline of crime on record "was led by an 11 percent drop in robbery and an 8 percent drop in homicide."[58]

The majority of African people in prison have not been locked up for homicide or robbery. They are nonviolent drug offenders who have been locked up for years for possession or low-level dealing. If they were white, they would more likely be in drug treatment centers.

Once convicted, African people are given much tougher sentences than white people. Eighty-three percent of federal crack defendants are African and 4.1 percent white, even though African people account for 38 percent of all crack users and white people account for 52 percent.[59]

It is well-known that five grams of crack cocaine gets the same federal mandatory minimum sentence of five years without parole as 500 grams of powder cocaine and 100 grams of heroin both of which are much more likely to be possessed by a white person.[60]

There are so many African people in prison that the weekend activity of many African families is prison visiting. The total inmate population today is almost six times that of 1972.[61] The prison population doubled between 1989 and 1999, more than a million Africans are now incarcerated. Blacks make up half of the total prison population. One newspaper article asserted:

> By 2000, roughly 1 in 10 black men will be in prison—a statistic with major social implications because prisoners do not have jobs, pay taxes or care for their children at home. And because many states bar felons from voting, at least one in seven African American men will have lost the right to vote....
>
> In the past five decades, the disparity between races has widened dramatically as minorities have replaced whites in the prison population....[62]

A *New York Times* article exclaimed:

> Every 20 seconds, someone in America is arrested for a drug violation. Every week on average a new jail or prison is built to lock up more people in the world's largest penal system....In the 1980s crack cocaine scared the country....But for all the havoc wreaked by crack the worst fears were not realized. Crack appealed mainly to hard-core drug users. The number of crack users began falling not long after surveys began counting them. A decade later, the violence of the crack trade has burned out, and murder rates have plunged....More whites than blacks use crack, according to surveys, but as the war on drugs focused on poor city neighborhoods, blacks went to prison at a far higher rate. Here in California, five black men are behind bars for each one in a state university.[63]

The prison population of the United States is so large that the state of California alone has the third largest prison population in the world[64]—far greater than enormous countries like Brazil and India. As of 1997, California had a total of 145,500 people in prisons that are operating at 189.8 percent of capacity. In addition, approximately 102,000 people are on parole in the state. With the prison population rising minute-by-minute, well over a quarter of a million people in California today are under the control of the California Department of Corrections.[65] Seventy percent of this captive population is African and Mexican.

CAGED LIKE ANIMALS

The conditions in the prisons are unspeakably brutal and genocidal. African men are caged like animals in the prime of their youth, bursting with energy and the desire to experience life, raise a family, express their talents. Many of these young people have been held in the camps since their teens and are sentenced to be there until they die. Others are destined by this colonial court system to be in and out of prison for years.

Families and friends of prisoners are also sentenced to brutal and degrading treatment by prison authorities. Women visiting men in prison are often subjected to strip searches as well as other insults and invasions of personal privacy. Impoverished families often find themselves having to travel a whole day across the state for a few hours of impersonal visitation with a loved one.

Inside the camps, more and more rights are being taken away from the inmates, and the rehabilitative programs instituted in the '60s and '70s are no longer existent. Prisoners are systematically being denied everything from college correspondence courses, to weightlifting, to TV. Without amenities, the true purpose of prisons is blatantly clear. They are institutions of genocide.

Across the country, reports surface from time to time of the conditions of physical and psychological torture endured by the largely African and Mexican prisoners. In New Jersey, a federal investigation of Bayside State Prison was launched after scores of inmates were "systematically beaten after a corrections officer was killed by an inmate there...."

> More than 100 inmates told *The Inquirer* last year that they were kicked, punched or beaten with nightsticks, in many cases while naked and handcuffed. They also said they were forced to walk a gauntlet of baton-wielding corrections officers in riot gear.[66]

California prisons are prototypes of sheer barbarity, with the super-max Pelican Bay State Prison being one of the meanest in the country. "Pelican Bay is now an international model of sensory deprivation and isolation," asserts one report on the prison in which half the inmates are locked in their cells 23 hours a day. In 1991, federal investigations revealed that guards had beaten an inmate's head with the butt of a gas gun and then framed the victim.[67]

One of the most notorious cases of abuse at Pelican Bay was one in which guards and medical staff "boiled an inmate alive," saying as they forcibly submerged him in scalding water until the top layer of his skin burned off, "We'll make a white man out of you yet." Other abuses include hog-tying prisoners to toilets or kicking them in the face after cell extractions, as well as the constant framing of inmates so that their sentences grow by decades with each year inside the prison.[68]

California's genocidal Corcoran prison is known as "one of the most violent institutions in the nation."[69] For sport, Corcoran prison guards set up "gladiator" fights in a bullpen between inmates, most commonly between African and Mexican prisoners. Armed guards stood on the tiers above them betting on the outcome of the fights.

During these "games," guards shot more than 50 prisoners, 7 of whom were killed.[70] The California Department of Corrections investigation, produced no criminal charges except the disciplining of the one guard who had provided evidence of guard brutality to federal authorities.[71]

More and more prisoners are being subjected to inhuman conditions in the maximum security prisons. According to an article in the *San Francisco Examiner*:

> About 57 maximum security units in 42 states now hold about 1 percent of the nation's 1.8 million prisoners....Started about 15 years ago, these prisons largely restrict prisoners to their cells 23 hours a day, and allow a prisoner to move outside the cell only with leg irons, handcuffs and an escort of two or three guards.
>
> Here, movement is regulated by 1,400 electronically controlled gates and watched over by 168 television monitors. With almost one prison employee for each prisoner, it costs about $50,000 a year to incarcerate a prisoner here, far more than the average cost in other prisons.[72]

In Florida, following the trend of many other states, there are more than 3,000 people under "close management," known as CM, a euphemism for the torture of long-term solitary confinement. The conditions in these concentration camps are so brutal that it is virtually impossible to remain sane. One prisoner described life in Florida's super-max control units in a *St. Petersburg Times* article:

> "Your mind turns in on itself. You literally talk to yourself, and the frustration makes you punch the door and walls...I've seen guys slice their wrist, their arms and their necks. I've seen guys bite chunks out of their arms trying to sever the main veins. I know guys who would

swallow bed springs, tooth brushes, strips of Coke cans, nails, razor blades, pens, pencils—anything that will puncture their insides just to get away from the CM cells."

The article continues:

Florida inmates and their advocates describe close management as nothing short of hell. They allege frequent mental or physical abuse by guards. They tell of summer temperatures reaching above 100 degrees, surrounded by the stench of feces, urine, body odor and, periodically, chemical agents used to force unruly inmates into compliance. They recount a constant struggle to keep their minds clear, and amid perpetual boredom, a never-ending build-up of anger.[73]

A white man wrote of his experience interviewing prisoners in New Folsom prison, another notoriously deadly institution in California, outside of Sacramento, the state's capital. Although his comments reveal a patronizing, anti-African and anti-Mexican arrogance, they also expose the angry sentiments and spirit of resistance of those captured colonial subjects who are being forced into today's concentration camps:

"I shouldn't be here" was a phrase I heard often, followed by an impassioned story about the unfairness of the system....Shirtless, sweating, unshaven...one inmate after another described the rage that was growing inside New Folsom. The weights had been taken away; no more conjugal visits for inmates who lacked a parole date; not enough help for the inmates who were crazy...not enough drug treatment, when the place was full of junkies; not enough to do—a list of grievances magnified by the overcrowding into something that felt volatile, ready to go off with the slightest spark.[74]

FREE ALL AFRICANS IMPRISONED ON DRUG CHARGES

Counterinsurgency is being carried out against African, Mexican and indigenous people in this country. It is not a conspiracy, as some white leftists proclaim. It is a popular war, public policy, taken for granted, voted in during every election.

Ultimately, as in any unjust war, the victims must exact justice and win reparations. Therefore, the National People's Democratic Uhuru Movement is waging a campaign to release all African people locked up on drug-related charges. A petition for the campaign reads:

> We, the undersigned, recognizing the role of the Central Intelligence Agency (CIA) in creating and distributing crack cocaine in the African community, demand that the U.S. government free all African men and women on drug-related charges. This includes all African people who are facing trial, locked in juvenile detention centers, on parole or probation, imprisoned under house arrest, held in city, county, state or federal prisons for any charges which are drug-related.
>
> We demand reparations to the African community to be used for community-run drug rehabilitation and treatment centers, and to repair all damage to the community as a result of the government and CIA-imposed drugs and resulting violence. Resources for reparations will also be used for viable economic development in the African community.[75]

Given the evidence, can any honest person refuse to support this demand?

Gary Webb is touted as a hero in white left and liberal circles. He makes revelations but no one has to take responsibility for it. There is no mention made of the wasted African lives, no call for justice. There is no price to pay.

Surely, in the white community, we have to do more than just listen to Gary and then go home.

African people are targets of an official counteroffensive being waged against their anti-colonial movement and their people. The *real* drug dealers are politicians, governmental officials, businessmen, bankers, brokers and lawyers who operate in the mainstream of white society. The real drug users are white people who are generally treated with sympathy in the press and offered a wide range of treatment options. White users do not, overall, spend the greater part of their lives in prison.

The beneficiaries of both the drug economy and the "prison industrial complex" are white people, just like us. Laundered money from the narcotics trade and the tremendous infusion of money spent on prison building are the lifeblood coursing through the strong U.S. economy that benefits the North American population. The million African people in prison are victims of a social system that needs someone else's suffering and exploitation in order to exist.

Impoverished Africans are not the criminals. They are oppressed colonial subjects. They are being stuffed into concentration camps with "crime" as the thinly veiled justification for genocide. As is usually the case, this genocide turns out to be a very lucrative proposition. Founded on slavery, slaughter and the theft of land and resources, the U.S. economy is as dependent on genocide today as it was in the past.

To look at the exposures of U.S. government drug trafficking—to just sit back and find it "interesting"—is complicity with this genocide. If we believe in justice, we must take responsibility and act. A campaign to release the millions of Africans incarcerated on drug-related charges is urgent. These are the "disappeared" of North America.

COUNTERINSURGENCY HAS MANY FRONTS

The prisons, police and the court systems are not the only places where the violent counterinsurgency plays itself out in the lives of African people in this country. Counterinsurgency is multifaceted. There is no aspect of black life that is not touched by this U.S. war.

For one thing, old-fashioned white citizen violence against African people, though less socially acceptable than in previous times, is an ever-present reality. The horrible murder of James Byrd Jr. in Jasper, Texas spawned many copycat attacks, and made national headlines:

> Dragged along a bumpy road by a chain around his ankles, James Byrd Jr. desperately shifted from side to side to ease the excruciating pain and was alive until his head was torn off by a concrete drainage duct, a patholo-gist testified...[76]

Byrd was kidnapped and murdered in a savage attack by three white supremacists.

Chairman Omali points out that the Jasper, Texas murder does not need "healing from the hatred," as called for by Jesse Jackson and white liberals who blamed racism for the murder. Yeshitela asserts that African people need *political power*. The answer lies in the ability to defeat a system in which the police and prisons are legally able to do to African people every day what the three white men did to James Byrd Jr. on June 7, 1998. In summing up the situation in Jasper, Texas, Chairman Omali stressed the urgency to build a movement to fight the counterinsurgency:

> Hatred ain't nothing but an emotion. It is because some-body has power over you that will allow them to act on that hatred and cause death....Some of the three white men in Texas have tattoos that identify them as members

of what is called a white hate group. People say, "See, this is the problem. If we can eradicate stuff like this, we can all just get along together."

But...throughout this country, we've got a situation where bankers wear suits and wouldn't be seen dead with a tattoo on them, because that's a statement of a lower class white person. But they make decisions that deny black people the right to have economic development in our own communities. They are more responsible for black people dying than three white men in Texas....

They'll have you chasing the Ku Klux Klan which is negligible next to the people who are making decisions about our lives and are responsible for us dying every day.[77]

African people in the United States are a people living in a warzone of police violence, oppression and poverty. Newspaper headlines sum up the reality:

- "Young Black Men 'Endangered'—Steep Rise in Violent Death."—This 1989 *San Francisco Chronicle* article states that African men between the ages of 18 and 24 years are killed at rates 7 times greater than white men.[78]
- "Low Life Expectancy Found in Poor U.S. Men"—This 1997 piece from the *Chronicle* shows that African men living in the impoverished inner city of Washington, D.C. have a life expectancy of just 57.9 years, "figures comparable to parts of Africa. Yet male Asians living in affluent counties in New York and Massachusetts live to an average age of 89.5."[79]
- "Grim State Report on Black Males," showed in 1997 that a five-year "study painted a bleak picture...of the lives African American men in California are living in comparison to men of other races and ethnicities." The statistics presented revealed that African men represent 3.7 percent of California's population,

but have an unemployment rate of 13.1 percent. African men accounted for 35 percent of state prison inmates despite being less than 5 percent of the total state population.[80]

- "Blacks Are More likely to End up on Death Row," from the *Chronicle* in 1998 reveals that Africans convicted of murder are nearly four times more likely to be sentenced to death than others who commit similar crimes.[81]

- "Maryland Troopers Stop Drivers by Race, Suit Says." According to the *New York Times* in 1998, the "race-based profile" has state troopers stopping African people more often than whites on the highway, prompting lawsuits and accusations all over the country.[82]

- "Teen inmates sexually abused, often beaten in Louisiana prison," headlines a 1998 *Oakland Tribune* article. Many of the captive predominately African youth "had cuts and bruises; one had been raped. Another boy pleaded with an investigator not to return him to his dormitory, where he said an inmate had been sexually abusing him for weeks."[83]

- "Blacks Left Out As U.S. Prospers, New Study Shows." This *San Francisco Chronicle* article in 1998 reported on a National Urban League study showing that the average African family owns "$43,000 less in wealth than the average white family."[84]

- "Health Disparities Remain Between Blacks, Whites," from the *Oakland Tribune* reveals statistics in which African children die of Sudden Infant Death Syndrome at a rate of 137.5 per 100,000 as opposed to 57.9 for white babies. African people are six times more likely to die of AIDS than whites and the death rate for cancer among black men is about 50 percent higher than for white men.[85]

- "Black Women Sue Over Strip Searches: They Say Customs Service is Biased." This 1998 *Chronicle* article talks about a class action suit filed by 80 African women who were singled out for strip searches at O'Hare airport in Chicago "because of race and gender. Sixty percent of those pulled aside last year (as they returned to the United States from another country) for body searches or X-rays were African American or Latino, Customs figures show."[86]

WAR AGAINST NATIVE PEOPLE

The Pine Ridge reservation in South Dakota is the national homeland of the Lakota and other people. The Lakota have heroically and brilliantly defended their sacred lands for hundreds of years, including in the 1970s when the FBI and other armed government agencies made a murderous assault on the reservation. Today the Oglala are struggling against political and economic conditions that constitute a continuation of the genocide that began in 1492.

Located near the Nebraska border town of Whiteclay, Pine Ridge is one of the most impoverished spots in the country with 60 percent of young people living below the poverty line. Twenty percent of the houses lack basic plumbing and unemployment is above 70 percent.[87] Life on Pine Ridge is not that different from other U.S. reservations where 59 percent of native people live in substandard homes, 29 percent are homeless and the remainder, only 14 percent, live in homes that meet federal housing standards. Fewer than half of all American Indians even have a telephone.[88]

Over the past several years dozens of murders of the Lakota people have gone uninvestigated around Whiteclay. Wilson Black Elk, Jr. and Ronald Hard Heart were bludgeoned to death in 1999 and their bodies dumped on the road. In September 1999, Robert Many Horses was beaten and dumped into a garbage can to die. Charges against four white teenagers accused of brutalizing Many Horses were dismissed.[89] Other native people whose recent killings in South Dakota have gone without investigation include Timothy Bull Bear Sr., Dirk Bartling, Lauren Two Bulls, Randell

Two Crow, Royce Yellow Hawk, Allen Hough, George Hatton and Ben Long Wolf.

In July 1999, hundreds of native people, including American Indian Movement members launched the first of several marches for justice through Whiteclay from the Pine Ridge reservation. In the midst of the struggle, President Clinton made a visit to the reservation to designate the area an "empowerment zone" that gives federal tax breaks to corporations and creates subminimum wage jobs for already impoverished people.

Alfred Bone Shirt, brother of the slain Robert Many Horses, stated, "We didn't need Clinton to come down here and empower us. Give us back our human rights and we will empower ourselves."[90]

WELFARE REFORM?

In 1996, under the Democratic president William Jefferson Clinton, the United States derailed "welfare as we know it." The Welfare Reform Act reversed 60 years of social welfare policy, including eliminating the responsibility of the federal government for guaranteeing cash assistance to America's poorest children. The law requires that by the year 2002, half of all adult heads of families on welfare must work. As a result, tens of thousands of people—mostly African women and children—have been pushed off the welfare roles in every state.

In the years since the passage of the bill, welfare "reform" has been touted as a resounding success. Most of those pushed into "welfare to work programs" however, are trapped in minimum wage jobs. *The Economist* magazine reported in 1999 that:

> A new study by the Center on Budget and Policy Priorities, a Washington think tank, suggests that America's poorest families, those headed by single women, have fallen more deeply into poverty.

Using statistics from the census, the study found that between 1993 and 1995 the income (including…benefits such as food stamps) of the poorest fifth of families with children headed by single mothers rose on average by almost 14 percent, or just over $1,000. Between 1995 and 1997, in contrast, this group's income fell by an average of nearly 7 percent or $580 per family. About 2 million families or 6 million people are affected.[91]

Forty-four percent of homeless people are *employed*, according to the latest statistics available from the Department of Housing and Urban Development. In addition, 67 percent of the adults who requested emergency food aid in 26 major cities in 1999 were working, almost twice the number of the previous year.[92]

AFRICAN CHILDREN, VICTIMS OF WAR

The lives of African and other oppressed children inside the United States today have been ravaged by the counterinsurgency. At very young ages they have seen their friends and family members shot down on the streets as a result of the violence stemming from the government-imposed drug trade. They are forced to attend schools in which they are despised, treated as criminals and told they are incapable of learning. African children see a future defined by few possibilities other than early death or prison. They grow up far removed from the lighthearted joys that white people generally associate with childhood. As early as preschool, young Africans are slandered as being "superpredators" and "problem children."

In the 1980s, the media began to rave about a so-called rash of babies who were supposedly physically and mentally impaired because their mothers took the crack cocaine that was being so freely distributed by the U.S. government. Medical studies on so-called "crack babies," have proven only "how really stressful the conditions are that inner city children are growing up in, and how destructive that can be with or without cocaine." A *Philadelphia Inquirer* article asks the question, "Coming up with the Wrong Answer: The crack baby reports were horrifying. But were they true?"[93]

The article discusses a study showing that the conditions of crack babies are in reality very little different than the conditions of African children as a whole. These infants, like their parents, are simply being criminalized by the chemical warfare employed by the U.S. government against African people.

The crack baby syndrome is used to send thousands of African babies into the foster care system, often so far away from their families that visitation is nearly impossible. Since 1982 when crack started to appear on the streets of black neighborhoods across the country, the numbers of children sent to the brutal foster care homes has skyrocketed. Today there are more than 540,000 children in the foster care system.[94]

"Forcibly transferring children of the group to another group"—a component of genocide as defined by international law—is one of the very vicious tactics that has long been used against colonized peoples. Indigenous children in the United States were forced into "boarding schools," essentially prisons for children, as part of the genocide against them.

Despite efforts by many African families to keep African children with other family members or within the African community, these children are often shipped out to distant, hostile white towns to be raised. Many of these children are terribly abused, even killed, and often the white foster parents are paid tens of thousands of dollars a year by the foster care system, receiving even more money if the infant is designated a crack baby or otherwise ill.

In 1996, more than 3,000 children were abused or neglected by foster parents and 14 died. In Philadelphia in 1998, a woman was charged with beating her 6 year old foster daughter to death. She stuffed the child's body into a duffel bag and tossed it into the river.[95]

In a famous Northern California case, Yvonne Eldridge, living in the posh white suburb of Walnut Creek, was given charge of scores of African babies through foster care agencies of Alameda and San Francisco counties.

Eldridge went so far as to build a new wing of her house where she set up an isolated infant dormitory outfitted with hospital cribs and medical equipment. Many of the babies were being fed intravenously.

Raking in $150,000 a year, tax-free from several different county foster care departments, Eldridge killed, maimed and tortured the African babies. Pressure from the African community led by the Uhuru Movement finally brought this vicious murderer and parasite to trial in 1996.

Honored in 1988 by former first lady Nancy Reagan for her "work with sick children," Eldridge specialized in "caring" for "medically fragile infants who were often born drug-addicted or to a woman infected with the AIDS virus."[96]

Eldridge killed three of the African babies and tortured numerous others, subjecting them to permanent disability by having doctors remove vital organs. The doctors were totally complicit, going along with Eldridge's demands to mutilate the children. In some cases, the doctors "surgically planted feeding tubes in [the infant's] stomach and even removed one girl's lower intestine."[97] Testimony also showed that Eldridge had starved some of the children and injected fecal material into the babies through intravenous feeding tubes. One article on the Eldridge case stated:

> A Walnut Creek foster mother may have administered poisonous amounts of minerals to seven children— including three who later died—to qualify for higher foster care stipends paid out for sick children, officials said yesterday.

Yvonne Eldridge, the foster mother who has cared for more than 40 sickly children over four years, was collecting as much as $10,000 a month in tax-free county payments when investigators shut her care home last October....[98]

When sick children were taken out of Eldridge's care, they prospered, doctors testified. An incredible crime, Eldridge was never charged with murder in the deaths of the babies and was given only a slap on the wrist for "child endangerment."

The media defended her by making the ridiculous claim that she had a psychological disease called "Munchausen's syndrome by proxy" in which "women make their children sick to establish closer relationships with physicians and hospitals...." Needless to say, Eldridge never suffered from the "syndrome" when raising her *own* three children.[99]

It is no wonder why young African children have a mortal fear of being taken away into the foster care system. One of the most poignant stories was the case of 9 year old Travis Butler in Memphis, Tennessee. Young Travis did not report the death of his mother until discovered by family friends more than a month later. After his mother died in their apartment, Travis went to school every day, did his own shopping and cooked his own food.

He told his friends that he kept his mother's death a secret "because he didn't want to be put in a foster home and he also didn't want his mother to be taken away."[100]

PROBLEMATIC SURVIVAL

Attacking the children of a population targeted for genocide has long been an imperialist method of annihilation. Certainly, survival of African children is problematic today. In 1995, the black infant mortality rate was 2.4 times higher than the white infant mortality rate, as compared to 1980 when African infants died twice as often as white children.

In 1994, 13.2 percent of African infants had low birth weight. That same year, the mortality rate for African children between the ages of one and four years, was 77.2 per 100,000. The average for all U.S. children in that age group was 42.9 per 100,000. Between 1985 and 1991, as crack was introduced by the government, the death rate for African adolescent males shot up from 125.3 to 231.6 per 100,000. In 1994, the death rate for young black men was 234.3 per 100,000, as compared to white male adolescent rate of 109.6 per 100,000.

African youths between the ages of 12 and 17 years are far more likely than adults to be victims of violence.[101] If they are not imprisoned as adults at the age of 13, they are left to die on the streets like young Christopher Sercye in Chicago. In 1998, the 15 year old lay mortally wounded from a gunshot wound on the steps of Ravenswood Hospital. Hospital workers, nearby on a smoking break, refused to bring him in to be treated. In typical American fashion, Christopher bled to death just steps away from the hospital.[102]

In Chicago, also, 7 and 8 year old African boys were falsely charged with rape and murder of a young girl. In their haste to criminalize two more African children, Chicago prosecutors ignored obvious evidence that such an act could only have been perpetrated by an adult. The children were interrogated by police and forced to "confess" to the murder. Their case was used as "proof" of the need to pass a juvenile crime bill. The children were held for months until DNA tests of the murdered child's underwear, available, of course, since the beginning, finally proved the innocence of the children.[103]

PUBLIC SCHOOLS IN THE WAR ZONE

If African children are able to survive their infancy and early childhood in the war zone produced by counterinsurgency, they face an incredible challenge within the colonial public school system. Increasingly, predominately African and Mexican public schools are children's prisons, militarized and patrolled by armed policemen. The children are taught mainly by white teachers and administrators who generally have great disdain for them. In these prison-preparatory institutions, African children are, given Ritalin, expelled, suspended or sent to juvenile halls at the drop of a hat.

As Chairman Omali Yeshitela has often said, "Crack cocaine has not done a millionth of the damage to our communities that is produced by one day in the public schools."

While the United States spends over $22,000 to keep a person in jail for a year, it allocates an average of only $5,700 to put a child through one year of public school in the United States.[104] All over the country African children are brutalized in the schools by teachers and administrators. For African boys, this begins with kindergarten.

In 1999, in Oakland, for example, a watchdog group blasted the "school district for suspending more than 10,000 students [the previous] year, including hundreds of children younger than third grade." The Oakland school district has 54,000 students, 20 percent of whom were suspended during one school year. In San Francisco, only 1,599 students were suspended out of a district of 61,000 children.

In Oakland—as is no doubt typical of majority black cities across the country—African children accounted for 72 percent of the suspensions but were only 52 percent of the student body. The report noted that among the suspensions were "381 for kindergartners and first- and second-grade students."[105]

All over the country, African and Mexican children are forced to attend these prison-preparatory schools, with substandard, Eurocentric curriculums that have no meaning for colonized children. They face the infamous "zero tolerance" rules at school that are justifications for expulsions and abuse.

Walk through a public school and you can hear white teachers screaming at children from every classroom. While in white schools, children are often given interesting and "challenging" projects geared to develop critical thinking and creativity, the public schools for black children are deadening, bleak institutions where the children are given tedious homework to be learned by rote.

African student "offenders" are being sentenced to abusive boot camps or prison. In Virginia, two fifth-graders who allegedly put soap in their teacher's water were charged with a felony. In Decatur, Illinois, six students were expelled for two years for their alleged participation in a scuffle that broke out after a school game.[106]

A recent study reveals a two-tiered educational system, one black, one white. Urban white children are now massively in private schools, but even within "integrated" schools, the paths of African and white children are vastly different. The *San Francisco Chronicle* reported:

> Racial segregation in U.S. public schools is accelerating, with the trend particularly notable among Latinos in California and elsewhere in the Southwest.
>
> As a result, 45 years after the U.S. Supreme Court outlawed segregation, minority students are increasingly likely to attend class in racial isolation and under "profoundly unequal" conditions, a study...finds.[107]

The answer lies not in school "integration," however. Often what is nominally called an integrated school simply employs tracking and educational segregation on the same campus. Integration of schools implies that African children cannot learn unless they go to school with white students. The struggle today, as it was in the sixties, is for African community control of their own schools, in which African children can be taught by caring African teachers in a supportive environment promoting black culture and history. Within the present repressive school systems, community control is impossible.

In New York City, in September 1998 the Board of Education voted unanimously to transfer control of security in the city's public schools to the New York police department—the same department that brutalized Abner Louima and killed Amadou Diallo, among hundreds of others. The vote came despite angry and impassioned opposition from parents who denounced the "prison-like atmosphere in the schools."

With its 80 percent white (mostly Italian and Jewish) teaching and administrative staff, the New York public schools system has only a 48.7 percent graduation rate. For many African and other colonized schools in some neighborhoods there is up to an 80 percent dropout rate for African and Latino students.[108]

Oakland—the city led by its new-style white power mayor, Jerry Brown—approved a plan in 1999 that doubled the size of its school police force. This measure was passed following the school shootings by white students in Colorado and Georgia. Such violence generally does not occur in African schools. Certainly nothing like what happened in Colorado ever happens in the predominately African Oakland public schools. A *San Francisco Chronicle* noted:

> The Oakland school board voted in April to run its own police force independently of the Oakland Police Department. Under a new plan the district plans to spend $1.1 million over the next three years to increase the number of officers from 14 to 32...[109]

One student, Tenisha Johnson, interviewed at East Oakland's Castlemont High School was representative of the sentiments of many when she asserted that she would rather have a school nurse than another police officer on campus. "I think [the additional police are] a waste of money," Johnson said.[110]

In St. Petersburg, Florida, site of the headquarters of the African People's Socialist Party, a key element of the Uhuru Community

Development Program is building an independent black community charter school. In St. Petersburg, public schools are not allowed to be more than 30 percent African, while many schools are all white. Consequently African children are bused all over the county, sometimes traveling more than an hour each way into hostile white neighborhoods. An article in *The Burning Spear* newspaper reads:

> Under these circumstances, African students are being pushed out of the schools at alarming numbers through unjust suspensions, expulsions and failings. Every day they are forced to walk into virtual battle grounds on school campuses where they not only have to contend with racist teachers and staff and arrogant white children but also the same police forces that brutalize and harass African people on the streets.[111]

The Uhuru Movement independent school programs are attempting to serve the needs of African children. The Uhuru-led Fred Hampton Saturday School offers tutoring, remedial education and training in arts and culture. The Malcolm X Special School serves African children tracked for behavioral programs and provides an education designed to stimulate highly inquisitive, energetic children.

GERM WARFARE

Another dramatic tool of the counterinsurgency against African people is the continuation of the germ warfare through the rampant AIDS epidemic. The virus is spreading like wildfire in the United States, Haiti, Africa and every place on the planet where African people are located.

African people in the United States make up 13 percent of the population, but account for 57 percent of all new infections of the HIV virus that reportedly leads to AIDS. Although the overall death rate from AIDS in the United States is dropping, the virus is now the leading cause of death among African people between the ages of 25 and 44.[112] Now that white gay men are apparently dying less often from AIDS, and as the illness is increasingly attacking the African community, news about it in the media is less common.

In his book, *Aids: Origin, Spread, and Healing*, the German doctor Wolff Geisler, purports the thesis that AIDS is in fact germ warfare targeting African people. Geisler traces the development of biological weapons by the United States since the Second World War that have resulted in the AIDS virus as race-specific germ warfare. Geisler raises many pertinent questions in this brilliantly researched book, which was first presented as a medical paper to the Zimbabwe International Book Fair in 1994.

Geisler asserts that 97 percent of persons with HIV "have been intentionally infected" through microbes in drinking water, medical measures and insects. Although the book looks primarily at AIDS in Haiti and on the continent of Africa, Geisler also talks about the town of Belle Glade in Southern Florida, which has long had the largest African concentration of AIDS cases in the United States.

According to evidence presented in the book, the U.S. military carried out exercises during the 1950s using mosquitoes in Florida, an experiment that was a probable source of the AIDS, according to Geisler. About 50 miles away from Belle Glade is an insect research station—the Florida Medical Entomology Lab and the Entomology Division of the University of Florida located at Vero Beach.

Tracing Japanese, German and then U.S. experiments on biological warfare, Geisler shows that AIDS viruses are targeting African people in Africa, in the United States and the Caribbean, including Cuba. He shows that HIV was developed from an infectious anemia virus of horses by biological warfare research being carried out in Germany and Japan until 1945. After the war, this research continued in the U.S. Geisler also posits that AIDS does not have to be fatal and that successful treatments and therapies for the disease can be found.[113]

Just as African people are clear about the source of crack, polls reveal that the black community also believes that AIDS comes from the government.

AFRICAN FIGHT-BACK

The information in this chapter only scratches the surface of the counterinsurgency against African people today. Documentation of this war could fill thousands of pages. The depth of this "unconventional" war against the African community is staggering and the data is undeniable.

Backed by a publicly supported policy of police containment of African people, the genocidal conditions in the black community are not the fault of African people themselves, or the result of an "unfortunate" breakdown of the American system, as the media portrays. The evidence is compelling, The United States is waging a planned, concerted war against African people to make sure Black Power never raises its head again.

But the struggle of African people is irrepressible, as we have seen on the pages of this book. It rises up again and again, despite all attempts to wipe it out. Today, the resistance of African people is on the upsurge. Demonstrations and rebellions against police brutality and prisons are taking place across the country. Organization is the key to the success of this resistance.

In 1991, the African People's Socialist Party formed the National People's Democratic Uhuru Movement (NPDUM) as a mass organization whose goals are to "expose and defeat the counterinsurgency" and to "defend the democratic rights of the African community." Led by the African working class and guided by its genuine interests of liberation, NPDUM is open to people of all nationalities who can unite with the organization's goals. Speaking of the despicable conditions for African people as a result of the counterinsurgency, Chairman Omali affirmed,

We don't have to live that kind of life. We can organize. We have to organize to overturn a foul rotten social system based on parasitism, genocide and slavery.

In response to the Black Revolution of the Sixties, the U.S. waged counterrevolutionary war against the struggling people around the world, and here as well. When the U.S. made war against Viet Nam and some other places they often pretended to observe some international rules of engagement that governed their conduct.

But in this country, it was a war without terms for the African community. There was nothing that they didn't do to put down the revolutionary movement in this country....

Sisters and brothers, we have to organize to stop the kind of things that are happening to African people today. But we have to get to the sources of the pain and understand the social system based on parasitism that requires our oppression for it to exist....

The National People's Democratic Uhuru Movement is an organization that we built because we felt it was necessary to do whatever we could to push back the State, to expose this war against our community that we refer to as a counterinsurgency, to open up the ability to allow the Africans and anybody else who would work with us to come into political life.[114]

Everyone, including the white community, can answer Omali Yeshitela's call to join NPDUM and organize to stand against this counterinsurgency. We must all come into political life. Let's begin to take responsibility for our complicity in the war against the African community, and support the right of African people for justice and peace.

Overturning the Culture of Violence

1. Omali Yeshitela, 1991, *Black Power Since the 60's: The Struggle Against Opportunism within the U.S. Front of the Black Liberation Movement* (Oakland: Burning Spear Publications), p. 17.
2. Quoted in: David E. Stannard, 1992, *American Holocaust: The Conquest of the New World*, (New York: Oxford University Press), p. 279.
3. Same as above, pp. 133-134.
4. Convention on the Prevention and Punishment of the Crime of Genocide, December 9, 1948, adopted by Resolution 260 III of the United Nations General Assembly.
5. Stannard, p. 256.
6. Robert Taber, 1970, *The War of the Flea: A Study of Guerrilla Warfare Theory and Practice* (New York: The Citadel Press), p. 11.
7. Dan Baum, 1996, *Smoke and Mirrors: The War on Drugs and the Politics of Failure* (New York: Little, Brown and Company), p. 250, quoting Jerry Adler.
8. Omali Yeshitela, 1982, *A New Beginning: The Road to Black Freedom and Socialism: The Main Resolution, Constitution and Program Adopted at the First Congress of the African People's Socialist Party* (Oakland: Burning Spear Publications), p. 29.
9. John L. Mitchell and Nora Zamichow, November 15, 1996, "CIA head speaks in L.A. to counter crack claims," *Los Angeles Times*.
10. Jonathan Schorr, January 19, 1997, "No doubt in Oakland about CIA-crack link," *The Oakland Tribune*.
11. Benjamin Pimentel, March 16, 1999, "CIA sued for failure to report drug trafficking," *San Francisco Chronicle*.
12. Olivia Woods, June 6, 1999, Testimony given at African Community Tribunal at the Uhuru House, Oakland, California.
13. Omali Yeshitela, 1996, "Resistance of African people: Crisis of Imperialism: Why we must build the National People's Democratic Uhuru Movement," (Chicago: National People's Democratic Uhuru Movement), p. 9-10.
14. Omali Yeshitela, May-June 1993, "Drugs, drug economy and neo-colonialism all part of U.S. war," *The Burning Spear*, p. 15.
15. Jack Norman, June 15, 1998, "View drug dealing as work, study says," *Milwaukee Journal Sentinel*.
16. Michael T. Klare, 1972, *War Without End: American Planning for the Next Viet Nams* (New York: Vintage Books), p. 268, quoting Byron Engle.
17. Edward J. Epstein, 1990, *Agency of Fear* (London: Verso), (www.douzzer,ai.mit.edu:8080/conspiracy/epstein/aofpro).
18. Same as above.
19. Tim Burtz, 1976, "Garden plot & swat," *Counterspy*, Vol. 2, No. 4, p. 21.
20. Klare, p. 244.
21. Same as above, pp. 262-264.
22. Same as above, p. 268.
23. Omali Yeshitela, November 1997-February 1998, "Excerpts from the keynote presentation at the Oakland Conference to Stop Police Brutality," *The Burning Spear*, pp. 7-30.
24. Baum, p. 277.
25. *Maryland vs. Jerome Edward Buie* [494 US 325]. U.S. Supreme Court Report, 108L Ed 2d.
26. Nat Hentoff, January 8, 2000, "Don't welfare recipients have rights?" *The Washington Post*.
27. Pierre Thomas, January 30, 1997, "Felony convictions cut black vote, report says," *San Francisco Chronicle*.
28. Sasha Abramsky, June 1991, "When they get out," *Atlantic Monthly*, Vol. 283, No. 6, pp. 30-36.
29. Baum, pp. 250-251.
30. Ron Harris, April 22, 1990, "Blacks take brunt of war on drugs," *Los Angeles Times*.
31. David Johnston with Steven A. Holmes, September 14, 1994, "Experts doubt effectiveness of the newly enacted Crime Bill," *The New York Times*.

32. "Blacks dissatisfaction with police," June 4, 1999, *The Wall Street Journal.*

33. P. Kraska and V. Kappeler, February 1997, "Militarizing American police," *Social Problems,* Vol. 44, No. 1.

34. Amnesty International, June 1996, "United States of America: Police Brutality and Excessive Force in the New York City Police Department."

35. Kevin Flynn, October 1, 1999, "Record payout in settlements against police," *The New York Times.*

36. Elaine Herscher, October 14, 1996, "Berkeley groups want pepper spray out of police hands," *San Francisco Chronicle.*

37. "Report charges police abuse in U.S. goes unchecked," July 7, 1998, Human Rights Watch, (www.hr.org/hrw/press98/july/polic707).

38. Angela Hill, March 2, 1997, "Man killed after traffic stop," *The Oakland Tribune.*

39. "Police officer kills suspect flashing gun," December 23, 1998, *The Oakland Tribune.*

40. Ben Charny, September 11, 1997, "Woman killed during struggle with policeman," *The Oakland Tribune.*

41. Christopher Reed, August 19, 1999, "Inquiry into LAPD 'death squad,'" *The Guardian* (England).

42. Yeshitela, "Stop Police Brutality," pp. 5-7.

43. Gerald Smith, Winter 1995, "The ones that are taking money are the ones giving the beatings," *Copwatch Report,* citing December 19, 1994, *The New York Times.*

44. Steven R. Donziger, ed., 1996, *The Real War on Crime* (New York: Harper Collins Publishers, Inc.), p. 167.

45. Mark Bouden and Mark Fazlollah, September 11, 1995, "Officer rode roughshod, got away with it," *The Philadelphia Inquirer.*

46. "Philadelphia feels effects of inquiry," March 24, 1996, *The New York Times.*

47. Paul Salopek, January 4, 1997, "Hints of a brutal trend," *Chicago Tribune.*

48. Toni Locy, May 22, 1996, "Dirty dozen leader gets 14 years," *The Washington Post.*

49. "Police get lesson in manners," April 8, 1999, *BBC News* (www.news.bbc.co.uk/hi/english/world/americas/newsid-314000/314171.st).

50. Dan Barry with Marjorie Connelly, March 6, 1999, "New York poll cites race bias in police acts," *The New York Times.*

51. Donziger, p. 20.

52. Bill Wallace, March 2, 1996, "Huge racial disparity in '3 Strikes' sentences," *San Francisco Chronicle.*

53. "Blacks more jailed report says," February 13, 1996, *The Oakland Tribune.*

54. "Prison guards union flexes powerful muscles," October 28, 1994, *The Oakland Tribune.*

55. "Experts say adult trials for young offenders no remedy," June 6, 1997, *San Francisco Chronicle.*

56. Joan Ryan, June 27, 1999, "Youth justice going forward or backwards?," *San Francisco Chronicle.*

57. William Raspberry, December 14, 1999, "Do we want to be a nation of prisons?," *St. Petersburg Times.*

58. Eric Drudis, May 17, 1999, "Crime rate in San Francisco falls yet again," *San Francisco Chronicle.*

59. United States Sentencing Commission, February 1995, "Cocaine and Federal Sentencing Policy."

60. Donziger, p. 27.

61. "Prison population hits 1.8 million," March 15, 1999, *San Francisco Chronicle.*

62. "Number of blacks in jail rising toward 1 million," March 8, 1999, *San Francisco Chronicle.*

63. Timothy Egan, February 28, 1999, "War on crack retreats, still taking prisoners," *The New York Times.*

64. Mike Davis, 1998, *Ecology of Fear: Los Angeles and the Imagination of Disaster* (New York: Metropolitan Books, Henry Holt and Company), p. 416.

65. "Population Statistics," *The Criminal Justice Consortium*, (www.wco.com/~aerick/edc), citing the California Department of Corrections Weekly Population Report for March 23, 1997.

66. "New Jersey prisoner abuse," April 24, 1998, *The Philadelphia Inquirer*.

67. Christian Parenti, June 1997, "Rural prison as colonial master," *Z Magazine*, Vol. 10, No. 6, p. 11.

68. Same as above.

69. Reynolds Holding, October 28, 1996, "Accusations of prison coverup," *San Francisco Chronicle*.

70. Same as above.

71. "Corcoran prison brutality," August 3, 1998, *San Francisco Chronicle*.

72. James Brooke, June 13, 1999, "Super max is home to 'worst' prisoners," *San Francisco Examiner*.

73. Adam C. Smith, December 5, 1999, "Life in lockdown," *St. Petersburg Times*.

74. Eric Schlosser, December 1998, "The prison-industrial complex," *Atlantic Monthly*, p. 72.

75. National People's Democratic Uhuru Movement, 1999, petition titled "Release All African Prisoners Incarcerated on Drug Related Charges NOW!". (For more information, contact: NPDUM, 1245 18th Ave South, St. Petersburg, FL 33705, 727-821-6620.)

76. "Doctor says victim was alive when dragging ordeal began," February 23, 1999, *San Francisco Chronicle*.

77. Omali Yeshitela, 1998, "A Lynching in Jasper, Texas: Thousands of Legal Lynchings Across the U.S.," (St. Petersburg: Burning Spear Uhuru Publications), pp. 2-4.

78. Ramon G. Mclend, February 23, 1989, "Young black men 'endangered'," *San Francisco Chronicle*.

79. "Low life expectancy found in poor U.S. men," December 4, 1997, *San Francisco Chronicle*.

80. Greg Lucas, March 20, 1997, "Grim state report on black males," *San Francisco Chronicle*.

81. "Blacks are more likely to end up on death row," June 5, 1998, *San Francisco Chronicle*.

82. Michael Janofsky, June 5, 1998, "Maryland troopers stop drivers by race, suit says," *The New York Times*.

83. "Teen inmates sexually abused, often beaten in Louisiana prison," June 29, 1998, *The Oakland Tribune*.

84. "Blacks left out as U.S. prospers, new study shows," July 31, 1998, *San Francisco Chronicle*.

85. "Health disparities remain between blacks, whites," November 27, 1998, *The Oakland Tribune*.

86. "Black women sue over strip searches," December 3, 1998, *San Francisco Chronicle*.

87. Joe Duggan, August 5, 1999, "Last call on Pine Ridge," *The Lincoln Journal Star*.

88. David P. Rider, Ph.D., July 1999, article circulated on internet.

89. "Judge drops charges in Mobridge case," September 28, 1999, *Associated Press*.

90. Joe Kafka, September 2, 1999, "Relations between Indians and whites often shaky in South Dakota," *Associated Press*.

91. "Off welfare, but poorer," August 28, 1999, *The Economist*, p. 23.

92. "Report: Many homeless working," December 21, 1999, *St. Petersburg Times*.

93. Susan Fitzgerald, June 15, 1997, "Coming up with the wrong," *The Philadelphia Inquirer*.

94. "Foster care agencies come under scrutiny," January 26, 2000, *St. Petersburg Times*.

95. Same as above.

96. Erin Hallissy, May 9, 1996, "Foster mom on trial for abuse," *San Francisco Chronicle*.

97. "Mother once honored by first lady faces child abuse charges," May 9, 1996, *The News-Times*.

98. Dan Reed, September 25, 1992, "Foster mother got $10,000 a month," *San Francisco Chronicle*.

99. Chris Lewis, August 9, 1996, "Rare illness may impact abuse trial," *The Oakland Tribune*.

100. "Boy found living alone with his mother's body," December 9, 1999, *St. Petersburg Times*.

101. "America's children: Key national indicators of well-being," August 1997, *Parent News* (http://npin.org/pnews/pnew897/pnew897g).

102. Lola Smallwood, May 18, 1998, "Witnesses say hospital refused to help dying teen," *Chicago Tribune.*

103. Steven Mills and Terry Wilson, September 23, 1998, "Assault charge, DNA linked man to Harris death," *Chicago Tribune.*

104. "The Hard Facts," Racism and Public Education, (www.nrc.org/Pages/Eanswers).

105. Jonathan Schorr, June 18, 1999, "Report takes aim at school suspensions," *The Oakland Tribune.*

106. Ellen Goodman, January 5, 2000, "Zero-tolerance rules come up empty," *St. Petersburg Times.*

107. Richard Lee Colvin, June 12, 1999, "Racial segregation growing in public schools, study finds," *San Francisco Chronicle.*

108. "NYPD in public schools," (www.saxakali.com/communitylinkups/NYCBDEd).

109. "Bay Area high schools look to police for safety, guidance," June 8, 1999, *San Francisco Chronicle.*

110. Same as above.

111. "Uhuru Community Development Program: Seizing control of our destiny," March-June 1998, *The Burning Spear,* p. 3.

112. "Blacks suffer most from AIDS of any group in the U.S." June 29, 1998, *San Francisco Chronicle.*

113. Wolff Geisler, 1994, *AIDS-Origin, Spread and Healing* (Koln:Bipawo Verlag).

114. Omali Yeshitela, "Stop Police Brutality," p. 30.

The massive imprisonment of African people generates a booming economy that benefits all sectors of white society. Credit: Photodisc.com

Millions of African people have been railroaded into a multi-billion dollar prison industry.
Credit: Imageworks.

6

A Mother's Cry

Rape and pillage resulted in our impoverishment and the destruction of whole civilizations. These were civilizations which gave rise to the pyramids of Africa...There were the Mayans and Aztecs and other civilizations in the Americas which were simply wiped out. Now we suffer and live in poverty. We are depicted as "lazy" or "wetbacks" or "spics" and the rest of it. It's so easy to hate somebody when your income and lifestyle comes as a consequence of their emiseration. We are talking about a parasitic relationship in which the rest of the world gets ripped off and the wealth comes to Europe and North America as a result.[1]

— Omali Yeshitela

Sharon, Maria, Pamela, Betty, Susan, Alma, Theresa, Barbara and Dorothy are mothers of sons who struggled to find the ways to raise their children in the embattled inner cities. Like millions of other African and Mexican women, these mothers had dreams for their sons and hoped to see the realization of their talents and aspirations: college, a job, a house, marriage, babies. They didn't ask for much; just a life for their children with a measure of love, dignity, and freedom from want. Isn't that the American dream?

These women loved their sons deeply and never wanted them to stray too far from sight. They knew it was a dangerous world for young African and Mexican men. The mothers appreciated their sons' humor and the way they made everybody laugh when times were hard. Part of large warm families who filled the house on Sundays and holidays, there were lots of relatives who loved these young men, too.

All these women lived with great stress and anxiety, as no doubt all African mothers do in this country. There was that weight, the ever-present fear of the nearly inevitable phone call. They had seen all too often how African men went out to the store and never came home as a result of violence imposed on their communities.

Pamela, Betty, Alma, Barbara, Dorothy—their sons are dead now. They were killed by the police; mowed down execution style. No investigation, no discipline of the officer, no apology. Their sons were then assassinated again in the media where they were slandered, criminalized and portrayed as worthless.

Maria, Sharon, Susan, Theresa—their sons have been framed up by hostile, colonial courts, victims of drug laws, the "three strikes," legislation and mandatory minimums. They are good sons, good men, fathers of infants and toddlers. Young and bursting with energy, these men now face life in the brutal prison cells, their manhood insulted, degraded, beaten down daily.

These women must live with their pain; there's an emptiness that can never be filled. There are tens of thousands of other mothers just like these. Many even have several sons who have been killed or are in prison. This is life in the war zone of America. This is the human face of counterinsurgency, a war with a massive political economy attached to it that makes a lot of money for all of us in the white community. The pain of these mothers and so many others; the sorrow, the death and violence suffered by African people—this is the price of our well-being.

In chapters 4 and 5 we presented the incredible devastation and the genocidal conditions imposed on African communities as a result of the U.S. government's counterinsurgency against them. What started out as COINTELPRO was extended to the entire African population to make sure it would never again rise up to become America's "greatest internal threat."

In this chapter, we look at the other side of the counterinsurgency—white people's relation to it. We examine the massive amount of wealth flowing into our pockets as a result of this counteroffensive. We see the white population's enthusiastic support for this war. And we expose the betrayal of African people by the white left and progressive sector—by those who proclaim to have the consciousness to struggle against injustice and man's inhumanity to man.

ECONOMY HOOKED ON DRUGS AND PRISONS

At least half of the two million people currently in prison are Africans. Millions more from black and other oppressed communities are under the control of the U.S. State through parole, probation and house arrest under which they are forced to wear electronic surveillance devices. Ten percent or more will spend their entire lives behind bars.

African prisoners are subjected to unspeakably brutal conditions which constitute violations of international law. Tens of thousands of people are forced to endure 23-hour lockdown year after year in tiny cells designed specifically for sensory deprivation. Others are beaten, brutalized or psychologically tortured, harassed, degraded—treated worse than rodents.

Animals, whales and redwood trees have movements defending their rights in this country; not so for African people in prison. Meanwhile jobs related to the prison industry are the economic mainstay of white communities all over the country.

At least 70 percent of the millions of African people tied to the prison system are there on drug-related charges. Yet the U.S. government has been exposed for bringing crack and other deadly drugs into the African community.

This suffering of African people fills our bank accounts, sends our kids to college and buys our cars. The *Detroit News* reported that as of July 1, 1999, the U.S. economy is doing fabulously: "A key gauge indicates the U.S. economy, already experiencing the longest peacetime growth in history, is on track to become the longest expansion ever...."[2]

Peacetime? The '60s' economic growth spurt took place during the U.S. war against the Vietnamese people; the '90s' during the war against African people inside the United States' own borders.

Michael Ruppert, former Los Angeles Police narcotics detective and researcher into government crimes, plainly states in his newsletter *From the Wilderness*: "The entire economy, and the entire political system itself, is currently hooked and dependent upon—drug money." And the massive wealth flowing from the prison economy, we might add. Ruppert continues:

> We have entered, at the end of the industrial age, a phase
> of growth where we must incarcerate an ever expanding
> number of people to sustain the growth of all the compa-
> nies profiting from law enforcement, crime, imprison-
> ment and war.[3]

How else are we evading the economic problems faced by the rest of the world that pundits call the "Asian flu," the Russian crisis or the Brazilian economic collapse?

In Volume II of the Hitz Report, the CIA admits it had direct ties to cocaine smuggling and drug money laundering.[4] So why are one million African people in prison, while not one CIA operative or government official has been brought to trial or even censured?

Although the complicity of every major Wall Street bank and brokerage firm in laundering drug money is obvious, they continue to operate, business as usual, getting richer and richer every day. There is hardly any sector of the white economy that is not fueled by money from drugs or prisons, yet it is the Africans who are called the "criminals" and marched off to the prison camps.

Eighty percent of drug users in the U.S. are white; only 12 percent are African. But white drug users are sent to treatment centers; they go to prison only in small numbers and for short periods of time. On the other hand, in 1997 the Justice Department estimated that 29 percent of African males born in 1991 will spend some time in prison. It's predetermined. Only four percent of white males are expected to be incarcerated,[5] yet white men commit 60 percent of all rapes, robberies and assaults. African men go to prison on these charges 17 times more often than white men do.[6]

So, every few seconds another African person is arrested, another slave is captured, another prison bed is filled, and the economy gets better and better. It goes without saying that these prison statistics are not about *justice* and have nothing to do with crime. African people are prisoners of the undeclared war being waged inside U.S. borders. They are interned in concentration camps, victims of "ethnic cleansing," enchained in modern-day human bondage.

ALL WE HAVE TO DO IS LOOK

Where is the movement from the "socially conscious" sectors of white society in opposition to this stark reality? Where are the anti-war demonstrators to stop the U.S. counterinsurgency war against African people right here?

The white left takes for granted that the masses of African people should continue to be in prison, albeit somewhat less brutal ones. Yet those responsible for the poverty, the prisons, the drugs whose profits flow to the white community enjoy a very lucrative freedom. Who are the real criminals in society whose whole economic well-being is based on the oppression of others?

While white people are better off than ever, African people experience a poverty rate of 26.5 percent of their population as opposed to 11 percent for white people, according to 1997 figures. Mexican people also have a poverty rate of 26.5 percent. The percentage of African families under the poverty line is 23.6 percent as opposed to 8.4 percent for white people.[7] In 1999, there were at least 1,060,000 homeless African people.[8]

But statistics aren't really necessary. All we have to do is look. Take a stroll down the main street of an African community in your city. You won't see any economic upswing there; it is a community under siege. Then, look around at your own neighborhood. You might not be wealthy, but there are no helicopters flying overhead, no SWAT teams patrolling the streets and breaking down doors. None of your neighbors are homeless and sleeping on the sidewalks.

Can any of us honestly say we are ignorant of this reality?

In California, since 1980, the state legislature has continually decreased funding for its state-run colleges and universities, resulting in 8,000 fewer jobs. In the same period, it created 26,000 new jobs in prisons and incarcerated 112,000 new prisoners.[9]

This did not happen without the enthusiastic backing of white California voters. In the face of California priority of prisons over education, state legislator and former '60s radical Tom Hayden, denied white voters' complicity with genocide, blaming it on the "law enforcement lobby." Hayden asserted:

> State politics has been handcuffed by the law enforcement lobby. Voters have no real idea of what they are getting into. They have not been told the truth about the trade-off between schools and prisons, or the economic disaster that will inevitably result. We dehumanize criminals [sic] and the poor in exactly the same way we did with the so-called gooks in Viet Nam. We put them in hell and turn up the heat.[10]

Yes, we put African and Mexican people in hell and turn up the heat, and certainly the "law enforcement lobby" put millions of dollars into African-incarcerating legislation. But the facts about this are no secret to anyone. They are on the front page of papers every day. The "trade-off between schools and prisons" are overwhelmingly voted in by the well-informed California electorate. White Californians know exactly what they are doing, and the economy is soaring off the charts as a result.

Republican California state legislator Frank Hill was much more truthful when he retorted, "If push comes to shove, the average voter is going to be more supportive of prisons than the University of California."[11]

DIRT UNDER THE RUG

The "inescapable dialectic" described by Omali Yeshitela continues today: the greater the devastation of the African community, the greater the affluence and wealth of the white population. The parasitic nature of our economy is exactly the same as during the period of slavery and land theft. Now it requires the suffering of others through drugs and prisons for our prosperity.

White people are happy with whichever president can keep the money flowing, regardless of the price in human terms to others. Both the Democrats and the Republicans have the same domestic policy attacking Africans. Clinton or Gore may be more white women-friendly, gay-friendly, environment-friendly than any of the Bushes, but when it comes to Africans, the liberals tend to be even more brutal than the Republicans. It was the Democrats who enacted "three strikes" laws, the juvenile crime bill, welfare "reform" and NAFTA.*

Since the Black Power Movement of the 1960s, direct white atrocities against African people—while they do occur—are less acceptable on the surface of American daily life. Lynchings and white mob attacks are no longer feasible on a mass scale. Perpetrators of such violence no longer go without censure. That was a powerful and irreversible ideological victory of the Black Power Movement of the '60s.

---

* The North American Free Trade Agreement enacted by Clinton in 1994. This bill further enhances the colonial domination of Mexico by the United States.

Nevertheless, the atrocities, carnage and lynchings necessary to maintain a parasitic social system are still there—even more so. It's just that the counterinsurgency lets the State do all the dirty work. Now as the victims of a genocidal counterinsurgency, African people, long regarded as an oppressed people by the international community, are portrayed as the violent ones.

The instigators of violence upon the whole world, we, the white people, suddenly become offended by the sight of brutality. If the beating of a Rodney King is caught on videotape, this is outrageous to white society. It tears our soul.

If millions of Rodney Kings are sent to the torture chambers called prisons by an unjust legal system, however, we refuse to see anything wrong with that. It's not our problem. Thus counterinsurgency does us a favor and sweeps the dirt under the rug for us.

The white left does not expose these realities; it unites with them. Occupying the vacuum created by the defeat of the Black Power Movement of the '60s, the white left has a clear stake in continuing to suppress an independent movement of African people. Its goal is to maintain white power by giving it a "kinder, gentler" face and enabling a greater percentage of the white population to share the stolen loot.

In the fall of 1998, the white left sponsored a national conference on prisons in Berkeley, California. Targeting the "prison-industrial complex," the conference was hosted by Angela Davis, the black radical of the '60s who was a longtime member of the Communist Party and favorite of the white left.

Hundreds of people attended. It was a feel-good affair with lots of speeches and workshops, although very little discussion of responsibility or strategy. The counterinsurgency and suppression of the Black Liberation Movement as the basis for the proliferation of the prisons today was not discussed. The conference pretended that "all" people were victims of current prison policies, as opposed to the reality of African and Mexican genocide. It was based on the opportunist politic that "it can happen to you too."

The focus was an evil prison-industrial complex, something far away and intangible. It let off the hook the whole white society that feeds on the drug/prison economy.

As one of its major goals, the conference resolved to set a national day of prison visiting for the following April.[12] Other than that, well, not much else seemed to come of the event. Meanwhile, newspaper headlines continue to announce the seemingly implacable hunger of the genocidal U.S. system of incarceration. As the clock ticks the number of Africans in prison grows.

What about a campaign supporting the National People's Democratic Uhuru Movement (NPDUM) demand for the release of all African people imprisoned on drug related charges? What about a march on Washington demanding reparations from the white community and U.S. government for millions of dollars gained from the drug and prison economies? What about arresting the real drug dealers? Or there could be a demand to end the public policy of police containment for African people and a call for real economic development of African communities.

But a national day of visiting people in prison? We don't think so. African prisoners are not animals in a zoo. They do not need our charity.

This is the white left, the voice of our self-interest. It is important that we look at its relationship to the struggle of African people over the past 30 years. If white people had mustered up the courage and honesty to raise our voices against the attacks on the Black Liberation Movement of the '60s, perhaps some of the effects of the counterinsurgency would be different today.

FRENCH DEFEATED BY VIETNAMESE

White left betrayal of their country's colonial subjects is not unique to the U.S. It happens all over the world—in Europe, Australia, South Africa. Wherever white people have settled outside of Europe, we have done so because genocide and colonialism would give us new "opportunities." Wherever we are, our parasitic relationship to colonized peoples is the same, and so are our left politics.

When French imperialism faced the liberation struggles in their colonies of Viet Nam and Algeria, the French left stood with their ruling class. The betrayal of the anti-colonial movements by the French left is a classic example of white left opportunism. The situation is remarkably similar to the North American left as it faced Black Revolution inside U.S. borders.

Just as in the U.S., the Vietnamese victory over their colonial masters in 1954 caused a tremendous social crisis inside of France, where Viet Nam was known as their "jewel of Indochina." Despite difficulties in winning its war against the Vietnamese, begun in 1946, the French government and people arrogantly believed that their army was undefeatable.

By May 1953, after a long succession of commanders in chief, General Henri Navarre was assigned to head up the French attempt to regain its lucrative opium colony from the hands of the national liberation movement led by Ho Chi Minh. Vo Nguyen Giap, the brilliant general of the Vietnamese liberation army, summed Navarre up as having "a sense of strategy."[13] Giap's comment, made later, was surely tongue in cheek. Certainly Navarre had a sense of strategy—a losing one.

Navarre was sent in to save the French after a string of defeats by the Vietnamese led by Giap. His famous last words reflected the classic imperialist denial: "A year ago none of us could see victory. Now we can see it clearly, like light at the end of the tunnel."[14]

Navarre's strategy was to concentrate strong mobile troops in Viet Nam's Red River delta to attempt to wear down the Vietnamese People's Liberation Army. At the same time the French would occupy Dien Bien Phu near Viet Nam's northwestern border with Laos. Dien Bien Phu would be the springboard from which to launch attacks on the people's liberated zones in the north. However, it didn't quite work that way.

General Giap summed up later that Navarre's greatest mistake was to underestimate the situation and the Vietnamese people:

> Navarre could not visualize the immense possibilities of the People's Army—the remarkable progress of the people and our army. He could see only the strong points of Dien Bien Phu and not its vulnerable points.[15]

Navarre was fighting a colonial war of a previous period, when the pith helmets and the khakis of the Foreign Legion were barely soiled during "battle;" when a thousand poorly armed colonial subjects could be annihilated for sport in a single afternoon followed by dinner with wine, cognac and cigars. Navarre was not prepared for the iron will of the organized Vietnamese revolutionary forces.

Navarre's fortified perimeter at Dien Bien Phu was in the shape of a giant foot with the big toe facing north. His battalions, made up largely of Vietnamese, Algerian and North African colonial subjects, were only 40 percent French. The army was led by the cream of the French military, such as, Christian Marie Ferdinand de la Croix de Castries, "aristocrat, dilettante, world-class horseman, gambler, lover," who wore colorful neckerchiefs and carried a "twitching riding crop."[16]

Navarre's men ensconced themselves in the Southeast Asian fortress with more than 50,000 bottles of French wine and two "mobile brothels," which consisted of 18 Vietnamese and Algerian women forced into sexual slavery for the pleasure of the French.[17]

Navarre considered the Dien Bien Phu fortress impenetrable, surrounded by thick rain forests and rugged terrain. But despite the French bombing of the Vietnamese army in the surrounding areas, the Viet Minh dug an incredible system of tunnels and trenches, with entrance holes only large enough for the small-boned Vietnamese to fit through. The Vietnamese soldiers fought during the day and dug tunnels through the night. The Central Committee of the Vietnamese Communist Party worked out its strategy:

> Keeping the initiative, we should concentrate our forces to attack strategic points which were relatively vulnerable. If we succeeded in keeping the initiative, we could achieve successes and compel the enemy to scatter their forces....[18]

Carrying out their strategy the Vietnamese began shelling the outposts of the fortification, which were hit hard and broken open. De Castries' airfield was exposed on three sides, making resupply his most critical problem. He was not able to reach many of his wounded men and airlift was impossible, so they had to stay where they were struck on the battlefield.

As they were breaking down the French barricades, the Vietnamese were also broadcasting political statements to the colonial soldiers in their own languages. Southeast Asians fighting on the side of the French were deserting in droves, and Algerians began to leave as well. The Vietnamese dug tunnels right up into the strongpoints of the French fortification and detonated bombs in the middle of them. By mid-May 1954, the French were vanquished with a total loss during the war of 172,000 casualties. The French wounded lay dying of gaping gangrenous wounds on their stretchers; there were few doctors and no medications. Dead bodies were piled up in heaps and buried at night.

Giap took prisoners, including de Castries himself. The wounded prisoners of war were treated in socialist order: first Vietnamese, then North Africans, followed by French NCOs and finally French officers. Most of the prisoners of war never returned to France or their home countries. They died, not from any brutality on the part of the Vietnamese. They simply perished from the conditions the French had imposed on the Vietnamese for a century: starvation, disease and lack of medical care.[19]

DEPRESSED IN FRANCE

Back in Europe, the French were devastated. "In France, people had to find excuses and scapegoats for this new and terrible hurt to their pride," writes one account.[20] The French were depressed: "mentally they were shattered, morally they were exhausted, financially they were bankrupt." Not only that, they were facing another anti-colonial struggle, this time in Algeria.

With the struggle of the Vietnamese against the French capitalist-colonial government, and with the threat of a similar fate in Algeria, the French left could have played a significant role. It could have galvanized the French workers to international solidarity from within the oppressor nation. Struggle at home would make France have to fight on two fronts, weakening and perhaps bringing down the capitalist rulers and bosses. Strikes, demonstrations and rallies could have fomented support inside of France in opposition to the aggression against the Vietnamese and the Algerians. With a cry of international solidarity, perhaps resources, medicines and arms could have been raised in aid of the Viet Minh and the National Liberation Front of Algeria.

But the left in France was no different from the white left in the United States and elsewhere. It was no different from the French colonial nation as a whole, which in the face of the Vietnamese victory, was "shattered," "exhausted," "bankrupt." The French left was adamantly against the liberation of the colonial peoples from French imperialism. Like white leftists in America, they believed that French colonial subjects were simply victims of racism and otherwise should be happy members of the French family. The French "progressives" patronizingly treated the anti-colonial movements like children.

In *Toward the African Revolution,* the Algerian revolutionary Frantz Fanon denounced the patronizing arrogance of white liberals and leftists who pretended that a change of attitude would change conditions. Being "nice" to colonized people does not end colonialism, Fanon pronounced, and personal relationships offer no solution for the political and economic oppression of a whole people. Fanon's observations continue to ring true today:

> The evocation of special classes of Frenchmen who are abnormally nice to Algerians does not modify the nature of the relations between a foreign group that has seized the attributes of national sovereignty and the people which finds itself deprived of the exercise of power. No personal relation can contradict this fundamental datum: that the French nation through its citizens opposes the existence of the Algerian nation.[21]

WHITE LEFT VS. BLACK POWER

Across the Atlantic, some 15 years after the Vietnamese defeated French colonialism, the African revolution inside the borders of the United States was waging military, political and ideological battles for its life. Like the Vietnamese and the Algerians, it was facing a patronizing, cowardly white left which united with its own government's attacks against it.

In 1967, African people held Detroit for seven days in the most powerful uprising since the Red Summer of 1919. Five hundred million dollars worth of damage to imperialist property was inflicted; 41 people were killed, 347 injured, 3,800 arrested, 5,000 made homeless, 1,300 buildings reduced to ashes, 2,700 businesses looted.[22] It is said that Ho Chi Minh himself recognized the military prowess and courage of the Detroit rebellion.

African rebellions were erupting in city after city. The Black Panther Party was formed; COINTELPRO implemented; black leaders killed. The cry for Black Power issued from within the African domestic colony. It was Viet Nam and Algeria inside the borders of the U.S.

A white movement called the "New Left" was claiming to distinguish itself from the old communist left by these very issues: the primacy of national liberation movements in the struggle against the capitalist system and the responsibilities of the oppressor nation to the oppressed. Pictures of Che Guevara, Ho Chi Minh, Mao Zedong hung on the walls of left leaning cafes, and "solidarity" was a word bantered about.

But when it came to the struggle of African people inside the United States, the white nationalism of the New Left was exactly the same as that of the old. Its stand was one of betrayal, opportunism, condescension and complicity with white power.

Despite the fact that the Student Nonviolent Coordinating Committee had sent its white membership back into the white society in 1966 to build support for the black struggle, not one former SNCC member actually did that. In general, the white left quickly forgot about any responsibility to struggling African people. It focused instead on campus "free speech" issues, and after a time it found the "anti-war" movement which would attempt to prevent white boys from returning to the U.S. in body bags.

The brutal attack on the Black Power Movement sent some of the members of Students for Democratic Society (SDS), the leading white radical New Left organization of the 1960s, running for cover. Like the Communist Party of the 1950s that it denounced, the white left of the '60s also went "underground," even though there were no specific government attacks against it. They spent years hiding out on rural communes or on houseboats on the San Francisco Bay.

In 1968, SDS issued a paper pledging its support to solidarity with the national liberation movements:

> We feel we have to respond to the black struggle for survival because it is a struggle against imperialism....We should give physical and financial aid to those black people now the object of State repression.[23]

In June of that year, Weatherman, an SDS offshoot, also issued a paper, making statements indicating possibilities for a principled white left relationship to the African movement. The Weatherman paper stated:

> The overriding consideration...is that the main struggle going on in the world today is between U.S. imperialism and the national liberation struggles against it...The primary task of revolutionary struggle is to solve this principal contradiction on the side of the peoples of the world. It is the oppressed peoples of the world who have created the wealth of this empire and it is to them that it belongs; the goal of the revolutionary struggle must be the control and use of this wealth in the interest of the oppressed peoples of the world.[24]

But such statements proved empty when it came to responding to the actual demands by the African revolutionary movement itself. When, in July 1969, the Black Panther Party called a conference in Oakland to build a United Front Against Fascism and mobilize white support against the escalating U.S. government COINTELPRO attacks against it, SDS refused to support it.

During the conference the Panthers called on everyone to participate in a BPP-led campaign for community control of the police who were terrorizing African people, just as they do today. The white leftists singled this campaign out as an excuse not to answer the Panthers' call for solidarity and defense of the movement for African liberation.

The SDSers stated that community control of police for African people was fine. They insisted that in the white community, however, a campaign for community control of the police "would not only undermine the fight against white supremacy," it would lead, according to them, to white vigilante bands.[25]

Building solidarity for the campaign for community control of police inside of white neighborhoods could have had tremendous possibilities. It could have been used to expose the true nature of the police and the fact that they have a completely different role for white people than they do in the African community.

Such a campaign might have opened up many issues in the white community concerning the repressive role of the State, the role of police in protecting white property and white power against a struggling, impoverished, colonized population. It could have raised up the right of African people to free speech and the ability to organize and assemble in their own interests without being attacked by the police.

But without a second thought, the white SDSers opted for self-interest and opportunism. Their betrayal left the Panthers and the black movement more isolated and vulnerable to attacks by the government.

Black Panther leader, Huey Newton was constantly in and out of prison during this period as a result of government frame-ups. Only five months after this conference, Fred Hampton was brutally murdered by the Chicago police department. The "militant" white left of the period took up no campaigns in defense of black revolutionaries facing deadly government attacks.

DAYS OF RAGE

During the summer of 1969, SDS members in Chicago clashed with members of the Black Panther Party led by Chairman Fred Hampton. Despite their lofty articulations of solidarity with the struggle of African people, the SDSers were building for "actions" in September, following by about a year the white youth riot at the 1968 Democratic convention in Chicago. This mobilization was to be called the "Days of Rage." The anarchistic, immature and rather ridiculous goals of "Days of Rage" were to gather white youth, who,

> ...fighting in a together way, smashing up induction centers, pig institutes, etc., and having been toughened psychologically, militarily and politically, would go back to their home cities and regions to create "two, three, many Chicagos"....then go to Washington, several tens of thousands strong, to tear apart that pig capital of U.S. pig power.[26]

In this same period, African people were putting real institutions on the ground to meet the needs of a desperately impoverished and oppressed people. The Black Power Movement was in the heat of a life and death struggle, literally facing the gun of the U.S. counteroffensive while fighting for real community power, with massive ramifications nationally and around the world. SDS, on the other hand, was a wild party of upper-middle class white kids playing at revolution. Inside the ranks of the student organization were

> ...communists, socialists of all sorts, 3 or 4 different kinds of anarchists, anarchosyndicalists, syndicalists, social democrats, humanists, liberals, a growing number of ex-YAF [the right-wing Young Americans for Freedom], libertarian laissez-faire capitalists, and of course, the articulate vanguard of the psychedelic liberation front.[27]

Like their counterparts in France, the "new" white leftists in the U.S. betrayed the Black Revolution in the most crucial moment. In the wake of the movement for the liberation of African people, SDS could have built a serious wide-ranging campaign in the white community in support of the Black Power movement and demanded that the U.S. military attacks on black people end. In fact the unruly and white nationalist white left became a problem for the Black Power Movement, and African organizations were forced to fight on a second front with the white left itself.

Akua Njeri (formerly Deborah Johnson), the widow of Fred Hampton and today the President of the National People's Democratic Uhuru Movement, remembers the struggles with the SDSers.

> SDS called for...the Days of Rage. In fact they wanted to go through the downtown area, break out windows in stores, throw balloons with urine at the pigs and they wanted the Black Panther Party to participate in that.
>
> Fred Hampton told them they were crazy, out of their minds, that's not what we talked about. We talked about organizing the community and ourselves to the point to get to armed struggle. That's not armed struggle. That's what he referred to as "Custeristic," anarchistic foolishness. They refused to listen to Fred Hampton.
>
> He continually denounced them because they allowed the pigs an excuse to bring oppression and brutality into our community, although not one single black person was involved in that craziness.[28]

Three months after the "Days of Rage," on December 4, 1969, Fred Hampton and Mark Clark were brutally murdered by the FBI and the Chicago Police Department who stormed their west side Chicago apartment in the pre-dawn hours. There was no outcry from SDS and the leaders of Days of Rage to one of the most brutal assaults against political activists ever recorded inside the borders of the U.S. The white anti-imperialist movement was silent.

There's a lengthy book summing up SDS. It's 726 pages long with endless anecdotes of the antics and intrigues of the new white left of the era. In that book, the assassination of Fred Hampton is only mentioned once, saying:

> In December Illinois Panther Chairman Fred Hampton was murdered in his bed by Chicago police—but there was no mass protest on campuses at all, no one to force the issue onto the white constituency, no one to call the rallies and make the connections and rouse the passions.[29]

It wasn't that the white left was dead, however. Exactly five months after the murder of Fred Hampton, on May 4, 1970, four white students were shot by the National Guard at Kent State University in Ohio during a demonstration against the U.S. bombing of Cambodia. In response to the murders of these white people there was a massive outburst of rallies and demonstrations on college campuses so militant that the U.S. government feared that the "revolution" had come. This time the "passions" of white people were indeed roused. Between May 5 and 8,

> [T]here were major campus demonstrations at the rate of more than one hundred a day, students at a total of at least 350 institutions went out on strike and 536 schools were shut down completely for some period of time, 51 for the entire year. More than half the colleges and universities in the country (1350) were ultimately touched by protest demonstrations, involving nearly 60 percent of the student population–some 4,350,000 people–in every kind of institution and in every state of the Union...[A]t 26 schools the demonstrations were serious, prolonged, and

marked by brutal clashes between students and police, with tear gas, broken windows, fires, clubbings, injuries, and multiple arrests...

The nation witnessed the spectacle of the government forced to occupy its own campuses with military troops, bayonets at the ready and live ammunition in the breeches, to control the insurrection of its youth; the governors of Michigan, Ohio, Kentucky, and South Carolina declared all campuses in a state of emergency, and the National Guard was activated twenty-four times at 21 universities in sixteen states, the first time such a massive response had ever been used in a nonracial crisis.[30]

That's what white students did in response to the murders of white students.

Ten days after the Kent State incident, two African students were killed and 12 wounded by white police during a demonstration on the black campus of Jackson State in Mississippi. In response there were protests on only 53 campuses, most of which were black. The New Left showed that it could stage an angry temper tantrum when white students were killed, in essence the "collateral damage" in the war against the Black Revolution. But the left would stare unblinkingly into space and do nothing when African people in the U.S. were struggling against the full weight of the U.S. State.

Today the media attempts to say that the "revolution" of the '60s was about hippies on Haight Street in San Francisco. But to link together African people struggling in the inner cities with crusty white pot heads putting flowers in their hair is obscene. There were two movements in the '60s: the Black Revolution allied with other anti-colonial struggles, and the white rights and white counterculture movements of alienated North Americans.

WHITE RADICALS RETURN TO THE PEDESTAL

The U.S. government had been very clear that the object of COINTELPRO was the black movement, not the white students. As a result of the counterintelligence program, courageous and articulate black leaders were dead; the Student Nonviolent Coordinating Committee and the Black Panther Party were crushed. The streets were silenced. The once exuberant African community was sullen and repressed. An atmosphere of quiet terror hung heavy in the air.

By 1970, with the counterinsurgency coming down against the African community, the New Left ran for cover, just like the old left of the 1950s McCarthy era. With the Black Liberation Movement destroyed by COINTELPRO, all pretense of white internationalism and anti-imperialism vanished. The draft was repealed ending all anti-war militancy a good four years before the Vietnamese actually won the war.

White students went to law school, or earned graduate degrees. Millions of other white youth flocked to the country to live as hippies, growing marijuana and organic vegetables. They conveniently left the embattled cities to the war-weary African and colonized populations who had no opportunity to remove themselves to the bucolic backwoods to recuperate from their battles.

"Burned out" by revolution, white leftists became environmentalists and feminists. The white progressives modeled their movements on the Black Revolution, naming their groups, for example, the women's and gay *liberation* movements, or the Gray Panthers. Everyone was getting liberated except African people.

Quickly the women's and gay movements won secure and lucrative places on the pedestal of white power. Today the white gender movements share a leadership role in the white rights movement in general, at the expense of the continuing emiseration of African people. Gay Liberation Day in San Francisco brings out tens of thousands of people to a hedonistic celebration of homosexual rights every year in the state where tens of thousands of African people are languishing in prison.

Chairman Omali Yeshitela describes the effect that the counterinsurgency had on both the African and white movements of the '60s:

> This terrorist reaction had an enormous impact on the black working class movement in the U.S. and the radicalizing process it had ignited throughout the various sectors of the population within the U.S.
>
> Many of the radical white intellectuals who had previously lent ideological support to the Black Revolution found themselves conveniently rethinking their positions to bring them more in line with the tepid traditional politics of the old left radicals who had always ignored the plight of black people.
>
> As anticipated by some black organizations, the hippies took baths, cut their hair and often became successful lower level capitalists, liberal Democratic politicians or overt, right wing, anti-black reactionaries.
>
> A sector of the North America women's movement began direct attacks on the imprisoned and death-ridden black working class movement...[31]

The call for solidarity from SNCC and the Black Panthers went unanswered. But a decade later the African People's Socialist Party created an organization giving white people an opportunity to answer that call in a solid organizational context. Chairman Omali Yeshitela explains the formation of the African People's Solidarity Committee in 1976:

> The Party has taken the demand by SNCC that the North Americans should struggle within their own North Ameri-

can communities a step further. We have also structured the relationship under the discipline of the Party so the strategic aims of the [Black] Revolution are never forgotten or dismissed by North American comrades whose different relationship to U.S. imperialism almost demands an opportunistic approach to every question that threatens the stability and future of a U.S. built off the life, blood and resources of the nonwhite, colonial, neocolonial and economically dependent peoples of the U.S. and the world.[32]

But in 1969 and '70 there was no African People's Socialist Party and no African People's Solidarity Committee. Without leadership, white people stirred by the Black Revolution were hopelessly lost in our "opportunistic approach to every question," as Chairman Omali puts it.

With the Black Power Movement defeated, and the white militants happily back on the pedestal of imperialism, the United States began its counterinsurgency against the entire African population. This meant drugs, prisons, police for Africans, and big money for white people.

DRUG-TAINTED MONEY

In 1994 a lawyer in Los Angeles representing someone accused of dealing drugs had his client's case dismissed by the Ninth U.S. Circuit Court of Appeals. The accused had been arrested by Los Angeles county sheriff's deputies after they stopped his car near an intersection in an LA suburb. On the front seat next to him was a plastic bag with more than $30,000 in cash, arranged neatly in ascending denominations and bound with rubber bands.

The deputies used a police dog which sensed drugs in the money and they arrested the man, even though no drugs were found in his car or home. Charges against him were dismissed, but the state wanted to keep the $30,000 as drug money under the asset forfeiture laws.

The lawyer won the case by raising a fact that has "been well-known in law enforcement and scientific circles for about 10 years," that more than three-quarters of all the paper money in the U.S. is tainted with drugs. Particles of cocaine or other drugs are stuck to it. According to the *Philadelphia Inquirer,* this case "vividly illuminates how extensively the drug trade touches mainstream commerce."[33]

While the African community is labeled as the "drug" community and represents the majority of drug prisoners, we cannot repeat often enough that the majority of all drugs are used and sold by white people.

Seventy-four percent of both federal and state prisoners on drug charges are African, yet they represent only 13 percent of illegal drug users in the U.S., according to the Sentencing Project's report of October, 1995.[34] Other evidence indicates that African people make up only 12 percent of users.

These statistics are even more astounding if one considers that in 1995 sixty percent of prescription psychoactive drug users were taking them illegally on a non-prescription basis. The laws against the use and sales of prescription drugs illegally are rarely if ever enforced, since such drugs are mostly used by white people.[35]

According to the U.S. Health and Human Services 1996 Household Survey on Drug Abuse, 13 million people in the U.S. were current illicit drug users. The report shows a decline in the percentage of African drug users between 1995 and 1996.[36]

Seven in ten people who used illegal drugs in 1997 had full-time jobs, a 1999 Department of Health and Human Services report noted. "A typical drug user is not poor and unemployed," drug czar Barry McCaffrey asserted. On the contrary, according to the report, "young adults, men, whites" were those "more likely to use drugs than other workers."[37]

Despite the statistics, the sentencing patterns are well-known: 5 grams of crack (read African) brings the same sentence as 500 grams of powder cocaine (read white).[38]

Thus, African people are stuffed into prisons, while the drug money flows freely through the U.S. economy to be enjoyed by white people. Drug profits do not just benefit drug dealers. Just as the profits from slavery extended far beyond the pockets of slave traders and plantation owners, drug money permeates the financial system, catapulting the stock market into its seemingly infinite and inexplicable upward spiral.

Drug money is estimated to generate $440 billion in profits worldwide, constituting 8 percent of total global exports. Since this drug revenue figure is estimated by the United Nations, functionally an agency of the United States today, the possibilities of underestimation are no doubt great. According to a U.N. International Drug Control Program report quoted in the *Seattle Times* "illegal drugs are bigger business than all exports of automobiles and about equal to the worldwide trade in textiles."[39]

The Underground Empire by James Mills, draws what is no doubt a far more accurate picture of the scope of the world drug economy, however:

> The inhabitants of the Earth spend more money on illegal drugs than they spend on food. More than they spend on housing, clothes, education, medical care, or any other product or service. The international narcotics industry is the largest growth industry in the world. Its annual revenues exceed half a trillion dollars—three times the value of all United States currency in circulation, more than the gross national products of all but a half dozen of the major industrialized nations...

Narcotics industry profits, secretly stockpiled in countries competing for the business, draw interest exceeding $3 million per *hour*.[40]

Writing in 1986, Mills claims the drug trade generated $500 billion a year then. As the "largest growth industry in the world," drug profits must be far greater today.

This money is not in the African community. A study cited in chapter 5 shows that street drug organizations in African communities make only about a $1,000 a week. On the other hand, billions of dollars of drug revenues flow into the U.S. mainstream economy benefiting white people, whether we are personally involved with drugs or not. It's the nature of parasitic capitalism.

The capitalist economy is amoral. Whatever the market will bear dictates the activities of parasitic capitalism, not morality. Oil, bananas, coffee, diamonds, uranium, drugs, sex—all are colonial commodities competing on the world market. Where lucrative, U.S. imperialism and Wall Street will attempt not only to control the source of the commodity in a "third world" country by any means necessary, they will always attempt to expand the market for that commodity. The current world economy can't stop doing that—it is the essence of parasitic capitalism.

For example, child prostitution is a growing multi-billion dollar industry of the world economy and is a key aspect of the popular sex tourism trade in Asia. Every U.S. politician would pretend to denounce this despicable practice, yet the U.S. founded this dirty business, consumes this commodity and no doubt controls the majority of its profits.

In colonized countries desperately impoverished by imperialism, people are forced to sell their own children as "commodities" which must be marketed in order to live. The profitable origin of this business is traceable to the U.S. military during the Viet Nam

War, "which facilitated sex between United States servicemen and young Asian girls."[41]

While drugs and child prostitution are particularly abhorrent aspects of the world economy, nothing about capitalism is clean. The suffering of those who produce coffee beans is no less genocidal than the effects of the drug and sex trade.

We cannot separate ourselves from drug money inside the U.S. or any aspect of the world economy just because we don't like it. Ignoring it makes it no less real. The world economy is based on genocide and slavery. As part of the white population we are the recipients, the beneficiaries of its revenues whether we want to be or not. The billions of dollars of drug money flowing through the U.S. financial system fill our pockets and checking accounts.

DIRTY MONEY AND WORLD POVERTY

Some analysts state that about $100 billion[42] of the $440 billion of worldwide drug money circulates inside the U.S. However this amount does not stand up to the report that U.S. "drug users buy about 60 percent of the world supply."[43] Sixty percent of $440 billion would be about $264 billion.

Michael Ruppert in "From the Wilderness" backs up this supposition. While United Nations and the Department of Justice estimate that $100 billion of drug money is circulating inside the U.S. every year, Ruppert asserts:

> [O]ther research, including material from the Andean Commission of Jurists...place the figure at around $250 billion per year. [Former investment banker and Assistant Secretary for the Office of Housing and Urban Development] Catherine Austin Fitts places the figure at $250 to $300 billion. Using her Wall Street experience as an investment banker, Fitts is then quick to point out that the

multiplier effect (x6) of $250 billion laundered would result in $1.5 trillion dollars per year in U.S. cash transactions resulting from the drug trade.[44]

Not surprisingly, the U.S. economy, as of the first quarter of 2000, continues to move along at a healthy clip. However, the situation is not really so pleasant. Indeed, how stable could an economy built on drugs, prisons, slavery and genocide be? The media obscures the crisis of imperialism and depth of the economic problems around the world. Canadian professor Michel Chossudovsky gives us a clearer picture:

> Humanity is undergoing in the post-Cold War era an economic crisis of unprecedented scale leading to the rapid impoverishment of large sectors of the world population....The crisis is not limited to South-East Asia or the former Soviet Union. The collapse in the standard of living is taking place abruptly and simultaneously in a large number of countries. This worldwide crisis of the late 20th century is more devastating than the Great Depression of the 1930s. It has far-reaching geo-political implications; economic dislocation has also been accompanied by the outbreak of regional conflicts, the fracturing of national societies and in some cases the destruction of entire countries. This is by far the most serious economic crisis in modern history.

According to Chossudovsky the manipulation of the world economy by private investors who hold monetary reserves that "far exceed the limited capabilities of the world's central banks," is redefining the world economy itself. He states that:

> In the late 20th century, the outright "conquest of nations," meaning the control over productive assets,

labor, natural resources and institutions, can be carried out in an impersonal fashion from the corporate boardroom: commands are dispatched from a computer terminal, or a cell phone. The relevant data are instantly relayed to major financial markets—often resulting in immediate disruptions in the functioning of national economies.[45]

Current International Monetary Fund (IMF) policies enrich the largest Wall Street commercial banks. These include Chase Manhattan, Bank of America, Citicorp and J.P. Morgan and the "big five" merchant banks. Goldman Sachs, Lehman Brothers, Morgan Stanley Dean Witter and Salomon Smith Barney. These institutions not only function as international speculators raiding the central banks of colonized countries in Asia, Latin America and Africa. The same Wall Street banks are also the *creditors* assigned by the IMF to bail out the colonial countries after the financial devastation which they themselves inflicted.

Just how did these Wall Street banks get more cash reserves than even the leading imperialist state banks? Chossudovsky links them to "hot" (speculative capital) and "dirty" (laundered) money.[46]

NORTH AMERICAN LAUNDRY

When African people are arrested on charges of drug sales, they are labeled "kingpins," and their pictures are splashed throughout the pages of the local papers. But as we know, African workers in the housing projects do not control the billion-dollar international drug trade. Notably, when ships laden with cocaine and other drugs are apprehended in the ports, there are neither pictures nor names attached to them. For example, a *St. Petersburg Times* article told of two cargo ships returning from Haiti that docked on the Miami River containing about 1,488 pounds of cocaine in November of 1999. "We have not made any arrests," a U.S. Customs spokeswoman is quoted as saying.[47]

While millions of African people are going to prison for life under some of the most stringent laws ever enacted, blatant "dirty" drug money laundering by prestigious corporate firms is completely acceptable. According to the New Jersey paper, *The Bergen Record:*

> While the federal government spends an estimated $16 billion a year on the war on drugs, less than 5 percent is devoted to following the trail of drug profits in and out of corporations, banks, and securities firms....The same imbalance can be seen in how the federal government punishes low-level drug dealers and big-time money launderers. According to court records, the money men who process millions of dollars in drug profits usually serve less than four years behind bars, while street-level pushers serve twice that amount.*[48]

Wall Street banks have long been implicated in drug money laundering. Scott Ehlers of *Foreign Policy in Focus,* writes that:

> Several services offered by international banks have been used by launderers. "Private banking," a little known and largely unregulated service, has been offered by Citicorp, Chase, and other U.S. financial institutions....This service can involve offshore accounts, moving large sums of money from one country to another, devising intricate networks of accounts, and helping to purchase homes, businesses, and investments with laundered funds. The service can also include setting up "concentration accounts," where funds from various individuals are com-mingled and their origins not identified. Citibank's private

---

* More often ten times that amount.

banking service, for instance, laundered tens of millions of dollars in drug money for Raul Salinas, the jailed brother of former Mexican President Carlos Salinas."[49]

How many tens of thousands of people are directly involved with drug money laundering, we do not know. But, we do know they are treated not as criminals but as "good white citizens," living in the suburbs. Scott Ehlers sums up:

> Although the U.S. is one of the world's leading money laundering centers, very few money laundering cases are actually filed—an indication that this crime is difficult to detect and/or that inadequate resources are being devoted to enforcement. In 1995, only 62 criminal money-laundering cases were filed with U.S. attorneys, of the 138 defendants, 52 were convicted.[50]

And how many thousands of African people went to prison on drug related charges that year?

In 1994 the *San Francisco Chronicle* reported that Bank of America had quarterly profits of $513 million. Asked how B of A planned to maintain its enormous profit margin, a bank spokesman replied, "trusts, *private banking* [italics mine] and mutual funds." In addition the article explained that "B of A created the empire by buying branches of busted S & L's."[51]

The Savings and Loans, which went bankrupt in the early '90s, were themselves tied to CIA drug laundering. *Houston Post* articles in 1990 detailed evidence that "at least 27 failed financial institutions—25 S & L's and two banks—had links to CIA operatives or to organized crime figures with links to the CIA."

According to a report by the Christic Institute, a Washington based watchdog group, "The owners of many of the thrifts had personal ties to the agency. In some cases CIA operatives or mob figures with ties to the CIA approved loans to their associates or obtained loans that were never repaid."[52]

BAGS FULL OF CASH

Drug money is an integral part of the entire U.S. economy. It is a major factor in the U.S. ability to continue to enjoy massive wealth while the rest of the world faces ever deepening poverty.

In 1995, in New Jersey, Colombian "exporters" reportedly used $3 million in cocaine profits to buy cars at BMW, Honda and Mitsubishi dealerships and export them through Port Newark. An article in *The Bergen Record* said, "Dozens of car dealers were approached with bags full of cash over a three-year period, yet only one notified the IRS."

Another example in the same article notes that Wilson Sporting Goods, which sells athletic equipment overseas, "thought nothing of getting a $10,000 stack of money orders—with no name and no return address except for a post office box—for an equipment order bound for Colombia. The money orders were later traced back to drug dealers in New York City."[53]

It seems that *all* of white America is awash in drug money. Everyone's got his or her fingers in the pudding. For example:

- In New York, Orthodox Jewish rabbis were charged with laundering and hiding $1.75 million for Colombian narcotics dealers by routing the cash "through the bank accounts of a synagogue and a yeshiv a in Borough Park, Brooklyn."[54]
- In California, at least 50 U.S. Marines and sailors were accused of "smuggling marijuana and cocaine into California for Mexican drug rings."[55]
- In Northern California, "A Napa Valley wine merchant has been indicted as a major cocaine dealer who allegedly sold his drug business to an associate in 1994..."[56]

- In Pennsylvania, even the seemingly stoic Amish have gotten into the act. Two Amish men admitted dealing more than $100,000 worth of cocaine to Amish youths. Despite sentencing guidelines that would have put African youth in prison for years, the Amish dope dealers were given a year in custody with work-release privileges. This means that the custodial term could be served in a local prison or a halfway house on nights and weekends.[57]

- In 1999, the wife of a senior U.S. military officer in Colombia was arrested on charges of shipping cocaine through official mail. The military officer, Colonel James Hiatt, was responsible for directing "200 U.S. troops operating in Colombia, including U.S. Special Forces on anti-drug missions." Six to eight other embassy staff and family members, in addition to Mrs. Hiatt, were investigated for using the Air Force Postal System to send drugs to the U.S. "Mrs. Hiatt is charged with conspiring to send at least six packages of cocaine, each containing about 2.7 pounds of the drug, with an estimated value of $235,000," according to *The London Times*.[58]

Like the police, prison guards have long been known to cash in on the drug trade. They have been caught dealing heroin, cocaine and marijuana in several California prisons including San Quentin, New Folsom and others where "dope...is a very lucrative business."[59]

One of the most revealing articles regarding the depth of the drug economy appeared in the *St. Petersburg Times* in 1989, in a series called, "No Questions Asked: Florida, Drugs and Money." This series examined how the economy of the entire state of Florida was dependent on the cocaine trade. The five-day series was unprecedented in its depth.

According to the series, Florida prosecutor William Norris stated:

If the drug business were to stop tomorrow, there'd be a crash in the Florida economy....[drug dealers] are flanked by attorneys who set up dummy corporations. They are made richer by bankers who help them hide the fact that the money was earned illegally. They are courted by real estate agents who blindly accept their cash. And they are tempted by a legion of sales people who peddle the kind of luxury that drug money routinely buys.

The articles show that approximately 9 percent of the state's economic activity was directly or indirectly related to drugs, and that drugs add between $6 billion and $7.5 billion a year to the South Florida economy [in 1989 dollars]. The series went on to note:

In cities and counties around the state, the drug money that pays for new homes, new shopping centers, new apartment complexes and new marinas provides local government with new tax revenues. That helps pay for schools and roads, and health and emergency services. The unifying factors in all these examples? In every deal, a lot of people who aren't drug smugglers make money.[60]

Involvement in the drug trade seems all-pervasive in white society. In Oakland, California an organization formed under the auspices of fighting drugs was in fact responsible for dealing drugs—on a world scale. The organization, Safe Streets Now, was headed up by a white woman, Molly Wetzel who had aspirations to build a national organization.

African community members came to the Uhuru House outraged that Wetzel and her organization, which were funded by the Oakland City Council, were working with the police to round up young Africans, take them off the streets and send them to prison. Houses of the families of these young Africans were then seized by police and bought by Safe Streets and Wetzel. Safe Streets was active in African neighborhoods desirable for gentrification for white people.

During this heated African community struggle with Safe Streets Now, a scandal broke out in which Safe Streets' leading paid organizer, Michael Simpson was arrested for buying and selling cocaine from the group's office. Newspaper articles exposed that Simpson was part of a larger drug ring with ties to the San Francisco police department, the Mafia and Colombian drug cartels. Of course, except for Simpson who is African, no other major arrests were made.[61]

GENTRIFICATION AND ASSET FORFEITURE

The dispersal and gentrification of African communities has been a key strategy of the counterinsurgency since the '60s when cities razed black neighborhoods under the guise of "urban renewal," or ran freeways through them.

Beginning in the '70s and '80s, urban African communities were targeted for "upgrading" as the white flight of the '60s began to reverse itself. Newspaper ads sought "pioneers," for gentrified brownstones in African sections of Brooklyn, in an attempt to draw white renters and buyers into an impoverished African community. In Oakland, the African People's Socialist Party summed up that the murder of Huey Newton on the streets of West Oakland in 1989 was the result of the local government's desire to eradicate the radical Panther image from Oakland. The legacy of the Black Panthers had long kept white investors from moving in.

The government's seizure of houses and cars from the African community is another highly lucrative offshoot of the drug economy which breaks up African neighborhoods and benefits white people. Between 1985 and 1995 the federal government, through the departments of Justice and Treasury, seized over $4 billion in assets from U.S. citizens, many of whom have never been charged with a crime. In 1994, the Drug Enforcement Administration (DEA) alone made 13,631 seizures with a total value of $646,786,850.[62] According to one report:

> Federal and many state forfeiture laws empower govern-ments to take people's private property without ever charging them with a crime. Legally, the property is accused of a crime, not the owner....Civil asset forfeiture laws allow the government to seize property without charging anyone with a crime, and keep it without ever having to prove a case. Seized property is presumed guilty and may be forfeited based upon mere hearsay, or even a tip supplied by an informant who stands to gain up to 25 percent of the forfeited assets.[63]

A *San Francisco Chronicle* article reports that by 1994 in California,

> Law enforcement departments have raked in more than $172 million in state asset-forfeiture funds. Since 1986, California law enforcement agencies have also landed nearly $270 million in asset-forfeiture money from the U.S. Justice Department, and more than $150 million from the U.S. Customs Service for their role in joint federal and state forfeiture cases.

This comes down to the government seizing the hard-earned houses of the parents or grandparents of African youth who are tar-geted by the counterinsurgency. Millions of dollars of the seized properties under the asset forfeiture laws go into the pockets of the police.

The *Chronicle* article informs us that the police rake in the money on the forfeitures:

[C]ounty governments and law enforcement departments have often milked the asset-forfeiture programs to fund other operation...overeager police have injured—even killed—innocent citizens in raids critics charge were motivated by the promise of asset-forfeiture booty...

Robert Sobel, a former Los Angeles County Sheriffs' Department sergeant, knows how lucrative asset-forfeiture can be. Sobel, a 20-year law enforcement veteran, says his department stole millions of dollars in forfeited money during drug raids in 1988 and 1989.[64]

More and more of such revelations are appearing constantly. In 1999 Catherine Austin Fitts, mentioned earlier, an investment banker formerly with the Department of Housing and Urban Development (HUD), made allegations about the role of HUD in the attack on the African community as a result of the imposition of crack.

Fitts is "convinced that the illegal drug trade, the enormous cheap capital it generates, and the CIA's role as enforcer/protector for the profits of that trade is a dominant factor in the economy of this country..."[65]

After leaving HUD in 1990, Fitts started her own investment company, the Hamilton Securities Group, which secured contracts with HUD through then-Secretary Henry Cisneros. Hamilton took defaulted HUD housing mortgages, repackaged them and auctioned them on the private market. Fitts' investment firm attempted to have these properties resold back to the African community.

Around 1996 Hamilton securities made "money maps" of HUD properties in the African communities that were financed by now defaulted HUD-held mortgages. About the same time that Fitts was doing this work, the "Dark Alliance" series by Gary Webb was appearing in the *San Jose Mercury News*, alleging that the CIA was responsible for crack in the African communities. Fitts found that the crack epidemic coincided with neighborhoods holding many HUD defaulted loans. These were areas which were desirable for gentrifi-cation. Thus, potentially very expensive property was being bought up by outside investors for almost nothing, while the African com-munity was being pushed out of their homes.

"The mathematical correlation is staggering," Fitts says. Every dot on the money maps represented a "HUD mortgage where the taxpayers lost money in a defaulted Federal Housing Administration (FHA) loan and where somebody else bought the property for pen-nies on the dollar. Most of those loans defaulted as the crack cocaine epidemic ravaged Los Angeles." Fitts continues,

> Exactly who bought and traded in properties throughout this area should be the subject of congressional hearings looking into corrupt HUD practices from the period and continuing to this day. I suspect that many of the same players connected to the Savings and Loan scandals, who have also been tied to Iran-Contra and CIA's drugs will surface yet again. Demographically it is also easy to see now that the racial composition of South Central has changed radically and that African-Americans have been geographically and politically fragmented as, I believe, an intended result. Their political power has been weakened.[66]

PRISON ECONOMY

In March 1999, some of us from the Uhuru Movement in Oak-land traveled to Folsom, California, outside of Sacramento to partici-pate in a demonstration called by the Barrio Defense Committee (BDC). The demonstration was held on the highway in front of the grounds of New Folsom prison where the son of BDC leader Maria Ortiz (now known as Quetzaoceloacuia) is imprisoned. Jose Luis

Aviña, faces life in prison after defending himself against a white man's attack in San Francisco in 1994.

Built in the late 1980s, New Folsom prison stands on the same plot of rolling hills as the old Folsom prison. New Folsom is one of California's notoriously brutal prisons. It is surrounded by a "death-wire electrified fence," set between two ordinary chain-link fences, that administers a lethal dose of 5,100 volts at the slightest touch. About a third of the inmates are serving life sentences. The prison was overcrowded even before it was finished and, like the 50 or so other prisons in the state, it operates at double its intended capacity.[67]

We knew that Folsom was a rural town about a two-hour drive from the Bay Area. The grandparents of one member of the African People's Solidarity Committee, Wendy Snyder, had lived in Folsom, and Wendy remembered visiting him there when she was growing up in the 1970s. In those days it was a poor town with mobile homes, beat-up old cars and not much commerce.

Driving to Folsom from the west, Wendy and others were struck, but not surprised to see a new, stylishly designed City Hall and police station, a sizable designer outlet mall, plenty of late-model four-wheel drive vehicles, espresso cafes, juice bars and upscale housing with hot tubs and pools. It seemed like a chic little Berkeley or Palo Alto in the middle of nowhere. During the demonstration out on the highway in front of the entrance, it was clear that the white people driving by in brand new cars were hostile. African and Mexican people in older cars, however, were honking supportively as they turned into the grounds to visit relatives.

After the demonstration, some of the protesters stopped at a juice bar for something to eat before the drive back home. Someone asked a teenage girl working there if a lot of people around there worked in the prisons. "Oh, everyone," she replied.

As an offshoot of the drug economy and a key element of the counterinsurgency, the prisons have opened up another tremendously lucrative market in the genocide of African people. From central California to upstate New York, from the panhandle of Florida to southern Illinois, rural white America is experiencing a new economic boom thanks to the massive prison building. In a situation very similar to that of plantation slavery, the suffering and labor of African people in the prison system benefit the financial well-being of white society today.

PRISONS BUILT BY LIBERALS

Liberals and Democratic Party elected officials are largely responsible for the prison boom. In California, Jerry Brown, the liberal governor of the '70s, passed "career criminal" prosecution programs which laid the basis for today's Three Strikes law. In Texas liberal Democratic governor Ann Richards added 100,000 new beds to that state's prison system within a very short time in the 1990s.

The same story is true for New York. On the heels of the militant African-led uprising at Attica Prison in 1971, Governor Nelson Rockefeller, a liberal Republican, first initiated mandatory minimum sentences for drug dealers and life without parole, the harshest drug laws in the United States. Following Rockefeller's lead, nearly every other state also enacted strict mandatory minimum sentences for drug offenses.

Federal mandatory minimums were then incorporated in the 1986 Anti-Drug Abuse Act which was engineered by Democratic Speaker of the House Tip O'Neil. According to the article "Prison Industrial Complex," published in the *Atlantic Monthly*, when liberal Democrat Mario Cuomo was elected governor of New York he took up Rockefeller's lead. Over the twelve years of Cuomo's governorship, he "added more prison beds in New York than all the previous governors in the state's history combined."[68]

The politicians built prisons as a conscious attempt to create jobs for white workers. It has been a strategy to shore up the economies in rural white areas that had gone sour years ago. It did not matter that this strategy required genocidal conditions against African and Mexican people in order to be successful. This, after all, is the legacy of America.

It was Democratic president John F. Kennedy who instituted the counterinsurgent capacity of the U.S. military and the police. Counterinsurgency in general seems to be the forte of liberals whose main goal is to put violence and genocide into the more remote hands of the State, and take it away from the daily activity of regular white citizens. It's genocide made nice. Clinton has done more to promote prison building than anyone, and has advanced the interests of the brutal private corporately owned prisons.

Along with the drug economy, prisons have proven to be one of the best methods of economic development for white people since Franklin Roosevelt implemented the Work Progress Administration (WPA) during the Depression years of the 1930s. The WPA "was designed to increase the purchasing power of [white] persons on relief by employing them on useful projects. WPA's building program included the construction of 116,000 buildings, 78,000 bridges, and 651,000 miles of road and the improvement of 800 airports."[69] The booming prison economy, pumping billions and billions of dollars into construction and other new jobs, functions in the same way.

The low unemployment rates being reported inside the United States today are the result of taking at least two million people out of the job market through incarceration. An article that appeared in the *Atlantic Monthly* in 1999 asserts, "Currently, among black men aged twenty-five to thirty-four with less than a high school education, the jobless rate is around 50 percent. If those in prison and jail are included, the figure rises above 60 percent." The article continues to expose that the only reason that

> ...[U.S.] unemployment statistics look so good in comparison with those of other industrial democracies is that 1.6 million [actually, it is 2 million as of this writing, Ed.]

mainly low-skilled workers—precisely the group least likely to find work in a high-tech economy—have been incarcerated, and are thus not considered part of the labor force. Rendering such a large group of people invisible...creates a numerical mirage in which unemployment statistics are as much as two percent below the real unemployment level."[70]

It can be no coincidence that the high-tech economy of Northern California has produced massive wealth for the white population there. But what is this wealth based on? Northern California was shown to be the center for crack and cocaine importation and distribution by Oscar Danilo Blandon, who is a primary CIA-backed drug dealer noted in Gary Webb's *Dark Alliance*. In addition, California has a prison system larger than almost every country in the world, including those with enormous populations.

Silicon Valley, the leader of the computer industry, is located around San Jose, part of the greater San Francisco Bay Area. According to a banner headline from the city's *Chronicle,* "S.F. Workers Rake in Fat-Cat Wages." In San Francisco, nearly 600 city employees made more than $100,000 in 1998, including 81 cops under the rank of captain.[71]

Alameda County, which includes Oakland and Berkeley, had a mean household income in 1995 of $74,300 with $81,400 projected for 2000. In Fremont, California, which is part of what is called Silicon Valley, the center of the computer software industry, 31 percent of household incomes in 1997 brought in between $50,000 and 75,000. The median income for all households in Fremont was $61,790 that year.

Although California has one of the most "diverse" populations in the country, resources generated by the computer industry stay in the tight-fisted hands of white people. There is no trickle down in the "digital divide," as it is called.

In San Jose, the contrast between the wealthy white population and the sizable impoverished Mexican population is staggering. The *San Jose Mercury News* reports, "Despite the raging prosperity in Silicon Valley, some people are still going to bed at night hungry. In the last fiscal year, Tri-City Volunteer's Emergency Food Services handed out 492,876 free meals..."[72] The San Jose organization helps 500 families on welfare and 1200 "working poor" families.

In Santa Clara County (where Silicon Valley is located), the *median* price of a home topped $410,000 in 1999, while the *average* price topped $500,000.[73]

THE PRICE OF PUNISHMENT

In 1994 the *Los Angeles Times* ran a series exposing the parasitic nature of the prison economy in enormous depth and detail. With at least 50 prisons in California at the close of the century, a quarter of a million mostly African and Mexican people are tied to the prison system in the state. Between the mid-'80s and the mid-'90s, California's prison budget grew from less than $730 million to more than $3 billion.

The *Times* series entitled, "The Price of Punishment: The Booming Business of Running California's Prisons," admits that the prison economy took the state out of deep economic depression and boosted the state's finances with an influx of billions of dollars. "With a minimal outside oversight," the series sums up, "California has spawned a multi-billion-dollar prison construction industry that extends from Wall Street money managers to hard hats who build the bastilles of concrete, steel and razor wire."[74]

The state of California constructs the biggest, most expensive, most brutal prisons in the U.S., packing away hundreds of thousands of African and Mexican people in concentration camps—and a broad sector of the white community makes money off it.

The state's prison building frenzy coincided with the imposition of crack cocaine into the African and Mexican communities in the early 1980s. Since that time, the California Department of Prisons has spent $5 billion on planning, engineering and construction of new prisons, and created a bond debt that will double to $10 billion with interest payments. Each California prison houses at least 4,000 people and costs $200 million or more to build. Each prison has 8 1/2 miles of razor wire surrounding it, 337 guns and a $2 million computerized alarm system.[75]

The same banks and investment firms that are involved in drug money laundering are some of the biggest winners of the California prison building spree. Institutions such as Morgan Stanley Dean Witter, Goldman Sachs, Solomon Smith Barney and Merrill Lynch and Co. are making billions by underwriting prison construction with private, tax-exempt lease revenue bonds. Being paid back at more than twice their original value, these bonds will be worth upwards of $6 billion.

MODERN-DAY GOLD RUSH

All sectors of white society have descended like vultures on this new gold rush of massive wealth at the expense of African and Mexican people. Consultants, architects and contractors are making millions off the prisons. The *Los Angeles Times* article clarifies,

> Nationwide, prison construction is a $5 billion-a-year business. It's a niche that has attracted large builders, including many that have done major projects for the Pentagon.

> "It has allowed us to have a reasonably steady flow of work," said Jim Thomas, regional head of CRSS Constructors, Inc., which has been construction manager at four California prisons...[76]

Real estate interests are finding a windfall in the prison boom. For example, Pleasant Valley State prison near Coalinga opened in 1994 on an expanse of flat, dry land. The property was owned by Triple D Farms which, in 1990, had bought the land from Bank of America at $374 per acre. The State of California paid $4,500 per acre to Triple D Farms, and then spent another $1,500 per acre supposedly for toxic clean-up, bringing the price up to $5,000 per acre. Farmland in the area generally sells for $2,000 per acre. Conveniently, this deal took place in the district of Assemblyman Jim Costa (D-Fresno). Costa is one of the two co-authors of the "Three Strikes" law and has six prisons in his district. Triple-D's partners have contributed to Costa's campaigns, giving him $3,000 in 1993.[77]

Even California's environmental movement is taking part in the parasitic feast. The state is paying $150,000 for anti-perching devices at each prison so that birds will not be electrocuted by the electronic fences. Mike Davis gives us a glimpse into the priorities in a state that assigns greater value to the life of waterfowl than to an African or Mexican people. In *Ecology of Fear* he describes the environmental struggle which emerged around Calipatria State Prison:

> The prison is just east of the Salton Sea—a major wintering habitat for waterfowl—and the gently purring high-voltage fence immediately became an erotic beacon to passing birds. Local bird-watchers soon found out about the body count ("a gull, two owls, a finch and a scissor-tailed flycatcher") and alerted the Audubon Society. By January, Calipatria's "death fence" was an international environmental scandal. When a CNN crew pulled into the prison parking lot, the Department of Corrections threw in the towel and hired an ornithologist to help them redesign the fence.

> The result is the world's only birdproof, ecologically responsible death fence. Paramo [the prison's public

relations officer] has some difficulty maintaining a straight face as he points out $150,000 in innovations: "a warning wire for curious rodents, anti-perching deflectors for wildfowl, and tiny passageways for burrowing owls." Calipatria has also built an attractive pond for visiting geese and ducks.[78]

Just about every white town in the U.S. is vying for some of the prison blood-money to bolster the income potential for their residents. A hundred and fifty years ago, white people ganged up to murder and lynch African people to get jobs. Or they moved west to kill indigenous people and steal their gold and land. Today, it is even simpler—get a prison, stuff it with African and Mexican people, enjoy an economic boom in your hometown.

Newspaper articles from around the country report on the excitement of white individuals and communities making a fortune off of the prison economy. In Susanville, California there is one state prison and another under construction.

"Where else in Susanville are you going to make $3,000 a month with a high school diploma," asks Dave Foster, chairman of the mathematics and science department at Lassen College and a former Susanville mayor. "It's allowed a lot of Susanville kids to stay here. This is our industry. Maybe that's ok."

> These jobs pay good money, an average of $41,000 a year, according to corrections officials...
>
> "It creates an economy," says [the] mayor pro tem of Adelanto, a rural California town which is still lobbying for a state prison after years of rejection. "The desert always has been notorious for not making jobs."[79]

In Crescent City, the home of the notorious Pelican Bay prison, the opening of that genocidal concentration camp led to an explosive economic growth. According to an article in the *San Francisco Chronicle*:

> Pelican Bay nearly doubled Crescent City's population of 4,500, when it opened in November 1989...bringing 20 years growth in five years....
>
> Annual county sales tax revenue...has jumped from $180,000 before the prison's opening to $570,000 today....
>
> The average $280 million prison brings with it an annual payroll of about $45 million, nearly as much as the entire budget of Siskiyou county.
>
> Most tantalizing to poor rural counties are the employment figures—up to 1,200 jobs at each maximum security prison, including professional positions for nurses, counselors, and administrators. There is typically one "spin-off" job in the community for every two in the institution.[80]

HOT JOBS

An article in the business section of the *San Francisco Chronicle* in 1997 listed the profession of prison guard under "Hot jobs for those who don't have a four-year degree":

> Due to California's "three strikes" law and other get-tough-on-crime measures, jails and prisons around the state will add nearly 17,000 new correctional officers between 1993 and 2005. The pay starts around $24,000 and goes as high a $46,000. This is one of the few well-paying jobs you can get with just a high school degree. The downside? You're dealing with criminals all day. And, competition for jobs is fierce. The state received 30,000 job applications last year alone.[81]

But lest you fear that living on $46,000 may be difficult with today's rising inflation, you can always make a bundle working overtime. The *San Jose Mercury News* reported that by working extra hours:

> Santa Clara County Jail Deputy Leo Mauro made a cool $141,500 last year—more than even the county's chief administrator. The Santa Clara county jail paid nearly $8 million in overtime in 1993, and for the deputies and correctional officers, the overtime is a perk. "One female deputy is paying off her BMW, one deputy wants to go on a vacation, one needs to put a down payment on a house," Mauro said, "I'm putting two kids through college."[82]

The situation is the same throughout the rest of the United States. The *Amarillo Daily News* exclaimed in 1994, "State dollars channeled through employment at Amarillo prisons are helping boost new housing starts and are pumping a consistent influx of cash into the city's economy..."[83]

The *Chicago Tribune* told how the prison population of the state of Illinois shot up almost 150 percent from 1980 to 1993, from about 150,000 to nearly 500,000. Consequently, rural towns all over the state have been in fierce competition for new prisons. The site for a brutal $60 million super maximum security prison was fought over by more than thirty white communities which petitioned the state Department of Corrections (DOC) in countless novel ways.

> "It got to the point we had to ask communities to tone down presentations," Howell (an Illinois DOC representative) said recalling fanfare that included welcome billboards, firetruck cavalcades, high school bands and roses.

Tamms, a community in downstate Illinois, won out with a package of inducements that, in addition to land, included two years of free water and sewer service and the extension of utility lines. Land is almost a standard giveaway today, Howell said.

Certainly, economics has played a major role in the warmer welcome. "It has finally dawned on city fathers that prisons bring a lot of jobs," said Rauch of the American Correctional Association.[84]

From the *Philadelphia Inquirer*:

In the 1950s, Charles Brayford's walk home from school took him past one of the humming textile mills in this tiny Schuylkill County borough. There he'd see 40 or 50 men who, having lost their jobs when the coalmines closed, were waiting to pick up their wives.

By the early '80s, most of the textile industry had vanished, too. Younger people either moved away or commuted long hours to work in Harrisburg or Allentown.

Now that sad slide into hard times seems, in the mid-90s, to be over. Brayford, 59, now the part-time mayor, sees new faces in the streets, old friends returning home to live, and at least some businesses turning a respectable profit.

"This town," he declares, "is coming back."

That's because Frackville sits smack at the center of one of Pennsylvania's few growth industries: prisons.[85]

From Georgia:

"Prisons are the real growth industry for rural Georgia," notes state Rep. Bob Holmes of Atlanta. "The rural counties are losing population; they have poor schools; they have no way to draw industry. Their bright kids are moving out. What the rural counties do have is lots of vacant land. They have dull kids who're just fine for prison guard duty. And often they have a long-term state legislator with sufficient power to land them a prison."[86]

The *Tampa Tribune* quoted an enthusiastic county official in Florida's rural Sumter County, where nearly one in every nine residents is a prisoner. County Administrator Bernard Dew was "delighted" with the parasitic benefits of the prison economy in his county:

> It's a good source of employment, particularly for younger folks....It's a clean, nonpolluting industry; it provides a market for local businessmen; and it provides many of its own services....We're able to count [inmates] in our population, which helps on some of our grant applications, and it has created support industries, too. I can't think of a negative.[87]

EVERYONE WORKS IN CORRECTIONS

"Who's in prison everywhere you see? It's Africans and Mexicans—it's slavery!" So goes a chant used by the National People's Democratic Uhuru Movement and the Barrio Defense Committee in their demonstrations. As has been shown, with all those Africans and Mexicans behind bars, the prison economy is the hottest thing going.

One observer remarked that the prison boom is a

> ...confluence of special interests that has given prison construction in the United States a seemingly unstoppa-

ble momentum. It is composed of politicians, both liberal and conservative, who have used the fear of crime to gain votes; impoverished rural areas where prisons have become a cornerstone of economic development; private companies that regard the roughly $35 billion spent each year on corrections not as a burden on American taxpayers but as a lucrative market; and government officials whose fiefdoms have expanded along with the inmate population.[88]

Upstate New York, like rural California, and the rest of the country, finds its economic opportunities through incarcerating African and Puerto Rican people in that state. "The Prison-Industrial Complex," an article in the December, 1998 issue of the *Atlantic Monthly* magazine, details the rise of the prison economy for New York's Adirondack North Country. People in this part of New York "tend to be politically conservative, taciturn, fond of the outdoors, and white...Twenty-five years ago the North Country had two prisons; now it has eighteen correctional facilities, and a nineteenth is under construction...." The article continues:

The traditional anchors of the North Country economy—mining, logging, dairy farms, and manufacturing—have been in decline for years. Tourism flourishes in most towns during the summer months...[T]he North Country's per capita income has long been about 40 percent lower than the state's average per capita income. The prison boom has provided a huge infusion of state money to an economically depressed region—one of the largest direct investments the state has ever made there.[89]

PRISON LABOR, MODERN-DAY SLAVERY

Today, industries operating inside the prisons are cashing in on the legal slavery permitted by the Thirteenth Amendment of the Constitution. Prisoners are being paid an average of about 35 cents an hour to produce well over $1 billion worth of products and services from office furniture to computer circuit boards to license plates to clothing to agriculture. In 1994 there were nearly 75,000 inmates working for the slave wages of the private sector employment in prisons. Slave labor in prison is not new. In the nineteenth century private prisons were common in this country:

> Prisoners were farmed out as slave labor. They were routinely beaten and abused, fed slops and kept in horribly overcrowded cells. Conditions were so wretched that by the end of the nineteenth century private prisons were outlawed in most states.[90]

Then the State took over as the slave master, and until laws were changed in the 1930s, almost all U.S. prisoners worked on state-run farms, factories, and public works projects or as laborers hired out to private business people.

In 1984, as the government was flooding crack into the African community, Congress created the Prison Industry Enhancement Program (PIE) which once again allowed state-run prison industries to sell their products on the open market and enabled private companies to again hire inmate laborers at nominal salaries under certain circumstances. Private industry is champing at the bit to fully exploit this new *captive* labor market. An article in the *Village Voice* queries:

> Booked a flight on TWA recently? Your call may have been taken by a young offender in the California Youth and Adult Correctional Agency. Bought any Microsoft software lately? It may have been packaged by prisoners

in Washington State. But private sector prison labor is only the tiniest tip of the iceberg; federal and state governments are far and away the biggest employers of locked-up laborers.[91]

In California prisoners on work farms produce milk, beef and eggs. They fight wildfires, make automobile licenses, produce eyeglasses for Medi-Cal, furniture used by government offices and neon signs for casinos.[92] In Oregon prisoners make millions of dollars for a blue jeans line, Prison Blues, which advertises that they are "made on the inside to be worn on the outside." According to Brian Bemus, administrator for Oregon's inmate work program, Prison Blues are now available in 300 stores across the U.S. and are hot sellers in Italy and Japan.[93] In addition:

Inmates now make articles such as clothes, car parts, computer components, shoes, golf balls, soap, furniture and mattresses, in addition to staffing jail house telemarketing, data entry and print shop operations. Some states have even begun assigning inmates to institutions after matching up their job skills with a prison's labor needs.[94]

Prisoners make socks, gloves, pants, desks and chairs. They grind prescription lenses, roast coffee and bake bread. They weld stainless-steel sinks, sew jeans and boxer shorts, raise chickens and package everything from three-ring binders to soapsuds.[95]

The return of treacherous chain gang labor in many states reflect not only intensified brutality and inhuman conditions for African people in prison, but more government-controlled slave labor. In Florida, minimum security prisoners do $10 million annually worth of road work. With the reinstitution of chain gangs in the state, that amount is growing.

By the year 2012, three to five million people will be behind bars at current rates, including an "absolute majority" of African men. "Because the prison system doesn't affect a significant percentage of young white men, we'll increasingly see prisoners treated as commodities," remarks one observer.[96]

Reflecting the African resistance to the involuntary servitude of the prisoners, one African woman in prison interviewed by the *Village Voice* noted, "'Most of us in here are minorities,' says 'Tee,' a young black woman doing 10 years...'The government just hauls us in here to make money off us. It's slave labor, exactly.'"[97]

PRIVATE PRISONS

With barely any legal supervision, private prisons are another aspect of the parasitic counterinsurgent economy which is reaping billions of dollars out of the suffering of African people. In fact private prisons are the fastest growing sector of the whole prison economy.[98] Operating in 28 states, private prisons hold at least 62,000 people in the U.S., and within the next decade the number of private prison beds is expected to grow to 360,000.[99]

The *Weekly Planet*, published in Tampa, Florida ran an article in 1997 on the private prison industry which noted:

> An...upbeat mood imbued a conference on private prisons held last December at the Four Seasons Resort in Dallas. The brochure for the conference, organized by the World Research Group, a New York-based investment firm, called the corporate takeover of corrections facilities the "newest trend in the area of privatizing previously government-run programs...While arrests and convictions are steadily on the rise, profits are to be made—profits from crime. Get in on the ground floor of the booming industry now!"[100]

In 1996 Attorney General Janet Reno announced that of seven new federal prisons being built, five will be private prisons. In addition private prison companies have also "begun taking charge of management at Immigration and Naturalization Service (INS) detention centers, boot camps for juveniles and substance abuse programs."[101]

The Corrections Corp. of America (CCA) out of Nashville, Tennessee is the largest private prison corporation in the U.S., controlling about half of the whole private prison market. According to the *Wall Street Journal*, CCA's 1997 revenue was $462.2 million, up nearly fivefold in five years, while earnings rose even faster.[102] CCA runs 46 penal institutions in 11 states. Founded by two Nashville businessmen with no previous experience in prisons, CCA's marketing strategy for promoting a private prison is, "You just sell [a prison] like you were selling cars, or real estate, or hamburgers."[103]

The second largest private prison company in the U.S. is Wackenhut Corrections, an offshoot of the Wackenhut Corporation which has long enjoyed U.S. government contracts and hired ex-CIA and FBI officials for its top level staff. Wackenhut Corporation has guarded nuclear weapons facilities and U.S. embassies abroad, and has been accused of being a CIA front.

A haven for retired military, CIA and diplomats, Wackenhut's top executives make astronomical salaries. The *Atlantic Monthly* reports that the current director of the Federal Bureau of Prisons, Kathleen Hawk Sawyer, is responsible for about 115,000 inmates. She makes a salary of $125,900. George C. Zoley, the chief executive officer for Wackenhut Corrections, is responsible for the supervision of about 25,000 state and federal inmates. His 1997 salary was $366,000, with a bonus of $122,500 and stock option grant of 20,000 shares. At least a half dozen other executives at Wackenhut Corrections were paid more last year than the head of the Federal Bureau of Prisons.[104]

Private prisons make money on every bed that is occupied each night. In some states, like Texas, which boasts some of the most rapid prison expansion in the country, too many prison cells exist. This creates whole new parasitic occupations off the backs of African and Mexicans: "bed brokers" and transport companies moving prisoners from state to state to fill the beds. As a result of interstate transport of prisoners in order to fill empty beds, Hawaii's third largest prison is in Texas.

Bed brokers, like Dominion Management of Edmond, Oklahoma, locate facilities with empty beds at a good price. The cost of a prison bed per night is $25 to $60 and bed brokers make a commission of $2.50 to $5.50 per person. When people are brought in from other states and counties, the host county gets a kick back of at least $1.50 a night for each prisoner.

CAPTIVE MARKET

It's a field day for the vendors and purveyors of products to be sold in or used by prisons. Selling everything from Dial soap to Lance peanuts, white people are drooling to compete for the captive market. A 1995 *Wall Street Journal* article reveals the enthusiasm of Rod Ryan, a Dial soap salesman: "I already sell $100,000 a year of Dial soap to the New York City jails. Just think what a state like Texas would be worth."[105]

Telephone calls from inmates generate a billion dollars a year. All the calls from prison are collect, often leaving impoverished families and loved ones of the youthful prison population deeply in debt. Desperate for contact with their children and spouses in the concentration camps, families often rack up monthly phone bills of a thousand dollars or more.

AT&T has a special prison telephone service called "The Authority." MCI's "Maximum Security" tacks a $3 surcharge onto every call from prison. Bell South's prison service is called "MAX," which has a promotional brochure with a picture of a heavy steel chain dangling from a telephone receiver instead of a cord. The brochure states that Bell South has "long distance service that lets inmates go only so far."

So much blood money is made on prisoner's phone calls to their families and friends that MCI installed its service throughout the California prison system at no charge and offered the California Department of Corrections a 32 percent share of all the revenues from prison phone calls. MCI and other phone companies have been exposed for overcharging the inmates; in one state MCI was adding an additional minute to every call.[106]

Atlantic Monthly sums up the mad rush to exploit the prison economy:

> What was once a niche business for a handful of companies has become a multibillion-dollar industry with its own trade shows and conventions, its own Web sites, mail-order catalogues, and direct-marketing campaigns. The prison-industrial complex now includes some of the nation's largest architecture and construction firms, Wall Street investment banks that handle prison bond issues and invest in private prisons, plumbing supply companies, food-service companies, health-care companies, companies that sell everything from bullet resistant security cameras to padded cells available in a "vast color selection."[107]

So, the more we incarcerate African people, the more money we make. But while 2 million people in prison makes for a booming economy, it doesn't do a lot for our emotional well-being. Paranoia is rampant and white people's anxiety has spawned a whole new counterinsurgency-related industry. The *Chicago Sun-Times* reported in 1994:

> Fear, and the alleviation of it, is now a $70 billion-a-year business—one of the fastest growing in the economy, according to experts—and well on its way to topping

$100 billion by the turn of the decade. That would be more than double the projected $44 billion annual outlay for law enforcement.[108]

The marketing of fear includes the growing sales of pepper gas sprays, home and car security systems, self-defense classes, latex dummies to ride in the passenger seats of cars, whistles, window bars, and of course guns of all sizes from petite pistols small enough to fit in a ladies purse to semi-automatic machine guns.

JOINING HUMANITY

It is a dirty business, this U.S. economy built on slavery and genocide, drugs and prisons. Everybody in white society gets something—from country prison guards who never graduated from high school, to urban middle class lawyers, architects and contractors, to the "elite" of Wall Street, the think tanks of Stanford and the highest levels of government. It's just capitalism plain and simple. It's the pedestal upon which white people sit. It's a parasite on the body of suffering humanity. It's America.

So much wealth is flowing into the general economy enjoyed by the white population that it is part of the fabric of everything we touch, eat, buy, wear, read, watch on television. It's the essence of all that we think and aspire to and make assumptions about. It's like those dollar bills tested in Los Angeles—they *all* have cocaine on them; they are all tainted with the blood and suffering of African and indigenous people.

Every day the newspapers back up what Chairman Omali and the African People's Socialist Party has been summing up for years about parasitic capitalism and the war against African people. All the data, the statistics, the facts spell genocide, terror and sheer cold exploitation of African human beings for our sake. The lives of millions are destroyed with our complicity and for our lifestyles. Is this any way to live? Is this reality a future that we want our children to grow up to experience?

In spite of our role as the world's prison guard, policeman and executioner, the African People's Socialist Party gives white people the opportunity to enter into a principled relationship with humanity. We *can* transcend opportunism and base self-interest. To do so we have to muster the courage to tell the truth, to draw correct conclusions from that truth, and to take action.

As Chairman Omali says, we can "stand on the forward side of history." In a presentation before the national convention of the National People's Democratic Uhuru Movement in 1996, the Chairman was very moving in addressing the stand that white people can and must take:

> The reality is the peoples around the world, I believe, can be won to struggle for the national liberation of African people—just like Africans can unite on the side of the people of Nicaragua and the side of the people of Viet Nam....
>
> You [white people] can take the right position. You must take the right position! All of us are going to make this struggle for the national liberation of African people. We are going to destroy white power because white power is the basis of oppression of everybody on the planet Earth. White power got its definition as a consequence of taking away the freedom and power of Africans, of the peoples of Asia and Latin America. It must be destroyed. It is the thing that gave rise to capitalism and imperialism and maintains it today.[109]

Overturning the Culture of Violence

1. Omali Yeshitela, November 1997-February 1998, "Excerpts from the keynote presentation by Chairman Omali Yeshitela at the Oakland Conference to Stop Police Brutality," *The Burning Spear,* p. 7.
2. Patricia Lamiell, July 1, 1999, "Economy: Leading index signals longest peacetime growth," *The Detroit News.*
3. Mike Ruppert, June 28, 1999, "Don't blink," *From The Wilderness*, Vol. II, No. 4, p. 1, (www.copvcia.com).
4. "Allegations of connections between CIA and the Contras in cocaine trafficking to the United States (1)(96-0143-IG)," Vol. 2: The Contra Story, CIA's report to Congressional investigation, (www.cia.gov/cia/publications/cocaine2/contents.html).
5. Sasha Abramsky, June 1999, "When they get out," *Atlantic Monthly,* Vol. 283, No. 6., pp. 30-36.
6. Mike Davis, 1998, *Ecology of Fear: Los Angeles and the Imagination of Disaster* (New York: Metropolitan Books, Henry Holt and Company), p. 417.
7. U.S. Census Bureau, September 24, 1998.
8. National Coalition for the Homeless, February 1999, "National estimates of homelessness," *NCH Fact Sheet,* No. 2, (http://nch.ari.net/numbers).
9. Davis, p. 416.
10. Same as above, p. 418.
11. Same as above, p. 416.
12. September 25-27, 1998, "Critical resistance: Beyond the prison industrial complex," (www.prisonactivist.org/critical/index).
13. Peter Macdonald, 1993, *Giap* (New York: W.W. Norton & Co.), p. 109.
14. Same as above, p. 124.
15. Same as above, p. 158.
16. Same as above, p. 134.
17. Same as above, p. 135.
18. Robert Taber, 1970, *The War of the Flea: A Study of Guerrilla Warfare Theory and Practice* (New York: The Citadel Press), p. 71.
19. Macdonald, p. 159.
20. Same as above, p. 161.
21. Frantz Fanon, 1967, *Toward the African Revolution* (New York: Grove Press, Inc.), pp. 83-86.
22. Dan Georgakas and Marvin Surkin, 1998, *Detroit: I Do Mind Dying* (Boston: South End Press), p. 13.
23. Kirkpatrick Sale, 1973, *SDS* (New York: Random House), p. 551.
24. Harold Jacobs, ed., 1970, *Weatherman* (Ramparts Press, Inc.), pp. 51-52.
25. Sale, p. 590.
26. Jacobs, p. 240.
27. Sale, p. 352.
28. Akua Njeri, 1991, *My Life with the Black Panther Party* (Oakland: Burning Spear Publications), p. 9.
29. Sale, p. 618.
30. Same as above, p. 637.
31. Omali Yeshitela, 1987, *The Road to Socialism is Painted Black: Selected Theoretical Works* (Oakland: Burning Spear Publications), p. 77.
32. Omali Yeshitela, 1991, *Izwe Lethu i Afrika (Africa is Our Land)* (Oakland: Burning Spear Publications), p. 96.
33. Alan Abrahamson, November 13, 1994, "Most money in L.A. is tainted by drugs," *The Philadelphia Inquirer.*
34. Marc Mauer and Tracy Huling, 1995, "Young black Americans and the criminal justice system," The Sentencing Project, (www.sentencingproject.org/policy/9070).

35. U.S. Office of National Drug Control Policy, 1996, "II: America's illegal drug profile," (www.whitehousedrugpolicy.gov/policy/98ndcs/iic).

36. U.S. Government Substance Abuse and Mental Health Services Administration Report, 1996, "Preliminary results from the 1996 National Household Survey on Drug Abuse, U.S. Department of Health and Human Services," (www.samhsa.gov/oas/nhsda/PE1996/HTTOC).

37. "Majority of drug users have jobs, study says," September 9, 1999, *St. Petersburg Times*.

38. Federal Mandatory Minimum Sentences, Governed by U.S. Federal Statutes 21 U.S.C. 841, 21 U.S.C. 844, 21 U.S.C. 960, cited by Families Against Mandatory Minimum (FAMM), (www.famm.org/about1).

39. Mark J. Porubcansky, June 26, 1997, "Drug dealing is 8% of all trade worldwide, the U.N. says," *The Seattle Times*.

40. James Mills, 1986, *The Underground Empire: Where Crime and Governments Embrace* (New York: Doubleday Company), p. 3.

41. Laurie Nicole Robinson, "The globalization of female child prostitution: A call for reintegration measures via Article 39 of the United Nations Convention of the Right of the Child," (www.law.indiana.edu/qlsj/vol5/no1/robinson.html).

42. Scott Ehlers, June 1999, "In focus: Trafficking and money laundering," *Foreign Policy in Focus,* Vol. 3, No. 16, (www.foreignpolicy-infocus.org/briefs/vol3/v3n16/au).

43. Julie Fields and Jim Haner, June 9, 1998, "Clinton, at U.N., leads call to halt flow of drugs, profits," *The Bergen Record*.

44. Ruppert, "Don't blink."

45. Michael Chossudovsky, 1998, "Financial warfare triggers global economic crisis," Third World Network, (www.twnside.org.sq/souths/twn/title/trigcn).

46. Same as above.

47. "1,488 pounds of cocaine found on two Haitian ships," November 27, 1999, *St. Petersburg Times*.

48. Ehlers, "Trafficking and money laundering."

49. Same as above.

50. Ehlers, "Trafficking and money laundering."

51. Kenneth Howe, April 21, 1994, "B of A reports quarterly profit of $513 million," *San Francisco Chronicle*.

52. Rick Emrick, Fall 1990, "S & L's funded covert operation," *Convergence: Journal of the Christic Institute,* p. 1.

53. "A failed war on drugs," June 7, 1998, *The Bergen Record*.

54. Robert D. McFadden, June 15, 1997, "Rabbis listed among suspects in laundering of drug profits," *The New York Times*.

55. "Servicemen suspected of running pot, cocaine," December 14, 1998, *The Oakland Tribune*.

56. Bill Wallace, July 31, 1998, "Napa wine merchant charged in cocaine deal," *San Francisco Chronicle*.

57. Jim Smith, July 1, 1999, "Sun shines on Amish in drug case," *Philadelphia Daily News*.

58. David Adams, August 17, 1999, "Embassy in Bogotá 'a base for drug smuggling,'" *The London Times*.

59. Jim Doyle, February 16, 1999, "Crackdown on drug traffic in state prisons," *San Francisco Chronicle*.

60. Geyelin, Finkel, Klien and Morgan, January 15, 1989, "No questions asked: Florida, drugs, and money," *St. Petersburg Times*.

61. Ben Charney, May 17, 1995, "Records: Activist dealt cocaine," *The Oakland Tribune*.

62. Human Rights Watch, 1995, "Civil Asset Forfeiture," (www.hr95org/Forfeit).

63. Same as above.

64. Sarah Henry, September 25, 1994, "The Thin Green Line," *San Francisco Chronicle*.

65.   Catherine Austin Fitts, May 21, 1999, "Government spends millions in campaign to silence former Wall Street banker, cover up connections to dark alliance stories and CIA Inspector General Report on Drug Trafficking," *From The Wilderness*, Vol. 2, No. 3, pp. 1-5.

66.   Same as above, p. 5.

67.   Eric Schlosser, December 1998, "The prison-industrial complex," *Atlantic Monthly*, p. 51.

68.   Same as above, p. 56.

69.   D.S. Howard, 1943, "WPA and the Federal Relief Policy," as quoted in website Excite Reference: "Work Projects Administration."

70.   Abramsky, pp. 30-36.

71.   Phillip Matier and Andrew Ross, June 22, 1999, "S.F. workers rake in fat-cat wages," *San Francisco Chronicle*.

72.   "Summer can be a rough time for the working poor," June 27, 1999, *San Jose Mercury News*.

73.   Broderick Perkins, May 14, 1999, "$400,000…and rising," *San Jose Mercury News*.

74.   Dan Morain, October 16, 1994, "The price of punishment: California profusion of prisons," *Los Angeles Times*.

75.   Same as above.

76.   Morain, "California profusion of prisons."

77.   Dan Morain, October 18, 1994, "The price punishment: Firm reaps profit from desolate prison site," *Los Angeles Times*.

78.   Davis, pp. 412-413.

79.   Dan Morain and Maria L. La Ganga, October 18, 1994, "The price of punishment: New prisons no panacea for ills of rural California," *Los Angeles Times*.

80.   Ann Bancroft, April 26, 1994, "Northern California wary of more prisons," *San Francisco Chronicle*.

81.   Ilana DeBare, March 3, 1997, "Good pay without a B.A.," *San Francisco Chronicle*.

82.   Melody Petersen, August 1, 1994, "Jail overtime still in millions," *San Jose Mercury News*.

83.   Danny M. Boyd, April 5, 1994, "Prisons have boosted economy of Amarillo," *Amarillo Daily News*.

84.   T.J. Becker, May 22, 1994, "Making corrections," *Chicago Tribune*.

85.   Julia Cass, May 20, 1996, "As public fears swell, so do Pa. prisons," *The Philadelphia Inquirer*.

86.   Neal R. Peirce, May 20, 1996, "Prisons are a growth industry--but at what price to the nation?" *The Philadelphia Inquirer*.

87.   Jim Tunstall, January 18, 2000, "Sumter site getting fourth federal prison," *The Tampa Tribune*.

88.   Schlosser, pp. 54-58.

89.   Same as above.

90.   Ken Silverstein, February 13-19, 1997, "Prisons, inc.," *Weekly Planet*, p. 21.

91.   Vince Beiser, May 21, 1996, "Look for the prison label," *The Village Voice*, p. 37-38.

92.   Dan Morain, October 17, 1994, "The price of punishment: California's profusion of prisons," *Los Angeles Times*.

93.   Beiser, p. 38.

94.   Silverstein, p. 21.

95.   Hobart Swan, June 1995, "Crime pays," *The East Bay Monthly*, Vol. XXV, No. 9., p. 15.

96.   Silverstein, p. 23.

97.   Beiser, p.40.

98.   Schlosser, p. 64.

99.   Silverstein, p. 21.

100. Same as above.

101. Same as above.

102. Greg Jaffe and Rick Brooks, August 5, 1998, "Hard time," *The Wall Street Journal*.

103. Schlosser, p.70.

104. Same as above, pp. 69-70.

105. Kevin Helliker, January 20, 1995, "Prisons a captive market," *The Wall Street Journal.*
106. Schlosser, p. 63.
107. Schlosser, p. 63.
108. "The marketing of fear," June 26, 1999, *Chicago Sun Times.*
109. Omali Yeshitela, 1996, "Resistance of African People: Crisis of Imperialism: Why we must build the National People's Democratic Uhuru Movement," (National People's Democratic Uhuru Movement), pp.22-23

Omali Yeshitela, Chairman of the African People's Socialist Party and leader of the Uhuru Movement, carries on the legacy of Malcolm X. Credit: © St. Petersburg Times

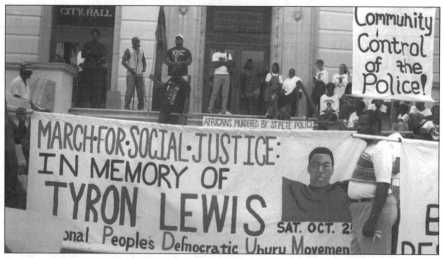

The police murder of 18 year old TyRon Lewis in St. Petersburg, Florida sparked a movement led by the African community. Credit: © Herb Snitzer

7

The Battle of St. Petersburg

In all the years of our struggles to end this existence of oppression and exploitation as a way of life... never has it been so clear that the era of liberation is upon us, that the era of the slave has arrived. Imperialism has lost all its vitality and is mired in the limitations imposed upon it by hundreds of years of the resistance by African people.[1]

— *Omali Yeshitela*

T he marine blue Tampa Bay is glistening in the Florida sun. Tropical breezes rustle the palmetto trees and lightly chop the waters. It's noon on a steamy July day in 1998. Inside the St. Petersburg Yacht Club building, nearly 200 members of the prestigious Suncoast Tiger Bay Club are waiting for the day's speaker to address their meeting. A current of nervous tension runs through the room as the guest lecturer steps up to the podium.

There's an interesting anomaly here. The wealthy white lawyers, bankers and politicians who make up the local capitalist power structure are about to hear a presentation by Omali Yeshitela, Chairman of the African People's Socialist Party, leader of the Uhuru Movement, African revolutionary. Yeshitela's brightly colored dashiki contrasts sharply with the conservative suits and ties worn by those in the audience.

"A little more than 30 years ago, Africans were often murdered in this country for simply attempting to register to join the Democratic Party," Yeshitela tells the gathering. He doesn't remind them that not too many years earlier, the town's first African City Council member, had been turned away when she showed up at a Tiger Bay

Club business luncheon in place of the mayor. And while it is now "integrated," we can be certain that no one from the FBI's black militant list has ever addressed the club before. Yeshitela continues:

> Yet today, a mere 34 years after the formal granting of civil rights and 33 years after formally winning the right to vote, Africans in the United States, especially the working class and impoverished youth, are characterized as vicious predators, an inarticulate and pathologically criminal community.
>
> A little more than 30 years ago, incessant struggle for democracy by our people had resulted in the primary public policy debate revolving around issues of black liberation. Today the public policy debate, while still involving African people, revolves around the most effective means of police containment of our increasingly impoverished community.
>
> This turn of affairs did not come about overnight. It came as a consequence of a process that saw thousands of young African militants arrested and killed throughout this country during the '60s.

Yeshitela goes on to sum up the powerful rebellions which ripped through St. Petersburg's south side twice following the police murder of a young African man in 1996. He talks about the oppressive economic and political realities which created the backdrop for these uprisings. For example, there was the razing, some years earlier, of vital African neighborhoods and business districts so that a freeway could be constructed. He points out the recent building of a huge sports coliseum in the middle of black community, and the importation of a major baseball team which seems to generate resources for the white community at the expense of the African community. Chairman Yeshitela says:

It was this reality that resulted in the broad daylight police execution of TyRon Lewis on October 24, 1996. It was this reality that has allowed us in the Uhuru Movement to say that although James Knight was the trigger man and, in our opinion, one who thoroughly enjoyed his work, the real issue is not Knight, nor even the cops whose cartoons mocked the death of Lewis, but the policy of police containment that established the conditions within which they function.

Some of St. Petersburg's so-called "movers and shakers" in the Tiger Bay Club are growing a little uneasy now. As the Chairman later remarked, he "took them to the very brink of disaster and then showed them the way out."

Yeshitela continues on an optimistic note:

I am convinced that the possibility for progressive change in St. Petersburg is greater than anywhere in this country. It is greater precisely because the primary contending social forces are quite conscious of what their material interests are and are therefore in a position to base their political relationship on these interests.

In other words, for the first time since the 1960s, African workers and poor people in St. Petersburg now have a power base and a voice that commands attention. Those demonized as the "inarticulate pathological underclass" have suddenly become quite eloquent, and confidently carry political weight. African workers had, through the two recent uprisings, demonstrated their ability to express their will by any means necessary. And they made clear who their leadership is: Omali Yeshitela and the Uhuru Movement.

On this afternoon, Yeshitela is at the table of the local rulers of white power, representing the oppressed African working class. For once he's holding a winning hand. Yeshitela affirms:

> The public police execution of TyRon Lewis ignited a popular rebellion that made it politically impossible to continue to ignore the African working class masses. The popular physical defense of the Uhuru leadership, under police attack at our office on November 13, 1996, was also a declaration by the people of the significance of the Uhuru Movement as the actual, on-the-ground, representative of the most dynamic sector of the African community.

> It was the perceived threat to tourism and an anticipated billion dollar baseball industry that led to the shooting of TyRon Lewis. This was another attempt at a unilaterally determined economic development that would come at the expense of the African community, as in the past.

> However, when this same perceived threat to the tourist and baseball industries led to recognition of the fact that the African community also has interests and aspirations which had to be considered, the stage was set for an honest relationship based on democracy and mutual respect. It holds out the possibility of replacing the failed policy of police containment of the African community with a policy of economic development that is the only path to social justice.

> We can no longer continue to do things and base relationships on political habits that do not recognize the value of black labor or which disregard the integrity of African opinions, aspirations and material interests.

The financial institutions of this city must end the economic quarantine of the African community....

We must admit to the failure of the disingenuous policy of police containment. It is, at best, a poor substitute for economic development. At worst, it is simply colonial occupation....

In closing, I would like to say that African people are good. We have played a central, that is to say critical, role in the development of the culture and economy of this country and this city.

Our demand today is that we be allowed to do the same for ourselves. To this end we are committed to relentless struggle. We welcome all who will join with us. Uhuru![2]

It is doubtful that anywhere else in the country—or perhaps the world—had a representative of the African working class and poor in recent times appeared before the white ruling class establishment and spoken from a *position of power* in quite the way that Yeshitela did on that July day in 1998. The following morning's *St. Petersburg Times* summed up for the whole city the essence of Yeshitela's brilliant presentation:

Omali Yeshitela walked into the heart of St. Petersburg's establishment Thursday and demanded a revolution.

He said nothing of violence.

"But this racially tormented city will never find peace," the leader of the National People's Democratic Uhuru Movement said, "until some fundamental patterns of local economics and politics are changed."

Yeshitela's speech at the St. Petersburg Yacht Club, bastion of all that is comfortable in this once sleepy resort town, was a revolution of its own sort....

Yeshitela offered an alternative: genuine economic development. Not jobs, not welfare, not even a few well-placed corporate relocations.

Yeshitela said street corner drug sales are just symptoms of the real problem that should be addressed—the underdevelopment of the African community. A community that offers real opportunity to young people is less likely to snare them in drugs and crime, he said.

There must be economic development—real community commerce—if we're going to move forward. Otherwise you have this problem of trying to contain a part of the community. And that's going to *always* lead to confrontations and conflict.[3]

AFRICAN LABOR BASIS OF TOURIST INDUSTRY

The South Florida town of St. Petersburg, located in Pinellas County, seems an unlikely spot for profound revolutionary transformation.

Nestled between the Gulf Coast and Tampa Bay, St. Petersburg has long been a tourist town, attracting in particular white retirees from Canada and the U.S. Northeast. These "Snow Birds," as they are known, traditionally descend on the city every year from November through late March. Dressed in t-shirts, bermuda shorts and clean white sneakers, they can be seen strolling about town or riding around on three-wheeled cycles. As they age, many Snow Birds stay on as full time residents of the city's large, lucrative nursing home industry. The south side of St. Petersburg is home to an impoverished, working class African community. The median per capita income in one of the poorest sectors of this area* is $5,576 a year in

---

* Specifically, this is the area immediately surrounding the Uhuru House on 18th Avenue South. The Uhuru House is the African community center headed up by Omali Yeshitela and the Uhuru Movement.

a predominately white county whose overall median per capita income is more than four times that. In this same area only 41percent of the adult population has graduated from high school, and 45 percent subsist below poverty levels.[4]

Although African people had populated Florida for centuries in their relationship with the Seminole people, much of the African community of St. Petersburg can trace its roots in the town to the period following the Civil War. Older sections of the south side are characterized by small wooden houses set up on stilts, shaded by enormous old live oaks dripping with Spanish moss.

Fleeing a brutal existence as sharecroppers in Georgia and other parts of the South in the years after Reconstruction, large numbers of African people were drawn to Florida. In these tropical regions, railroads were being built and a tourist industry was being developed. Africans came to South Florida any way they could. Some even walked the long, hot, dusty and hostile roads with their scanty belongings bundled into a pack. The *St. Petersburg Times* reported:

> Freed slaves were among the early homesteaders who dotted the Pinellas peninsula.
>
> Later, as the city of St. Petersburg was born, African-Americans helped* build the railroad that brought people here. In the boom years before World War I and in the 1920s, white contractors imported hundreds of black laborers to help build the town's streets and homes.
>
> They and their descendants endured generations of rigidly enforced segregation and second class status. There were lynchings, as well as quieter forms of violence that stunted their hopes.[5]

---

* "Helped?" Who else but Africans did the backbreaking labor building the railroads?

Over the years, St. Petersburg's "town fathers" sought a docile, subservient African population willing to work for subsistence wages in the city's tourist and retirement trade. The white power structure attempted to officially implement an apartheid system that closely resembled a concentration camp. The *St. Petersburg Times* commented:

> For decades, the city had been obsessed with maintaining a "sanitized social environment"—i.e., no Negroes—for the tourists. In 1936, City Council voted to force all black people to live in a 17 block area west of 17th Street and south of Sixth Avenue South.
>
> The plan for a black internment zone proved unworkable, but the message in St. Petersburg was clear. African-Americans could not swim at its beaches, try on clothes in its department stores or sit on its famous green benches.[6]

Generations of African nursing home workers have made a meager living ministering to old white people sent by their children to St. Petersburg to die. On the south side, police and white repression was the order of the day. Poverty was a given. For African people there was no ladder of success to climb; only houses to clean, decrepit bodies to wash, food to cook—all for subminimum wages.

Despite the incredible difficulty of their conditions, many African people survived with dignity and a profound sense of humanity. African people had raised the babies of white people for hundreds of years; now they tended to their dying. It was a common story that white children were often nurtured and loved far more by African women domestic workers than by their own cold, distant mothers.

Now infirm, alone and often abusive, the aged white people relied on African caregivers for their very lives, many times receiving no other human warmth or contact. Sometimes African nurses even fought for the interests of the moribund whites against some of the elderly's own uncaring relatives and profiteering nursing home owners.

Benefactors of a parasitic social system, the oppressor's soul shrivels like the body. The spirit of the oppressed remains expansive and open, and the rich African culture prevails in the face of brutality. Such was the situation in St. Petersburg. As Chairman Omali Yeshitela put it very simply: "African people are good."

Yeshitela has said in summing up the political economy of the town:

> [St. Petersburg sought African people] for the exact purpose of providing a cheap labor force for this tourist industry. Our significance as a cheap labor reserve force grew to include the nursing home industry that was an offshoot of tourism.
>
> From the beginning there was a built-in tension to this relationship. On the one hand, our cheap labor was seen as essential to a profitable tourist industry. On the other hand, there was the irrational fear that our black presence was a threat to this same tourism. The resolution to this quandary has been police containment of the African community.[7]

RACIST MURAL TORN DOWN

For years, St. Petersburg's city hall reflected the source of its prosperity and spelled out in no uncertain terms the town's philosophy regarding the place of African people. In the lobby of City Hall, visible to all who entered the building, hung a pair of eight-foot-long paintings. One of them depicted white picnickers on the beach being entertained by grotesque musicians, caricatures of African people. These paintings had been commissioned by the state during the Depression as part of the effort to bring economic resources to Florida's white population, including its artists.

By the end of the second imperialist war, the world was changing. Oceans away, oppressed colonized peoples, whose existence was not so different from that of the residents of South St. Petersburg, had begun to organize and fight U.S. imperialism. At the same time, throughout the U.S. South, resistance was in the air. Powerful mass leaders like Fannie Lou Hamer and Rosa Parks, sharecroppers and domestic workers, began to stand up to white power. The "built-in tension," inherent in a system constructed on the backs of African people, began to rise to the surface, even in this placid Gulf Coast town. Blatant symbols of white supremacy would no longer go unchallenged.

On the day after Christmas in 1966, at the height of St. Petersburg's tourist season, 24 year old Joseph Waller (now Omali Yeshitela) marched into City Hall and tore down that offensive painting. An article in *The New York Times,* written 33 years later, described Yeshitela's drive to destroy that image:

> Every time Mr. Waller, a young black man, saw it, anger and humiliation scorched him deep inside.
>
> In December 1966, he tore it down. With police officers in pursuit, he ran through St. Petersburg's downtown, the ripped painting flapping in his clenched fists like the captured flag of some oppressive government. To him, it was.
>
> Some historians in this city on Tampa Bay have called his action the start of the Civil Rights Movement in St. Petersburg.[8]

The movement sparked by Yeshitela on that day proved to be far more profound and wide reaching than any one could have predicted. It brought to the African community consciousness, organization and a vital link to the broader revolutionary movements of the world.

For his act, Omali Yeshitela was charged with a felony and thrown into prison, serving two and a half years of a five year sentence. Six months of that sentence was spent in isolation in the St. Petersburg jail. In prison, Yeshitela organized JOMO, the Junta of Militant Organizations, and a few years later formed the African People's Socialist Party. Despite the ravages of COINTELPRO and counterinsurgency against the Black Power Movement of the 1960s, the black working class movement in St. Petersburg was never eradicated. For more than 30 years, the Uhuru Movement has had an uninterrupted presence in the town. Today the influence of Uhuru is so great that the situation provides an inspiring model for the possibilities of liberation and political power for African people everywhere.

While all around the country the police run roughshod over African people, in St. Petersburg, Police Chief Goliath Davis gives the black power salute and instructs his force to show respect to black residents. In nearly every city large and small, city leaders implement counterinsurgent policies to rid the streets of Africans.

In St. Petersburg, Mayor David Fischer has promised resources for African economic development, and stated for the record his opposition to the policy of police containment. City leaders and representatives of major banking institutions have participated in an African community conference on economic development. Regardless of the sincerity on the part of these city officials, the strength of the African working class power base makes taking such stands a political necessity.

In 1998, the community-based Concerned Citizens for Action organization brought a proposal before the city council to put up a plaque on the still empty spot where the racist mural once hung on the city hall landing. In a tenuous moment of rare unity, the council passed the motion. The plaque would apologize to the African com-

munity for the offensive painting, and to Omali Yeshitela for perse-
cuting him for his actions 32 years earlier.

The leading local newspaper, *The St. Petersburg Times,* editorialized regarding struggles in the City Council concerning the apology
to Yeshitela:

> For that act of conscience, Joe Waller was convicted of a
> felony and locked in prison for two years. Now the city is
> proposing a plaque explaining the event—considered a
> turning point in the local Civil Rights Movement—and
> apologizing. But the squeamishness of some city officials
> threatens to undermine any benefit that could come from
> the apology.
>
> The mural, which hung prominently in the grand stair-
> case of City Hall, depicted outrageous racial caricatures of
> African-American musicians performing for whites on the
> beach. Its presence in the seat of local government was a
> sign of the racist, segregationist times, and should not be
> forgotten. Neither should the actions of Waller, now
> known as Omali Yeshitela.[9]

A Remarkable Child

The transformation of St. Petersburg from a typical bastion of
white power to an emerging center of black self-determination is a
remarkable and historic one.

The architect of this change is Omali Yeshitela, without whose
leadership the events of October 24, 1996 would have been insig-
nificant and TyRon Lewis just one more forgotten African victim of
police murder.

Yeshitela was born Joseph Waller in 1941 in the Gas Plant Area
of St. Petersburg. A thriving and vital black neighborhood, the Gas
Plant was part of the larger African community where everyone

knew each other in the backdrop of a rich African culture. It was a community of people with unique, colorful personalities and multiple talents expressed within the confines of an oppressed colony. There was Mr. Elijah "I Got 'Em" Moore, who, dressed in full tails and a top hat, sold produce from his garden by going door to door.

There was the Chairman's Uncle Sammy who could "hit harder than a Georgia mule kicking downhill." Uncle Sammy became a legend for his fearless willingness to fight the police whenever the occasion called for it. Once when the police tried to arrest him, Sammy wrestled the cop, snatched the cop's gun, threw it up on the roof of a two story building and then caught a taxi home.

Yeshitela grew up in an African community like many others, where in the midst of poverty there was humor, wit and exuberance. It was a society of dignified matriarchs who wore magnificent hats to church, wise old men who gathered under the oak trees exchanging stories, beautiful young women with an incredible sense of style, and dashing young men ready for life. There were masses of children playing on the streets. In this society, the distinction between siblings and cousins and friends was unimportant—it was all family.

There were social clubs where, in the 1950s, Ray Charles and other greats used to sometimes play. There were barber shops and small businesses which met the needs of the residents. The community's all-black schools were staffed with brilliant African teachers who gave the students a sense of pride and brought out their best.

The Gas Plant Area was perhaps representative of many African communities throughout the United States, and the Chairman attributes much importance to its embracing African culture. But like so many other established black neighborhoods, the Gas Plant Area was torn down, destroying a long standing cultural and economic base which had nurtured generations of African people. Powerful white businessmen had determined that the land was to be used for a baseball coliseum, today known as Tropicana Dome.

Typically, it didn't matter that the price of the Dome was the well being of thousands of African people. Today the hideous structure stands surrounded by an empty wasteland. So many lives destroyed once again so white people could make money.

Throughout Yeshitela's youth, however, the Gas Plant was a vital part of a community in which conditions prevailed for the upbringing of a remarkable child. He was the oldest of seven children born of Lucille and Joseph Waller Sr. The elder Waller was a hard working railroad worker. The Chairman's mother was a beautician who owned several salons over the years. Lucille was an interesting, entrepreneurial woman, and as her children were growing up she became a nurse. At the same time she created social justice programs based in the Pentecostal Church to which she belonged.

Young Joseph displayed leadership qualities at an early age. His mother once commented that she could not remember a time when he could not read. "When I was no more than four years old, Aunt Jessie, my mother's sister who was living with us at the time, taught me to read," the Chairman tells us in his pamphlet, "Social Justice and Economic Development for the African Community: Why I Became a Revolutionary." His Aunt Jessie spent hours with him sitting on the living room floor with the newspaper.

> Needless to say, my reading lessons contained horror story after horror story of Africans being lynched or suffering some other atrocious injustice.
>
> I read…voraciously—everything from the *St. Petersburg Times* to Black Hawk and Captain Marvel comic books to encyclopedias; from Plato and Nietzsche to Dostoyevsky, Shakespeare and Richard Wright. I read Thomas Paine and the American Declaration of Independence.[10]

As an elementary school child, Yeshitela quit a job shining shoes for white people in disgust when the white boss attempted to make him dance on the sidewalk in order to drum up business.

Tracked into classes for more "promising" children, Yeshitela left high school after encountering teachers who operated on the assumption that Africans had to "prove" themselves to white people in order to become free. Believing that it would offer an opportunity to experience the world, Yeshitela joined the army in 1959. He was sent to Berlin, Germany where, despite all its contradictions, "life...was freer than it had ever been in the United States."

In 1962, Yeshitela was reassigned to Ft. Benning, Georgia "as the Civil Rights Movement was heating up and the racial polarization that exists in this country was pushed to the surface."[11] As his political consciousness developed, Yeshitela began writing and posting on the battalion bulletin boards leaflets which denounced the conditions of African people in the military and in the United States as a whole. For his activities he was sent to a psychiatrist who pronounced him quite "sane." "You're just a Garveyite"—a follower of the earlier Black Power leader Marcus Garvey—the doctor told him.

With his new political consciousness developing rapidly, Yeshitela "went on strike. For all practical purposes I quit the army." He was court-martialed. Conducting his own defense, Yeshitela successfully "turned the proceedings into a trial of the treatment of Africans in the U.S. Army." In an unprecedented move, the Army found him not guilty and he was discharged from service.[12]

COMMITMENT TO SOCIAL JUSTICE

Freed from the military, Omali Yeshitela returned to St. Petersburg ready to experience life and to plunge into the whirlwind of political struggle emerging in the early '60s. The dynamic African youth was hungry for justice and eager to make his mark on the world. He began to look into various black organizations which were cropping up as the Civil Rights Movement heightened.

A striking figure, tall and thin and, in those days, usually wearing sunglasses, Yeshitela displayed a penchant for boldness and astute political clarity early on. He proved to be a powerful and moving speaker and his leadership abilities were soon apparent. By the time he was 24, he had made his life-long commitment to struggle for the liberation of African people, and his characteristic impatience with any obstacle that got in the way of justice had manifested itself.

In 1966 Yeshitela joined the Student Nonviolent Coordinating Committee. It was the same year that SNCC had put forward the electrifying slogan, "Black Power." While a SNCC organizer, Yeshitela led a group that tore down the 8-by-4 foot racist mural from the City Hall.

In prison after being found guilty of "destruction of public property" for tearing down the painting, Yeshitela conceived his idea of forming JOMO (the Junta of Militant Organizations):

> a massive organization made up of the young African workers who are essentially considered useless by the government. The basic policy of the government was to use the police as a disciplinary force to control the young Africans who could not be absorbed into St. Petersburg's service-based political economy. The situation was pretty much the same as it is today.[13]

In 1972, after COINTELPRO hit the Black Revolution with a vengeance and the counterinsurgency was besieging the African community, Yeshitela united two other black organizations to form the African People's Socialist Party. It is this Party which leads the Uhuru Movement today. Yeshitela tells us about the reason for this transformation:

It became clear to me that what we refer to as racism is essentially the ideological underpinnings of a repressive, colonial system. Africans do not suffer injustices because people don't like us, but because we do not have the power to render their hatred or dislike impotent.

Therefore, it is a waste of time to struggle against racism which is essentially the ideas in the heads of white people. What has to be struggled for is the power to prevent the ideas in the heads of white people from harming us. Many white people have a problem with this conclusion because it takes white people out of the center of the issue and allows African people to set out on a self-defined course independent of the feelings and opinions of whites.[14]

JOMO adopted the greeting "Uhuru," popularized by the Mau Mau liberation movement led by Didan Kimathi in Kenya in the 1950s. It was during the time of JOMO that the movement encompassed by the leadership of Chairman Omali Yeshitela began to be called the "Uhuru Movement" as it is today.

Although the Black Revolution of the '60s was crushed by a government attack, Omali Yeshitela never wavered from the cause of African freedom. A brilliant and talented man, who could have been successful in any profession he chose, Yeshitela never abandoned his commitment to justice for African workers and poor people. As a result of this commitment, the Chairman struggled for many years in poverty and relative isolation.

While always maintaining a local organization in St. Petersburg, Yeshitela organized at different times in Gainesville and Tallahassee, Florida, as well as Atlanta, Georgia and Louisville, Kentucky. He focused on publishing *The Burning Spear* newspaper and building popular campaigns around local issues which affected the African working class.

From the very earliest days of the Party, Yeshitela wrote profound theoretical works while in the thick of political struggle. Aware of the significance of economic institutions in the hands of African workers, he opened the Ujaama restaurant in St. Petersburg and African Connection bookstore in Louisville during the Party's formative years.

OAKLAND YEARS

In the late 1970s, after establishing the African People's Solidarity Committee, Omali Yeshitela opened a branch of the African People's Socialist Party in San Francisco, California. A few years later, after a brief respite in Louisville, the Party then moved its national office to nearby Oakland, where it remained for about 12 years. Because of the liberal, affluent and international character of the San Francisco Bay Area, Yeshitela always referred to Northern California as the Party's "rear base."

Oakland turned out to be an excellent base of operation during that period when most black liberation organizations had been silenced by COINTELPRO, and the African working class was staggering under blows of a brutal U.S. government war against it. These fertile California years provided an expansive backdrop for Yeshitela, who has the ability to incorporate widely disparate influences into his own worldview.

In Oakland, he deepened his political theory profoundly, waged groundbreaking political campaigns of far-reaching impact, consolidated his Party and the African People's Solidarity Committee, and built successful economic institutions. These included Spear Graphics, a typesetting and printing enterprise, and the tremendously popular Uhuru Bakery Cafe on Oakland's Telegraph Avenue, which served natural foods until it was closed by an arsonist's fire on the same day in December 1989 that the United States invaded Panama.

When the Party arrived in Oakland, they found little evidence of black power in a city in which, not too many years earlier, the Black Panther Party had been born. Yeshitela has commented on the notable devastation of the African community as a result of the counterinsurgency.

Little more than a decade earlier, African people in berets and black leather jackets had proudly set the pace for an organized black revolutionary movement that shook the world. Now, Africans in the city of the Panthers were dazed, suppressed and beaten down under tremendous poverty and a militaristic police presence. Tens of thousands of Africans were homeless or lived in substandard housing.

Operating out of an Uhuru House organizing center in the heart of impoverished East Oakland, the Party went into tireless action, bringing back a '60s style of high profile struggle. The goal was to force the interests of the African working class back onto the political agenda of the city. Homelessness was a crisis in the African community ignored by the media and politicians. The Party staged a successful Tent City for the Homeless for more than three months in a downtown park, followed by a people's takeover of an abandoned house in the African community. In 1984 and '86 they launched ballot initiatives calling for community control of housing which won 25,000 votes each time. Through these bold campaigns the question of homelessness was forced into the public policy debates nationally.

It was in Oakland that the Party first popularized the understanding that the massive influx of crack cocaine on the streets of the black community originated from the government. The Uhuru Movement exposed the U.S. government's "war on drugs" for what it was—a "war on the African community."

It was during these years as well that the African People's Solidarity Committee became consolidated to a principled relationship under the Party's leadership. Organized around reparations to the African community, APSC began building successful, politicized fundraising institutions in the white community, which, for the first time, brought meager though steady resources to the Party's work.

While in California, Chairman Yeshitela established lasting international relationships with representatives of the revolutionary movements of Nicaraguan, Salvadoran, Chilean, Palestinian, Filipino, Mexican and other indigenous peoples. These reciprocal relationships broadened Yeshitela's political vision, while exposure to the Chairman's brilliance and political clarity profoundly deepened every international revolutionary movement he touched. Many revolutionaries from around the world looked to Chairman Omali for leadership, and genuine solidarity.

During this same period, Yeshitela traveled several times to England to meet with Africans about building the African Socialist International, an organization uniting African people everywhere. He twice spoke at the United Nations and served as the People's Advocate for the Party-led World Tribunal on Reparations for African People in New York, an event that was subsequently held annually for several years in various U.S. cities. In 1991 he founded the National People's Democratic Uhuru Movement (NPDUM) in Chicago. NPDUM was a historic organization built for the express purpose of pushing back the effects of the counterinsurgency on African people.

In Oakland, Chairman Omali adopted a long view about his own health and survival. He gave up cigarettes and beer, took up running and weight training and adopted a vegetarian diet. He made a remarkable transformation from a noticeably thin person to a muscular body builder. In his usual manner, he made an unwavering commitment to healthy living. Today he looks at least 10 years younger than his 58 years.

In the early '90s, Yeshitela began to sense the growing militancy which was once again manifesting itself in the African communities throughout the country. His days in the rear base were coming to an end, and he was traveling across country on speaking tours constantly. He felt the urgency of relocating east of the Mississippi River where most Africans in the United States are concentrated. Yeshitela made the strategic decision to return to St. Petersburg where an active base of African community support existed since the '60s.

In 1993, he and the leadership core of the African People's Socialist Party made that move. He opened up an Uhuru House on 18th Avenue South, in the heart of the African community, where members of the local Party unit were out on the streets daily, organizing against the rampant police brutality in the town. Yeshitela also opened Uhuru's Black Gym, a community fitness center, on the first floor of the building. His instincts proved correct. Three years later when the police killed TyRon Lewis 3 blocks from the Uhuru House, Omali Yeshitela was well-situated to lead the African community in bringing about substantial changes in St. Petersburg, Florida.

TyRon Lewis: One Victim Too Many

At eighteen, there was very little that the world had to offer to TyRon Lewis. Bright, bold and attractive, TyRon had a taste for experiencing the fullness of life. According to his stepfather, the youth simply "wanted a little bit of what everyone else had." Poor and African in a hostile white world, Lewis had very few tools to make his dreams a reality.

Like so many others coming into their manhood in the '80s and '90s, TyRon Lewis was dealt the crushing blow of experiencing childhood in an African community under siege. A deadly drug trade, controlled by the white-controlled U.S. and local governments, was one of the many factors that hit his neighborhood hard, robbing his family of the stability that a child so desperately needs. The future possibilities were grim, and by the time he was barely out of diapers he had to learn to fend for himself.

Born in the decade after Martin Luther King and Fred Hampton had been murdered by government assassins, TyRon had no opportunity to experience the exuberance of the Black Power Movement of the 1960s. All he knew was there wasn't enough money to pay the bills—for long periods of time there was not even electricity or running water at his house. From every street corner loomed the ever present reality of a thuggish police force that taunted, tormented and insulted him and his friends.

While we mostly know TyRon only through the biased eyes of the white nationalist media, it seems clear that there was a spirit in the youth that never allowed him to submit quietly to the conditions he faced. Though emotionally wounded by the war zone environment in which he found himself, he was nevertheless courageously defiant in the face of the brutal authority of white power. At age nine he is said to have "cursed" the police and made it very clear that he was not afraid of them.

An "A" student when he wanted to be, TyRon was sentenced at the age of 12 to a school for "mentally impaired or severely emotionally disturbed children" in Pinellas Park, a neighboring white town known for its hostility to African people. These oppressive "special education" programs have long been used to crush the spirit of smart, spunky African children like him. They are institutions that serve to prepare black youth for prison.

With an understandably irrepressible anger welling up inside him, young TyRon reportedly "threatened" a teacher at the special education school. As a result he was "involuntarily committed to a state hospital" and placed on medication, according to the *St. Petersburg Times.*[15] Like prisons, brutal mental institutions are used to lock up African people who dare to resist their conditions.

And so, like many millions of other young African men in America who are victims of the U.S. counterinsurgency, TyRon Lewis' fate was sealed. He could be sure of life in prison, or early death.

As it turned out, two months after his eighteenth birthday, TyRon Lewis was gunned down by white cops because he refused to leap out of a car and deliver himself into the hands of the hostile armed police force. In a fateful example of the cycle of African oppression from generation to generation, TyRon was killed on the same corner that in 1978 had been the scene of another police murder of a young African man. TyRon was two weeks old when Willie James Daniels was assassinated by white cops on the intersection of 16th Street and 18th Avenue South.

If TyRon had been a white teenager from the serene and affluent north side of town, the media would most likely have played on our sympathies. We would be asked to consider his turbulent childhood, his troubled past, his wit, talents and creative potential snuffed out at such an early age. We would have been presented the image of a "good kid" as seen through the eyes of those who loved him. His grieving mother, his distraught sister and fond friends, who remembered how he defended the neighborhood children from bullies, would have been interviewed. We would have had a picture of a human being unjustly murdered in the prime of his youth.

Because he was African and impoverished, TyRon was portrayed as nothing but a criminal who deserved to die. He was killed twice. First he was murdered by the police in St. Petersburg. Then his character was assassinated by the media. The *St. Petersburg Times* ran months of articles detailing his "court records," presented in a slanderous way and accompanied by unflattering mug shots.

Ultimately, the St. Petersburg Police Department blamed TyRon for his own murder because, they say, he did not immediately get out of the car.

In only three weeks a grand jury exonerated the white policeman who executed TyRon. His stepfather, who raised Lewis, charged,

> Knight shot my son down in cold blooded murder like a
> dog in the street and can walk away from it with the help
> of his white superiors with no remorse for the black man,
> or his family, and without any fear of God....Justice has
> not come for the black man of St. Petersburg.[16]

But TyRon Lewis' death was one police murder too many in this Florida town. African people rose up in anger and in response to his execution. The 18 year old African was not going to be just another nameless victim of the policy of police containment of the black community. Profound changes for black people would be won as a result of his death. The Uhuru Movement and the African working class of St. Petersburg would make sure that the name of this martyred youth would be permanently enshrined in the hearts and memories of the African community and all progressive minded townspeople.

In life, TyRon Lewis was part of the African working class so despised by white power. In death he became a symbol of the heroic resistance of the oppressed, a galvanizing force for social justice, and a reminder that, yes, African people are good.

POLICE MURDER

Sixteenth Street South near the corner of 18th Avenue is the site of St. Petersburg's central African community commercial district. Notably absent are the antique shops, clothing boutiques, book stores, bakeries, greengrocers and cafes which generally dot the streets of white community shopping areas.

Here one sees the distinctly undercapitalized small businesses that can be found in African communities everywhere—high-interest mortgage and loan companies, check cashing services, real estate and insurance offices alongside convenience stores, barbecue stands and take-out fish restaurants. Up the block is the uninviting local NAACP headquarters, which is usually closed. On the northwest corner of 16th Street and 18th Avenue South is a car detailing establishment.

On any given day, there is a continuous flow of traffic around this corner.

The afternoon of October 24, 1996 was seasonably warm. At 5:30 p.m., 18 year old TyRon Lewis was driving with a friend along

18th Avenue South in a Pontiac LeMans, said to have tinted windows, an accessory which has proven dangerous for many African people. When he stopped for a red light at Sixteenth Street, he was approached by two white St. Petersburg police officers, James Knight and Sandra Minor. Knight had four complaints on his record[17] and belonged to a force in which 283 allegations of police misconduct had been investigated during the previous year.[18]

According to Knight and Minor, Lewis was stopped for "speeding." Many might argue that he was stopped for "driving while black."

Knight and Minor later claimed that Lewis and his passenger refused to unlock their doors or roll down their tinted windows. In front of more than 30 onlookers Knight drew his Glock and stood in front of Lewis' car. Many witnesses, including cousins Eddie and Willie Graham, asserted to the media that it was possible to see through the tinted windows, and that both Lewis and his passenger had their hands up.[19] Sandra Minor took out a baton and began bashing in some of the car windows.

James Knight claims that the "car lurched forward several times, knocking him onto the hood," an allegation which nearly all 30 witnesses denied.[20] According to Lisa Craft, who watched the murder, Sandra Minor yelled for Knight to fire his gun. "She just told him to shoot and that's what he did."[21] Knight aimed and fired through the windows, striking TyRon twice in the right arm. A third shot hit him squarely in the chest.[22]

The young man who had faced such oppressive conditions throughout his short life died in the ambulance on the way to the hospital.

AFRICAN WORKERS DEFEAT THE POLICE

Quickly, the restless and increasingly angry crowd on 18th Avenue South grew. Photographs of the scene reveal teenagers and children, adults and babies, people of all ages gathering at the intersection in response to the blatant execution. It was part of the collective memory of the community that Willie James Daniels had been killed by a white cop on exactly the same corner years before.[23]

Someone ran to alert organizers from the Uhuru House, located three blocks east on 18th Avenue. The building which houses the national and local offices of the African People's Socialist Party, an auditorium and the Uhuru's Black Gym and Fitness Center was known to the community as a center of very vocal defense of the rights of the African community. The Uhuru movement had been struggling against police violence for more than a generation, and had been there on the scene in 1978 protesting the murder of Daniels. So, when TyRon Lewis was murdered, people knew just where to go.

Upstairs in the center, a young leader of the African People's Socialist Party, Sobukwe Bambaata, was sitting in front of a computer working on the new issue of *The Burning Spear* newspaper. In minutes he and other comrades were in the thick of the crowd as fire trucks, ambulances and more policemen began to arrive at the scene. Sobukwe courageously leapt up on top of a car and gave a powerful speech laying out the roots of the police violence that was ripping the African community apart.[24]

By 6:45 p.m., African men and women were "taunting officers and chanting," according to the papers, and many began to "throw rocks and bottles at police." The people were tired of life in a militarized war zone of martial law and thuggish armed police. A night of insurrection ensued. The rebellion turned out to be not "random violence," but rather a conscious insurrection approaching guerrilla warfare.

On October 26, the *St. Petersburg Times* reported at least 28 fires had been set during the night in a broad area between First Avenue North and 26th Avenue South, and 49th Street South and 4th

Street South.* The targets of arson were remarkably well chosen, and black owned businesses were spared. An assessment in the paper showed that the damage was limited to banks, police substations, white and other foreign owned businesses, media vans and police cars.

Badcock Furniture, a white-owned furniture store in the heart of the south side, was reduced to rubble. One police car, a Channel 44 TV satellite van and two of the station's cars were destroyed by fire. White-owned Sun Liquors was a "total loss," and Sun Bank reported "medium to heavy damage." A fire was set at the downtown post office.[25] A Molotov cocktail was tossed into the local probation and parole office.[26]

Newspaper photos capture scenes of hand-to-hand combat between civilians and the police as tensions erupted. Reportedly, the street fighting in the area surrounding the murder was fierce enough for an "entire platoon of officers [to keep] its distance until riot gear [was] brought in Friday." Three to five hundred police were called to the city from the surrounding area, including the neighboring Hillsborough County Sheriff's Department and its canine unit. At least eight other fire departments were brought in, all of whom proved incapable of putting down the African resistance.

The *St. Petersburg Times* wrote that the fire department was first called for the Badcock Furniture Store fire at 9:26 p.m., but "firefighters retreat a short time later because they do not think the area is secured by police." At 10:45 p.m., "Engine 1 is back at the Badcock fire site, which is now surrounded by police. Firefighters… dive for cover behind the engines when police see a man perched in a truck, pointing a small device at them. It turns out to be a video camera." On Friday, 200 Florida National Guard troops were brought in on a standby basis.[27]

The Burning Spear newspaper described the rebellion:

---

* In St. Petersburg streets run north and south, avenues east and west.

Hundreds of courageous young African workers were immediately transformed into fearless freedom fighters who fought police in pitched battles in the streets, reduced sections of the city owned by parasitic merchants to ashes and strategically targeted South St. Petersburg police substations and command centers for destruction.

Hundreds of police from law enforcement agencies throughout the state of Florida were deployed to crush our rebellion. National Guard troops stood at the edge of our community awaiting orders from the white rulers to attack.

Unafraid of this arrogant and vulgar display of deadly force, the courageous warriors of African liberation in St. Petersburg fought them like seasoned urban guerrillas. Armed with makeshift weapons, guns and unflinching revolutionary heroism, these warriors camouflaged themselves in the shadows that landscaped the pitch dark streets, and suffered no casualties while making the oppressors pay a dear cost for their decades of crimes against our community.[28]

NO JUSTICE, NO PEACE!

The Uhuru Movement went into immediate action. Within hours, leaflets summing up the situation had been produced and handed out widely. The day after the killing, a demonstration was held on the steps of the police station at which people chanted, "No justice, no peace! Tired of going to the graveyard. Black power's back. Fight back!"[29]

Within a week, a tribunal was held in front of a packed audience at the Uhuru House. The tribunal served as a people's court which put the killer police officers James Knight and Sandra Minor along with the mayor and the police chief on trial for genocide, using United Nations documents defining the crime for its basis.

Ministers and black community activists served as tribunal judges, with Omali Yeshitela acting as the people's advocate. Testimony was heard from witnesses of the murder of TyRon Lewis, as well as from others who had been brutalized by the police themselves. When the jurors went out to deliberate they found the accused not only guilty of genocide but of first degree murder. All four were sentenced to the death penalty by means of the Florida state electric chair.

Rev. Clarence Davis, who delivered the verdict to the tribunal after deliberation by the judges, found the mayor and police chief as guilty as the killer cops because they "showed a dereliction of duty."[30] In a country that had enslaved, lynched and executed African people without need for evidence for hundreds of years, this verdict was the closest thing possible to justice for African people.

People's Advocate Omali Yeshitela had defined the question of justice in his opening remarks at the tribunal:

> When we talk about justice in this instance, we make a distinction. There is no such thing as justice in general. The reality is that if you are born in an era of slavery, there is one justice for the slave and another justice for the slave master. In reality, it was illegal under slavery for the slave to escape. According to the system of justice of the slave master, if you try to escape, you have broken the law...you have deprived the slave master of his property. While justice for the slave master was to hold the slave in bondage and catch and punish him, justice for the slave was to run away, to end his bondage, even though it was against the law.[31]

Though no representatives of the establishment media were permitted to witness the tribunal, reporters and cameramen were milling around outside, soon catching wind of the verdict and the sentences. The death penalties were greatly played up in the media.

The newspaper reports neglected to mention that this African people's tribunal had no power to enforce the capital punishment, because, naturally, African people have no control over the use of Florida's electric chair. By not mentioning this fact, the media conveniently gave the impression that the Uhuru Movement was calling for assassinations and executions in the streets. This deliberately falsified impression would be used to justify later attempts to literally wipe out the Uhuru Movement and, if necessary, the surrounding residents.

The city government thought it could simply wipe out the Uhuru House in a military-style assault similar to the attack on the MOVE collective in Philadelphia in 1985. In that murderous onslaught, eleven women, men and children were burned alive, and more than 60 houses in the surrounding neighborhood were burned to the ground.

In the days and weeks following the killing of TyRon Lewis, the Uhuru Movement continued to raise protest on every front possible. A picket was held outside of Lewis' funeral, which was attended by neocolonialist Rev. Joseph Lowery who was called into town to smooth over tensions. By October 30, the U.S. Commission on Civil Rights had sent in a panel to investigate the situation and to hold public hearings. The Commission found that the city "must attack deepseated economic and social problems to avoid the type of violence that broke out last week," the local paper reported.[32]

On November 4, the African-American Leadership Coalition was formed, comprised of a wide spectrum of political, religious and business leaders committed to defending the interests of the African working class. The Coalition issued a statement demanding prosecution of the killer cops, reparations for the family of TyRon Lewis, as well as "hands off the Uhuru Movement," which was coming under increasing attack by the city. Omali Yeshitela was being demonized in the media daily, and the mayor had proclaimed that he would never sit down at the same table with the Uhuru leader. There was a groundswell of African sentiment that South St. Petersburg should secede from the city.

Chairman Omali assessed the context in which this "battle of St. Petersburg" was taking place:

> The U.S. government waged counterinsurgency against our movement...When this movement was crushed, the U.S. government waged a campaign against black working and poor people and, by extension, against the whole African community. A campaign of slander and demonization was initiated. So today, no one remembers that Africans are oppressed and exploited; now Africans are the problem for everyone. We are the criminals. White people are afraid of us.
>
> Today, they don't have to listen to black folks. They can let whole communities be wiped out. The devastation in the African community is not explained today as a consequence of the oppression by white people or the government. Now, "they brought it on themselves."
>
> It affects whole federal and local budgets. You don't have to spend that money on the needs of the African community now if you can put it in places to shore up white power. You don't have to worry about infant mortality or anything else that happens to black people. You can create economic institutions to feed white people by putting African people in prisons. You don't have to pay any attention to poverty or homelessness, because there's no spokesperson. Nobody speaks for the African community.

That makes it easy for the U.S. government to kill people in the streets and not have to explain it...Nobody has to pay any attention to the African community anymore. Just lock them up and put them in jail if they don't act right. Put police on the campuses to lock the children up...So they can kill TyRon Lewis in broad daylight and even if there's a brief uprising, they can handle that too...they can crush it. In fact, the rebellion justifies a greater kind of repression...TyRon Lewis was supposed to die.

But what happened in St. Petersburg was that a revolutionary organization was on the ground. We intervened in the process and helped the people to understand what it meant that TyRon Lewis had been killed.

As a consequence, there was profound struggle that jumped off. This was crucial. The African working class, which had been pushed out of political life by the terror of the government with the defeat of the Black Revolution of the '60s, thrust itself with a fury back into political life.[33]

KILLER COPS EXONERATED

Every Wednesday at 6:30 p.m. the regularly scheduled meeting of the local branch of the National People's Democratic Uhuru Movement is held at the Uhuru House in St. Petersburg. Just three weeks after the rebellions which shook the city, Uhuru organizers expected the meeting on November 13 to be well attended. It was the day that the grand jury findings on the murder of TyRon Lewis by police officers James Knight and Sandra Minor were expected to be handed down. The community was going to want to discuss the decision, whatever it might be.

Police Chief Darrel Stephens had other plans. He knew that an exoneration of the killer cops by the grand jury could anger a community that had already proved its capability of defending its rights.

His solution was not to attack the injustice but to attempt to silence those who spoke out against it.

With the backwards view that the cause of the October 24 rebellions was somehow the Uhuru Movement and not the police murder of an African youth, Stephens instructed his troops to begin arresting members of the Uhuru Movement in the morning before the grand jury decision was made public. It was a typical kind of imperialist move that betrays the ignorant assumptions of the oppressor. It was a decision that would ultimately destroy his career in policing in St. Petersburg.

Stephens not only made proactive arrests. During the days prior to the verdict, he sent garbage trucks through the streets of the south side to pick up rocks and bottles which he claimed had been "stock-piled for use as weapons" against the police.[34] Feelings about the police by south side residents were at an all-time low.

Around noon, word had come to the Uhuru House that comrade David Willard had been arrested for a traffic violation. At about 2:30 p.m. Uhuru activist Mtundu Stewart was headed to the Uhuru House on 18th Avenue South. As he pulled up to the building, seven heavily armed members of a special weapons team swooped in, surrounding him. Stewart's crime: "driving with an expired tag."[35]

As Mtundu was being arrested, Omali Yeshitela drove up with Linzy Williams, another comrade in the movement. By this time the Uhuru House was surrounded by 27 policemen and seven carloads of the Green Team, a special weapons force that wears camouflage gear and is used against the African community. They tried to grab Williams and arrest him for "violation of probation."[36] A crowd of African people gathered. Angry at the flagrant military attack on organizers in front of the Uhuru House, the crowd began chanting, "murderers, murderers!"[37]

"Then the police rushed us," Omali Yeshitela recalls. "They pushed us back up against the wall, pepper-sprayed me in the face, pepper-sprayed Kinara Zima, who was the leader of our local organization here, and then took Linzy to jail.

By now people are highly offended. Hundreds of people are standing on both sides of the street in front of the Uhuru House....Now the pigs start running amok, driving up and down with the doors of their cars partially open with their guns sticking out. Obviously they were either thinking they were going to intimidate somebody, or that they were going to provoke a situation allowing them to justify a military attack on us."[38]

Meanwhile the grand jury had released its statement:

This grand jury finds that Officers Knight and Minor were in the lawful performance of their duties when they attempted to effect a traffic stop of the Pontiac for excessive speed and possible reckless driving...Further, the grand jury finds that Officer Knight was in reasonable fear of imminent death or great bodily harm at the time he decided to use deadly force...Therefore, we have determined that the death of TyRon Lewis was the result of a justifiable homicide under the laws of the State of Florida.[39]

During the afternoon of November 13, after the grand jury report was issued, members of TyRon Lewis' family planted a wreath at the intersection where the eighteen year old had been shot. They were incensed at the grand jury report. "Some were weeping," the local paper noted. During an interview with Truman Smith, TyRon Lewis' stepfather, the *St. Petersburg Times* asked him if he thought that the Uhuru Movement was "using Lewis' death to advance its own political agenda." The paper reported:

Smith rejected that conclusion. "This Uhuru group is only doing what is best for the black man. And it's groups like this that the white man fears. For they (the Uhurus) know that this, and all black murders, are caused by the white police and must be brought to the public's attention. Without the Uhuru group everything would be hush, hush, under the table."

Smith responded to the grand jury statement that his stepson had crack cocaine in his possession when he was shot. "We people in St. Petersburg—I mean the black people in St. Petersburg—are sectioned off in communities in which the white man pushes all his dope, coke and everything else into the black community to make it the only way a black man can make a living."[40]

The November 13th grand jury report not only fully relieved the murderous police of any responsibility in the killing of Lewis, it actually put blame on the Uhuru Movement:

"We are concerned that a certain group in St. Petersburg continues to advocate violence as a remedy for perceived or real social problems,"[41] the report arrogantly read, as if the violence isn't perpetrated by the armed representatives of U.S. State power. The Uhuru Movement, whose goal is to *stop* the centuries-old violence against African people, was accused of "advocating violence."

These grand jury "findings" were meant to be a justification for literally killing the leadership of the Uhuru Movement and destroying its center. As Omali Yeshitela pointed out, "The grand jury that was supposed to be dealing with the cops actually indicted us! The cops walk, we're dead, and the explanation from the grand jury is *we* were the ones who started everything."[42]

But things didn't quite work out as planned for the white ruling class of St. Petersburg. The one factor which white power never counts on defeated their plans: the will and power of the oppressed African community. What was to have been the all-too-common assault on black revolutionary leaders and organizations turned out quite differently, and soon the balance of power in the town would undergo a radical shift.

THE PEOPLE DEFEND THEIR LEADERS

After the initial arrests and pepper spray attacks, the police presence around the Uhuru House remained heavy for the rest of the afternoon of November 13, 1996. They closed off 18th Avenue South between 13th and 16th streets, threatening people with jail if they entered the Uhuru center.

Nevertheless, hundreds of people continued to join the crowd gathering around the building as word of the grand jury verdict and the attack on Omali Yeshitela got out. Party organizers began distributing a leaflet which read "Killer Cops Set Free." It called on the community to attend the 6:30 meeting of the National People's Democratic Uhuru Movement that evening. Despite the police intimidation, about 100 people, including babies and children managed to get into the hall as the NPDUM meeting was called to order. Hundreds more were outside.

Declaring it an "unlawful assembly," the police yelled out over bullhorns outside the doors that people would have 5 minutes to get out of the Uhuru House or tear gas would be shot into the building.[43] People began moving towards the doors, but almost immediately the police started to fire tear gas into the hall.

Wanda Grant was one of the people who braved the military occupation to come to the 6:30 meeting. She told the *St. Petersburg Times* how "the police set off tear gas at the front and back exits of the house. Everyone ran, a frightened crush of people trying to flee the gas. Babies and small children gasped, she said."[44] Omali Yeshitela related later:

I began to tell the people to be calm, that we are going to walk calmly out the rear door. Thirty seconds [later, the police] begin shooting tear gas into the building. They had already started moving on our forces who were telling everyone trying to come in, "You *can* come to the meeting…"

The police were spraying pepper spray into the faces of the people. They surrounded the front door so that the door couldn't be shut to keep the tear gas out and at the same time pepperspraying the faces of the people. They were actually shooting the tear gas under the door and in the cracks.

The police flooded this room with tear gas. There were babies in this room, and children. There were women and men in this room, and the police had total disregard for the lives of those people. According to the news, the police used all the tear gas they had in the city of St. Petersburg against us. They ran out of tear gas.[45]

In the back of the building police fired the explosive canisters at a tree, several branches of which quickly went up in flames. The tree was obviously ignited intentionally since it lay in the opposite direction of the door into which police were shooting their canisters. The burning tree could have easily—and from the standpoint of the police, conveniently—ignited the Uhuru van parked underneath it, potentially creating an explosion big enough to destroy the Uhuru House and several homes behind it.

Omali Yeshitela tells how "courageous young brothers and sisters in the community came and snatched the branches, dragged them out of the trees as they were on fire. As they tried to put the fire out, the police would shoot tear gas at them to drive them away so the building would burn down. But the community did it anyway. They put the fire out."

Another nightlong battle ensued with African workers engaging in well-executed guerrilla warfare. A helicopter was brought down and the army-like police forces retreated in fear. As the Chairman described it, the "brothers and sisters kicked their asses!"[46] And so the community people successfully defended their center and forced the police to withdraw.

The *St. Petersburg Times* wrote in the next morning's edition:

> As night fell, some streets in St. Petersburg sounded like a war zone...
>
> Police officers took cover from automatic gunfire, but one officer was shot in the leg.
>
> Police helicopters circled looking for rooftop snipers, but one helicopter was hit by gunfire in the windshield and floor. A bullet grazed the pilot's elbow.
>
> Officers raced in groups from intersection to intersection trying to get control of the streets, but they ducked Molotov cocktails, rocks and bottles.
>
> Police counted at least 50 rounds of gunfire at one intersection alone.
>
> "If need be, take the troops out!" one scared officer screamed over his radio. "They can't take heavy gunfire out there!"
>
> Police officers pleaded for more backup, more riot gear, more tear gas. "We don't have shields!" one yelled. "Some of us don't have gas masks!"[47]

And so the community defended its voice, the Uhuru Movement, and defeated the armed assault. No one knows how many people fought or who they were. In a true revolutionary style they represented a cross-section of the population: children and women and men, some of them with bandanas on their faces like the guerrilla fighters in the Sandinista Revolution in Nicaragua. When Chairman Omali asked a young child on the streets near the Uhuru House where he was during the November rebellion, the boy replied, "I was out there throwing." Yeshitela summed up the events of the night of November 13, 1996:

> The police are supposed to be so bad. They have all the guns, and they run around threatening people. They catch one person by themselves and beat them to death. But the community put some guerrilla warfare on them, and made all those guns useless. The police couldn't do anything because they suffered a political defeat. They couldn't kill us like they planned to.[48]

The *St. Petersburg Times* reported on Friday that 29 arsons and 74 smaller fires had broken out during the night of rebellion.[49]

RIFTS IN WHITE POWER STRUCTURE

The rebellions that rocked St. Petersburg gained national and international notoriety. Scenes of the fierce resistance were played repeatedly on CNN for days. Reporters and correspondents flocked to the city from around the world. In this period when the brutal will of the oppressor is inflicted on the African working class with impunity, the situation was truly unique. Like it or not, the African working class now had a place at the bargaining table, and was represented by a very articulate spokesman—Omali Yeshitela.

From those days in the autumn of 1996 up until today, there has been no more business as usual. In this time of re-emerging white power around the country, the black power base in St. Petersburg continues to grow its roots deeper and deeper, as an increasingly intractable African working class demands justice. There is no going back to the old days when actions could be taken based on slander and the criminalization of African people. There will be no more well-being for white people at the flagrant expense of Africans—at least not without a struggle.

The African working class community now has an increasingly strong voice with the ability to shape the political agenda in the city. Because of this situation—predictably—splits and rifts within the white ruling structure became apparent almost immediately following the rebellions.

One of the first to suffer the consequences of this new fissure in the pedestal of white power was police chief Darrel Stephens. While Mayor David Fischer praised Stephens' "restraint," reactionary white sectors of the police department attacked him from the right. Within a week of the October 24th uprising the Police Benevolent Association (PBA) filed a class action grievance against the chief, essentially for—in their opinion—responding too mildly to the rebellion. Stephens was being held responsible for much of the police "bungling"—ineptitude which was in reality the retreat of his men in the face of a superior force.

The local paper cited some of the rather slapstick antics of the police on that night. For example, the cop sent back to the station for tear gas returned with the wrong box, and the guns used to launch the tear gas canisters initially malfunctioned.[50]

A proponent of the policy of community policing, in reality a more insidious form of counterinsurgency and police containment of the African community, Stephens became increasingly exposed on all sides as a wishy-washy liberal who pleased no one. The Police Benevolent Association represented those on the force who preferred the old-style of policing—straight up thuggery. "The chief split the baby, so to speak" complained Jack Soule, the head of the PBA. "He had to try to appease certain factions without making others too angry. It didn't work. There comes a time as chief of police that you need to stand up and be counted."[51]

As *The Burning Spear* newspaper noted:

> The feud between the PBA and Police Chief Darrel Stephens is rooted in two contending philosophies on policing. One, the traditional form, employs maximum naked force and sheer terror, and the other more strategically aimed at dismantling African resistance, and more cleverly disguises this naked force and terror of the police beneath a less antagonistic veil.[52]

In November 1996, Chief Stephens further dug his own political grave by announcing that killer cop James Knight would be suspended from the force for 60 days without pay. The suspension was *not* because Knight had just murdered a young, unarmed African, however. Knight was suspended for "violating departmental guidelines" by placing himself "in a position of danger" when he allegedly stood in front of TyRon Lewis' car.

The next day the headlines in the local paper cried, "Police morale sinks after suspension."[53] The force was angered by any censure of Knight. At the same time the African community was offended and angered at the blatant disregard for the real issue— James Knight had murdered an unarmed African youth; he had not endangered *himself.*

Once again, Stephens could please no one.

TESTING THE LIMITS OF FREE SPEECH

Police Chief Darrel Stephens was facing another crisis as well, again resulting from struggle raised by the African community for his actions on the afternoon and evening of November 13. The police chief was not only catching flak for the department's "pre-emptive strikes"—arresting Uhuru Movement members in advance of the grand jury decision. He was under fire also for "provoking a riot" by militarily assaulting the Uhuru House and its community supporters. Many objected to the department's use of excessive and unnecessary force when they brutally tear-gassed the Uhuru House during the meeting, creating a frightening and potentially deadly situation.

Stephens had justified his military attack on November 13 by using the grand jury's blame of the Uhuru Movement for the uprisings. He claimed that the courageous public outcry orchestrated by Uhuru in protest of the police killing had crossed the limits of constitutionally-guaranteed free speech, constituting a criminal offense. In newspaper articles, Stephens was reported as stating that he "believes Uhuru political speech—which encourages a black rebellion against the white power structure—'contributed to the atmosphere' of racial tension and violence. Their speech, he contends, fomented both nights of rioting."[54]

The *St. Petersburg Times* backed up the chief's openly anti-democratic and anti-black allegations, again citing the tribunal verdict which sentenced Knight and Minor to capital punishment. On November 15, a *Times* editorial criticized Omali Yeshitela and other Uhuru leaders for shouting "jail the killer pigs." The *Times*, stated, "This has gone beyond exercising First Amendment rights and engaging in civil disobedience. This is a calculated pattern of behavior that simply cannot be tolerated. It is an intentional effort to spark violence that endangers the lives of the black residents the Uhurus claim to represent."[55]

Meanwhile, State Attorney Bernie McCabe was determined to indict members of the Uhuru Movement for "inciting a riot." However, the State Attorney was forced to admit that he had carefully listened to tapes of Uhuru leader Sobukwe Bambaata speaking before the city council. McCabe was quoted in the media as saying that— apparently much to McCabe's dismay—Bambaata had *predicted* violence if conditions facing African people were not changed, as opposed to inciting or committing violence.[56]

Lengthy debates raged in the local press and the city council meetings about whether the first amendment rights applied to the Uhuru Movement and the African community. But while politicians and media pundits were discussing whether freedom of speech should apply to the African working class community, the Uhuru Movement continued to raise strategic struggles and campaigns that kept the city's attention focused on the essential questions.

Omali Yeshitela demanded that economic development for the African working class community must be seen as the solution to the problems, not an intensified police presence. Genuine economic development was needed to replace the prevailing public policy of police containment, the policy that was responsible for the death of TyRon Lewis, as well as the rampant police brutality around the country.

Yeshitela galvanized the burgeoning Coalition of African-American Leadership, which was made up of African clergymen, businessmen and professionals. The coalition had originally formed to calm the post-rebellion situation, and to put some of the money the government had promised for the rebuilding of St. Petersburg into their own pockets.

Omali Yeshitela used the militancy of the African masses as leverage to bring the coalition to a position of unity. For once, the black middle class was going to have to achieve its own interests *not* at the expense of African workers. The newly emerging political power of the African working class would set the coalition's agenda. The organization agreed to raise the demands, put forward by the Uhuru Movement, calling on the city to prosecute the killer cops, to give reparations to the family of TyRon Lewis, and to keep all destructive "hands off the Uhuru Movement."

The Coalition of African American Leadership, which is still in existence as of this writing, has wrought one of the most profound examples of cross-class unity ever to emerge from the African community. It was this unity which prevented the government, the police or the media from isolating the Uhuru Movement and further attacking it. On November 13, even as the police were surrounding the Uhuru House, the coalition called a press conference condemning the grand jury's verdict exonerating the homicidal cops.

"The coalition will not be split until we see justice," asserted Sevell Brown, the local head of the Southern Christian Leadership Coalition. The coalition called for economic boycotts, lawsuits against the police, marches and civil disobedience to challenge the grand jury's findings.[57] This united bloc of almost the entire African community played a key role in the transformation of sectors of the ruling class that was about to manifest itself.

"THE UHURUS SHOULD NOT BE SCAPEGOATED!"

United African community struggle brought about a dramatic turnabout in the *St. Petersburg Times*. Departing from its previous editorial position commending the police attack on the Uhuru Movement, on November 20 the *Times* came out against Stephens' handling of the November 13th attack. The editorial defended the right of the Uhuru Movement to have peaceful assembly, calling the police attack "a heavy handed show of force that confirmed some black residents' worst fears of the police." The editorial stated that "Stephens and other police officials owe the community some answers…What possible justification can be made for the tear gassing of a peaceful assembly of black residents?"[58]

Lawyer Robyn E. Blumner, a former head of the local ACLU, wrote in her column in the *St. Petersburg Times:*

> [The] fundamental distinction between lawful and lawless conduct was not understood by the St. Petersburg police department on the night of Nov. 13, the night the grand jury failed to indict officer James Knight in the shooting death of TyRon Lewis. It is a distinction, however, this

community's police force (and the *St. Petersburg Times* editorial board) has a duty to learn.

It is hard to know from the press reports whether the members of the National People's Democratic Uhuru Movement are a syndicate of criminal thugs or a grass-roots public interest organization. But, either way, one thing is clear: They, like the rest of us, have a First Amendment right to say the most provocative things at the most sensitive times. And any police force that engages in pre-emptive arrests designed to silence those revolutionary messages violates what is inviolate.

If the Uhurus engaged in vandalism, trespass or arson on the night of the first melee in St. Petersburg, then they should have been arrested for those crimes. Instead, St. Petersburg police rounded up Uhuru leaders weeks later, within hours of the grand jury's decision and on charges unrelated to the initial disturbance, in an admitted attempt to prevent the group from vocalizing its dismay over the judgment and whipping up community outrage...

The Uhurus should not be scapegoated by St. Petersburg officials as instigators of social unrest when the real culprit lies in their own house. Obviously, the black community was seething with resentment against the police before the shooting.

By arresting the Uhurus into silence, St. Petersburg police did more than merely gag extreme speech; they defied a great American tradition and created some of St. Petersburg's first political prisoners.[59]

While the ruling class media and judicial circles were defending the rights of the Uhuru Movement and questioning the legality of the police attack on November 13, the white left of the Tampa Bay Area remained characteristically silent in the face of violence against the African working class-led movement.

Even the African People's Socialist Party's own organization, the African People's Solidarity Committee, failed to organize any actions from the white community to defend the Uhuru House. Once again, white "progressives" stood by and did nothing as the government nearly murdered Omali Yeshitela and scores of African human beings whose only "crime" was to struggle for justice and liberation.

THOUGHTFUL VOICE

In this climate of struggle, African workers gained a modicum of power for the first time since the '60s. The government sent then-Secretary of Housing and Urban Development (HUD) Henry Cisneros into St. Petersburg. He spent three days in the city investigating the situation.

Cisneros came prepared to set up an interagency task force, a citizen's advisory board, to further the "healing process" between the African community and the white power structure. In what would normally have been just more perfunctory lip service to a "racial disturbance," Cisneros' input turned out to be surprisingly insightful. During his stay, the HUD Secretary met with different sectors of the African community, walking through the housing projects and talking to people on the streets of the south side.

Following his investigative meetings, Cisneros stated that he found the situation in St. Petersburg to be among the "most racist in the country."[60] As a result of talking to the African community, Cisneros reported that—much to the dismay of some of the St. Petersburg ruling class—"every road led back to Omali Yeshitela,"[61] acknowledged by nearly everyone as the people's leader. Cisneros came to the conclusion that Yeshitela was a "person who touches lives in a serious way,"[62] and "singled him out as a thoughtful voice who should be heard,"[63] recommending that Yeshitela participate in the advisory board.

Because of Cisneros' urging, the mayor who had vowed that he would never sit at the table with Omali Yeshitela, was forced to agree to a meeting that included Uhuru representatives. City Council President Edward Cole conceded that "it was very important" for the Uhuru Movement to be part of meeting with the city. The mayor and others were now finding it in their growing interest to look to Yeshitela for solutions to the town's problems. "'We have racial problems, we have police problems, we have economic problems,' Fischer said, repeating the assessment of outsiders such as Cisneros," the *St. Petersburg Times* reported. "'We either come to grips with it or we just can't make this city proceed.'"[64]

The Burning Spear reported:

> On November 23, the mayor sat with defeat morbidly engraved on his face as the Coalition [of African American Leadership], alongside Chairman Omali Yeshitela and the Uhuru Movement, met with Henry Cisneros.[65]

Now, just weeks after the rebellions and the demonization of the Uhuru Movement in the media, Omali Yeshitela was named to sit on the community advisory board, headed by a representative of HUD, in partnership with the St. Petersburg City Council. "Race talks may include Uhurus," local headlines huffed. The advisory board continued to function for the next year.

Thanks to the brilliant leadership of Chairman Omali Yeshitela and the heroic resistance of the African masses, the police were not able to wipe out the Uhuru Movement. The federal government was not able to set up neocolonial puppets over the situation. The local powers were not able to do what is generally done after rebellions—send in more police and clamp down on an already terrorized community.

Within a year of the rebellions in Los Angeles, for example, the repression was far worse than before, the inner city economy was devastated and the just uprising by African workers was but a distant memory. In St. Petersburg, Chairman Yeshitela and the "Uhurus" have seen to it that the murder of TyRon Lewis and the "battle of St. Petersburg" have remained in the forefront of the town's consciousness. A profound change had indeed taken place and things were never going to quite go back to the way they had been prior to October 24, 1996.

By the end of the year, the *St. Petersburg Times,* which had once criminalized the Chairman, was hailing him. "Uhuru leader honored for work," headlines now announced, reporting on a banquet honoring Omali Yeshitela by African community leaders. The article quoted Peggy Peterman, a retired *Times* writer, one of the first African journalists for the paper, who spoke at the event, paying tribute to Yeshitela. "Dwell on his goodness and his heart. He hates injustice, and I do, too. The occasion is not only Omali Yeshitela. It is us, for he is us."[66]

ENDING POLICE CONTAINMENT

Step by step, the African working class, through its voice—the Uhuru Movement—was building its base of power. It was unraveling the dominant policies of counterinsurgency, which have been used against African communities around the country since the defeat of the Black Power Movement of the '60s. The Uhuru Movement united as many diverse forces in the town as possible. It seized the moral high ground, showing all citizens how they could benefit from ending this bloody and oppressive practice of police containment of the African community. The Uhuru Movement called for economic development instead. If resources would be poured into the African community, conditions could be changed positively for the whole city.

In this highly charged atmosphere of transformation after the rebellions, the contradictions surrounding Police Chief Darrel Stephens deepened. Criticized from both right and left, his days were numbered. Few failed to notice that the balance of power was shifting in the town.

Six months after the rebellions, Stephens was removed from his position as police chief. He was replaced by the city's first African chief, Goliath Davis, a veteran policeman who, by his own description, grew up poor on the city's south side. Holding a doctorate in criminology, Davis was known throughout his years on the force for his intercession "on behalf of black officers and criminal suspects if he disagrees with the way other officers are treating them."[67]

By the time the local papers were summing up the first anniversary of the rebellions in the autumn of '97, Chief Davis had already made his mark as a leader. Davis had stated his commitment to overturn the policy of police containment. He immediately instructed his officers "to treat the Uhuru headquarters as an 'embassy in Washington, D.C.' and do not attempt to arrest or subdue suspects there," according to the *St. Petersburg Times*.[68] It was an awesome concession to the growing political power base on the south side. No one could remember the last time the African working class had its own embassy.

Chief Davis ended the "tough guy" stance of officers, banned all profanity and demanded that he be informed of every instance in which the police "barge into a house and serve a search warrant."[69] As time went on, complaints of police brutality and misconduct declined significantly and, as of this writing, no one has been killed by the police since the murder of TyRon Lewis. During 1998, Davis' police force got more praise from the African community than complaints. Nearly 242 letters and phone calls of support came in, as well as 205 formal complaints, "most saying an officer was rude or didn't do enough about a particular problem," reports the *St. Peters-*

burg Times. Complaints of excessive force were down from 37 in 1997 to 15 in 1998, the paper stated.[70]

All of this is not to say that the African People's Socialist Party and the Uhuru Movement now believe in the police and the white power system. *The Burning Spear* newspaper reminds us,

> It does not matter whether there are good police or bad police. The police are there to protect the property and political power of the ruling class by violence and force. And African workers victimized by poverty and desperation are constantly resisting the political and economic domination of the ruling class, whether it is through the form of unconscious resistance which is called street crime, or through conscious class struggle and revolution. So the police are doing their job when they violate our people. Police brutality is the official policy of the white power State in its constant war to keep African people enslaved.[71]

After the rebellions, the city wanted to beef up the police force with increased personnel. It purchased $600,000 worth of riot equipment and also has considered buying a "military armored personnel carrier."[72] It applied to be part of Weed and Seed, a federal counter-insurgency program based on models used in colonized countries around the world.* Not surprisingly, the Weed and Seed target zone was the area immediately surrounding the Uhuru House.

During the transition from Chief Stephens to Chief Goliath Davis, the Uhuru Movement was in the middle of a campaign of massive opposition to Weed and Seed in the African community. It put fliers on 10,000 doorsteps, staged demonstrations, and regularly spoke out

---

* A full discussion of Weed and Seed can be found in Chapter 4. See also November 1997-February 1998 issue of *The Burning Spear*, "The City of African Resistance: Weed and Seed," in the Special Supplement.

in opposition at the Weed and Seed meetings held in African community centers and housing projects. As a result, the meetings were empty except for a few demoralized paid Weed and Seed organizers. The African working class had become clearly informed about the nature of the program.

Early in 1998, Chief Davis and Mayor Fischer officially came out against Weed and Seed, making St. Petersburg the first city to attempt to officially withdraw from the insidious program. Although the federal government later forced the city into a compromise position on Weed and Seed, it was possibly a national precedent for the police chief to oppose the program.*

On several occasions, Goliath Davis has publicly stated his feelings that police containment of the African community is no solution to the social problems which exist in the African community and the city.[73] Davis participated on a panel sponsored by then-governor Lawton Chiles, along with Florida State NPDUM Branch Chairman Chimurenga Waller and several other activists. From the podium of the forum, Davis united with Waller's assertion that economic development and not police containment must be the official policy of the government if "racial relations" are to improve.

Davis' actions lived up to his words as well. For example, he showed profound restraint, respect and professionalism by ordering his force to wait for seven hours for a reportedly armed African man to come out of a building. The man had allegedly just robbed two stores. Then he ran into an apartment building to evade the police. As *The Burning Spear* notes, "normal procedure would have been to raid the apartment and kill."[74]

---

* The federal government forced St. Petersburg to implement Weed and Seed throughout the entire city, including the white community. This solution was ridiculous on its face since we have yet to see the multi-agency police forces sweeping the people off the streets of white neighborhoods. The Weed and Seed "community meetings" continue to be held predominately on the African south side.

The police chief went so far as to purge the department's vice squad of some of its most thuggish and anti-black cops. Several were fired, including the officer responsible for coordinating the Weed and Seed program. These bold actions struck a nerve within white ruling circles. Reactionary sectors of the city council and the media have attacked him ever since. Some backwards leaning columnists have accused Davis of being under the leadership of Omali Yeshitela.

The Burning Spear explains the material reasons behind Davis' stand:

> We must not be fooled. The job of the police is to kill and maim the oppressed and starving African community and to protect the property and wealth of the white rulers who live on our backs. Goliath Davis could not change this even if he wanted to. However, the APSP realizes that when the movement of the oppressed people has become strong, the philosophy guiding the resistance sometimes invades the ideological sanctuary of the rulers like a virus, and contaminates it. When this happens, the system becomes fractured, and elements within ruling class go to war with each other. This is happening in St. Petersburg as we speak.
>
> The African masses created this crisis with the October and November rebellions of 1996, and the subsequent political battles which have molded and shaped this community into a fortress of militant resistance. This resistance will not go away...the policy of police containment will not be tolerated. It will be resisted. We will never go back![75]

SELF-DETERMINATION

The years subsequent to the murder of TyRon Lewis have been characterized by constant political motion led by Omali Yeshitela. An ongoing stream of African community conventions, economic development conferences, protests, forums, marches and public campaigns have kept the issues of the African working class in the forefront of all of the city's public policy debates and city council agendas. Articles about Uhuru-led campaigns or related issues often appear in the local papers several times a week or more.

The regular Wednesday evening National People's Democratic Uhuru Movement meetings, led by Branch President Chimurenga Waller, often turn into an impromptu people's court. Every week Africans come for leadership on a myriad of issues, from abuse of their children in the schools, to discrimination in housing and employment. A backdrop for all its political campaigns have been the Uhuru Movement-led institutions serving the needs of the African working class community. These include the Uhuru Black Gym and Fitness Center and the Uhuru food buying club.

The Uhuru-led African Festival Market, featuring vendors and musical groups, takes place every Saturday in a community park. Developed by the Uhuru Movement as an institution to forward economic development on the south side, the festival market was endorsed by the city after months of opposition from reactionary sectors of the white power structure. Some hostile African businessmen also opposed it. Ultimately community pressure won over a majority of the city council to vote in favor of the project. When the issue twice came before the city council in an open hearing, it drew hundreds of people expressing their support.

The head of the St. Petersburg Chamber of Commerce came out for the African Festival Market. One councilman from a mostly white part of town stated in the council meeting that he supported the market and endorsed a policy of economic opportunity over "containment" in the black community.[76]

The city's commitment to the African Festival Market was not backed up by any resources, making the road to success a rough one. If it were a white project it would have been well funded with money for coordinators, vans, musicians and promotion. Nevertheless, the market represents a powerful political victory for the Uhuru Movement and carries out a vision for black community economic self-reliance. The market and other Uhuru Movement victories are signs of the emerging African working class power base.

This power in the hands of African workers has become so apparent in the city that in May of 1999, one area newspaper, the *Weekly Planet,* did a cover story with full color picture of African people in front of the red, black and green African flag. The article was entitled "Power shift: St. Pete's black community moves toward self-determination." In it, author Susan Eastman astutely summed up the unique new balance of political power in St. Petersburg, which came about as a result of the leadership of the Uhuru Movement and the Coalition of African American Leadership:

> In the aftermath of the disturbance that rocked the city in 1996, new alliances formed in the black community among a new generation of leadership—mostly African Americans from the baby boom generation who came of age imbibing the social critique of Dr. Martin Luther King Jr., Stokely Carmichael and Malcolm X. People from what had been regarded as a radical fringe, such as Omali Yeshitela joined forces with business people such as Lou Brown, who owns a real estate firm, and Grady Terrell III, a fuel oil dealer, who had not been actively involved in politics. Social activists Gwendolyn Reese and Marva Dennard also joined the group, as did representatives from African American churches with social missions, like

the Rev. Manuel Sykes of Bethel Community Baptist Church, and Bishop John Copeland of the Macedonia Freewill Baptist Church. Together these citizens formed the Coalition of African American Leadership Inc...

The 1996 uprisings will have marked a change in the black community, the Coalition of African American leadership believes, if the community becomes conscious of its political clout.

The Coalition flexed its muscles repeatedly in the two years following the civil disturbance. Its members endorsed mayor David Fischer's reelection, criticized the federal Weed and Seed anti-drug program, consistently backed decisions of Police Chief Goliath Davis, including his rejection of Weed and Seed money, and raised questions about the funding of the Jordan Park redevelopment project. The coalition also backed the African Market Festival idea. This week the coalition questioned whether racism is motivating complaints that Chief Davis interfered in an internal affairs investigation of a black officer accused of dealing cocaine.

"The real issue is whether we can come into the discussion with our interests recognized," Yeshitela said. "We have a responsibility and a right to be a self-interested and self-determining people. Anything less goes against human nature."[77]

MARCUS GARVEY ACADEMY

In 1999, the Uhuru Movement submitted an application for an all-African charter school. The proposal for the Marcus Garvey Academy came out of an ongoing tutorial program for African children, which is held twice a week at the Uhuru House.

The Uhuru-led educational programs are desperately needed as an alternative to the Pinellas County school system that destroys African children. In the public schools nearly 52 percent of African 5th graders, for example, read below grade level, a figure that rises to 60 percent by the time they reach the 7th grade.[78] The longer African students stay in the school system, the less they are educated. In addition, physical and psychological abuse by white nationalist teachers is widespread if complaints brought to the Uhuru House by distraught parents are any indication.

Scheduled to open in the fall of 2000, the charter school will be headed up by African People's Socialist Party member and high school math teacher, Amina Camara. The academy's focus will be on African children who have been failed by the white power school system. When the charter school is finally on the ground, it will provide a supportive learning environment with a foundation of African history and culture for the students.

Amina Camara is an energetic, dynamic young woman and a first class teacher passionately dedicated to the education of African youth. She is currently under fire at Gibbs High School where she teaches, because she is an outspoken proponent for the rights of African students. She refuses to be intimidated by the white power school structure and is openly aligned with Uhuru. Months of early morning Uhuru Movement demonstrations in front of the school successfully pressured the principal and school officials to back down from their attack on Camara.

While school board members have acknowledged that the charter school application is well written and makes an excellent case for addressing the specific needs of African children, the proposal for the Marcus Garvey Academy is meeting fierce opposition from the board as well as the NAACP. They are using as the basis for their contention that the charter proposal does not meet the county's racial quotas, which permit no more than 30 percent of any student body to be African children. There are many *all white* schools in the district, but an all African school for children who have been pushed out of the colonial school system is not allowed.

This NAACP-enforced quota, in effect since the school desegregation orders of the 1960s, has prevented African people from having control over its own community's schools. It has sentenced a generation of young Africans to as much as an hour and a half of daily busing into hostile white schools in Northern Pinellas County.

Currently, the National Peoples Democratic Uhuru Movement is gearing up for a battle with the school board and has initiated a struggle against the NAACP for its anti-African, do nothing stance.

Camara believes that the Marcus Garvey Academy "would have an amazing effect, and be a positive turnaround for the education of black children. They'll know we love them and are concerned for them. Our children are capable of learning without Ritalin, without Prozac and without labeling."

Whether or not African workers in St. Petersburg win the right to operate their own charter school this time around remains to be seen. But, as one of the many fronts of Uhuru-led campaigns in the city, there is victory in the struggle. The right of African parents to educate their children in a nurturing environment that provides them true knowledge of African history has become a rallying cry for many.

St. Petersburg Goes Uhuru

In the process of the transformation of St. Petersburg, Omali Yeshitela has become acknowledged as a man of great stature. In 1997, Yeshitela was given several pages in the St. Petersburg Times for an autobiographical piece called "A 'revolutionary' speaks."

A few months later, the St. Petersburg Times alleged that Omali Yeshitela had moved into the "mainstream." The article stated that "Mayor David Fischer, whom Yeshitela's group once condemned as being guilty of genocide, has held several meeting in which Yeshitela was a key player. The mayor even invited Yeshitela into his office last week for a one-on-one, 45 minute chat."[79] Chairman Omali responded that it was the mayor who had declared that he would never sit down in the same room with the Uhuru Movement; Omali Yeshitela had never said that he would not meet with the mayor. "It seems to me," Yeshitela observed, "that I have not gone mainstream; rather the mayor has gone Uhuru!"

By the end of '97, Yeshitela was named one of the most important people of the Tampa Bay Area by the *Weekly Planet*. The paper noted that:

> [Yeshitela] seems to be the one leader able to effectively express the deep anger and frustration of the urban poor relating to economic empowerment. The St. Pete power structure knows that if it can begin to address Yeshitela's concerns, then maybe it can finally ease the racial and economic tensions confronting the community. Love him or hate him, Omali is a tremendous force for change in St. Pete and brings a lot of hope.[80]

The January 2, 2000 edition of the *St. Petersburg Times* featured photographs of the racist mural which once hung at city hall and of Omali Yeshitela being arrested by a white policeman after tearing it down. These pictures were selected as a part of a small group of objects defining life in Florida today that the paper would elect to be buried in a time capsule until the next millennium. "Perhaps, 1,000 years from now," *Times* writer Eric Deggans editorialized, "these photographs will seem like ancient relics from America's bitter adolescence—symbols of a conflict long solved and hardly understandable.

"But in the here and now, these 30 year old photos look like they could have been taken yesterday."[81]

THE MOVEMENT GROWS

As the movement develops in St. Petersburg, a growing force of experienced and dynamic leadership is rising up. Gaida Kambon, National Secretary of the African People's Socialist Party; Sobukwe Bambaata, brilliant young editor of *The Burning Spear;* Chimurenga Waller, president of the National People's Democratic Uhuru Movement; Amina Camara, director of the Marcus Garvey Academy; Connie Burton, Tampa community activist and radio personality; and so many others are making their own marks upon the emerging political landscape of the area.

In the unfolding situation, the African People's Solidarity Committee has begun to carry out the role envisioned by Chairman Omali. Its mission is to provide the white community a means to find the road to peace and unity by supporting the work of the Uhuru Movement. APSC makes the call for black community economic development one that white people can participate in. It creates the ability for white citizens to contribute resources to the Uhuru institutions. It lets the white residents echo the demand for an end to the brutal policy of police containment and to express opposition to backwards members of the City Council who take such a negative view. APSC calls for an end of the white tradition of finding the well being of white society at the expense of African people.

In one of its brochures, APSC calls on the white community to help "right the historical wrong," and "to end the divisiveness found in our city, not by blaming the victim, or by covering up well-known historical truths. Instead, we can soberly recognize the reality of the relationship between African and white people and its basis, taking steps to change this relationship."

In 1999, APSC headed up a successful effort to get a new roof and to make some renovations on the Uhuru House with donations and support from the white community. Responding to a favorable article in the *St. Petersburg Times* about the project, a major company donated all the necessary materials and labor for a new roof on the building.

In the fall of 2000, APSC plans to open Uhuru Furniture on the north side of St. Petersburg. APSC already coordinates two similar stores in Oakland and Philadelphia, as part of the Party's broader group of economic development institutions. The Uhuru Furniture stores accept excellent quality furniture and collectible items from supportive donors as a way of making reparations to the African community and supporting the call for economic development in a down-to-earth way. The stores then attract a large base of shoppers, many of whom come out of conscious political support.

Jeanette Shihadeh, a member of the solidarity committee, was quoted in a *Times* article:

> We're actually answering the call of the Uhuru Movement as a concrete way we can take responsibility for the history of white people in this country toward black people and the continuation to this day of the economic embargo.[82]

St. Petersburg, Africa, the World

Taking off from the Tampa International Airport on a clear day is stunning. Rising up over the bay as it flows into the Gulf of Mexico to the Atlantic Ocean, one feels the expansiveness of a world beyond the boundaries of the mundane workaday reality of capitalist America. There is a link with all those who share this equatorial climate and these sparkling timeless waters, the peoples of the Southern Cradle, as Cheikh Anta Diop put it. One senses the spiritual bond of all the places united by the same legacy of slavery and genocide, the lands where ancient civilizations hover on the edge of time, waiting to reemerge. One can almost see them just beyond the horizon: the Caribbean Islands, Mexico, Venezuela, the coast of Africa.

In the flat tropical landscape below, St. Petersburg seems undifferentiated from any of the other coastal towns which ring the periphery of Florida. From the air there is nothing to indicate that the political situation for African people in that little tourist town is unique and transformational, and that the influence and impact of the Uhuru Movement is being felt on far distant shores.

But, in London, or Kinshasa, in Chiapas, Kingston or Manila, someone is reading a wrinkled copy of *The Burning Spear* newspaper or listening to a tape of Omali Yeshitela speaking. There is an energy beaming outward like a radio wave, resonating like a drum. On the savannas, mesas and deltas, in the rain forests and deserts, in the rugged mountains and on the windy flatlands, in the ghettos, the barrios and prisons, people are picking up the signal. Along the Nile, the Congo, the Euphrates, on the Yangtze, the Ganges, the Amazon, on the Rio Grande and the Mississippi: the message comes through. The time for liberation is here.

The work to concretize the vision of Marcus Garvey, to unite African people everywhere and liberate the motherland, has been the lifelong aspiration of Omali Yeshitela and a central goal of the African People's Socialist Party. In 1981, at the First Congress of the Party, a resolution was passed to build an African Socialist International (ASI). Its objectives were to create "one all-African international socialist association which would enhance our ability to realize our historic mission to free and unite our people and motherland, and to defeat imperialism and issue in a new day of peace, freedom and world socialism."[83]

Over the years Chairman Omali traveled to London to speak to audiences of African people from throughout the world about the dream of the ASI. In time Nzela Kinshasha, a Congolese refugee, joined the Party and began organizing others of the diverse African community in Britain and Europe. In August 1999, the years of groundwork paid off when a three week long speaking tour in England was organized for Yeshitela. The tour ended with a highly successful Organizing Conference for the First Congress of the African Socialist International to be held the following year.

Yeshitela spoke almost nightly in an exhausting but exhilarating series of talks with audiences full of enthusiastic Africans speaking with every possible kind of accent. In almost every audience there was an atmosphere of unanimous endorsement of Yeshitela's theme, "Touch one, touch all." It opened up possibilities of an end to struggles waged in isolation and the strength of a reunited Africa. There was now hope for the continent and the people that have been ravaged by Western imperialism for five hundred years.

The compounded effects of a half millennium of imperialist rape of Africa created the basis for the genocidal conditions which exist there today. African people are catching unmitigated hell. AIDS alone is killing 2 percent of the population of a number of African countries each year. A newborn baby in Zimbabwe can expect to live only 39 years. Within the next decade, that will drop to 31 years.[84]

In many countries, 80 percent of grown men do not have full time jobs and the vast majority of people cannot read or write. In an area the size of England, on land with some of the richest mineral subsoil in the world, 40 percent of the population subsists on less than 65 cents a day.[85] In the Ivory Coast, an incredibly mineral rich country, tens of thousands of people live and die on the streets. One of the leaders of the Socialist Union of the Ivory Coast, an organization participating in the building the ASI, told Sobukwe Bambaata, editor of *The Burning Spear* newspaper:

> The poverty in Ivory Coast is a shame. We've got a lot of resources in Ivory Coast. We've got oil, we've got ore, we've got timber, we've got everything that we need for our own survival! But still, the people perish and are crushed by poverty. This is the fault of the government which tries to extract our resources for the benefit of

French imperialism. Our resources are taken away from us. From Ivory Coast our resources are going to France to benefit the French population. What a contradiction! It is a shame. Today, the conditions of the people of Ivory Coast are unacceptable! [86]

Life is so difficult in Africa that in August 1999, two teenagers from Guinea hid in the wheel wells of a Sabena A330 Airbus taking off from the Conakry airport to Brussels. Yanguine Koita, 15, and Fodé Tounkara, 14, dressed in all the clothes they owned and wearing only flipflops on their feet, slipped into the space above the wheel of the jet and huddled together for the flight. They perhaps did not fully realize that the air at 40,000 feet drops to subzero temperatures and the oxygen levels plummet. But the boys were on a mission to try to redeem Africa. They were prepared to deliver their message to the world despite any eventualities of the dangerous trip.

Their decomposing young bodies were not found until 10 days later in the Brussels airport. In the one of their pockets was found a moving letter:

> Messrs the members and leaders of Europe, we appeal to your sense of solidarity and kindness to come to the rescue of Africa. Help us, we suffer too much in Africa, help us, we have problems and a lack of many rights for children.
>
> Regarding the problems, we have: war, illness, food etc....As for the rights of the child, in Africa and especially in Guinea we have too many schools but a big lack of education and teaching...So if you see us sacrificing and risking our lives, it is because we have too much suffering in Africa and we need you to fight against poverty and end the war in Africa...[87]

The two courageous young patriots are now called "the martyrs of Africa."

On August 28 and 29, representatives from 10 African countries and Africans from Sweden, France, England and the United States came together in London to make a united fight for Africa's very life. "We can see the urgency of the situation," Nzela stated, speaking of the need for Africans from the Congo where he is from, to join together to liberate Africa.

> People may say, you are talking about many years...But everything depends on how hard and how fast we work...The only solution is the African Socialist International, the revolutionary unity of African forces. We can have, as the Chairman was saying, the Lumumba Trail, the Marcus Garvey Trail! The material basis is there. It is ours to unite and to do our work![88]

Chairman Omali stated at the conference:

> In the African People's Socialist Party, we are convinced that the struggle for African freedom has reached its limitations within the borders defined for us by imperialism. That is true whether those borders are in Africa itself, or whether those borders are in places like England, or the United States or the Caribbean. These imposed borders serve effectively to keep African people separate, one from the other. They serve as effective means of extracting wealth and value from Africa. Thus, even today, in 1999, the latest figures I have seen indicate that only seven percent of all trade in Africa occurs among Africans ourselves. This means that the vast majority of the "formal" trade—as they characterize it—

is the theft of value and resources from Africa by Europe, North America and, increasingly, Japan…

Today, the crisis of imperialism is reflected in the crisis of neocolonialism which is deepening the misery of African people worldwide. Reports given at this meeting today will reflect this crisis and the growing emiseration of our people throughout the world. The reports will also reflect the fact that the African working class aligned with the poor peasantry represents the social force of the future, absolutely necessary for our advancement as free people into the next millennium…

The current crisis of imperialism demands that we Africans come together to assume responsibility for our fate.

Hence the call to build the African Socialist International, a worldwide organization for African liberation, fighting on many fronts around the world in strategic unity. The ASI must be based on revolutionary principles with the objective of liberating and unifying Africa and all her children who have been dispersed throughout the world. It must be a party, which has as a fundamental objective the elevation of African workers and toilers to their rightful role as leaders in society.

Truly the world is open for the advancement of Africa, if we would but seize the opportunity. This is the time. Let's take it on.[89]

The two-day proceedings ended with a spirit of optimism and hope. Plans were laid and work assigned. There was a new sense that in whatever corner of the globe African people were struggling, they were no longer alone. A new era was dawning, and the deaths of Fodé and Yanguine would not be in vain. The African Socialist International and the liberation of the African homeland were that much closer; the very foundation of the pedestal of the parasitic capitalist system was that much weaker. Everyone suffering under the tentacles of imperialism was that much nearer to freedom. "Free Africa and we will free the world," asserted Yeshitela.

When he returned to St. Petersburg at the end of August, Chairman Omali and Party members summed up to a packed house the victories of the trip to England. The theme "touch one, touch all," was embraced as enthusiastically by Africans in Florida as it was by others abroad. The battle of St. Petersburg was set in the greater context of African people everywhere. In the meeting hall of the Uhuru House on 18th Avenue South, everyone understood that in this little backward Southern town history was truly being made.

The following January, at the Party's annual Plenary conference, Chairman Omali captured the essence of this new period in which victory seems so much nearer:

> Revolutionaries are optimistic. We can actually envision a new world. We see a new world. All the pragmatists and all the empiricists are opposed to us because they find all the reasons why this new world cannot happen. It is we who are the optimists. It is we who will not allow our vision for the future to be determined by what is real today.[90]

Overturning the Culture of Violence

1. Omali Yeshitela, unpublished manuscript.
2. Omali Yeshitela, July 9, 1998, Presentation at the Suncoast Tiger Bay Club, St. Petersburg, Florida.
3. James Harper, July 10, 1998, "Activist says economic, political change needed in city," *St. Petersburg Times*.
4. Monica Davey and Kitty Bennett, October 26, 1996, "Census: Area's residents mostly low-income, black," *St. Petersburg Times*.
5. James Harper, October 27, 1996, "Violence in St. Petersburg: A wary coexistence," *St. Petersburg Times*.
6. Susan Aschoff, July 27, 1999, "Civil rights, civil matters," *St. Petersburg Times*.
7. Yeshitela, July 9, 1998, Suncoast Tiger Bay Club.
8. Rick Bragg, July 3, 1999, "Effort to heal old racial wounds brings new discord," *The New York Times*.
9. "A sincere apology is overdue," June 16, 1999, *St. Petersburg Times*.
10. Omali Yeshitela, 1997, "Social Justice and Economic Development for the African Community: Why I Became a Revolutionary," (St. Petersburg: Burning Spear Uhuru Publications), p. 3.
11. Same as above, p. 7.
12. Same as above, pp. 8-9.
13. Same as above, p. 16.
14. Same as above, p. 17.
15. Craig Pittman and Tim Roche, February 13, 1997, "Records show teen's violence, instability," *St. Petersburg Times*.
16. David Barstow, November 15, 1996, "Violence in St. Petersburg: Grand jury enrages man who reared Lewis," *St. Petersburg Times*.
17. "Mayor says calm restored in Florida city," October 27, 1996, *The New York Times*.
18. Tim Roche, October 30, 1996, "Chief's policy thrust into debate," *St. Petersburg Times*.
19. Tim Roche and Craig Pittman, November 13, 1996, "Case in jurors' hands," *St. Petersburg Times*.
20. Leanora Minai, Craig Pittman and James Harper, March 24, 1998, "Discipline in driver's shooting is rejected," *St. Petersburg Times*.
21. "Four days' highlights," November 13, 1996, *St. Petersburg Times*.
22. Tim Roche, November 14, 1996, "Grand jury: Police officer's action justified," *St. Petersburg Times*.
23. Harper, October 27, 1996, "Change needed."
24. "One year later: Then and now," October 20, 1997, *St. Petersburg Times*.
25. Bill Adair, et al., October 26, 1996, "Violence in St. Petersburg: Timeline of tension," *St. Petersburg Times*.
26. David Ballingrud, October 26, 1996, "State of emergency," *St. Petersburg Times*.
27. Adair, et. al., October 26, 1996, "Violence in St. Petersburg."
28. "Organized resistance shakes St. Pete," Special Edition, 1997, *The Burning Spear*, p. 2.
29. Sue Landry, October 26, 1996, "Violence in St. Petersburg: Uhurus protest police treatment of blacks," *St. Petersburg Times*.
30. David Barstow, November 20, 1996, "Violence in St. Petersburg: Uhuru rhetoric tests limits of free speech," *St. Petersburg Times*.
31. "Tribunal finds police guilty of murder," Special Edition, 1997, *The Burning Spear*, p. 27.
32. Adam C. Smith, Craig Pittman and David K. Rogers, October 31, 1996, "Rights officials say problems remain," *St. Petersburg Times*.
33. Omali Yeshitela, November 1997-February 1998, "The city of African resistance: St. Petersburg," *The Burning Spear*, Special Supplement, pp. A-E.
34. Bill Adair and Sue Landry, November 14, 1996, "Violence in St. Petersburg: Police planned to get Uhurus off the street," *St. Petersburg Times*.

35.   Omali Yeshitela, 1997, "Point of the Spear: Police attack on Uhuru House helps unify African community," Special Edition, *The Burning Spear,* p. 6.
36.   Sue Landry, Monica Davey and David Barstow, November 14, 1996,"Violence in St. Petersburg: Mayhem again," *St. Petersburg Times.*
37.   Yeshitela, 1997, Special Edition, "Point of the Spear," p. 6.
38.   Same as above.
39.   "The full text of the grand jury's report," November 14, 1996, *St. Petersburg Times.*
40.   Barstow, November 15, 1996, "Grand jury enrages man."
41.   "The full text of the grand jury's report," November 14, 1996.
42.   Yeshitela, November 1997-February 1998, Special Supplement, "City of African resistance," p. F.
43.   Yeshitela, 1997, Special Edition, "Point of the Spear," p. 6.
44.   Landry, Davey, Barstow, November 14, 1996, "Violence in St. Petersburg: Mayhem again."
45.   Yeshitela, Special Edition, 1997, "Point of the Spear," p. 6.
46.   Same as above, p. 7.
47.   Landry, Davey, Barstow, November 14, 1996, "Violence in St. Petersburg: Mayhem again."
48.   Yeshitela, Special Edition, 1997, "Point of the Spear," p. 7.
49.   "Violence in St. Petersburg: After a night of fire, fear," November 15, 1996, *St. Petersburg Times.*
50.   Roche, October 30, 1996, "Chief's policy thrust into debate."
51.   Adam C. Smith, November 14, 1996, "Police morale sinks after suspension," *St. Petersburg Times.*
52.   "As African community unites, police factions fight," 1997, Special Edition, *The Burning Spear,* p. 10.
53.   Smith, November 14, 1996, "Police morale sinks after suspension."
54.   Barstow, November 20, 1996, "Uhuru rhetoric tests limits of free speech."
55.   "The rule of law," November 15, 1996, *St. Petersburg Times.*
56.   Barstow, November 20, 1996, "Uhuru rhetoric tests limits of free speech."
57.   Mike Jackson, November 14, 1996, "Violence in St. Petersburg: Coalition leaders condemn decision, consider boycotts," *St. Petersburg Times.*
58.   "The Uhurus' rights," November 20, 1996, *St. Petersburg Times.*
59.   Robyn E. Blumner, November 24, 1996, "Lawless and lawful speech," *St. Petersburg Times.*
60.   Peter E. Howard, June 12, 1997, "St. Pete shake-up: Davis named city's first black chief," *The Tampa Tribune.*
61.   "Organized resistance shakes St. Pete," 1997, Special Edition, *The Burning Spear,* p. 3
62.   Same as above.
63.   Adam C. Smith, November 27, 1996, "Race talks may include Uhurus," *St. Petersburg Times.*
64.   Same as above.
65.   "Organized resistance shakes St. Pete," 1997, Special Edition, p. 3.
66.   Kelly Ryan, December 15, 1996, "Uhuru leader honored for work," *St. Petersburg Times.*
67.   Stephen Thompson, June 12, 1997, "St. Pete shake-up: Policeman born poor, rises fast," *The Tampa Tribune.*
68.   Tim Roche, October 20, 1997, "Rebuilding's foundation rests on promises," *St. Petersburg Times.*
69.   Same as above.
70.   Mike Brassfield, August 29, 1999, "When a brush with the law becomes a push," *St. Petersburg Times.*
71.   "The police are the iron fist of the white power state," 1997, Special Edition, *The Burning Spear,* p. 11.
72.   Roche, October 20, 1997, "Rebuilding's foundation rests on promises."

73. "War erupts within St. Petersburg police force as African community defeats police containment!" February 1999-April 1999, *The Burning Spear,* p. 33.
74. Same as above.
75. Same as above.
76. Susan Eastman, May 20-26, 1999, "Power shift: Emerging alliances," *Weekly Planet,* p. 22.
77. Same as above, pp. 19-20.
78. Statistics for 1995-96 from the Pinellas County School Board.
79. James Harper, October 12, 1997, "Uhuru leader move into mainstream," *St. Petersburg Times.*
80. "The Best of the Bay: Omali Yeshitela, 56, Chairman, National People's Democratic Uhuru Movement," October 10-16, 1997, *Weekly Planet.*
81. Eric Deggans, January 2, 2000, "The photographs," *St. Petersburg Times.*
82. Jon Wilson, February 21-23, 1999, "Uhurus seek unity in roof project," *St. Petersburg Times.*
83. Omali Yeshitela, 1982, *A New Beginning: The Road to Black Freedom and Socialism* (Oakland: Burning Spear Publications), p. 57.
84. Gwynne Dyer, November 10, 1998, "Commentary: Despair of a continent," *The Philadelphia Inquirer.*
85. Alex Duval Smith, September 1, 1999, "The boys who froze to death at 40,000 feet," *The Independent.* (London).
86. "Interview with People's Socialist Union of the Ivory Coast," May 1999-April 2000, *The Burning Spear.*
87. Smith, September 1, 1999, "The boys who froze to death at 40,000 feet."
88. Nzela Kinshasha, May 1999-April 2000, "Building the ASI in the Congo," *The Burning Spear.*
89. "Omali Yeshitela speaks at the African Socialist International," May 1999-April 2000, *The Burning Spear.*
90. Omali Yeshitela, January 2000, Presentation at African People's Socialist Party Plenary.

Omali Yeshitela has said, "Free Africa and we will free the world." The future of the planet is in the hands of African people. Credit: © Herb Snitzer

African People's Solidarity Committee-led March Against Genocide in Oakland, California, an expression of white solidarity with African Liberation.

8

Reparations Now!

Here for instance is a lovely British home, with green lawns, appropriate furnishings and a retinue of well-trained servants. Within is a young woman...fingering the ivory keys of a grand piano and pondering the problem of her summer vacation, whether in Switzerland or among the Italian lakes; her family is not wealthy, but it has a sufficient "independent" income from investments to enjoy life without hard work. How far is such a person responsible for the crimes of colonialism?

It will in all probability not occur to her that she has any responsibility whatsoever, and that may well be true. Equally, it may be true that her income is the result of starvation, theft, and murder; that it involves ignorance, disease, and crime on the part of thousands; that the system which sustains the security, leisure, and comfort she enjoys is based on the suppression, exploitation, and slavery of the majority of mankind. Yet...she is content to remain in ignorance of the source of her wealth and its cost in human toil and suffering.

The frightful paradox...that a blameless, cultured, beautiful young woman in a London suburb may be the foundation on which is built the poverty and degradation of the world. For this, someone is guilty as hell. Who?[1]

— *W.E.B. DuBois*

The most poetic of all historians, W.E.B. DuBois wrote about the deeper philosophical questions surrounding the relationship of a young, seemingly innocent English woman to the masses of oppressed peoples of the world. It was 1946. White people had not yet heard the cry of the Mau Mau, the chant of the Black Panther, the song of Bob Marley, the rap of Tupac Shakur—the powerful voice of Africa that rocked the bastions of the parasitic capitalist system. Though twilight had begun to fall over the empire upon which the sun was never supposed to set, DuBois wrote at a time when English imperialism still dominated much of the world.

Today, because of the proliferation of the just revolutionary movements of colonial peoples over the past decades, the place of white people in the world is less secure. Not quite as many things can be taken for granted. Anxiety abounds. Lifestyles have changed, and technology now dictates our experience of wealth. In an era of microwaves and dishwashers, traffic jams, e-mail and faxes, few of us can imagine the leisurely life on an English estate. Not many of us have grand pianos in our living rooms or a "retinue of well-trained servants" to pick up our dirty socks, wash our toilets and cook our dinner.

But the ultimate issues of guilt and responsibility are still there, and the principle raised by DuBois so long ago remains applicable. The majority of the world's wealth is in the hands of Europeans and North Americans. Meanwhile, the billions, the masses, the majority of living, breathing human beings on Earth face unmitigated suffering, political terror, malnutrition and death at an early age. For them the issue of survival is pressing.

For most of us, regardless of the economic stratum, our dominant problem is where to spend our weekends—Tahoe or Yosemite? Where to have dinner—Italian or sushi? Which car to buy next—Honda or Volvo? Any honest observer could safely deduce that there's a relationship here.

Appearances may have changed, but the parasitic relationship is the same. DuBois' question of more than a half century ago still awaits an answer. Someone is "guilty as hell." Who?

HEIRS OF THE SLAVEMASTER

Looking at the "culture of violence," through the eyes of the colonized instead of through the blinders of the oppressors, we can begin to arrive at the truth. After examining the disquieting reality presented on these pages, we come now to our own place in the world.

This book invites us to cross a threshold, to question everything we learned from white power, from our teachers, scoutmasters and Sunday school instructors. It requires from us a response. It is a cry to lower our defenses, expand our minds and open our hearts. Hear the voice of Africa and the world, see the vision for the future. Join it. Move forward.

Generally, our first reply is, "*I* didn't do it!" Or, "I'm not rich." "I'm a woman." "I'm gay." "I'm Jewish." "I'm Irish." "I'm oppressed myself."

But we have seen, as Omali Yeshitela has so carefully proven, a whole social, political and economic system constructed and maintained on slavery, genocide and colonial oppression. This exploitation creates a pedestal upon which all white people sit—North Americans, Europeans, Canadians, Australians and those of us who have settled in Africa, Asia and South America. We are the citizens of the oppressor nation.

It is true that we do not all sit equally on capitalism's pedestal, but we are all there enjoying the feast as best we can. For most of us, our lifelong ambition is to get more. As innocent or oppressed as we may perceive ourselves, or as well-intentioned our sentiments, nevertheless our very lives, built on the backs of everyone else, constitute a hate crime against humanity. No alternative lifestyle can change that. Nor does our denial make it go away.

White people destroyed whole civilizations and wiped out a world culture imbued with respect for all living beings. What remained—the empty land, the forced labor, the plundered resources and the stolen scientific knowledge—was greedily appropriated.

A share of this loot was extended to all those whom white power defined as fully human—other white people. Those who were designated as only "three-fifths" of a person were part of the spoils, commodities to be bought and sold, or slaughtered at will.

This process created and maintains the pedestal of the capitalist system, providing the whole white world with the promise of "life, liberty and the pursuit of happiness"—and wealth—at the expense of others. It is this promise that cemented our undying loyalty to imperialism, asking from us only one thing: our complicity in genocide and oppression.

So here we all are, sitting on this pedestal built on the backs of humanity, battling it out over who's going to get what and how much. Should white women get as much as men? Should white gays have the same democratic rights as heterosexuals? Meanwhile, the question of those stuffed in the pedestal under our feet is ignored.

We are not plantation owners or slave ship captains. We may not be the Rockefellers or Bill Gates, the owners of prisons, or the CEOs of multi-national corporations. We may not control Congress or work as agents of the CIA.

But yes, we are guilty. We are the children of the slave masters facing the children of the slaves. We inherited the wealth and power of a parasitic social system, they the poverty and oppression.

THE CHALLENGE

"Culture" in America is an empty shell of consumerism, devoid of spirit, genuine human relationship and meaningful endeavor. We feel personal loss at the death of parasitic Princess Di whose fortune came from the terrors of British colonialism. The latest African victim of police murder is a nameless statistic. His or her death means nothing to us.

Our pets receive top veterinary care and better food than millions of humans on this planet. We are indifferent to the fact that Mexican babies, whose mothers must carry them on their backs while picking our vegetables, go hungry and die of treatable diseases. We demonstrate more concern about the redwood trees than about the dire conditions of the indigenous peoples to whom this land and those trees rightfully belong.

Descriptions of the annihilation of colonized peoples are written in the cold, "objective" third person. There is no *Diary of Anne Frank* by a native child, and if there was one it would probably gather dust on the bookshelves. Unlike the majority of warmly hospitable world cultures before the European invasion, we tend to identify only with our own experience.

Thus we condemn ourselves to monotony, homogeneity and boredom. For stimulation we look to violence and loveless sex. If we seek out other societies it is only to culturally colonize them, extracting interesting exotic snippets from their lives to enrich ours—

world beat, the blues, ethnic clothing, international foods, hip-hop style, slang, dance. We strip other cultures bare like an abandoned car left on the streets. Their arts and talents become more goods for us to exploit at their expense.

Our lives are measured in increments of time, slots of work and blocks of vacation days. The passing of years is marked by credit card payments, mortgages, investments, savings, retirement, inheritances. Personal worth is gauged by our portfolio of assets, marketable skills and physical attributes. Denial gets us through the day; it takes alcohol, drugs or mind-numbing TV to get many through the night.

White power must suck the lifeblood of everyone else in order for blood to flow through our veins. Not only are we dependent on the suffering of oppressed peoples for our prosperity, we also require their docility for our sense of security. When the ground under our feet becomes unsteady because of the earthquake of African and colonial resistance, we become fearful. With every tremor our anxiety grows.

How healthy can the life of a tapeworm be? How happy, peaceful or fulfilling? By the time a child has reached middle school, she has witnessed tens of thousands of murders and violent episodes on TV. For the purposes of white power, she is thus conveniently immune to human suffering. Violence bears no consequences. Like the cartoon characters, the wounded and dead are supposed to just happily pop up off the ground and resume life.

Such violence is not a symptom of the corruption of our society, as some believe. Nor is blood on the screen the cause of violence in real life. It's the other way around. Violence in the media simply reflects our history of genocidal and murderous assaults against African and indigenous peoples. TV violence did not create the Columbine High School murders. Columbine students were bringing back home what white people have always done to others.

When did our society *not* have violence as its main form of entertainment? Before the festive lynchings and castrations of African men? Before the hands of African babies were chopped off by the thousands in the Congo for sport? Before the uteruses of indigenous women were cut out and used as saddle horns by laughing white men?

As we begin to look honestly at the world, other things become clear to us as well—for example, that *we* are the "minority" population. Caucasians constitute less than one-fifth of the world's people, and the fraction is declining. No wonder we see the mad scramble for white babies. Hundreds of thousands of dollars are paid for the ova of young, blond athletic women with high SAT scores.

Even our own genes seem to be rebelling against white power. Costly tests for infertility, in vitro fertilization, sperm banks, grandmothers becoming pregnant—it takes a lot these days to keep our genetic pool from drying up. We see forced sterilization and birth control for African women; outlawed abortion for white women.

Examining reality, we begin to comprehend the extent of our arrogance about who we are in the world. We see the obscenity of the notions of freedom and democracy in a society built on torture, bondage, rape, murder and the destruction of truly democratic societies, for our benefit.

If we look at the reality squarely and honestly, we can start to tackle the question of our culpability. There is a path to redemption.

We must begin by acknowledging the reality without defensiveness. We can listen to the call for justice from the colonized and look to them for solutions to the world's problems. It is on our shoulders to accept the challenge to change the course of our history.

Given this history, some of which we have seen on the pages of this book, accepting that challenge should be a welcome choice.

THE GAP

"Consumers see reasons to cheer," blared the headlines during the 1999 Christmas shopping season. "Strong paychecks, low inflation and a surging stock market lead the consumer confidence rate to a 31-year high." Given that confident consumerism is one of white America's foremost talents, we have certainly outdone ourselves. Jobs are plentiful, inflation low and stocks are sky-high. Not counting brief periods of "correction," the Dow and the Nasdaq close at record highs day after day.[2]

In early February 2000, *The New York Times* reported excitedly that the U.S. economy entered its 107th month of uninterrupted economic growth, "beating the old mark of 106 months set during the 1960s." Almost 400,000 new jobs had been added to employer payrolls in January—the biggest gain since September 1997. The average hourly wage was now $13.50. The largest areas of growth came from the service, construction and business services sectors.[3]

White baby boomers are happy because over the next 40 years they stand to inherit a staggering $10 trillion to $136 trillion from their parents, according to an article on the business page of the *St. Petersburg Times* in December 1999. Defined as people who are now between their mid-30s and early 50s, the baby boomers, most of whom are already well-off, are coming in for a windfall as their parents die. "The wealth that's been accumulated by people over 70 has become huge," reports the paper, and every bank in the country is scrambling to attract some of this money.[4]

Things have never been better for America, it seems, and the state of the economy is a big news story. But, oh, by the way, as it turns out there are quite a few people who are not basking in the glow of all these riches circulating through the U.S. financial system.

Despite the booming economy and income growth in most American homes, black family wealth *declined* over the past five years, a 1999 University of Michigan study found. The net worth of the median African family decreased from $8,400 to a mere $7,500 between 1994 and 1999. During the same period, the net worth of the median white household increased to $59,500. That means that "for every dollar of wealth the median white household had in 1999, the median black household held barely 9 cents."[5]

Additionally, the increasing numbers of people in prison conveniently lowers the unemployment rate. *The Tampa Tribune* cites a *Wall Street Journal* article:

> The strong economy has pushed U.S. joblessness to the lowest levels in three decades. But a grim factor also is helping improve the numbers: a record 1.7 million [make that 2 million, Ed.] people are currently imprisoned in the United States.
>
> Since most inmates are economically disadvantaged and unskilled, jailing so many people has effectively taken a big block of the nation's least employable citizens out of the equation.
>
> And because minorities are jailed at a much higher rate, black unemployment...would likely be as high as 9.4 percent.[6]

A 1999 study found that in New York, Arizona, New Mexico and Wyoming the rich got significantly richer while the poor grew increasingly impoverished over the past two decades. The largest increase in the gap between rich and poor is found in New York where between the mid-1970s and the mid-1990s, "the poorest families [lost] $2,900 in real income while those at the top gained nearly $108,000 per family."[7]

In New York City, a staggering 1.8 million people, or 24.3 percent of the population, are officially poor, living on a nearly impossible income of $16,665 or less for a family of four.[8]

"Oh well," remarked Martin Feldstein, an economist from the National Bureau of Economic Research, one of the co-authors of the study.

"What public policy should be concerned about is poverty, not inequality. If the total is getting bigger and it's growing at the top, that isn't a bad thing," he said, "so long as it does not come at the expense of those at the bottom."[9]

Where else, Mr. Feldstein, would it come from?

By mid-2001, the government-imposed five year limit for welfare benefits—a key point of the President Clinton's welfare reform—will hit millions of current recipients. Already more than six million people have been pushed off welfare. "More former welfare recipients are working," boasts the government. So what? Their salaries add up to less than the benefits lost.

The New York Times reports that two million people in America work full time all year while living below the poverty line. Seventy percent of poor children live in families in which someone has income from work. "Lousy pay from work is the biggest source of poverty for people who aren't elderly," comments *The Times* writer Peter Elderman.

The numbers of people making *half* the poverty-level income increased to 14.6 million people in 1997 from 13.9 in 1995.[10]

Currently in the United States, the richest 2.7 million Americans—the top 1 percent—have as many after-tax dollars to spend—$620 billion—as the bottom 100 million Americans. Between 1977 and 1999, the income of everyone making $40,000 or more a year (read white people) increased, while the income of everyone making $30,000 or below (read African) went down.[11]

WORLD POVERTY

Around the world, an estimated 1.5 billion people live on less than one U.S. dollar a day, and the number is rising. The United Nations Human Development Report states that 40 percent of people in South Asia and Sub-Saharan Africa live in poverty.[12] The World Bank notes "significant increases in poverty" in East Asian countries.[13]

But while the World Bank reports on the poverty, in reality the bank and its twin institution, the International Monetary Fund (IMF), were instrumental in bringing it about.

The Economist Cheryl Payer explains,

> The International Monetary Fund is the most powerful supranational government in the world today. The resources it controls and its power to interfere in the internal affairs of borrowing nations give it the authority of which United Nations advocates can only dream....Since its founding at the end of the Second World War, the IMF has been the chosen instrument for imposing imperialist financial discipline upon poor countries under a facade of multilateralism and technical competence.[14]

Back in 1975, then-President Jimmy Carter authorized a study, *Global 2000,* funded by the CIA and its Bank of Credit and Commerce International (BCCI). The BCCI was later exposed as a massive worldwide CIA front for drug money laundering and a funding base for covert action. Given the backers of the study, its aims should be clear.

Global 2000 predicted what the devastation of life in the colonized world would be by the end of the millennium—all of which has come about and more. Essentially the report was a kind of reckoning of what it would take worldwide to maintain the lifestyle of the West. *Global 2000* states in part:

> In...South, East and Southeast Asia, poor areas of North Africa and the Middle East, and especially Central Africa, where a calamitous drop in food per capita is projected—the quantity of food available to the poorest groups of people will simply be insufficient to permit children to reach normal body weight and intelligence

and to permit normal activity and good health in adults. Consumption in the LDCs [lesser developed countries, Ed.] of central Africa is projected to be more than 20 percent below the FAO [Food and Agriculture Organization of the United Nations] minimum standard, assuming no recurrence of severe drought.[15]

Of course there have been years of severe drought in that region, but far more deadly are the policies of the U.S.-controlled IMF. Under IMF "guidelines," impoverished countries are forced to stop growing food to supply their own people's needs and to sell cash crops to the United States and Europe instead. The book *Food First* describes this phenomenon:

> How do those who blame drought and an encroaching desert for famine in the Sahel* explain the vast amount of agricultural goods sent out of the region, even during the worst years of drought? Ships in the Dakar port bringing in "relief" food departed with stores of peanuts, cotton, vegetables and meat. Of the hundreds of millions of dollars' worth of agricultural goods the Sahel exported during the drought, over 60 percent went to consumers in Europe and North America and the rest to the elites in other African countries, principally in the Ivory Coast and Nigeria. Marketing control—and profits—are still by and large in the hands of foreign, primarily French, corporations.[16]

---

* The Sahel is an area of Africa extending from the Sudan in the east to Senegal in the west and separating the Sahara from the tropical regions of western and central Africa.

ECONOMY BASED ON GENOCIDE

Today nearly all the physically accessible forest in Africa has been destroyed by colonialism. On an oil-rich continent in which African people have no access to their own resources, the people are forced to use wood as their main source of fuel for cooking and heating. In rural areas of Central Africa, families must assign someone the full-time daily task of finding firewood. In some cities, Africans spend 20 to 30 percent of their incomes on wood.

As the wood shortages continue to grow, Africans are increasingly forced to burn fertilizer for fuel, thus exacerbating an already existing fertilizer shortage and contributing to the inability to produce food. It is a vicious downward spiral of poverty, dependency and the inability to produce life—so that *our* families can have heat or air conditioning any time we want.

Clearly, the ability to enjoy our North American lifestyle means genocide in most of the rest of the world, especially Africa. Indeed, Africans, Asians and South Americans *combined* have been using only 7 percent of the world's aluminum production, 9 percent of its copper and 12 percent of its iron ore, according to *Global 2000*.

The one-quarter of the world's population that inhabits industrial countries is projected to continue absorbing more than three-fourths of the world's nonfuel mineral production.[17]

And then, of course, there's AIDS, predicted to kill two percent of the population of several African countries each year throughout the indefinite future. According to a 1999 United Nations report, up to 25 percent of the population of a number of African countries are HIV positive on the continent on which 91 percent of the world's AIDS deaths have so far occurred. This can be shown in human terms. For example, two-thirds of the women of childbearing age in Zimbabwe could die of AIDS in the next 10 years, and so could most of their children.

In this country, drugs have saved the lives of thousands of white AIDS patients, but, as one article reports, "no African country can afford to pay for anti-retroviral drugs for its population, and few sufferers have enough means of their own."[18] Generally speaking, now that AIDS has declined in the white gay community, we hear less and less about it.

And so, pundits marvel at the economic wonder for white America. How is it that the economic indicators just go up and up and up? In his New Year's Day column, economist Robert J. Samuelson reminded his readers that he has been predicting an economic collapse for the past several years. Economists have predicted the fall of Wall Street since the early '80s, and yet the U.S. economy seems to have unlimited growth potential.

What does it take to keep the United States economy healthy? The answer is simple: genocide. Babies with AIDS and starving mothers with no milk throughout Africa. It takes drugs on every corner of the African community of America, and millions of Africans tied to the prison system. It takes children playing on glass-strewn streets in front of burnt out houses and homeless Mexican families hunted down by the *migra*.* It takes child prostitution in Asia, torture in South America, political terror in Indonesia. Alcoholism and poverty on the concentration camps they call Indian reservations, and people freezing to death on the streets of the wealthiest country on Earth.

You

are not forgiven
no matter what you say

you are not   you are not   no matter what

---

* Mexican term for the Immigration and Naturalization Service (INS).

Reparations Now!

The way a man is followed by his shadow, like a three-
     legged stray,
down all the afternoon streets

so you are followed by our blood
smeared across your teeth

And we are throwing our heads back
dancing still and anyway and almost completely

without you   and your innocence
and your good shoes

No matter when you arrived it was better
before then   Though the words you brought for us
are now inside us

Sometimes I look   and a crowd has gathered   laughing
at someone tied to a tree   and both his arms
are broken   and his clothes are soaked in gasoline

and though it helps
no one now   forgives nothing   now—not at all…[19]

This excerpt from Tim Seibles' powerful and moving poem, "You," raises the specter that haunts white people—the knowledge, just under the surface, that what we have done to African and other colonized peoples is unspeakable and unforgivable. Someday an accounting must come from the oppressed. Will retribution, we wonder with dread, take the forms that we have so easily dispensed for others: prison, enslavement, torture, appropriation of property, capital punishment, random slaughter? Will they lynch us, brand us, burn us alive, cut out our hearts and impale our infants with bayonets, as we did to them? Will they exact from us a payment for centuries of opulence bought with their blood?

We cannot say what the future will bring, but we could probably predict that one day the bottled rage and pain and loss and sorrow of half a millennium will erupt in an explosion capable of making the rebellions of the 1960s seem like child's play. Someone will stand for our crimes against humanity—if not us, our children or our children's children. Justice will be served one way or another.

Ultimately, if we wanted to respond with integrity, we could anticipate that day of reckoning by making our self-criticism, paying the restitution and accepting the consequences. It would be an opportunity to join with the just movement for the liberation of African people, accept its leadership and, by extension, enter the embrace of all the struggling peoples of the Earth. We could cast our lot with the oppressed for the first time by helping to tear down this bloody pedestal of suffering on which we sit.

We might begin to learn the meaning of genuine solidarity, put down our arrogance, struggle to stop the exploitation, pay our dues, make our reparations, return the stolen goods, acknowledge the truth, break our bonds with this parasitic system, forge our bonds with the planet and its people. We could take responsibility to right the historical wrong.

We could unite others like ourselves inside the belly of the beast to seek our future with the oppressed instead of at their expense. In that process, we might discover something of our own humanity. We might stumble upon a life that is truly worth living. We might find peace, harmony and goodwill among people. And just possibly we might earn a modicum of respect from the world community. Maybe even someday, an ounce of forgiveness.

THE PRICE

Unfortunately it is a more common response to statements like those in Tim Seibles' poem that we make no plea for forgiveness. We suppress the honest expression of our guilt and utter the whine of the fearful but unrepentant: will they do to us what we did to them?

The irony in our often articulated fear is that African people do not lynch and slaughter us. While there is a proud history of colonial resistance, there is no tradition of wanton vengeance, as justified as it may in fact be. The humanity of oppressed peoples is generally too great.

In reality, *we are doing it to ourselves.* We inflict violence on our own society. The life of colonial brutality turns in upon itself, and for all our prosperity and self-admiration, the ultimate price is our own self-destruction. What we dish out comes back at us from within our own ranks. Is that what you call karma?

Take Timothy Thornton, for example. On July 17, 1999, Thornton, along with three other white prison guards, brutally beat inmate Frank Valdes to death at the Florida State Prison in Starke, Florida. Reportedly, the guards took special pleasure in the beating. The autopsy report showed that Valdes' ribs were broken, there were boot marks on his upper body and his testicles were swollen. The guards claim that Valdes was fatally injured because he threw himself off his bunk. As it happens in most such cases, the guards will probably not serve much time, if at all, and they have been released on reduced bail.

This case is a microcosmic example of the entire history of the United States—a modern lynching in modern form in the great American tradition. Starke is in Bradford County where 17 major prisons provide jobs to 8,200 people out of a total population of 24,777.[20] That means that the majority of adults work in a prison-related job. Like many counties throughout the country where prisons are the main source of revenue, everyone knows someone who works in corrections.

Beverly Lee, ex-wife of Thornton, told the *St. Petersburg Times*, "They bring it home with them. You try to treat your family the same way as prisoners: controlling them. You tend to back away from caring about people."[21]

A society built on 500 years of genocide and slavery does not produce particularly nice people. While it has been noted that even "good" white people participated in lynch mobs, collaboration with colonialism generally creates an unbridgeable dichotomy in people's lives. It eats away at our souls like acid. Can someone really be a brutal prison guard on weekdays and a sweet, loving father and spouse the rest of the time?

This contradiction is not limited to prison-related occupations, however, or even to the businessmen, bankers and executives whose decisions have genocidal consequences for the lives of the oppressed every day. Seemingly benign jobs are equally as violent in their own way. Teachers whose job it is to police the predominately African public schools. Professors whose universities buy land in the inner cities, displacing oppressed populations. Lawyers who make a bundle by sending thousands to prison. Social workers who are assigned to break the spirit and will of bright, confident African children who show resistance to their repressive schools. Even entrepreneurs in the growing alternative lifestyle industry—mellow masseuses, herbalists or yoga teachers who walk past hungry and homeless African people to get to their peaceful white studios.

No matter what we do, we can't escape it. The reality behind our parasitic existence comes back to haunt us.

THE CRISIS

Given the reality that we have looked at in this book, it's no wonder white society is in a crisis.

It's understandable that we are depressed. Americans spend $44 billion annually on Prozac and other antidepressants.[22] For those who prefer to go natural, there's St. John's Wort. By the millions we are going to shrinks, filling support groups and flocking to 12-step programs. We are looking for answers in self-help books. We are learning to breathe deeply, affirming our self-worth and meditating.

Or we are numbing our depression with narcotics. After all, we make up three-quarters of the illegal drug users in this country.

But when we, or our children, are caught using drugs, we are treated with empathy in the media. "San Francisco, the epicenter of the [heroin] epidemic, is where most young suburban users come to get their dope. With the invulnerability of youth throbbing inside them," the *San Francisco Chronicle* rhapsodizes in an article about young, white upper-class junkies, "they don't know what they're getting into."[23]

When Mark Garcia was brutally killed by San Francisco police in 1996, he was falsely accused of being a crack addict even as no drugs were found in his system. Garcia was vilified. No media wrote of the "invulnerability...throbbing inside him."

In a story about a reformed white crack addict, the *St. Petersburg Times* portrays sympathetically a good middle-class white man who said he had to "talk with a guttural growl" when buying the drug on inner city streets. "Words edged with attitude helped him melt into gritty Tampa neighborhoods where he bought his crack. And the words masked roots in a white Ohio suburb where his father was a sheet metal journeyman, his mother stayed home and he and his twin brother wanted for nothing."

We are supposed to feel for this guy. The drug addiction isn't the problem here. It's the fact that he had to go to the "gritty" inner city streets every day and try to disguise his whiteness that's portrayed as the tragedy.

But, the article admits, "While profiles tend to paint a picture of crack users as poor, inner city minorities, experts say McNutt, a white man from a middle-class upbringing, is more common."[24]

In addition to drugging ourselves, we are battering, abandoning and abusing our children.

In 1994, there were more than three million children who were reported as abused. In the state of Florida, "so many new cases of child abuse and neglect are being reported to Florida authorities that the state may be heading toward a 'child protection emergency.'" Since June of 1999, emergency shelter placements for abused or neglected children have increased by 80 percent.[25]

In Exton, Pennsylvania, in 1999, Richard Kelso, a successful chief executive of a $500 million-a-year chemical company in suburban Philadelphia, and his wife Dawn, abandoned their 10 year old son who has cerebral palsy.[26] In Houston, Texas, 13 babies were found abandoned during 1999.[27] In Memphis, Tennessee, that same year, a couple was accused of leaving their 18 month old son to die in the wilderness. They are also suspected of tossing his two and a half year old brother to his death in a lake.[28]

In Pittsburgh, a 37 year old man bludgeoned his 5 year old twins to death with a sledgehammer in 1998 because they weren't getting ready for day care fast enough. Neighbors said that the man seemed the ideal father. His little son was found in a pool of blood on the couch and his daughter was in front of the TV with her skull battered. After killing his children, he called the police and waited on the porch for them to come, cell phone in hand.[29]

Then there was Ronald Shanabarger who fathered a child with the intention of later killing the baby to get revenge against his wife. He allowed seven months for his wife to bond with the child, then suffocated the baby with plastic wrap in 1999. He harbored anger for his wife, dating from an incident before they were married, when she did not return home promptly from her vacation after Shanabarger's father died.[30]

Notorious cases of infanticide by white moms made headlines in the late '90s. In Philadelphia, Mary Noe murdered eight of her own babies and was sentenced to 20 years probation. In New Jersey, Melissa Drexler strangled a baby she gave birth to in a bathroom at her prom. Amy Grossberg gave birth in a Delaware motel, then handed the baby over to her boyfriend who tossed the newborn into a dumpster. Darlie Routier of Texas stabbed her two sons in her home, then claimed that the boys were killed by an intruder.[31] Another man injected his son with HIV so that he could avoid paying child support.[32]

In some cases, children kill their parents, like the Menendez brothers or the twin 11 year old boys in North Carolina who were accused of murdering their father and wounding their sister and mother in a shooting rampage in their home.[33]

SOCIAL SUICIDE

Let's face it, we're killing each other. We are serial killers, sexual abusers, thrill killers, post office murderers, cannibals, road rage shooters, high school slaughterers, body choppers and woman torturers. Stories about these kinds of crimes fill the daily papers.

When we've finished attacking our families, we take our guns to work and school. Two million of us every year experience violence at the workplace.[34] School killings in Colorado, Mississippi, Kentucky, Arkansas, Oregon and many other places are well-known and becoming more common.

"Unprecedented stress making Americans sick,"[35] headlines scream. So we relax with violence, as did Christopher Churchill in Illinois. He admitted to killing his half-brother, his brother's girlfriend and her three children "to relieve stress," a 1999 newspaper article noted.[36]

On the weekends, there's murder for fun, like the ex-Marine in California who killed a boy "just to see what it felt like"[37] in 1997, and the guy who was convicted of murder in the "thrill killings" of two pizza deliverymen in New Jersey in 1999.[38]

Attacking women is a favored pastime for men such as the Yosemite murderer in 1999 who stuffed the bodies of his victims in the back of their rental car and burnt it. There's the sex torture case in New Mexico where who knows how many women were held captive in chains, raped and subjected to electric shocks.[39]

Don't forget the man released in New York after 20 years in psychiatric hospitals for killing and eating a teenager. He "no longer presents a danger to society," a 1999 *New York Times* article assured us.[40]

The Oakland Tribune reported the same year that a man "left out crucial facts" when police interviewed him about his girl-friend's disappearance. The man had failed to mention that he stabbed his girlfriend, then dismembered her body and buried the pieces in his yard.[41] In a more everyday kind of incident, Arthur James Cox Jr., in Fremont, California, was arrested after he repeat-edly dragged his 29 year old girlfriend by her hair, struck her with his belt and kicked her."[42]

Consistently, these unthinkable acts are white on white crimes.

The Philadelphia Inquirer speculated that we're doing this because:

> [I]t all comes down to entitlement. Many white men [and white women, we might add, Ed.]...are raised with the belief that they are entitled to economic success, social leadership and personal happiness. And when they miss the mark in some or all those areas, their frustration may fester into murderous rage.[43]

Put simply, it's black power rising, white power falling. The thought of someone else being free terrifies us.

THE FEAR

If we identify with white power we must nervously watch our backs. Everything about white power is in a deep crisis. There's pollution and car accidents, nuclear attacks, militia bombings, AIDS, herpes, breast cancer, asbestos, tainted water, second-hand smoke, saturated fat and ticks bearing Lyme disease to worry about.

The proliferation of horror movies expresses our fears. The Blair Witch, the Scream and all those who know what we did last summer are coming to get us. Or is it our own conscience?

From the bars on our windows to our car alarms to the cans of mace in our bags, our security has been shaken as the colonized rise up and demand what is rightfully theirs. Even nature is rebelling against the destructive force of white power: elephants are killing their trainers and killer bacteria are resisting antibiotics. There's E. coli, staphylococcus, salmonella, shigella, ebola, mad cow disease and flesh-eating bacteria lurking around every corner.

As we enter the new millennium, war, mass killings, anxiety and fear grip not just the United States, but much of the white world. We weren't sure if Y2K would bring about Armageddon and the "end of civilization as we know it," as some predicted. Somewhere in the minds of white people is the recognition that 500 years of the death and destruction of white power is enough. Retribution is overdue.

Yet, as Omali Yeshitela tells us, these are good times, excellent times. Indeed, they are, if looked at through the eyes of the slave. Not that the masses of people around the world are not suffering and struggling. But the crisis of imperialism indicates to all who want to see it that the parasitic capitalist pedestal is weak. U.S. imperialism in not able to extinguish the fires of resistance—throughout the Arab states, in Mexico and Colombia, in Africa and Asia. Nor can imperialism any longer control the internecine warfare and fratricide which is emerging inside of Europe as the northern continent reverts back to rivalrous tribalism for which it has been known for millennia.

CRISIS IN EASTERN EUROPE

"Why are the Chinese happier than Germans?" goes a joke making the rounds in Berlin. "Because they still have their wall."[44]

In November 1989, the Berlin Wall came down and imperialism cheered. In Catholic school in the 1950s, the Sisters of Providence had us pray for the conversion of Russia from godless communism, which we all did fervently. Meanwhile, the CIA and U.S. government-imposed economic sanctions helped erode the structure of the country. But perhaps, the most significant factor in the collapse of the Soviet system is that the majority of white people of Russia and Eastern Europe wanted to join the rest of the white world on the pedestal of colonial exploitation and share the loot.

Not that they hadn't already been doing that to a certain extent. It was always notable that the leaders of the former Soviet Union were white, yet white people were a minority in the USSR. Soviet magazines and books targeted for the West featured the European art, ballet and classical music found in Moscow and Leningrad (now St. Petersburg). When would someone from Turkmenistan or Uzbekistan replace Khrushchev as the head of state, one wondered.

The majority of countries and national territories that made up the Soviet Union were former colonies of imperialist Russia. After the Bolshevik Revolution, their relationship changed little, and most of the resources of those areas continued to flow towards the white Russian provinces.

At the same time, the Soviet Union always attempted to control the liberation movements in Africa and Asia where struggling organizations desperately needed resources. The white chauvinism of the USSR is said to have been one of the dominant factors in the rift between the Soviet Union and China. In South Africa and Zimbabwe notably, the Soviets funded only the liberation organizations that would guarantee a subservient relationship with them once the country was independent.

A genuine concern for the liberation of African people seemed to be absent, and few of the Soviet-backed movements in Southern Africa ever won. When they did, as in Angola and Mozambique, they soon became neocolonialist regimes, and the oppression of the masses actually increased. Regardless of their opportunist motives, however, the Soviet subsidy of revolutionary movements in Africa and Asia threatened U.S. imperialism.

Thus, the real target of the Cold War, led by the United States ostensibly against the Soviet Union, was control of the colonial countries.

Chairman Omali gets to the heart of the contradictions of the former Soviet Union. "The real locus of the class contradiction in the real world exists in the contest between capitalism born as a world system, and the 'pedestal' upon which it rests," he explains. White workers sitting on the pedestal of imperialism cannot overthrow the parasitic capitalist system. The burden of that historical task is left to Africans and others upon whose shoulders white power rests. If we want to see an end to capitalism, we have to commit ourselves to their leadership.

In the early twentieth century, before its revolution, backwards Russia was excluded from most of the benefits of the white world. Some called Russia "capitalism's weak link." In some ways, the revolution provided for white Russia its "primitive accumulation of capital," as the Soviets attempted to create a socialist economy which would contend with the Western-controlled, capitalist economic system. Given the worldwide nature of the parasitic capitalist system, that was impossible. Yeshitela explains in his book, *Izwe Lethu i Afrika*:

> Hence the 1917 revolution in Russia was not a true socialist revolution since the real historical basis for socialism, which is the destruction of the pedestal upon which capitalism rests and which is required for its existence, had not occurred. What happened in Russia in 1917 was the

existence of conditions, which constituted the *political basis* for socialists to seize state power.

However, this seizure of state power by socialists did not change the reality that the world economy—even the world economy within which Russia existed—was, and continues to be, a capitalist world economy. It is the same world economy created by the slave trade and augmented by other facts of parasitic or "primitive" accumulation that transformed the vast majority of the peoples and countries of the world into great reservoirs of human and material resources largely for European and North American exploitation.

Through the capture of state power, socialists in Russia were able to effect some important changes in the lives of the Russian/Soviet peoples. Immediately they were able to pull Russia out of the terrible first imperialist world war, although the Russian people would suffer imperialist-supported civil war and actual imperialist invasion, [in 1918] which caused immeasurable human suffering and economic damage.

The Russian revolution also resulted in the destruction of Tsarism or Russian feudalism. The great feudal estates of the Russian nobility were seized, and this facilitated the ability of the revolution to address the starvation, oppression and land deprivation of the peasants...

The Soviets were not able to understand that the colonial peoples were to be the real makers of anti-imperialist revolution. Also, they were not able to comprehend why they as communists continued to experience the same kind of economic problems that were associated with capitalism. The Soviets hid their contradictions and "eventually became demoralized and perhaps even corrupted by failures they apparently did not fully understand." Yeshitela continues:

> Therefore, it was the Soviets who capitulated first, before other [Eastern] European industrial societies, opting to join the capitalist world economy. Thus the heirs to the first great attempt at socialism joined the feast of the flesh of the world's oppressed peoples in order to solve its own economic and political problems...
>
> Hence, the mad rush by the Russians and 'Eastern' Europeans into the orgy of consumerism that characterizes their rich white kith and kin of Western Europe and the United States. The domestic struggle against Russian and Eastern "communism" continues to reveal itself as the struggle for the possession of "things"—VCR's, color TVs, and the like—that other white people long ago accepted as their just right, due to them because of their whiteness...
>
> [T]he Russians and Eastern Europeans have chosen...to abandon the cause of the wretched toilers of Africa, Asia, Latin America and the internal colonies of the white capitalist countries. They have chosen to join the privileged white world in its losing attempt to keep the parasitic pedestal of capitalism, which is to say, white power in place.[45]

Today there is ethnic cleansing, fratricide, war and violence as various groups which lived peacefully side by side under communism now brutally vie for a taste of imperialism's loot stolen from the colonies. Left without the free schools and health care, and lacking the subsidized jobs and housing of the white communist society, death rates in Eastern Europe now surpass birth rates. In the Ukraine, population growth is negative since the end of the communist system. Because of "recent social and economic crisis conditions," states a web site on Ukrainian health, the number of deaths exceeds the number of newborns in the Ukraine by a quarter of a million people.[46]

The same trends are found in the rest of the former Soviet bloc. Martin A. Lee's *The Beast Reawakens,* says of the former East Germany: "The euphoria of their newfound freedom quickly faded as the standard of living among easterners plummeted." Lee continues:

> When the better times promised by Chancellor Kohl showed no signs of arriving, many Easterners became disillusioned with democracy and nostalgic for the bad old days of the GDR [East Germany, Ed.], with its guaranteed work and social services. The number of marriages dropped, birthrates fell, crime soared, and health care centers were inundated by people unable to cope with the angst of an uncertain future.[47]

Today, feuding and resentment abound in Germany as the Westerners resent having to share their robust economic benefits with their former communist brothers and sisters.

Murderous white nationalist skinheads and neo-Nazis are running rampant throughout Russia and Eastern Europe. Following the lead of white workers in America who always viciously attacked Africans in order to win more economic gains for themselves, by 1991—only two years after the fall of the Berlin Wall—there were more than 40,000 white nationalist "extremists" in Germany. During 1992, more than 4,500 white nationalist assaults killed 17 African and other colonized people and injured hundreds.[48]

RESPONSIBILITY

For the West to disclaim responsibility for what it so clearly did is to make every white man alive on Earth today a criminal. In history, as in law, men must be held strictly responsible for the consequences of their historic actions, whether they intended those consequences or not. For the West to accept its responsibility is to create the means by which white men can liberate themselves from their fears, panic, and terror...[49]

—*Richard Wright*

Richard Wright wrote these words in 1957 in his book *White Man Listen!* His statement of so long ago appeals to us to take responsibility for being the children of the slave master, for lives built on the genocide and suffering of others. He is correct that it is in accepting the historical burden of truth that we can free ourselves from our fears, panic and terror. It is in the act of reparations that we find redemption. We can break down the long-standing isolation from others that we have imposed upon ourselves and begin to see the possibility for the future as it is being projected by the oppressed of the Earth.

"It can be said that the white man is at bay. Never have so few hated and feared so many." In the introduction to *White Man, Listen!*, John A. Williams cites this quote by Wright and adds:

These words, written by Richard Wright three years before his untimely death on November 28, 1960, in Paris, have more meaning today than when they were first set down. The white man, Wright meant, has been brought to bay by his own conscience, by the juggernaut, economics, and by the ceaseless pressure brought to bear upon his grim penchant for insisting that the world was his and his alone; the pressure has come from all over the world: China, Africa, Latin America, the rest of Asia, and in America itself. Nonwhite pressure.[50]

Williams and Wright were writing in the 1960s when national liberation movements throughout the world were the "main trend," as Omali Yeshitela says, threatening the foundations of the capitalist system. White people had indeed been brought to bay.

In this era of imperialist counterinsurgency, the viciousness of white power has again been unleashed on humankind. But the revolutions of 30 years ago have not gone away. Crushed by imperialist counterinsurgency, they remain to be completed. Conditions for colonial peoples are worse than ever. It is only a matter of time until the widespread proliferation of revolutionary organizations again threatens imperialism's pedestal, and "nonwhite pressure" again reins in white power, bringing it to bay once more.

As the world lies on the cusp of inevitable transformation, it is time for us to stand for the consequences of our historic actions, which Richard Wright called for so long ago. We are offended by those who call such a stance "middle-class self flagellation." Wright's statement is true. There is no statute of limitations for crimes against humanity.

Acknowledgement and reparations are moral and ethical responses to the reality around us. We have to begin by admitting that, yes, we are all part of this. No one is exempt.

WHITE WORKERS: GUILTY

While the ruling class directs and the middle class grows fat, white workers are imperialism's eager attack dogs. As workers we have always been ready to brutalize African people in the hopes of being rewarded with a greater share of the stolen loot.

This is our "ladder of success," with a body of an African on every rung. Whether it's the Marines or the Ku Klux Klan, the militias, southern sheriff's deputies, Irish gangs, Italian mafia, Western posses or just the good old lynch mob, white workers have always been the enthusiastic storm troopers of white power. Violence against African and indigenous people is our rite of passage with which we prove our whiteness. This is the essence of the American dream, of the fact that any white kid, no matter how poor, can become wealthy or be elected president.

Few of us are more than a generation or two away from the stratum of white laborers. All of our grandfathers *and* grandmothers did the same thing to join the middle class—stepped on the backs of African, Mexican or indigenous people, one way or another. We didn't take up class struggle; we took up genocide and terror. We didn't lynch the boss, we hung Africans from trees; we didn't burn the White House, we torched the homes and bodies of Africans; we didn't seize the means of production, we stole the land of the indigenous people.

Consequently we are the richest workers in the world. And there we are, ridiculed by the white rulers whose bidding we do and hated by colonized peoples whose lives we terrorize.

It is a rather pathetic trait of white workers that even when the government and ruling class turn their backs on us, we still love America! Viet Nam Vets, families of the guards who Rockefeller killed at Attica prison, people dying of cancer after working in government-owned nuclear plants, exploited workers of Appalachia— where are you? The rulers of white power don't care about you. Once you've done their dirty work, you're disposable.

There *is* a future for us if we join the struggle of the colonized toilers of the world.

As Chairman Omali said, the exploitation of white workers is not in the context of black power. It exists in the framework of *white power*. If we are interested in destroying the basis of our oppression as workers, let's join with African and other oppressed peoples who are going to free themselves of the deadly system sitting on their backs. That, by the way, is the very same system that exploits us.

WHITE WOMEN: GUILTY

We instigated countless murders of African men by charging rape, mostly to cover over something we didn't want our husbands to know about. We were there at the lynchings and burnings and mutilations of African people. We were egging white men on. We dressed in our best outfits, brought our children and, grinning, we had our pictures taken in front of the tortured corpses.

We fought for our democratic rights at the expense of African people. As nineteenth century feminists, we said that it would be better for an African woman to be the slave of an educated white man than of a "degraded, ignorant black one."[51]

In the 1960s, we built a white women's "liberation" movement off the impetus of the Black Liberation Movement. The black movement was destroyed by government terror. The African population was assaulted in a counterinsurgent war against the whole people. We got power and money within the system at black people's expense. Now we are 36 to 39 percent of all executives, administrators and managers in wholesale, retail, entertainment and banking. We're 40 to 50 percent of executives in insurance, education and hospitals, and 66 and 67 percent of executives in social service and health service. We got what we wanted through the affirmative action laws that came as a government concession to the life and death struggles of African people in the '60s. Now, African people are still impoverished and white women are tired of affirmative action. Almost 80 percent of women polled no longer support it.[52]

Through our movement for women's liberation, we've gained power and money in the capitalist system. We've proven that we can be as good as white men in ruling white power. But do we have "liberation"? The degradation and objectification of women is greater than ever. We're raped and abused in greater numbers. Our bodies sell cars and jewelry and dish detergent from every TV screen and billboard. Hollywood holds up hideous visions of anorexic white women with facial surgery and nose jobs, artificially inflated breasts and lips, capped teeth, bleached hair and vacant looks in their eyes.

Our women's liberation movement, built off the back of the Black Power Movement, mirrored the actions of white workers as a whole. We sold out black people and opportunistically went for ourselves. What we got was the power to be good oppressors next to men and some of the stolen wealth. But we changed nothing in a society that is built on slavery and genocide and takes the exploitation of women for granted.

JEWISH PEOPLE: GUILTY

What Europeans did to other Europeans under Hitler had been practiced for hundreds of years against African, indigenous and Asian peoples. No white people, including Jews, protested when Africans and other colonized peoples were being slaughtered by the millions by European and American powers. What was inflicted on Jews by Nazi Germany was an outgrowth of centuries of genocide against other peoples. Only when the atrocities were carried out against other white people, was any outrage registered by Europeans.

Despite experiencing some of what colonized peoples have been subjected to for so long, most Jews did not stand with the oppressed. Instead, they stole the land of the Palestinians and created the Israeli state. Now, the fiercest imperialists in the Middle East, Jews engage in slaughter of Islamic peoples. W.E.B. DuBois wrote:

> The concept of the European "gentleman" was evolved: a man well bred and of meticulous grooming, of knightly sportsmanship and invincible courage even in the face of death; but one who did not hesitate to use machine guns against assagais [light spears used by Southern Africans, Ed.] and to cheat "niggers"; an ideal of sportsmanship

which reflected the Golden Rule and yet contradicted it—
not only in business and industry within white countries,
but all over Asia and Africa—by indulging in lying, murder, theft, rape, deception, and degradation, of the same
sort and kind which has left the world aghast at the
accounts of what the Nazis did in Poland and Russia.

There was no Nazi atrocity—concentration camps,
wholesale maiming and murder, defilement of women
or ghastly blasphemy of childhood—which the Christian
civilization of Europe had not long been practicing
against colored folk in all parts of the world in the name
of and for the defense of a Superior Race born to rule
the world.[53]

The African scholar Walter Rodney had this to say about European fratricide, reiterating the theme that our own colonial violence,
so freely dished out to others, comes back against us:

In the short run, European racism seemed to have done
Europeans no harm, and they used those erroneous ideas
to justify their further domination of non-European peoples in the colonial epoch. But the international proliferation of bigoted and unscientific racist ideas was bound to
have its negative consequences in the long run. When
Europeans put millions of their brothers [Jews] into ovens
under the Nazis, the chickens were coming home to roost.
Such behavior inside of "democratic" Europe was not as
strange as it is sometimes made out to be. There was
always a contradiction between the elaboration of democratic ideas inside Europe and the elaboration of authori-
tarian and thuggish practices by Europeans with respect to
Africans.[54]

The mass murder of Jews in Nazi Germany is used to further attack African people. A Jewish member of the Alameda County Board of Supervisors broke into tears once when the Uhuru Movement in Oakland went before the board to protest the abuse of African children in the foster care system as genocide. Genocide only happened to Jews, she said.

Steven Spielberg once came to the nearly all-African Castlemont High School, located in East Oakland, down the street from the Oakland Uhuru House. His purpose was to force African children to watch the movie *Schindler's List*.

One wonders why anyone would make a film glorifying a Nazi who saved a tiny percentage of people from death by putting them in slave labor in his factory. In any case, Spielberg and others were incensed when the Castlemont students laughed at the movie. Certainly the thought of any white people trying to tell Africans about genocide is patronizing and outright ridiculous.

Holocaust museums have opened in Washington D.C. as well as in many other U.S. cities, but the wholesale murder of Jews never took place inside the United States. Genocide against African and indigenous people was carried out here. Jews are getting reparations by the trillions of dollars from Germany and Switzerland while reparations to African people is laughed off by white society.

Where are the Jews who are willing to use their experience in Germany as an opportunity to stand in solidarity with African and colonized peoples?

AFRICA COMES BACK STRONG

Resting on the foundation of the plunder of Africa, white power always looks to Africa for its solutions when facing a crisis. Resource rich and underdeveloped, Africa is imperialism's trump card. To paraphrase what colonizers once said about the Philippines, white power wants Africa; it does not want the Africans. That is why the

renewed scramble for Africa is responsible for the almost unimaginable genocidal devastation that continent faces today.

The African People's Socialist Party is building the African Socialist International (ASI) however, something the cleverest imperialist
never banked on. As an international organization uniting African
formations everywhere, the ASI has the potential to rapidly unite and
strengthen African people under its slogan, "Touch one, touch all."
With the possibility of elevating the suffering people out of their
demoralizing isolation, a new ray of hope is radiating. A viable strategy for liberation is unfolding across that ravaged continent. The
African homeland can be liberated.

With the existence of the ASI, new generations of African revolutionaries all over the world will have Yeshitelism to look to for direction, instead of the European communists of old which led them
right back under the imperialist whip.

Without a doubt, the twenty-first century will be characterized
by the successful struggle for the liberation of Africa and the repos-
session of its stolen resources.

Imperialism has come to the end of its rope. It has enslaved,
annihilated, raped and pillaged too many and too much. It has
destroyed the Earth itself, threatening life at every level, from extinct
species of trees to endangered animals and mutated micro-organisms.
With its bloody hands, it has disrupted every thing from the ozone
level of the atmosphere to the genetic infrastructure of life itself.

We live in a time, however, when the mass of struggling humanity will not go quietly to their demise. They are bolstered and given
hope by a clear and powerful strategy—a liberating analysis of the
world as it really is—explained by Omali Yeshitela.

Africa was the cornerstone of the imperialist pedestal. The continent provided the slave trade and the gold, diamonds, resources and
oil essential to create imperialism and necessary to maintain it.
Therefore, a liberated Africa and a healthy Western imperialism cannot stand side by side; one must cancel out the other.

"No one knows," Marcus Garvey said, "when the hour of Africa's redemption cometh. It is in the wind, it is coming. One day, like a storm, it will be here. When that day comes, all Africa will stand together."

Liberated Africa represents life and health and the vibrancy of a positive culture. America stands for death, destruction, lynching and genocide. Omali Yeshitela has remarked:

> They kill us in great numbers. Everybody is accustomed to black people dying in great numbers, just like so much trash scattered across the Earth. They kill us like that not only because the ideology of imperialism is based upon great hatred for African people, but also as a part of a counterinsurgency, a part of the effort to keep Black Revolution down. That is why they kill us the way they kill us.
>
> The idea is that with every mass death, we should be so demoralized that we'll never fight again. They say, "Look, every time you fight we will kill you. We will kill your leaders. We will mutilate them. We will rape your women. We will commit every unimaginable crime against you." The idea is to demoralize the people so the people will never have the courage and the will to resist again.
>
> But it doesn't work. It can't work. So, even after so much murder and mayhem against our people and our Revolution, we see Africa always coming back strong. Whether it's in the streets of Philadelphia or whether it's in Azania itself, Africa always comes back strong.[55]

Sobukwe Bambaata, the editor of *The Burning Spear* newspaper, asserted on the journal's pages:

The entire continent of Africa is being rocked by violent upheavals which will transform its politics and its people forever. There is not a regime on the Continent which is safe from this whirlwind. Nor will the white imperialist slavers survive in the long run. The convulsions shaking Africa are the opening salvoes of a new era: the era of Africa's redemption, liberation and unification under the rule of the African working class and poor peasantry.

African microstates burdened by decades of imperialist-imposed debt and economic rape have begun to crumble and collapse. Armed clashes between competing camps of the African petty bourgeoisie have reduced numerous states to lawlessness and chaos, while various conflicts between competing African states threaten to destabilize the entire Continent.

Within this powder keg which is Africa, the imperialist powers, particularly the United States and France, have become engaged in a new "scramble for Africa" to determine which slave master will rule over the impoverished and downtrodden masses. At the same time, Africa's workers and poor peasants, who have borne the brunt of Africa's rape and pillage by white power, are waking up and becoming ever more determined to shake off the modern-day enslavement which has bound us to a life of misery, famine and death.[56]

Is there a place for us in this future world in which all those formerly colonized for our benefit ascend to their rightful places of freedom and control of the Earth? What becomes of us?

What About the White People?

"What are you talking about?" asks Omali Yeshitela in a presentation in Oakland, California in 1996.

> Hell, you take your chances just like everybody else.
>
> Why do we have to promise the white people something? Everybody else is wondering where the next meal is going to come from, wondering whether the police are killing their children or locking them up when they are 10 or 15 minutes late coming into the house. And we are supposed to worry about the white people?
>
> We say to white people that you should end your own self-imposed segregation and isolation from the rest of humanity. Join with us because imperialism and white power will be destroyed. Participate in destroying it and building a new world. The question for everybody on the planet Earth is, what side are you going to be on when it comes down? Down with imperialism! White power has to go![57]

In another speech, Yeshitela also addressed the concerns of white people facing the prospects of a liberated world:

> We're saying that the entire relationship is parasitic. Therefore all the people who want to see a new world—everybody including the poor white people—must turn loose their whiteness. Join with the struggle of black power to overturn white power, which is the social system within which the poverty of white people occurs...The poverty of white people does not occur within any kind of black power system.

So what white people have to do is fight against white power. They have to unite with the struggles of black people whose oppression and exploitation is the basis for the existing system that is oppressive and exploitative to everyone.[58]

THE FORWARD SIDE OF HISTORY

It is not a matter of well-wishing, but of sharing the very same fate whether in victory or death.

— *Che Guevara*

On the last weekend of September 1976, some comrades and I jumped into a beat-up Ford and drove all night from Louisville, Kentucky to St. Petersburg, Florida for the founding conference of the African People's Solidarity Committee (APSC).

A month or so before, a friend of mine had told me that there was going to be a speaker in Louisville whom "you've got to see." I had just returned from kicking around France for a couple of years, something white people do to "find" ourselves. It was the period when Eldridge Cleaver and a coterie of ex-Panthers and their followers still lived in the French capital, giving it a progressive feeling. The Black Revolution of the '60s was still in the air, despite the deadly counterinsurgency that had silenced its core.

It was the years of the victory of the Vietnamese over U.S. imperialism. Peace talks were taking place in Paris. Liberation struggles in Mozambique, Angola and Guinea Bissau were defeating imperialism as well. French imperialism was vying with the United States for power, so it liked to expose the atrocities of the U.S. government, even as it committed the same atrocities itself. Because of this I learned more about what was really happening in Asia and Africa from reading the newspaper *Le Monde* than I had ever been aware of before. When I returned to the United States, I felt the importance of supporting the struggle of African people here.

On an August evening in 1976, my friend took me to the predominately African west side of Louisville to the YMCA where a forum sponsored by the African People's Socialist Party was being held on the second floor. Party members were evident in their beautiful dashikis and African dresses. A small portable record player played John Coltrane, and on the wall was a large map of Africa.

Omali Yeshitela gave a brilliant presentation going over the current political situation in just about every country in Africa. While doing so he summed them up in the context of parasitic capitalism. Never having been an active leftist, I knew nothing about theoretical socialism and communism. I just knew, however, that what Omali Yeshitela was saying made sense of the world. There were no leaps of faith required. Everything just came into focus.

During his visit to Louisville, Yeshitela announced an upcoming conference at the end of September in Florida to build the African People's Solidarity Committee (APSC). The APSC would be a new kind of organization which would enable white people to work directly under the leadership of the African Liberation Movement itself.

When the Party was formed in 1972, just following the apex of the devastation of the Black Power Movement of the '60s, Chairman Omali was able to see the role that the white left had played in uniting with the government attack. Chairman Omali understood clearly that white people, left to our own devices, would never be able to take a principled stand in relation to the struggle of African people. The Party realized that a principled stand *might* be possible, however, but only under the correct political conditions.

The existence of white people on the backs of colonized peoples created a material basis for European opportunism, including that of the white left. Therefore, white people interested in true solidarity and unity with African people must be organized under the leadership of African workers. In order for the interests of African workers to not be sold out, as we have done over and over again throughout history, we white people must be organizationally tied to their very same interests.

Since there are actually only two poles to stand with: imperialist white power or black power—which is the power of the people— the organizational relationship makes sense. We have worked under white power's leadership for centuries, and look what it has brought us. The idea of working under the leadership of black power seems refreshing and hopeful.

The specific work of the African People's Solidarity Committee is to organize a strategic base of the African Revolution within the North American population. The existence of APSC serves to erode the historic loyalty of the white population to the parasitic capitalist system, and point the way for a broader sector of the white popu- lace to find its genuine human interests in a future characterized by the liberation of suffering humanity.

About 40 people attended that founding conference, coming from across the country, including Maine, Massachusetts, Florida, Alabama, California and Kentucky. We were made up mostly of white contacts the Party had made over the years in the course of various political campaigns. During the two-day conference, Chair- man Omali gave a riveting 11-hour presentation on dialectical mate- rialism and political theory. Other Party members conducted workshops on just about every aspect of Party work.

For me, it was a life-changing event. The level of discussion was exciting and filled with the potential for human possibilities beyond anything I had ever imagined.

SOLIDARITY

We were a shaky group of white people who joined the fledg- ling African People's Solidarity Committee that weekend. It was to be expected, I guess, considering the "material basis of opportunism," but APSC's first statements of purpose dealt a great deal with the struggles of white workers, women and gays, and very little about solidarity with the Black Liberation Movement. Nevertheless, a whole new process was set in motion.

Though it was a long time before any real concept of solidarity was grasped by APSC members, that September conference was historic. It was the first time that a revolutionary African organization had formed a group of white people under its leadership who committed to go to the trenches with "black power" as *our* slogan.

The existence of APSC has profound significance for the world revolutionary struggle. The African People's Socialist Party turned the relationship of Europeans to Africans right side up. No longer would African people have to be held hostage to the charity or fleeting political whims of white people, who have always used our access to resources to attempt to control the direction of anti-colonial movements. In the 1960s, for example, when the Student Nonviolent Coordinating Committee (SNCC) took a stand in support of the Palestinian liberation movement, they found that most of their contributions from Jewish liberals suddenly dried up.

We joined the African People's Solidarity Committee because of our unity with the aims and goals of the African People's Socialist Party. The interests and aspirations of African workers thus became *our* interests and aspirations. Yeshitelism is embraced as our political worldview. Omali Yeshitela becomes our leader and "Uhuru" becomes our slogan. Under the leadership of black power, the vision of a liberated Africa and social system under which all living beings could once again live in peace and prosperity becomes our future.

Many years after that weekend in 1976, Chairman Omali summed up the profound significance of the formation of the African People's Solidarity Committee:

The fact is, the Party has taken the demand by SNCC* that the North Americans should struggle within their own North American communities a step further. We have also structured the relationship under the discipline of the Party so the strategical aims of the Revolution are never forgotten or dismissed by North American comrades, whose different relationship to U.S. imperialism almost demands an opportunistic approach to every question that threatens the stability and future of a United States built off the life, blood and resources of the non-white, colonial, neocolonial and economically dependent peoples of the United States and the world.

The Chairman continues in his book *Izwe Lethu i Afrika:*

This deep opportunism manifests itself as a near total self-alienation of white people from the vast majority of the world's peoples. This alienation is expressed in many ways, but none so significantly as the inhumane, barbaric, treatment white people have participated in and/ or encouraged against other peoples. Often, the only "provocation" for the actions of white people has been the desire of whites to take or keep possession of ill-gotten resources which have become essential to the white way of life.[59]

RACISM OR REPARATIONS?

At the founding conference, the African People's Socialist Party called on APSC to adopt the case of Dessie Woods, an African

---

* The African-led Student Nonviolent Coordinating Committee evicted its white members in 1966, calling on them to go back into the white community to win solidarity with the struggle of black people. Notably the white people found every other kind of issue *except* that one.

woman in Georgia who was serving a 22 year prison sentence for killing a white man with his own gun who tried to rape her. The Party's slogan, "Free Dessie Woods, Smash colonial violence," was eventually known all over the world and a massive movement was built which eventually did free Dessie Woods in 1981.

Responding to the call, two members of the young organization formed a Dessie Woods Defense Committee in San Francisco. Soon the Party sent organizers to form a Party unit there, and the solidarity committee grew. Eventually, in 1981, the Party moved its national office to neighboring Oakland, the predominately African city that had once been the home base of the Black Panther Party.

During the 12 years in which the national office of the APSP was in Oakland, the Party, APSC and the Uhuru Movement went through tremendous transformations. The Party's deepening relationship with APSC led to the growing understanding of the nature of parasitic capitalism as a whole. Over the years, every possible white opportunist attack on the Party arose from within the ranks of the solidarity movement itself. Thus the Party's efforts to struggle against this opportunism and unite ASPC both strengthened the solidarity committee and deepened the Party's own political theory as well.

The essence of the struggles in APSC revolved around the question of what we call "material solidarity"—raising money and resources. Clearly it isn't enough for us in APSC to just spend our time simply "educating" white people about the conditions imposed upon African people. We live in a world in which white people control 75 percent of the world's resources while the African community is impoverished. The African People's Socialist Party was in dire need of resources just to be able to carry out its campaigns in the African community. The realities of parasitic capitalism must be addressed in our work. Thus, our job must involve winning white people to unleash those stolen resources and turn them back over to Africa.

Most of us were enmeshed in a politic of lifestyle-based rejection of white society, seeking not transformation but an alternative way of living. We espoused the downwardly mobile idea, popular at the time, that to cut ourselves off from consumerism and the mainstream of white society was a significant political statement. This politic was also a way of denying that we sat on the pedestal of the oppressor nation. It was an attempt to try to equate our own experience with that of colonized people.

Struggle by the Party demanded that we grow up, however, and go back into the belly of white society to try to transform it. Instead of rejecting its lifestyle, we had to take responsibility for white power. It was these struggles which brought us to the fundamental questions. The question was not racism, the changeable ideas in our heads, but the objective reality of parasitic capitalism.

Taking on racism is easy. I can go to workshops dealing with my bad thoughts about African people, then get into my Volvo and drive back to my lovely house in the white neighborhood. I can have black friends and lovers, grow dreadlocks or hang out at blues clubs. African people are still filling the prisons, being shot down by the police and making less than half of my income. The colonial oppression of African people remains intact.

The stand called for by the African People's Socialist Party is quite different. It goes right to the dialectical relationship between human bondage and wealth, genocide and land ownership, suffering and well-being, justice and atonement. It takes us to the deepest recesses of our own souls to find out if we are prepared to carry out in practice what we express in words. It brings us to the question of reparations.

THE MOUNTAIN

In the late 1970s, when the solidarity committee was first building in Northern California, the revolutionary Sandinista movement from Nicaragua was also organizing there. Almost instantly, the Party and the Sandinistas formed a deep bond, and representatives of the FSLN* spoke at nearly all Party forums regardless of the subject.

The diminutive but dynamic Sandinista leader, Carmen Olivares, who was nearing the end of her pregnancy in the last months leading up to the FSLN victory, spoke passionately at APSP-sponsored events. More than support from white people, she called on North Americans to give "militant solidarity." She often said that the best thing white people could do for the Sandinistas was to support the movement for African liberation inside U.S. borders.

The Sandinistas always spoke of the Nicaraguan mountains, the training ground and rear base from which they launched their revolution.

The mountains were key for their forces to build.

Omali Yeshitela adopted the analogy of the mountain in defining the Party's work with the solidarity committee in California:

> Before we came to San Francisco, California, we were trying to free Dessie Woods, within the context of a strategy that we understood could liberate black people...It was a struggle that was most often complicated by the colonialist attacks by the government on the one hand, and to a great extent, counterattacks by North Americans on the other. It was a struggle that was complicated by the tremendous poverty of our Party and of our people, so that often our struggle was composed equally of attempts to just feed the members who constitute our Party, as well as to do the other work. Often our struggle was complicated by the most ridiculous need to pay a light bill in the office

---

* The Frente Sandinista de Liberación Nacional (FSLN) led a successful revolution against the U.S.-backed Somoza regime in 1979. The revolution was heavily attacked by the United States, militarily, economically and politically. In 1990 with much help from the CIA, the revolution was overturned.

where we did work; by the most obscene need to pay the rent in the office where we worked...

Our decision to come to San Francisco was partially influenced by these difficulties...We understood that we needed a rear base area. There are no mountains within the colonial territory to which we can escape, develop resources, repair our engines, and then return again to attack our enemies. So therefore we had to create the mountain. From various utterances and signs of solidarity that we received from North American left forces in San Francisco, California—and from the evidence of the material resources that we could see here—we saw the possibility of creating our mountain here.

We perceived the possibility of being able to bring leading Party forces to the San Francisco area whose primary responsibility would be to develop the unity with the North American forces in this area, in accordance with our strategy for liberation for our people. And as a consequence, and in relationship to developing that unity, seek out the resources which would be available to help the forces who are doing work to make revolutionary struggle within the actual African colony in this country. So that there could be a *Burning Spear* newspaper...So that there could be an office where the work to free Dessie Woods was being led...So that we could maintain a telephone in our office which would allow us to maintain relations with other revolutionary nationalist forces within this country, and with each other. So that we could have the ability—from this mountain that San Francisco constitutes for us—to go into other areas to provide the same kind of leadership for our struggle that we feel we've been providing in the places where we already do work...[60]

The relationship of APSC to the Party was attacked viciously by the white left of the San Francisco Bay Area, where, since the defeat of the Black Panther Party, they were entrenched in a lucrative political economy and control over much of the electoral politics of the area. The absence of any revolutionary African movement gave them unchallenged access to jobs, offices and even international revolutionary organizations. They had resources to go to Nicaragua and Cuba for "revolutionary" vacations.

They could demonstrate in Berkeley by the thousands against what the United States was doing in Central America. At the same time, the "progressive" Berkeley mayor and city council were sending out heavily armed police, helicopters and RVs to suppress the African community in Berkeley. The city set up a curfew which permitted no African youth on Telegraph Avenue near the University of California campus after nightfall.

In all the years that we were in the Bay Area, not once did the white left answer a call for political or financial support for the campaigns being waged by the Party on the brutal war-torn streets of East and West Oakland.

But then, many of the same struggles were still inside of APSC, as our own opportunism reared its ugly head in resistance to the question of material solidarity, the control of the resources. Even when we did raise money, we did it on our timetable, not with the urgency dictated by the pace of an anti-colonial struggle led by the Party. This was just another form of charity, and the African People's Socialist Party was not interested in that.

In the early 1980s, the Party was making a fierce effort to put the issues of the suffering African working class back on the political agenda of Oakland. The Party fought tirelessly, often on many fronts at once, addressing the questions of homelessness, housing, police brutality, education and democratic rights for the black community. It was the tempo of fierce struggle which set the timetable for material solidarity. It is a demanding timetable. The resources needed for the liberation of African people never diminish; oppression takes no vacation.

For North Americans used to doling out money at will, raising funds according to our own laid-back agenda, and generally controlling the flow of resources to revolutionary movements, the timetable of the African Revolution is quite a challenge. It is a challenge that could only be met by embracing the understandings of Yeshitelism as our own, and broadening our base in the white community.

It took many years for this to happen.

In 1980, we opened Paper Tiger, a xeroxing and print shop in San Francisco which was supposed to be a fundraiser for the Party's work. Instead, the shop went deeply into the red while we promoted it as a "women's collective business." APSC then attempted to seize the resources of the print shop outright and to "renegotiate the terms for our relationship to the Party." The APSP responded to this outrageous opportunism from its own solidarity organization by wresting control of the shop out of the hands of the renegade APSC forces and calling together other white supporters to help reorganize the solidarity movement. Paper Tiger was closed, and this struggle resulted in the temporary disbandment of APSC in 1981.

UHURU FOODS, UHURU FURNITURE

It wasn't until 1985 that APSC was finally re-formed. By this time the solidarity organization had made a decisive breakthrough. We determined to establish solid institutions which were clearly owned by the Party, which we would use to raise resources in the white community for the Uhuru Movement.

The most successful of these reparations institutions, as we call them, have been Uhuru Foods, and Uhuru Furniture and Collectibles, which have proved to be successful long-term vehicles for generating resources. These institutions have provided a springboard for a more penetrating relationship with a broader sector of white society.

Uhuru Foods started out around 1980 selling everything from tofu-kabobs to Polish sausages at the annual San Francisco Gay Liberation Day and the Haight Street Fair. Throughout the '80s, we sold food and giant chocolate chip cookies to stoned Deadheads at Grateful Dead concerts and had food booths at nearly every fair, large and small, in Northern California.

Occasionally a fair bombed, causing us to lose every cent. Once we had a fire in the booth, and sometimes we were reprimanded by the promoters for the revolutionary literature that we gave to every customer. But by the late '80s we had learned how to run an established, well-respected professional business. In 1987, the Party opened the Uhuru Bakery Cafe which served natural foods, had a successful catering component and baked its own breads. It was extremely popular until a fire in the roof of the building closed it in 1989. APSC participated in this institution which gave us a lot of experience in the food business.

Today Uhuru Foods is known by many for its successful annual booths at the Monterey jazz and blues festivals, Afribbean, reggae concerts and many other local fairs. People come year after year to the Uhuru Foods booth in support of the movement, often donating more money than the cost of the food item they just bought. Every winter Uhuru Foods also sells delicious holiday pies to supporters from Marin County to Silicon Valley. Scores of people volunteer to help make each pie season happen and there are many repeat buyers for whom an Uhuru pie for the holidays is a tradition. Uhuru Foods operates similarly in Philadelphia as well.

Uhuru Furniture and Collectibles is another very significant institution run by the African People's Solidarity Committee, in Oakland for more than ten years and Philadelphia for five. Uhuru Furniture was instituted in the early 1980s, when comrades began selling donated thrift items at the Ashby Flea Market in Berkeley as a fundraiser for the movement.

In 1989, we got a truck and opened our own store in Oakland. When our original site was damaged by the 1989 earthquake, we moved to our present location on Grand Avenue. In Philadelphia, we are located in Center City. Both stores are highly successful with a crew of volunteers who help pick up furniture and sell it, as well as a large base of donors and shoppers who come out of political support.

The impact of these political institutions of black power reach into the suburbs and have been important in winning the battle of ideas in the white community. Everyone we meet at the furniture store or food booth receives brochures and fliers that explain what the Uhuru Movement stands for. Thus the question of reparations to African people begins to penetrate more and more deeply into white society.

These institutions operate within the context of much political work in campaigns led by the Party or the National People's Democratic Uhuru Movement. APSC leads study groups, marches, forums and teach-ins in the white community constantly to win other white people's participation in finding our future on the forward side of history.

One of the most important APSC campaigns is the annual March Against Genocide which involves the white community taking a stand against the genocidal conditions faced by African people today. This march is also a fundraiser, with friends and family making pledges to sponsor the marchers.

CRUCIAL WEAPON FOR BLACK LIBERATION

Chairman Omali said of the African People's Solidarity Committee:

In 1976, four years after its founding, our Party opened a new front of struggle within the North American society itself, with the creation of the African People's Solidarity Committee. The African People's Solidarity Committee was founded as an all-white organization. And while we were unclear of all its possibilities in 1976, it has come to be a crucial strategical weapon in the arsenal of our Party and the African Liberation Movement.

Historically the presence of whites in the African liberation movement has been as arrogant colonialist interlopers—ideological imperialists or Ku Klux Communists as we refer to them—or as patronizing liberal integrationists of one stripe or another.

In addition, the historical relationship of Africans to whites in the United States and much of the world, from colonial slavery through capitalist colonialism and neocolonialism, has undermined the self-confidence of Africans in organizational and political associations with whites. In most instances, such associations shore up the assumption of the supremacy of whites in all relationships...

However, the African People's Solidarity Committee works directly under the leadership of the Central Committee of our Party. It achieves its strategical leadership from our Party and its work is a reflection of the strategetical objectives and programmatic thrust of our Party and movement. In addition, all of the economic projects that it creates and/or manages are owned by the African People's Socialist Party. This is because we are materialists and recognize that in the real world, ownership and control of the material resources determine the balance of power in relationships, notwithstanding expressions of goodwill.

Our relationship with the African People's Solidarity Committee is a reflection of our understanding that white people do exist in the real world...Our Party was able to provide a scientific explanation for our relationship to white people with our elaboration of the concept of parasitic capitalism. That is capitalism that is not only characterized by the contradiction of private ownership and socialized production. It is characterized by the more profound and significant contradiction of private ownership and socialized production resting upon—and relying for its continued existence on—a basis of stolen land, resources and labor.[61]

I can only say that this political relationship has been an inspiring, exuberant and ever-deepening experience. It is true that we still carry with us the legacy of white power, and our own white arrogance and opportunism continue to raise their heads. But we have broken with white power and stepped into the unfolding human drama to be played out by the masses of oppressed peoples.

From rather typical alienated middle-class white lives, all of us in the solidarity movement are now united in an almost tangible bond with the majority of the Earth's people. Despite the grim state of the world we see around us, we have faith in the future and optimism for tomorrow. We have seen the words of Omali Yeshitela, which to some white people seem "radical" or far fetched, embraced enthusiastically as common sense by colonized people of almost every nationality.

Someday the vision of Yeshitelism and the truth about parasitic capitalism will sweep the world. Then, indeed, the moment of Africa's redemption will come, and with it the redemption of all people, including those Europeans who choose to share the very same fate with those upon whose backs we have rested for so long.

STOP THE VIOLENCE

It is interesting that as the perpetrators of violence against the whole world, there are many of us who are vehemently against the inevitable use of violence by African people in the process of liberating themselves. Most of those who espouse the nonviolent philosophy—the Quakers, for example—have supported the armed revolutionary movements in Viet Nam and Nicaragua, we might note. But when such resistance comes home, they arrogantly denounce it, raising hypocritical platitudes and invoking the names of Mohandas Gandhi and Martin Luther King.

When another African person is shot down by the police, these Quakers and their ideological fellow travelers are nowhere to be found. When African children are slapped by white teachers, when their parents are forced into homelessness by the welfare system or when African foster children are abused by white people, we don't see any of them out there taking a stand against the violence.

The brutality of a colonial, parasitic prison system elicits no response from the peaceful soft-spoken Friends—as the Quakers are called—whose meeting houses, lest they forget, were founded by slave owners. If they were sincere, they would demonstrate daily against the brutish history and violent present reality of this country. Instead, they demand that African people turn the other cheek and subscribe to their principles of civil disobedience.

It is safe to say that African people and other oppressed peoples hate violence. It is antithetical to their cultures. Their distaste for engaging in violence may be one reason why imperialism has continued to exist for so long. They want to live, love and enjoy life in peace. It is violence that prevents them from doing so.

The Uhuru Movement does not engage in, nor has it ever engaged in violence. It has done the long hard work "above ground" to win the battle of ideas and destroy the legitimacy of the U.S. government and system in the eyes of African people. The Uhuru Movement exposes the heart of the truth, sharply and sometimes painfully, and this is why some white liberals dislike "Uhuru tactics." These tactics never involve violence, not because of a philosophical commitment to nonviolence, but because the time is not ripe for such actions.

One day, however, African people will fight. They must fight to end the violence. Like all colonized peoples, Africans have a human right to defend and liberate themselves by any means necessary, regardless of where they are located in the world. It is only just. Grandmothers and children, youth and adults will pick up the gun, and we will begin to experience daily life as it is lived in Beirut, Kosovo or Kinshasha.

Imperialism will never give up its power peacefully, and the lines will be sharply drawn. Peace will come in the armed unraveling of this system born of violence.

Point number 10 of the platform of the African People's Socialist Party states:

We want the right to build an African People's Liberation Army.

> We believe that true freedom, although often taken away, cannot be given to a people. We believe that African people are our own liberators, and that we have a right and obligation to build an African People's Liberation Army to defend our political gains, our freedom fighters and communities, and to win our actual freedom from our oppressive colonial slave masters. We believe that neither meaningful freedom, nor guaranteed political and social gains, nor genuine liberation are possible without the assuring existence of an African People's Liberation Army....[62]

Henry David Thoreau, the father of civil disobedience whom many uphold for his nonviolent stands, encapsulates powerfully the necessity for the use of violence to gain justice. In discussing John Brown's raid on Harper's Ferry in 1859, Thoreau asserts:

> I do not wish to kill nor to be killed, but I can foresee circumstances in which both these things would be by me unavoidable. We preserve the so-called peace of our community by deeds of petty violence every day. Look at the policeman's billy and handcuffs! Look at the jail! Look at the gallows!…We are hoping only to live safely on the outskirts of *this* provisional army. So we defend ourselves and our hen-roosts and maintain slavery.
>
> I know that the mass of my countrymen think that the only righteous use that can be made of Sharpe's rifles and revolvers is to fight duels with them when we are insulted by other nations, or to hunt Indians, or shoot fugitive slaves with them or the like. I think that for once the Sharpe's rifles and the revolvers were employed in a righteous cause. The tools were in the hands of one who could use them…The same indignation that is said to have cleared the temple once will clear it again. The question is not about the weapon, but the spirit in which you use it.[63]

Well said. Uhuru!

BUILDING A NEW WORLD

"This is our period," affirms Omali Yeshitela, looking over the top of his wire-rimmed glasses from behind his desk at the St. Petersburg Uhuru House. Behind him hangs a map of the world turned right side up. An old Ray Charles record is playing. On his laptop computer, he receives e-mail from Africa, London, New York. The phone rings constantly: reporters, members of the Coalition of

African American Leadership, African workers with problems to be solved, family, children, grandchildren. On the streets below there are signs everywhere that these are Uhuru streets, liberated African territory. Even the police department acknowledges this building as "the embassy," with its own diplomatic immunity. No one is to be arrested here.

A few blocks away there's the new building, purchased a few months ago, which will house an Uhuru health food store as well as the gym and fitness center now located on the first floor of the Uhuru House.

There's the struggle for the Marcus Garvey Academy Charter School. The school board said the charter application was the best they'd ever seen. "But," said the all-white board, "no, you can't have an all-black school." African children are being failed by the colonial school system which permits all-white schools in the northern part of the county. Even in the white community, many see this as unjust.

On the north side of town, the African People's Solidarity Committee is dropping leaflets calling for the defense of Omali Yeshitela who has received death threats in recent months. The Chairman is attacked politically by two reactionary City Council members, one of whose husband once worked on the campaign to elect George Wallace for president. APSC is opening its own office downtown and plans to open an Uhuru Furniture in the next few months. It is extending Uhuru territory into the white neighborhoods.

Since the police murder of TyRon Lewis and the subsequent rebellions three years ago, nothing's been the same. Omali Yeshitela and the Uhuru Movement seized the reins of the struggle, fighting for the interests of the African working class. Most people thought the African working class would never be able to articulate for itself again. The murders of Malcolm X, Fred Hampton and Huey Newton were supposed to take care of that.

But in St. Petersburg, Uhuru has been building and campaigning on every front. They have drawn the lines and the town is polarized.

Many who dismissed the needs of African poor people for so long are listening: African preachers, businessmen, white people of all stripes—educators, housewives, students, workers, professionals, even businessmen who sometimes make significant contributions to the south side projects.

There are increasing numbers of white people in the city who see the Uhuru Movement providing solutions to problems and possibilities for the future of their town. Yeshitela welcomes everyone to join in the experiment of building an African working class power base. His only stipulations are that the public policy of police containment against the African community be overturned and that the well-being of the white community not come at the expense of African people. Yeshitela defines this period:

> We intend to build. Imperialism destroys everything—destroys lives, freedom, the environment. There is nothing that imperialism has not destroyed. We are not the destroyers, we are the builders. That's what our job is in the world. We are trying to take care of all those problems left on the world by imperialism and free the world of that blight so that we can all live a decent life.[64]

The Chairman is confident about the future. This struggle in St. Petersburg is incredible. The situation is unique. There's also the work in London to build the African Socialist International. There are Uhuru fronts in New York and Philadelphia and California.

There is burgeoning struggle around the country: African resistance to police brutality, to their deadening economic conditions, to being carted off to prison every day. There is the demand for reparations for the attacks on African people in Tulsa, Oklahoma in 1921 and the successful struggle for reparations for the murders of Africans in Rosewood, Florida in 1923. There is vocal opposition to the attack on affirmative action.

The indicators are good. A movement is afoot. Omali Yeshitela is determined to build. Everyone who unites with justice for African people is welcome to come along.

> People don't join revolutions to destroy something. People join revolutions to build something—build a New World. You join a revolution because a social system you are now involved in prevents us from living, prevents us from producing, prevents us from developing. We are not the destroyers; we are the ones who fight so that we can live. Malcolm X said, "I'm not for violence. I want to stop the violence."
>
> This New World has all kinds of practical manifestations. It is a world without oppression. It requires us then to fight for democracy and freedom. It is a world in which African people can be reattached to our motherland, our homeland.
>
> We believe that peace is possible and there can be tranquility, but there is a price that has to be paid for it. There must be genuine justice in the world for that to occur. Justice is defined by the interests of oppressed peoples being realized in the world. In order for there to be peace, the oppression and exploitation of African people have to end; the indigenous peoples of the Americas have to have ownership of the land and resources. There can be peace for white people. They can take the alarms off their cars and houses. They can become rational human beings. It can be a different kind of situation in the world. That is what we are struggling for.[65]

REPARATIONS AND REDEMPTION

Throughout the pages of this book we have tried to take responsibility for the past in order to truly see our future. We believe that the conditions exist to construct a genuinely internationalist movement among the North American population for the first time.

Tied organizationally to the leadership of the African working class we can do something that no white left movement has ever done. By joining the African People's Solidarity Committee, we can build a citizens' movement for reparations to African people. We can do everything in our power to see that the interests of oppressed peoples are realized. We can participate in ending the gap between the haves and the have nots. We can help end a system based on slaves and masters, oppressed and oppressors. We can support the life-giving movements of oppressed peoples and end the white power system. "Uhuru" can be our freedom as well.

Reparations, self-criticism, acknowledgment are necessary. But this must be done in the process of changing real conditions in the world. It is not a maudlin, internalized process. Nor is it intellectual and academic. It is a process to be played out exuberantly under the spotlight of emerging history, in touch with the vibrancy of the organized oppressed.

Everything that belongs to Africa must be returned: the money, the gold, the art, the skills, the minerals, the people, the talents. In return, a world is created without the built-in tension brought about by the system of masters and slaves.

"Free Africa and we will free the world," says Omali Yeshitela. When this system of slavery and genocide is overturned then Africa, Asia and the Americas can flourish once again. In the freeing atmosphere of a new world, the pressing problems created by white power can be solved: The end of oppression, slavery, genocide, unjust imprisonment and police brutality. Food, housing, health care and education for everyone. Equality for women, the cherishing of children, respect for the elders. The flowering of world culture, peace on Earth, societal harmony, personal serenity. Optimism, humor and hospitality. Science, mathematics and technology put to beneficial use. Popular expression of art and beauty.

A healthy environment, the survival of whales, a patch for the ozone layer, a cleansing of waters, irrigation of deserts, the stability of the human population. A cure for AIDS and other deadly diseases. Love, the joy of life. An end to violence.

The late brilliant African scholar Cheikh Anta Diop expressed his belief that a liberated Africa will bring about such a new approach to life. He believed that,

> The universe of tomorrow will in all probability be imbued with African optimism.
>
> It can be deduced… that most of the future African scientists, taking into account their cultural past, will belong…to the category which adopts a reasoned optimistic viewpoint.
>
> Perhaps they will consider that once earthly humanity accomplishes itself, instead of dying of boredom in the most complete idleness, man will realize that his task has only begun. He will discover then that it is absolutely within his possibilities…to tame the solar system and to reign there as far as the peripheral planet Pluto, in a practically eternal manner…Life would thus in its own way have triumphed over death, man would have made an earthly paradise which would be almost eternal, and at the same time would have triumphed over all the pessimistic philosophical and metaphysical systems, all the apocalyptic visions of the destiny of the species…[66]

The challenge is before us. We can join this future exploding with the energy of a re-emerging humanity so long suppressed for our sakes. Or we can go down with the sinking ship of white power.

We in the Uhuru Movement believe that the twenty-first century is dawning as a new era of liberation, and represents an end to a millennium of oppression and death. At the juncture that we unite in solidarity with the African Revolution, we cease to be voluntary agents of oppression, and we participate in building a hopeful future for all mankind, ourselves included. Uhuru!

Reparations Now!

1. W. E. B. DuBois, 1972, *The World and Africa* (New York: International Publishers), p. 41.
2. "Consumers see reasons to cheer," December 29, 1999, *St. Petersburg Times*.
3. "Unemployment rate dips to 30-year low of 4% in January," February 4, 2000, *The New York Times*.
4. "Banking on the inheritance bubble," December 19, 1999, *St. Petersburg Times*.
5. Ismail Turay Jr., "Black family wealth declines despite robust economy, study finds," February 4, 2000, *The Tampa Tribune*.
6. "Inmate rate helps lower joblessness," February 1, 2000, *The Tampa Tribune*.
7. Nina Bernstein, January 19, 2000, "Widest income gap is found in New York," *The New York Times*.
8. Nina Bernstein, October 7, 1999, "Poverty persists in city despite boom," *The New York Times*.
9. Bernstein, January 19, 2000, "Widest income gap."
10. Peter Edelman, July 8, 1999, "Clinton's cosmetic poverty tour," *The New York Times*.
11. David Cay Johnston, September 5, 1999, "Gap between rich and poor found substantially wider," *The New York Times*.
12. United Nations Human Development Programme, Human Development Report (www.undp.org/hdro/)
13. Paul Lewis, June 3, 1999, "World Bank says poverty is increasing," *The New York Times*.
14. Cheryl Payer, 1974, *The Debt Trap: The International Monetary Fund and the Third World* (New York and London: Monthly Review Press), pp. ix-x.
15. Gerald O. Barney, 1988, *Global 2000: The Report to the President Entering the Twenty-first Century* (Maryland: Seven Locks Press), p. 17.
16. Frances Moore Lappe and Joseph Collins, 1978, *Food First: Beyond the Myth of Scarcity* (New York: Ballantine Books), p. 89.
17. Barney, p. 27.
18. Gwynne Dyer, November 10, 1998, "Despair of a continent," *The Philadelphia Inquirer*.
19. Tim Seibles, 1999 *Hammerlock*, (Cleveland: Cleveland State University Poetry Center) p. 59.
20. Matthew Boedy, February 4, 2000, "Guards' backers crowd court," *St. Petersburg Times*.
21. Adam C. Smith, July 23, 1999, "Prisons are field that feeds a region," *St. Petersburg Times*.
22. Amy Weintraub, November/December 1999, "The Natural Prozac," *Yoga Journal*.
23. Kevin Fagan and Neva Chonin, January 8, 1999, "Young, rich and strung out," *San Francisco Chronicle*.
24. Sarah Schweitzer, November 29, 1999, "Former addict finds escape from crack," *St. Petersburg Times*.
25. Curtis Krueger, November 25, 1999, "Child abuse numbers rising," *St. Petersburg Times*.
26. "Why did they do this?" December 30, 1999, *St. Petersburg Times*.
27. "Abandoned babies in Houston area number 13," December 26, 1999, *St. Petersburg Times*.
28. "Couple suspected of leaving 2 boys to die," September 9, 1999, *St. Petersburg Times*.
29. "Dad beats 5-year-old twins to death with sledgehammer," June 5, 1998, *The Oakland Tribune*.
30. "The lowest of the low?" June 29, 1999, *Philadelphia Daily News*.
31. "Killer moms," June 30, 1999, *Philadelphia Daily News*.
32. "Man who injected son with HIV could get life," December 7, 1998, *The Oakland Tribune*.
33. "Twin boys charged in killing father, wounding sister," April 7, 1999, *San Francisco Chronicle*.
34. George Lardner Jr., July 27, 1998, "Violence at work affects 2 million," *San Francisco Chronicle*.
35. "Unprecedented stress making Americans sick," August 17, 1996, *San Francisco Chronicle*.
36. "Teen convicted of killing 5 in drunken rampage," March 13, 1999, *San Francisco Chronicle*.

37. "Cops say ex-Marine killed boy just to see what it felt like," October 3, 1997, *San Francisco Chronicle.*

38. "Thrill killer convicted," April 24, 1999, *The Tampa Tribune.*

39. Zelie Pollon, April 5, 1999, "Sex-torture case stuns small town," *San Francisco Chronicle.*

40. Charlie LeDuff, April 22, 1999, "Jury says man hospitalized in cannibalism killing can go free," *The New York Times.*

41. Josh Richman, March 23, 1999, "Trial includes re-enactment of stabbing," *The Oakland Tribune.*

42. Alan Zibel, April 6, 1999, "Hayward man charged with imprisoning girlfriend," *The Oakland Tribune.*

43. William R. Macklin, August 15, 1999, "White males and mass violence," *The Philadelphia Inquirer.*

44. Martin A. Lee, 1997, *The Beast Reawakens* (New York: Routledge), p. 264.

45. Omali Yeshitela, 1991, *Izwe Lethu i Afrika! (Africa is Our Land)* (Oakland: Burning Spear Publications), pp. 49-56.

46. Ukraine Human Health (www.freenet.kiev.ua/ciesin/envinfo/health/popheal.htm)

47. Lee, p. 263.

48. Same as above, p. 275.

49. Richard Wright, 1964, *White Man, Listen!* (New York: Doubleday & Company, Inc.), pp. 2-3.

50. Same as above, p. ix.

51. Robert Allen, 1983, *Reluctant Reformers: Racism and Social Reform Movements in the United States* (Washington, D.C.: Howard University Press), p. 147, quoting Elizabeth Cady Stanton.

52. Derrick Z. Jackson, April 10, 1995, "White women: The wild card in the affirmative action debate," *The Oakland Tribune.*

53. DuBois, *World and Africa*, p. 23.

54. Walter Rodney, 1981, *How Europe Underdeveloped Africa* (Washington, D.C.: Howard University Press), p. 89.

55. Omali Yeshitela, March/April/May 1990, "No sell-out! No negotiated settlement! Remember Sharpeville!," *The Burning Spear*, Supplement, p. D.

56. Sobukwe Bambaata, February-April 1999, "Africa in upheaval! On the eve of revolution!," *The Burning Spear*, p. 15.

57. Omali Yeshitela, August 1995-February 1996, "Where do we go from here?" *The Burning Spear*, p. 32.

58. Omali Yeshitela, February/March/April 1989, "Dual power-the black working class recapturing our resources," *The Burning Spear,* Supplement, p. O.

59. Yeshitela, *Izwe Lethu*, pp. 96-97.

60. Omali Yeshitela, 1979, "Report from the Mountain" (San Francisco: African People's Solidarity Committee), p. 9.

61.' Omali Yeshitela, January 15-16, 2000, "Turn our weaknesses into strengths! Forward to the new millennium!," Political report at the African People's Socialist Party National Plenary in St. Petersburg, Florida.

62. African People's Socialist Party, February-April 1999, "What we want-what we believe," *The Burning Spear,* p. 5, adopted September 23, 1979.

63. Henry David Thoreau, 1993, *Civil Disobedience and Other Essays* (New York: Dover Publications), p. 45.

64. Yeshitela, January 15, 2000, Presentation at the African People's Socialist Party National Plenary in St. Petersburg, Florida.

65. Same as above.

66. Cheikh Anta Diop, 1978, *The Cultural Unity of Black Africa: The Domains of Patriarchy and Matriarchy in Classical Antiquity* (Chicago: Third World Press), p. 197.

UHURU!

Selected Bibliography

Acuña, Rodolfo. *Occupied America: A History of Chicanos*. New York: Harper Collins Publishers, 1988.

African People's Socialist Party. *The Burning Spear*. St. Petersburg: Burning Spear Publications.

Alexander, Fran, ed. *Oxford Encyclopedia of World History*. New York: Oxford University Press Inc., 1988.

Allen, Robert. *Reluctant Reformers: Racism and Social Reform Movements in the United States*. Washington, D.C.: Howard University Press, 1983.

Anderson, Jon Lee. *Che Guevara: A Revolutionary Life*. New York: Grove Press, 1997.

Aptheker, Herbert. *American Negro Slave Revolts*. New York: International Publishers, 1987.

Avery, Ron. *City of Brotherly Mayhem: Philadelphia Crimes & Criminals*. Philadelphia: Otis Books, 1997.

Barney, Gerald O. *Global 2000: The Report to the President Entering the Twenty-first Century*. Maryland: Seven Locks Press, 1988.

Baum, Dan. *Smoke and Mirrors: The War on Drugs and the Politics of Failure*. New York: Little, Brown and Company, 1996.

Bennett, Lerone Jr. *Before The Mayflower: A History of the Negro in America, 1619-1964 Revised Edition*. USA: Johnson Publishing Company, Inc., 1978.

Boyer, Richard O. and Herbert M. Morais. *Labor's Untold Story*. New York: United Electrical, Radio & Machine Workers, 1973.

Bradley, Michael. *The Iceman Inheritance: Prehistoric Sources of Western Man's Racism, Sexism and Aggression*. New York: Kayode Publications, Ltd., 1991.

Breitman, George, ed. *Malcolm X Speaks: Selected Speeches and Statements*. New York: Grove Weidenfeld, 1990.

Brown, Dee. *Bury My Heart at Wounded Knee: An Indian History of the American West*. New York: Holt, Rinehart and Winston, 1971.

Carroll, Peter N. and David W. Noble. *The Free and the Unfree: A New History of the United States*. New York: Penguin Books, 1988.

Carson, Clayborne. *In Struggle: SNCC and the Black Awakening of the 1960's*. Massachusetts: Harvard University Press, 1981.

——. *Malcolm X: The FBI File*. New York: Carroll & Graf Publishers, Inc., 1991.

Chinweizu. *The West and the Rest of Us: White Predators, Black Slavers and the African Elite*. New York: Vintage Books, 1975.

Churchill, Ward. *A Little Matter of Genocide: Holocaust and Denial in the Americas 1492 to the Present*. San Francisco: City Lights Books, 1997.

Churchill, Ward and Jim Vander Wall. *Agents of Repression: The FBI's Secret Wars Against the Black Panther Party and the American Indian Movement*. Boston: South End Press, 1988.

——. *The Cointelpro Papers: Documents from the FBI's Secret Wars Against Dissent in the United States*. Boston: South End Press.

Cockburn, Alexander and Jeffrey St. Clair. *Whiteout: The CIA, Drugs and the Press*. New York: Verso, 1998.

Convention on the Prevention and Punishment of the Crime of Genocide, December 9, 1948, adopted by Resolution 260 III of the United Nations General Assembly.

Cruse, Harold. *The Crisis of the Negro Intellectual: From Its Origins to the Present*. New York: William Morrow & Company, Inc., 1971.

Davis, Mike. *Ecology of Fear: Los Angeles and the Imagination of Disaster*. New York: Metropolitan Books, Henry Holt and Company, 1998.

Desroches-Noblecourt, Christiane. *Tutankhamen: Life and Death of a Pharaoh*. London: Penguin Books Ltd., 1963.

Diop, Cheikh Anta. *The African Origin of Civilization: Myth or Reality*. Westport: Lawrence Hill & Company, 1974.

——. *Black Africa: The Economic and Cultural Basis for a Federated State*. Westport: Lawrence Hill & Co., 1978.

——. *The Cultural Unity of Black Africa: The Domains of Patriarchy and of Matriarchy in Classical Antiquity*. Chicago: Third World Press, 1978.

——. *Precolonial Black Africa: A Comparative Study of the Political and Social Systems of Europe and Black Africa, from Antiquity to the Formation of Modern States*. Trenton: Lawrence Hill & Company, Africa World Press Edition, 1987.

Donziger, Steven R., ed. *The Real War on Crime*. New York: Harper Collins Publishers, Inc., 1996.

Drechsler, Horst. *Let Us Die Fighting*. London: Zed Press, 1966.

DuBois, W.E.B. *The Suppression of the African Slave-Trade to the United States of America, 1638-1870*. New York: Shoken Books, 1969.

——. *Black Reconstruction in America 1860-1880*. New York: Antheneum Press, 1972.

——. *The World and Africa*. New York: International Publishers, 1972.

Fagan, Brian M. *Rape of the Nile: Tomb Robbers, Tourists and Archaeologists in Egypt*. Rhode Island: Moyer Bell, 1975.

Fall, Bernard B., ed. *Ho Chi Minh On Revolution: Selected Writings, 1920-66*. New York: The New American Library, Inc., 1968.

Fanon, Frantz. *Toward the African Revolution*. New York: Grove Press, Inc., 1967.

Foner, Eric and Olivia Mahoney. *America's Reconstruction: People and Politics after the Civil War*. Baton Rouge: Louisiana State University Press, 1995.

Foner, Philip S. *The Black Panthers Speak: The Manifesto of the Party: The First Complete Documentary Record of the Panther's Program*. Philadelphia: J. B. Lippincott Company, 1970.

——. *Organized Labor & the Black Worker 1619-1973*. New York: International Publishers, 1976.

Forman, James. *The Making of Black Revolutionaries*. Washington, D.C.: Open Hand Publishing, Inc., 1985.

Foreign Policy in Focus (www.foreignpolicy-infocus.org).

Foster, William Z. *The Negro People In American History*. New York: International Publishers, 1976.

Selected Bibliography

Franklin, John Hope and Loren Schweninger. *Runaway Slaves: Rebels on the Plantations*. New York: Oxford University Press, 1999.

Galeano, Eduardo. *Open Veins of Latin America: Five Centuries of the Pillage of a Continent*. New York: Monthly Review Press, 1973.

Geisler, Wolff. *AIDS-Origin, Spread and Healing*. Koln: Bipawo Verlag, 1994.

Georgakas, Dan and Marvin Surkin. *Detroit: I Do Mind Dying*. Boston: South End Press, 1998.

Gerberg, Mort. *The U.S. Constitution for Everyone*. New York: The Berkley Publishing Group, 1987.

Ginzburg, Ralph. *100 Years of Lynchings* Baltimore: Black Classic Press, 1988.

Grant, Joanne, ed. *Black Protest: History, Documents & Analysis 1619 to Present*. New York: Fawcett Premier, 1968.

Hamdun, Said and Noël King. *Ibn Battuta In Black Africa*. Princeton: Markus Wierner Publishers, 1998.

Harris, Joseph. *Africans and Their History, Revised Edition*. New York: Mentor Books, 1987.

Herodotus. *The Histories*. Vermont: Charles E. Tuttle Co., Inc., 1997.

Hill, Robert A. and Barbara Bair, eds. *Marcus Garvey: Life and Lessons*. Berkeley: University of California Press, 1987.

Hochschild, Adam. *King Leopold's Ghost: A Story of Greed, Terror, and Heroism in Colonial Africa*. New York: Houghton Mifflin Company, 1998.

Holzer, Howard, ed., *The Lincoln-Douglass Debates*. New York: Harper Collins Publishers, Inc., 1994.

Innes, Brian. *The History of Torture*. London: Brown Packaging Books Ltd., 1998.

International Covenant on Civil and Political Rights, December 16, 1966, adopted by the United Nations General Assembly.

Jacobs, Harold, ed. *Weatherman*. Ramparts Press, Inc., 1970.

Jacobs, Paul and Saul Landau with Eve Pell. *To Serve the Devil, Volume I: Natives and Slaves*. New York: Vintage Books, 1971.

Jaffe, Hosea. *A History of Africa*. London: Zed Books Ltd, 1988.

Jacques-Garvey, Amy, ed. *Philosophy & Opinions of Marcus Garvey*. New York: Atheneum, 1971.

Johansen, Bruce E. *Forgotten Founders: How the American Indian Helped Shape Democracy*. Boston: The Harvard Common Press, 1982.

Jordan, Winthrop D. *White Over Black: American Attitudes Toward the Negro, 1550-1812*. New York: W.W. Norton & Company, Inc., 1968.

Katz, William Loren. *Black Indians: A Hidden Heritage*. New York: First Aladdin Paperbacks, 1997.

Klare, Michael T. *War Without End: American Planning for the Next Viet Nams*. New York: Vantage Books, 1972.

Kolko, Gabriel. *Anatomy of a War: Viet Nam, the United States, and the Modern Historical Experience*. New York: The New Press, 1997.

Lappe, Frances Moore and Joseph Collins. *Food First: Beyond the Myth of Scarcity*. New York: Ballantine Books, 1978.

Lee, Martin A. *The Beast Reawakens*. New York: Routledge, 1997.

Lenin, V.I. *Against Revisionism*. Moscow: Progress Publishers, 1972.

——. *Imperialism, The Highest State of Capitalism*. Peking: Foreign Language Press, 1975.

——. *On Proletarian Internationalism*. Moscow: Progress Publishers, 1976.

Lindqvist, Sven., *"Exterminate All the Brutes": One Man's Odyssey into the Heart of Darkness and the Origins of European Genocide*. New York: The New Press, 1996.

Littlefield, Henry W. *History of Europe Since 1815*. New York: Barnes & Noble Inc., 1957.

Loewen, James W. *Lies My Teacher Told Me: Everything Your American History Textbook Got Wrong*. New York: Touchstone, 1995.

Macdonald, Peter. *Giap: The Victor In Viet Nam*. New York: W.W. Norton Company, Inc., 1993.

Marx, Karl. *Capital: A Critique of Political Economy, Vol. 1*. New York: International Publishers, 1979.

Marx, Karl and Frederick Engels. *The Communist Manifesto*. New York: Pathfinders, 1988.

Massimo, Teodori. *The New Left: A Documentary History*. New York: Viking Penguin, Inc., 1968.

McCoy, Alfred W. *The Politics of Heroin In Southeast Asia*. New York: Harper & Row, 1972.

——. *The Politics of Heroin: CIA Complicity in the Global Drug Trade*. New York: Lawrence Hill Books, 1991.

McEvedy, Colin. *The New Penguin Atlas of Medieval History*. London: Penguin Books, 1992.

Mills, James. *The Underground Empire: Where Crime and Governments Embrace*. New York: Doubleday Company, 1986.

Moody, Roger, ed. *The Indigenous Voice: Visions and Realities, Vol. I*. London: Zed Books Ltd., 1988.

Morris, William, ed. *The American Heritage Dictionary, Second College Edition*. Boston: Houghton Mifflin Company, 1982.

Nevins, Alan and Henry Steele Commager with Jeffery Morris. *A Pocket History of the United States*. New York: First Washington Square Press, 1986.

Njeri, Akua. *"My Life with the Black Panther Party."* Oakland: Burning Spear Publications, 1991.

O'Reilly, Kenneth. *"Racial Matters": The FBI's Secret File on Black America 1960-1972*. New York: The Free Press, 1989.

Patterson, William L., ed. *We Charge Genocide: The Crime of Government Against the Negro People*. New York: International Publishers, 1971.

Payer, Cheryl. *The Debt Trap: The International Monetary Fund and the Third World*. New York and London: Monthly Review Press, 1974.

Pirenne, Henri. *Economic and Social History of Medieval Europe*. New York: Harcourt, Brace & World, Inc., 1937.

Poe, Richard. *Black Spark White Fire: Did African Explorers Civilize Ancient Europe?* California: Prima Publishing, 1997.

Raper, Arthur F. *The Tragedy of Lynching*. New York: Dover Publications, 1970.

Selected Bibliography

Reeves, Nicholas. *The Complete Tutankhamun: The King, The Tomb, The Royal Treasure*. London: Thames and Hudson Ltd., 1990.

Rodney, Walter. *How Europe Underdeveloped Africa*. Washington, D.C.: Howard University Press, 1981.

Roediger, David R. *The Wages of Whiteness: Race and the Making of the American Working Class*. New York: Verso, 1999.

Royko, Mike. *Boss, Richard J. Daley of Chicago*. New York: E.P. Dutton & Co., 1971.

Sakai, J. *The Mythology of the White Proletariat: A Short Course In Understanding Babylon*. Chicago: Morningstar Press, 1983.

Sale, Kirkpatrick. *SDS*. New York: Random House, 1973.

Scammell, G.V. *The First Imperial Age: European Overseas Expansion c. 1400-1715*. London: Unwin Hyman, Ltd., 1989.

Schivelbusch, Wolfgang. *Tastes of Paradise: A Social History of Spices, Stimulants, and Intoxicants*. New York: Vintage Books, 1992.

Schlosser, Eric. "The prison-industrial complex," *Atlantic Monthly*, December 1998.

Shapiro, Herbert. *White Violence and Black Response: From Reconstruction to Montgomery*. Amherst: The University of Massachusetts Press, 1988.

Soukhanov, Anne H., ed. *Encarta World English Dictionary*. New York: St. Martin's Press, 1999.

Stanley, Jerry. *Digger: The Tragic Fate of the California Indians from the Missions to the Gold Rush*. New York: Crown Publishers, Inc., 1997.

Stannard, David E. *American Holocaust: The Conquest of the New World*. New York: Oxford University Press, 1992.

Taber, Robert. *The War of the Flea: A Study of Guerrilla Warfare Theory and Practice*. New York: The Citadel Press, 1970.

Thomas, Hugh. *The Slave Trade: The Story of the Atlantic Slave Trade: 1440-1870*. New York: Touchstone, 1997.

Thoreau, Henry David. *Civil Disobedience and Other Essays*. New York: Dover Publications, 1993.

Tolnay, Stewart E. and E. M. Beck. *A Festival of Violence: An Analysis of Southern Lynchings, 1882-1930*. Chicago: University of Illinois Press, 1992.

Turner, Frederick, ed. *Geronimo: His Own Story*. New York: Penguin Books, 1996.

Twombly, Robert C. *Blacks in White America Since 1865*. New York: David McKay Company, Inc., 1971.

Tzu, Sun. *The Art of War*. Boston: Shambhala Publications, 1991.

Universal Declaration of Human Rights, December 10, 1948, adopted by the United Nations General Assembly.

Van Sertima, Ivan. *They Came Before Columbus: The African Presence in America*. New York: Random House, 1976.

Vincent, Ted. *Black Power & the Garvey Movement*. Oakland: Nzinga Publishing House, 1988.

Warner, Sam Bass Jr. *The Private City*. Philadelphia: University of Pennsylvania Press, 1971.

Weatherford, Jack. *Indian Givers: How the Indians Transformed the World*. New York: Ballantine Books, 1998.

Williams, Eric. *Capitalism and Slavery*. New York: Capricorn Books, 1966.

Williams, Jay. *Knights of the Crusades*. New York: Harper & Row, Publishers, Incorporated, 1962.

Williams, Juan. *Eyes on the Prize: America's Civil Rights Years, 1954-1965*. New York: Viking Penguin, Inc., 1987.

Wright, Richard. *White Man, Listen!* New York: Doubleday & Company, Inc., 1964.

Yeshitela, Omali. *The Struggle for Bread, Peace and Black Power: Political Report to the First Congress of the African People's Socialist Party*. Oakland: Burning Spear Publications, 1981.

——. *A New Beginning: The Road to Black Freedom and Socialism: The Main Resolution, Constitution and Program Adopted at the First Congress of the African People's Socialist Party*. Oakland: Burning Spear Publications, 1982.

——. *Not One Step Backwards!: The Black Liberation Movement from 1971 to 1982*. Oakland: Burning Spear Publications, 1982.

——. *Reparations Now! Abbreviated Report from the International Tribunal on Reparations for Black People in the U.S.* Oakland: Burning Spear Publications, 1983.

——. "A Political and Economic Critique of Imperialism and Imperialist Opportunism." Oakland: Burning Spear Publications, 1987.

——. "Complete the Black Revolution of the Sixties." Oakland: Marcus Garvey Club, 1987.

——. *The Road to Socialism Is Painted Black: Selected Theoretical Works*. Oakland: Burning Spear Publications, 1987.

——. *Black Power Since the 60's: The Struggle Against Opportunism within the U.S. Front of the Black Liberation Movement*. Oakland: Burning Spear Publications, 1991.

——. *Izwe Lethu i Afrika! Africa Is Our Land*. Oakland: Burning Spear Publications, 1991.

——. "Defeat the Counterinsurgency: Main Resolution to the Founding Convention of the National People's Democratic Uhuru Movement." Chicago: National People's Democratic Uhuru Movement, 1993.

——. "Resistance of African People: Crisis of Imperialism: Why we must build the National People's Democratic Uhuru Movement." Chicago: National People's Democratic Uhuru Movement, 1996.

——. "The Dialectics of Black Revolution: The Struggle to Defeat the Counterinsurgency in the U.S." Oakland: Burning Spear Uhuru Publications, 1997.

——. "Social Justice and Economic Development for the African Community: Why I Became a Revolutionary." St. Petersburg: Burning Spear Uhuru Publications, 1997.

——. "A Lynching in Jasper Texas: Thousands of Legal Lynchings Across the U.S." St. Petersburg: Burning Spear Uhuru Publications, 1998.

Zinn, Howard. *A People's History of the United States 1492-Present*. New York: Harper Collins Publishers, 1995.

Index

Index

Index

Index

Index